GOVERNMENT AND BUREAUCRACY IN INDIA
1947–1976

GOVERNMENT AND
BUREAUCRACY IN INDIA
1947–1976

B. B. MISRA

DELHI
OXFORD UNIVERSITY PRESS
BOMBAY CALCUTTA MADRAS
1986

Oxford University Press, Walton Street, Oxford OX2 6DP

NEW YORK TORONTO
DELHI BOMBAY CALCUTTA MADRAS KARACHI
PETALING JAYA SINGAPORE HONG KONG TOKYO
NAIROBI DAR ES SALAAM CAPE TOWN
MELBOURNE AUCKLAND
and associates in
BEIRUT BERLIN IBADAN NICOSIA

Filmset and printed by Rajbandhu Industrial Co.
C 61 Mayapuri, New Delhi 110014
Published by R. Dayal, Oxford University Press
YMCA Library Building, Jai Singh Road, New Delhi 110001

Preface

This study attempts to examine in some depth the problems of governance within the framework of popular consent and parliamentary democracy as envisaged by the transfer of power from British to Indian hands. It throws light on the constitution and management of the civil service and covers a general analysis of the administrative changes introduced from time to time in order to improve efficiency and raise the standards of administrative morality.

The task of running the administration of India on democratic lines is not easy. It is beset with serious constraints under which the government and its bureaucracy have to function. These constraints proceed in the first instance from the historical tradition of 'bureaucratic despotism' which had developed in India under British rule and taken firm roots in the entire field of administrative hierarchies. The second important source of constraints was the authoritarian and caste-ridden character of Indian society, which knew of no 'social contract' and basically recognized only 'status' as a guide to social relationships. The experience of history before Independence and the division of society into mutually exclusive elements were in fact both opposed to democracy, though from two different premises. For while the bureaucratic administration was rule-bound and based on custom, democracy, which is a contract-based ideology, found support only among the western-educated middle-class elites who used it as a lever to forward their political objective of representative government. And since this middle-class ideology remained over the years bereft of any social and economic content, its appeal did not extend beyond a small minority of educated Indians who used politics to promote their employment opportunities in the government. Even on the transfer of power the bureaucarcy continued to be sceptical about the soundness of a democratic constitution; society remained generally indifferent and showed little or no interest in the removal of the wide gap existing between the community and the administration.

True, the leaders of the several renaissance movements did emphasize from time to time the need for integrity of conduct and a contractual approach to social organization in order to sustain modern government and administration. But their basic concern was either ethical or cultural. There was no distinct economic dimension underlying those movements that might lend support to the liberalism of their social philosophy. Religion in the Indian situation did not lead to the rise of capitalism as an instrument of modernization and social change. The teachings of religious leaders served as examples to be occasionally quoted but not socially applied. They could not bridge the gap that had developed under British rule between society and administration, which continued to be governed by the mutually exclusive principles of status and contract respectively. Even Indians in the civil service and the learned professions, whom Macaulay had visualized as a social link to unite the community with the administration, could not fill the gap. Recruited from the upper layers of society, they appeared as rulers, not as servants of the people. They governed but did not guide.

The growth of industry and the working class in the first few decades of the twentieth century gave rise to left parties in politics, more especially as an aftermath of the Russian Revolution of 1917. Their efforts at direct contact with workers and peasants as well as their international affiliations raised hopes of a social reconstruction based on socialism, the removal of economic disparities and establishing an identity of approach between the people and government. But imperialism helped the vested interests of the Congress party and combined with it to curb the rising influence of the Communists and Revolutionary Socialists. It was in these circumstances that power was transferred to the Congress to prevent the Communists and other radical elements from becoming a menace to British interests.

In the reorganization of the political and administrative apparatus of the state, structural refinements and personnel expansion occurred, rather than policy radicalization involving a thorough restructuring of service conditions as well as a corresponding change in the constitutional and legal safeguards of the public services. In the absence of any fundamental change in the character of social and economic policy, the old administrative structure continued with such quantitative additions as extended functions of the state demanded. That perhaps is the reason why the bureaucratic machinery of government, which changed but little even in terms of attitudinal responses, failed generally to secure popular participation in projects for rural development. At the instance of the Prime Minister a Community Development programme was launched in 1952 to ensure that participation, but it yielded disappointing results.Doubtless steps were periodically taken to cleanse administration by providing for administrative vigilance and punishment of corruption. But the administration could not be freed from this malady. With the extended functions of the state there arose a vast field of administrative action in which administrators might act outside the strict scope of law and propriety, without the injured party being in a position to obtain any effective redress. The evil at the level of Plan implementation was even more evident. As there had been in the past a considerable time-lag in the progress of rural societies in terms of education and economic development, no organized and responsible public opinion or pressure could grow as a corrective to administration at the grass roots level. Indeed, the absence of organized resistance to corruption at that level has led to a steady decline in the standards of administrative and political morality.

The neglected state of villages in the fields of education, agriculture and money-lending constitute a sad reflection on democracy itself. Gandhi realized the danger of rural backwardness and tried to meet the situation by an emphasis on 'basic education', village industry and 'constructive programmes'. These formed part of his concept of a democratic decentralization intended to promote managerial self-reliance and economic self-sufficiency. But the results could not meet the expectations. Within the framework of imperialism even Curzon at the start of the century had tried to promote primary education for villages and co-operatives as a mode of rural financing. But these were all palliatives and did not touch even the fringe of the problem of rural reconstruction. In the face of stark disparities between the rich and the poor, democracy after 1947 fell far short of its objectives as far as the Indian villages were concerned. It was realized that if the disparities were to go the concept of democracy must of necessity be invested with social and economic content, without which the rule of law and liberty had little or no relevance for the weaker sections of society. The abolition of privy purses, the extension of the public sector and bank nationalization were all measures effected in response to the popular urge for the removal of iniquities. A further remedy suggested was to circumscribe Fundamental Rights and restrict the operation of the judicial processes which were supposed to benefit only those who wished to defend property and privilege. The introduction of the Emergency under Article 356 of the Constitution in June 1975 and the subsequent enactment of the forty-second constitutional amendment in 1976 were both sought to be justified on the score of social and economic progress. The Twenty-Point Programme of the Prime Minister came in the same context. But the opposition held a contrary view, especially in respect of the Emergency and the constitutional amendment. They declared the Emergency as wholly uncalled for and rejected the contention of the ruling party that its social and economic objectives could not be achieved except by a curtailment of democratic freedoms.

The controversy so occasioned was not without a corresponding analogy in the history of British rule in India. Several cases of social injustice, for instance, occurred where people had to suffer from the rigidity of judicial procedure. An eminent administrator like Holt Mackenzie and his school of civilians in the the 1820's pressed for executive review of judicial decisions to make justice available to the poor. Later in the 1870's, the Lieutenant-Governor of Bengal, Sir George Campbell, reiterated the same principle. In a letter of 15 July 1873 he explained to the Government of India the manner in which the rich and litigous class of zamindars and money-lenders was raising lawyers to a dominant position in Indian society and causing the ruination of the cultivating community by fraudulent transfers of land effected in satisfaction of bonded debts. Another school of equally eminent civil servants was led by A. C. Lyall, Secretary to the Government of India, who expressed himself strongly in opposition to executive control of the judiciary. It is not that the Government of India did not appreciate Campbell's concern for protection against too literal an enforcement of legal contracts. It did realize the inadequacy of judicial action in securing justice to the needy. Even so, Lyall pointed out in a letter of 26 March 1874 that the proposed executive control would set up an arbitrary will in the place of law, substitute a rapid conjecture for methodical examination and destroy the very notion of fixed and sovereign law paramount over individual will and power. Historically, therefore, both the viewpoints claimed and found support in the administration of the country under British rule. It was the general and sustained respect for the Cornwallis Code of 1793 that allowed the balance to remain tilted on the side of the judiciary.

However, the concept of the freedom of the judiciary in the Indian situation (as in the British model) never signified independence of the legislative authority. Ever since the Restoration of 1660 sovereignty in England remained vested in the King-in-Parliament and judges in their judicial conduct were to be guided by the laws enacted by Parliament. This principle of legislative supremacy constituted the cornerstone of the King's Courts set up in India under parliamentary enactment. The Supreme Court, first established at Fort William in Bengal in 1774, and the several High Courts established later in 1862 could, with the approval of the executive government, frame their rules of business for their own guidance or for the guidance of their subordinate courts. But in no case were these rules to be repugnant to the laws enacted by the sovereign legislature. The Federal Court established under the Government of India Act, 1935, could likewise make rules to regulate generally the practice and procedure of the courts, including rules as to the persons practising before the court. But these rules, as before, were to be with the approval of the Governor-General, and in no way contrary to the Act passed by the British Parliament, which established the Court.

Though essentially a Constitution Act establishing a supreme federal authority in India over provincial governments, the Government of India Act, 1935 did not invest the Federal Court with powers to adjudge the constitutionality or otherwise of a measure enacted by the Federal Legislature. All that the Court was authorized to do under the Act was merely to 'report' upon a question of law, and that, too, only when the Governor-General felt called upon to consult it 'in his discretion' on an issue which he considered to be of such a nature or of such public importance that it was 'expedient' to obtain its opinion for consideration'. Though federal in form, the 1935 Act was in fact unitary in spirit and content. It was a logical sequence of a historical development that had taken place since the Regulating Act of 1773. As indicated in the first chapter of this study, the Constitution of 1950 was in principle as well as in certain details based on the Government of India Act, 1935.

Even so, the judiciary in the post-Independence period became involved in several clashes with the government on jurisdictional grounds and in constitutional term. There was, of course, a loss of historical perspective that led to such a development. But it proceeded even otherwise from a number of distortions. Indian federalism was, for instance, wrongly sought to be viewed as a variant of the American prototype based on the separation of powers and with provisions for judicial review. This has led to a number of legislative measures of social and economic importance being declared judicially *ultra vires* of the Constitution on the alleged ground of interference with fundamental rights to property or privilege. The ruling Congress party, too, has not been free from its own share of responsibility. Much of the trouble would have been obviated if only the rights so defined, instead of being incorporated into the Constitution as an ornament to satisfy ideological whims, had been allowed to remain as part of the regular codes of law on the analogy of the erstwhile British pattern of functioning in India. Their transfer to constitutional categories encouraged the judiciary to bring them under its purview.

The sources used for this work are in general archival, including for the most part the original files of the Ministry of Home Affairs in the Government of India as well as those of the Department of Personnel and Administrative Reforms, Cabinet Secretariat, which had in addition made a highly useful study on the Management of the Indian Administrative Service. The manuscript sources were supplemented not only by select documents, official publications as well as annual reports of relevant departments and organizations, but also by the reports of the several Study Teams of the Administrative Reforms Commision, which I found far more enlightening than the reports of the Commission itself. The information gleaned from newspaper clippings and learned journals was used with caution as a secondary source. But this study is on the whole based on a scrutiny of the facts and views expressed in 'Notes' and correspondence on the relevant files themselves.

Of the several persons who lent their co-operation in the completion of this work, mention must especially be made of L. P. Singh and Govind Narain, both of the Indian Civil Service, who as Secretaries to the Government in the Ministry of Home Affairs were the first to encourage me and permit access to the official files of the post-Independence period. I am also deeply grateful for the co-operation extended to me in this regard by Mr. T. C. A. Srinivasavardan, then Joint Secretary in the Ministry.

As regards permission for the use of source material available in the Department of Personnel and Administrative Reforms, I am deeply indebted to the initiative and encouragement of the former Cabinet Secretary, B. D. Pandey, also of the Indian Civil Service. It was here that Mr. R. N. Haldipur of the Indian Administrative Service, then Joint

Secretary in the Department, came to my immediate help and extended necessary permission for the use of files.

I am grateful to S. N. Prasad, Director, National Archives, and his staff for the assistance ungrudgingly extended to me in the pursuit of my researches. I shall be failing in my duty if I omit to acknowledge my deep gratitude to N. Mukerji, keeper of records in the Ministry of Home Affairs, whose unstinted help and co-operation left a memorable impression on me.

B.B.M.

Contents

CHAPTER I

The Government

This chapter will discuss some aspects of the Government at the Centre. It will restrict itself to a review of the Government's parliamentary and federal character, emphasizing its declared objectives and the directive principles of State policy. A reflection on the form of the Government and its declared goals is essential for two main reasons: to throw light on the gap, if any, between precept and practice, and, in addition, to provide a fresh perspective for a clear understanding and assessment of the bureaucracy in the post-Independence period.

A new perspective flowed from the transfer of power and the consequent socio-political change that occurred in the complexion of the Government. This led to the formal separation of the bureaucratic element from the democratic and decision-making political executive. It was a radical change. Structurally, the bureaucracy suddenly ceased to be the Government. In the early periods of British rule, there had existed no wall between the common people and the officers of the Government. Judges and Collectors were the only agency through which popular complaints were heard and remedies supplied. They alone could be looked upon as the people's representatives (even if not elected) and were invested not only with the protection of life and property or the execution of certain development schemes, but also with the promotion of such relief measures as provided, for instance, against famines and epidemics. There were no elected representatives to interpose between these officers and the people. However, the bureaucratic claim to represent the interests of the common people began to be questioned in the closing decades of the nineteenth century and seriously challenged after the outbreak of the first World War. The principles of representative government introduced in 1892 and extended later in 1909 were an expression of the struggle for supremacy between the forces of democracy and the perscriptive claims of the bureaucracy for direct access to the people without any intervention from politicians. The position steadily changed in favour of the latter and the Government of India Acts of 1919 and 1935 tightened the hold of the elective element over popular sentiments. The elected non-officials acquired through politics a degree of legitimacy which the bureaucracy could not but acknowledge.[1] Civil servants none the less continued as Executive Councillors and formed part of the political machine until the Interim Government came into being in September 1946 and excluded them from any share in political authority. The bureaucracy became reduced to the position of a subordinate administrative instrument, separate and distinct from the political apparatus, and was replaced by a political leader as the spokesman of the people. It is mainly in the context of free India's social and political ecology that an analysis of bureaucratic change will be attempted here. But since an appreciation of this change is immediately related to an understanding of the new Government, this chapter will first briefly review its formal constitution and then discuss the functioning of its Ministers and Governors. Other chapters will study the bureaucracy itself.

The India (Provisional Constitution) Order, 1947

Under the Cabinet Mission Proposals of 16 May, 1946 the Constituent Assembly was invested finally to frame the Constitution of India. It began its first sitting on 9 December, 1946 and completed its proceedings on 26 November, 1949. The Constitution so settled was put into force on 26 January, 1950. In the meantime, on 3 June, 1947, the British Government announced its plan to partition British India into two independent Dominions of India and Pakistan. Consistent with this plan, the Indian Independence Bill was introduced on 4 July and formally enacted on 18 July and the Independent Dominion of India came into existence on 15 August, 1947. The constitutional arrangement, which remained operative after the transfer of power and before the inauguration of the new Constitution, followed as closely as possible the provisions of the Government of India Act, 1935, and was extensively adapted to suit the new circumstances created by the declaration of India's independence. In exercise of the powers conferred on him by the Indian Independence Act, the Governor-General issued on 14 August an order called the India (Provisional Constitution) Order, 1947. It made such ommisions from, additions to, and adaptations and modifications of the Government of India Act, 1935,[2] as seemed to him to be necessary. For instance, the control of British Government and the means by which it had been exercised in the past under the 1935 Act was no longer to remain valid. The Constituent Assembly became the sovereign Dominion Legislature in place of the British Parliament. It was empowered not only to frame the constitution of the new Dominion of India, but also temporarily to perform the limited legislative function of the erstwhile Central Legislature swept away by the order. The order-making powers of the Governor-General which applied also to the partition of certain provinces as well as to the administration of the common services and other Central functions, were, however, not absolute. These were not to extend beyond 31 March, 1948 and were, in addition, limited by the right of the Dominion Legislature to repeal or amend any order, and to deprive the Governor-General of his order-making power itself by passing a law to that effect.

Another important adaptation which the order of 14 August 1947 effected was to convert the Executive Council of the Governor-General into a Council of Ministers to aid and advise the Governor-General in the exercise of his functions. Members of the Interim Government were thus to be called Ministers and their Council came to be cited as a Cabinet on 15 August, when they took the oath of office.

Adapting the pattern of the self-governing Dominions of the Commonwealth, the King, on the advice of the Indian leaders, appointed Lord Mountbatten to be the Governor-General of the Dominion of India. In the presence of the Members of the Cabinet the Chief Justice of India administered on 15 August the oath of allegiance and the oath for the due execution of office. He then took his seat under a salute of 31 guns.

The Council of Ministers appointed by the Governor-General consisted of: Jawaharlal Nehru, Prime Minister, External Affairs and Commonwealth Relations, Scientific Research; Vallabhbhai Patel, Home, Information and Broadcasting, States; Dr Rajendra Prasad, Food and Agriculture; Maulana Abul Kalam Azad, Education; Dr John Matthai, Railways and Transport; Sardar Baldev Singh, Defence; Jagjivan Ram, Labour; C. H. Bhabha, Commerce; Rafi Ahmad Kidwai, Communications; Raj Kumari Amrit Kaur, Health; Dr B. R. Ambedkar, Law; R. K. Shanmukham Chetty, Finance; Dr Shyama Prasad Mukerji, Industries and Supplies; N. V. Gadgil, Works, Mines and Power.

As regards relations with the Indian States, the Cabinet Mission in its Memorandum of 12 May 1946 had assured them that the British Government would in no circumstances transfer paramountcy to an Indian Government. But the pledge could not be kept. The projected transfer of power soon made it impossible for Britain to carry out its obligations towards the States, obligations which depended for their fulfilment on its continuing responsibility for the Government of India. The Indian Independence Bill therefore provided that from the date when the Dominions of India and Pakistan were set up the treaties and agreements which gave Britain its suzerainty over the States would become void. The appointments and functions of the Crown Representative and his officers would naturally from that moment terminate and the States become masters of their own fate, free to stand alone or to associate with one or other of the Dominion Governments. However, in his speech in the House of Lords on 16 July 1947 the Secretary of State welcomed the setting up by the Interim Government of a States' Department to carry on negotiations with the States. He appreciated the assurance by Sardar Patel, the Home Member, that the Congress had no desire to use its political strength to meddle with the domestic affairs of the rulers. In fact the British Government's proposal of 3 June which embodied the decision to partition India led its leaders to recognize the necessity of a federal constitution with a strong Centre. They were, therefore, anxious to have the co-operation of the States by limiting their accession in respect of only such subjects as defence, external affairs and communications. Naturally, the Indian Independence Act did not consider any of the States to be separate international entities. And, in keeping with the federal framework of the Act of 1935, the India (**Provisional Constitution**) Order also declared that the **Dominion of** India 'shall, as from the fifteenth of August, 1947, be a Union comprising, (a) the Provinces hereafter called Governor's Provinces, (b) the Provinces hereafter called the Chief Commissioners' Provinces, (c) the Indian States acceding to the Dominion (by fresh long-term agreements), (d) any other area that may with the consent of the Dominion be included in the Dominion'. Cumulatively, these developments contributed to the process of merger and integration of the States, which began with the circulation of the Draft Constitution in February 1948. Their old position that they would accede to the Union through voluntary instruments changed rapidly; and the position which finally emerged was that the States would occupy the same position as the other federating units with their internal constitutions being determined by the same Constituent Assembly. Even the operation of the fundamental rights and adult franchise were extended to them.

As regards the civil service, two new all-India services had come to be evolved in October 1946 to take the place of the Indian Civil Service and the Indian Police, the Indian Administrative Service and the Indian Police Service. They were organized on the basis of an agreement between the Government of India and the Provincial Governments. The principles on which these new Services were constituted were comparable to those of their predecessors. They were to be non-political. Their recruitment, conditions of service and disciplinary control were to be governed by professional considerations of merit, discipline, efficiency, diligence and honesty, not by political considerations of allegiance to party. These principles were recognized by the Home Member Vallabhbhai Patel as a *sine qua non* of sound administration under a democratic régime even more than under authoritarian rule. They were settled at a conference of Provincial **Prime Ministers on 21 October 1946, and the details** were later worked out, through correspondence, with the Provincial Governments. Even before the transfer of power the Government of India, with the aid and advice of the Federal Public Service Commission, thus held competitive examinations, made recruitments, issued rules governing recruitment, discipline, control and conditions of service, and, finally entered into agreements with candidates for these Services.

The Interim Government also carried on negotiations with the British Government relating to guarantees given to the former Secretary of State's Services and to the newly created all-India Services. The position of the Services after the termination of the Secretary of State's control was discussed and it was agreed by both sides that the existing rights of all members of these Services, whether European or Indian, should be guaranteed if the officers were willing to continue and were retained by the new Governments. It was also agreed that a scale of compensation decided upon by the British Government should be paid to those Europeans of the all-India Services who wished to retire prematurely, or whom the new Government did not want to keep. Indian officers were expected generally to continue in service, but they were given a joint guarantee by the Central and Provincial Governments that their subsisting rights would be duly safeguarded. These Governments, however, retained the right to retire any individual officer even if he was willing to serve. The Indian officers so retired were to be entitled to the same scale of compensation as was admissible to their European counterparts. In a circular letter of 18 June 1947 the Government of India thus undertook to safeguard the pay, pension and other subsisting rights of all the officers who continued in service. And having regard to these commitments, the Home Ministry was in honour bound to include the necessary safeguards in the Constitution itself.

At the request of the Interim Government the Indian Independence Act expressly guaranteed that Judges and members of the Secretary of State's Services, European and Indian alike, who continued to serve the Government of the new Dominion, would enjoy their existing privileges as regards pay, leave and pension. In accordance with the assurance held out even to all-India Service officers as had not been appointed by the Secretary of State, the India (Provisional Constitution) Order of 14 August 1947 confirmed that, subject to any general or special orders or arrangements affecting his case, any person who immediately before 15 August 1947 held a civil post would be deemed duly appointed to a corresponding post in the new set-up.

The Drafting Committee of the Constituent Assembly accordingly provided safeguards for the rights of all offices of the all-India Services. The article drafted by it in October 1948 did so in respect of the Secretary of State's Services as well as the Indian Administrative Service and the Indian Police Service. This, however, evoked considerable controversy, and the scope of the safeguard was finally restricted to the Secretary of State's Services only.[3] Even this restriction failed to escape criticism. It was argued that members of the Secretary of State's Services were rulers under the old régime and that the guarantee provided would enable those still in service to continue to be so in the new régime also. But Vallabhbhai Patel decisively intervened in defence of the article designed to protect the rights of the Secretary of State's officers.[4] He also took the opportunity to express appreciation for the Indian Civil Servant.

Today my Secretary can write a note opposed to my views. I have given that freedom to all my Secretaries. I have told them, 'If you do not give your honest opinion for fear that it will displease your Minister, please then you had better go. I will bring another Secretary'. I will never be displeased over a frank expression of opinion. That is what the Britishers were doing with the Britishers. We are now sharing the responsibility. You have agreed to share responsibility. Many of them with whom I have worked, I have no hesitation in saying that they are as patriotic, as loyal and as sincere as myself. . . . These people are the instruments. Remove them and I see nothing but a picture of chaos all over the country.[5]

The conditions of service guaranteed by the Constitution had in fact already been anticipated by the India (Provisional Constitution) Order. Another important change which the Order effected was the abolition of the 'reservations' and the 'safeguards' provided under the 1935 Act to enable the Governor-General to act 'in his discretion', or to exercise 'his individual judgement'. Even the law made by the Governor of a Province under Section 93 of that Act was directed to be omitted in the schedule to this Order.

Indeed, the Act of 1935 and its adaptations under the India (Provisional Constitution) Order served as a draft for the framing of a number of chapters of the Constitution of India. The Constitution makers not only largely followed the scheme of the Government of India Act with suitable modifications, but also adopted its language in a number of cases.

The Constitution of India

The Constituent Assembly took nearly three years to frame the Constitution. B. N. Rau, an eminent constitutional lawyer who assisted the founding fathers in their task, travelled far and wide to collect the necessary information for their guidance. His reports and suggestions, which influenced the conclusions of the Assembly, accounted for the variations made to remove the inadequacies of the Government of India Act. Following the Irish model, for example, it framed the basic rights of the citizens which were justifiable, and the Directive Principles of State Policy which were to be guidelines for legislative and executive action by the State. It recognized the difficulties of the U.S.A. in evolving the doctrine of judicial review, and made provisions for more certainty in the interpretation of the Constitution by restricting the scope for evolving new doctrines by judicial interpretation. However, the form of government envisaged in the Constitution remained parliamentary and the form of the Constitution federal. These were two important features which were embodied in the Government of India Act, 1935.

The Form of Goverment: Parliamentary

The Constitution created a sovereign democratic republic, with an Executive responsible jointly to the Legislature in accordance with the British tradition. The Constitution of India accordingly provided that 'there shall be a Council of Ministers with the Prime Minister at the head to aid and advise the President in the execution of his functions'. The Prime Minister was to be appointed by the President, and other Ministers were to be appointed by the President on the advice of the Prime Minister. Thus the executive power of the Central Government, though in law 'vested in the President of the Union' was sought to be exercised by, or on the authority of, a Council of Ministers called the Cabinet which would be collectively responsible to the lower chamber of the Central Legislature, the Lok Sabha, elected by adult franchise.

This ministerial responsibility to Parliament is enforced, in the first place, by a general election to the Lok Sabha where most Ministers have to face the electorate. The day-to-day responsibility of the Minister, on the other hand, is enforced by votes in Parliament on all questions which come up before it in the form of resolutions, bills for legislation, requests for grant of money out of the consolidated fund, and to an extent by interpolation. And since a Minister's responsibility is joint, no Minister should publicly criticize a decision of the Cabinet. He should resign if he wants to air independent opinion. On the analogy of the 1935 Act it was of course suggested by the Constitutional Adviser, B. N. Rau, that the President might be invested with certain special powers to be exercised by him in his discretion. It was stated that although under responsible government the Head of State mostly acted 'on the advice of Ministers responsible to the legislature, nevertheless there are certain matters in which he is entitled to exercise his own discretion'. These matters, it was pointed out, included the choice of a Prime Minister under certain circumstances, the dissolution of Parliament, the prevention of a grave menace to the peace and tranquility of the Union, the safeguarding of the financial stability and credit of the Union Government, and safeguarding the legitimate interests of minorities. After due consideration, the Union Constitution Committee decided without reservation in favour of the parliamentary form of executive where the President would have no special powers vested personally in him but would exercise all his functions, including the dissolution of the lower chamber of Parliament, only on the advice of his Ministers. He could do nothing contrary to their advice, nor could he do anything without their advice. The Constituent Assembly finally accepted the principle of a parliamentary government where the President, like the King of England, was the Head of State, not of the Executive.

Most of the modes of parliamentary government had already been developing in India along the lines of British practice, even in the presence of what Lord Minto described as 'constitutional autocracy'.[6] The functioning of the Indian Legislature in accordance with the established rules of procedure, even though under official majority, brought constitutional advance to the threshold of the parliamentary system. Questions, resolutions and motions in the Legislative Council acquired a greater significance and became more and more frequent when within the restricted field of transferred subjects in the Provinces. The Act of 1919 laid down the principle that the Governor should be guided by the advice of his Ministers unless he 'sees sufficient cause to dissent from their opinion, in which case he may require action to be taken otherwise than in accordance with that advice'. In fact, the Act introduced in the provincial field contains the rudiments of the cabinet system of government. For it made provision for a minister to be answerable to the legislature and his continuance in office dependent on the confidence of that legislature. The Act of 1935 which carried the process of the transfer of power a step further, rendered ministerial responsibility in the Provinces subject to much stricter legislative control. The administration of a Province was entrusted to its Council of Ministers, fully accountable to a wholly elected legislature. The Governors were of course invested with 'special responsibilities' in the exercise of individual judgement and discretion. But they took care not to invoke them in spite of popular attempts to set up parallel governments in the districts.[7] The policy of the British Government was to see that the responsibility introduced in the governance of the Provinces remained for all practical purposes inviolate and unimpaired. Under the scheme of federation contemplated in that Act a certain measure of responsibility was to be transferred at the Centre also, although that scheme did not materialize.

Indeed, the administration of India over several decades had drawn largely upon the traditions of British constitutional law and Indian leadership had looked up to the British model as by far the best. The Constitution of the Dominion Government of India which had already been functioning in accordance with the India (Provi-

sional Constitution) Order of 1947, thus commended itself immediately as a suitable model for the Constituent Assembly to adopt. It
is interesting to note that, while the Constitution Act of 1935 had
earlier been decried by Congress leaders as a charter of slavery, the
Order based on it was later used by them to form the essential
ingredients of the Constitution of free India.

The Form of the Constitution: Federal

The task of constitution-making in India under British rule was
governed by practical considerations of social and political ecology,
not by abstract principles. The parliamentary enactments of the
past in many cases either imparted statutory sanction to existing
realities or devised an instrument of government best fitted to meet
imperial and political exigencies. The whole approach was pragmatic, not theory-bound.

Historically, the rise of imperialism lent itself to a number of
important developments. The exploitation of Indian resources to feed
British manufactures called for an organization of the machinery of
government invested not only with the direction of political affairs,
but also with administrative, financial and legislative control. The
Government of India Act, 1833 provided for a highly centralized
unitary government to facilitate economic exploitation.

When the Crown took over from the Company under the Government of India Act, 1858, the situation did not materially change. It
did not affect the unitary character of government but, on the contrary, reinforced it by means of functional rationalization which, in
effect, meant not only centralization but also an extension of the
activity of the State within the framework of economy and efficiency.
This extended activity, however, suggested the expediency of a progressive devolution of authority to the provinces in the administrative,
financial and legislative fields. Even so, the provinces had till 1919 no
legal rights and continued to be no more than agents of the Central
Government, which in turn was subordinate to the Secretary of State.

Apart from the exigencies of imperial finance dictating the need for
progressive decentralization, two other factors had in the meantime
been operating to produce a similar effect. The first was an increasing
provincial bias since 1854 in the behaviour even of officials representing their respective provinces in the Indian Legislative Council. They
were generally prone to put across provincial interests and viewpoints
and to persuade the Centre to accept them. The second was the

growth of Indian nationalism which sought to secure for Indians an increasing share in the country's administration and to ensure constitutional advance in the provinces as a step towards self-government and social and economic development.

The Government of India Act, 1919, provided, for the first time, for the division of the field of administration into two spheres, the Central and the Provincial. Defence, communications, external affairs, customs, income-tax and criminal administration were among the more important subjects retained by the Centre. Certain other subjects like agriculture, education, industry, land tenures, local self-government, medicine, public health and public works were made wholly provincial. Some scope for ministerial responsibility was created in the provincial field by a transfer of the so-called nation-building subjects to the charge of Indian ministers. Certain sources of revenue too were in consequence handed over to the provinces to fulfil the responsibilities entrusted to them.

Thus the Government of India Act, 1919 introduced, though unconsciously, some form of federation based on a division of the list of subjects. The immediate object was of course to meet the demand of politics and an attempt to restrict political concessions to the provincial sphere. It was not to make the provinces autonomous federating units. But since this demand for the transfer of power, however limited, could not be met except by a division of subjects for administrative purposes, the division so effected tended to impart to the arrangement a federal form. It remained unitary in spirit. For the actual division was effected by a series of devolutions from the Governor-General-in-Council who remained 'in undisturbed responsibility to Parliament and fully equipped to fulfil that responsibility'.[8] The Indian princes, too, remained outside the scope of administrative reorganization, retaining their old forms of government.

The period after 1919 and before the enactment of 1935 was dominated largely by mass politics representing both revivalist reaction and left sectarianism. The Congress Party, which had declined to work the Constitution of 1919, became subject to the influence of both. Its non-cooperation movement raised the emotional content of politics to a height which clouded reason and split its leadership. The aftermath of the movement produced serious repercussions on the Muslim attitude and British policy in India. While the British moved away from the goal of dominion status envisaged in the announcement of 20 August 1917,[9] the Muslim League, right from its Lahore Session of 1924 onwards, took up a definitely separatist stand to prevent the Congress from seizing power. However, the idea of all-India federation had in the meantime come to be generally mooted. While the League demanded reservation of seats in legislatures and a federal form of government with a limited Centre, the Nehru Committee (1928) recommended a strong Centre and no reservation of seats for religious minorities. The committee was not particularly keen on the accession of the Indian States. But even if they agreed to join an all-India federation, the Centre, it was emphasized, must continue to be strong. The Simon Commission (1930) recommended full provincial autonomy with ministerial control over the whole field of administration including law and order. But it did not suggest an all-India federation including the Indian States. This was raised and discussed in some depth at the Round Table Conference (1930–2), when an all-India federal scheme was in principle accepted as a condition for the establishment of responsible government. Dominion Status still remained a future goal, as announced by the Viceroy in his statement of 31 October 1929.

The Government of India Act (1935) that followed represented a clear break with the unitary concept of India's administration. It prescribed a federal union of autonomous provinces which no longer derived their authority, political and fiscal, by devolutions made by the Centre, but obtained as a direct grant from the Crown under statutory provisions, specifying three distinct lists of subjects, Federal, Provincial and Concurrent. The authority of the provincial governments could not be abridged or withdrawn at pleasure by the Centre. Their administration was entrusted to their Councils of Ministers which were fully answerable to wholly elected legislatures.

However, the federal structure so created had serious limitations. The federating units were merely the Governors' Provinces, where the Governor remained invested with unusual powers in the exercise of his 'special responsibilities', subject to the overriding authority of the Governor-General over the entire field of administration, including the demarcated sphere of provincial jurisdiction. This was a remnant of the old unitary system intended to ensure imperial control over the Government of India and counteract any centrifugal tendencies that might arise from the grant of provincial autonomy. The 1935 Act was an attempt to convert a unitary state into a federation.

However, the concept of an all-India federation was considered incomplete without the princely States as constituent units. A proposal for their entry was made by a White Paper, which recommended that a new polity should be created in which both the British India provinces and the Indian States would be federally united. Unlike the provinces of British India, the Indian States possessed sovereignty in varying degrees. This sovereignty was by itself an impediment to accession. For the rights, authority and jurisdiction which were to be exercised on behalf of the Crown by the Central Government, did not extend to any Indian State, unless the Ruler himself agreed to their exercise. In other words, the accession of an Indian State could not take place without its consent. The Constitution Act could not itself make any Indian State a member of the Federation, but it could prescribe a method of accession and indicate the legal implications involved. It was, however, recognized that the Indian Federation, with the acceding Indian States as its constituent units, would present a model which would be 'unique in character among the Federations of the world'.[10]

The provisions relating to the provinces came into force in 1937. But negotiations with the princes under the Instrument of Accession became protracted and the war intervened in 1939 to interrupt their continuance. Writing about the failure to set up a federation, R. J. Moore thus observes:[11]

That Churchill delayed the Act of 1935 and aroused hostility among Indian nationalists is clear . . .he also encouraged princely truculence after 1935 by insisting that the princes should not be bullied into acceding to the federation. There were sufficient diehard respecters of treaty rights among the Tories to make Neville Chamberlain fearful for party unity. In consequence, Linlithgow was held tightly in leading-strings from home and cannot be adjudged primarily responsible for the failure to hustle the prince.

The Cabinet Mission expressed itself against the transfer of paramountcy to any government in India, although it emphasized the importance of preserving India's unity within the framework of a federal system based on a Centre limited functionally to defence, communications and foreign affairs. In its anxiety to maintain that unity the Congress Party also reconciled itself to the idea of weak Central Government. But when the scheme of Partition was announced on 3 June 1947, the thinking of the Congress changed. The immediate result of the declaration of Partition was a decision by the Union Constitution Committee and the Provincial Constitution

Committee of the Constituent Assembly that India would be a federation with a strong Central Government and Legislature; that there would be three Legislative Lists (Union, States and Concurrent) on the lines of the 1935 Act; and that residuary powers would vest in the Centre. The 1935 Act and the India (Provisional Constitution) Order adapted from it were in fact already serving as a suitable guide for a federal constitution within the framework of a strong and powerful Centre.

Some of the peculiar features of the Indian federal constitution were exhibited in the manner in which legislative powers were distributed between the Union and States. The Union List, for instance, shows that notwithstanding its numerous legislative items, it contemplates the exercise of residuary powers to legislate on any matter not provided for in the State or Concurrent Lists. Besides, the Constitution made express provision that, in the event of legislative conflicts in the Concurrent field, the law made by a State would be treated as void to the extent that it conflicted with the Union law. A State, however, has the freedom to legislate with the approval of the President to modify the Union law in its application to the State.[12] In certain cases Parliament can legislate on a matter classified in the State List itself, provided it is necessary to do so in the national interest.[13] Though recognizing a federation as a dual polity based on a division of authority in the distribution of legislative, executive and judicial powers, the framers of the constitution sought to ensure that the elements of duality did not impair the unity of the country. They thus introduced uniformity in all basic matters within the framework of federalism. The means adopted to preserve that unity and uniformity were the continuance of the integrated legal and judicial system which the British had built for imperial purposes, as well as a common all-India Civil Service which they had, in addition, designed to man key positions and serve as watch dogs for the Centre in the various provinces. The office of the Governor, too, was intended to maintain the hold of the Centre over the States. For, as an appointee of the President, he was expected to act as an agent or representative of the Centre, which he actually does through his powers to constitute the local legislatures and shape the formation of the State Ministries.

Since the Governor is authorized to give or withhold his assent to every bill, or return it to the legislature for reconsideration, or preserve it for the consideration of the President who may likewise call for revision or amendment, they can both use discretion to enable the

Union to supervise and control legislation by States in their exclusive field.[14]

Though exercised only when both Houses of Parliament are not in session, the legislative powers of the President (Article 123) to promulgate an ordinance having 'the same force and effect as an Act of Parliament', a relic of the 1935 Act, are an encroachment on the supremacy of the legislature, which enables the executive to legislate when Parliament is not in session. Ordinances have in fact been issued almost immediately after Parliament has recessed, which creates an impression that the executive can legislate on issues where the Government wishes to avoid discussion in Parliament. And as an ordinance has the same force as parliamentary legislation, the executive can manoeuvre to repeal even laws passed by Parliament, although for a period not exceeding six months, the maximum limit for Parliament to remain recessed. The executive authority over Parliament is likewise secured by Article 240 of the Constitution which empowers the President to make regulations 'for the peace, progress and good government' of specified territories. Any regulation so made may repeal or amend any Act of Parliament, or any existing law applicable for the time being to the Union territory. These provisions, though justified under the 1935 Act, cannot but be viewed as repugnant to the accepted concept of parliamentary democracy.

There is, in addition, a separate chapter dealing with 'Emergency Provisions', covering such situations as a national emergency, a failure of the constitutional machinery in the States and a financial emergency. The President is invested under Article 352(1) with powers to proclaim a state of emergency whenever he feels that the security of India or of any part of its territory is threatened by war, external danger or internal disturbance. A Proclamation so issued (a) may be revoked by a subsequent Proclamation, (b) shall be laid before each House of Parliament; and (c) shall cease to operate at the expiration of two months unless before the expiration of that period it has been approved by resolutions of both Houses of Parliament.

When a Proclamation is made, not only the executive power of the Union but also the power of Parliament to make laws is extended to all matters in the State List.[15] The substance of this provision is borrowed from the 1935 Act and further extended to include external aggression. A proclamation can be issued even if there is no actual threat but the danger of a threat developing. When a proclamation of emergency is in operation, the rights of citizens to freedom of speech, movement, etc. is suspended. The President may even by order declare that the right to move any court for the enforcement of any fundamental rights will also remain suspended.[16]

Indeed, the emergency powers of the President, which the Government of India exercises on his behalf, converts the federation into a unitary state, concentrating in the hands of the Union Government all executive, legislative and judicial powers. The Constitution can in fact be both unitary and federal to suit particular requirements or circumstances, a feature which was designed originally to give it resilience and adaptability, but which can also be turned to the advantage of a ruling party.

The arrangements which provided against the failure of constitutional machinery in the States were designed not only to ensure stability in the governance of the States, but also to give extended powers to the Union Government to control them. It is laid down that if, on receipt of a report from the Governor of a State, the President is convinced that its government cannot be carried on in accordance with the Constitution, he may by proclamation assume to himself such powers and functions of government as he deems fit or necessary. Even the powers of the local legislature can under the direction of the Union Government be declared exercisable by or under the authority of Parliament. Proclamations under this provision have been issued on several occasions when parties in State legislatures have been unable to form stable governments. The concentration of power at the Centre has sometimes been responsible for deliberately creating instability in the States.

The President's power to ensure the financial stability or credit of India or any part of its territories is yet another source of strength to the Centre. Once he is satisfied that a state of financial emergency has arisen, he can declare so by proclamation, authorizing the Union Government to direct any State to observe such canons of financial propriety as it may deem necessary to meet the situation.[17]

The integrated system of the judiciary which combines the judiciary of the Union and the States, operates as an additional reinforcement to the authority of the Centre. In terms of the jurisdiction of the courts there is in fact no demarcation between Union laws and State laws. The Supreme Court of India, the apex of the entire judicial system, functions as a court of both original and appellate jurisdiction. In its former capacity the Supreme Court resolves disputes between the Union and the States as well as between the several

States. As an appellate court in constitutional, civil and criminal cases, on the other hand, it adjudicates on appeals from the High Courts of the several States. This integrated system of judicial administration follows the pattern that prevailed under the Government of India Act, 1935.

The control of the Centre is further entrenched by the right vested in it to make appointments to the higher State judiciary. Every Judge of a High Court is, for instance, appointed by the President after consultation with the Chief Justice of India, the Governor of the State and the Chief Justice of the High Court concerned. Indeed, the appointing authority is the Union Government itself. The removal of a Judge of the High Court likewise proceeds from the Centre. The State legislature or the State executive has no say in the matter.

Territorial Reorganization

By far the most important constitutional provision that tends to reduce the States to subordination is that which gives Parliament its power to change their areas, boundaries or names. Articles 2 and 3 of the Constitution invest Parliament with full powers to alter or even destroy the identity of a State mentioned in Schedule I. Parliament can also form new States by separating territory from a State or by uniting any territory to a part of another State. Thus Hyderabad was under the States Reorganization Act (No. 37 of 1956) divided between the territories of Mysore and Andhra Pradesh, and Sikkim was made into a new State in 1975.

In introducing these provisions, the founding fathers were guided by the imperial precedents of the British Government. In his decisions to reorganize territorial divisions the Governor-General in Council was not fettered by anything except considerations of administrative convenience, financial viability or strategic significance. Though all the provinces had after 1833 become in a sense agents of the Central Government, their different categories remained none the less distinguishable. By the close of Lord Dalhousie's administration (1848–56), there had already come into existence three forms of provincial governments, namely, those under a Governor and Executive Council, those administered by a Lieutenant–Governor and those placed under a Chief Commissioner.[18] Most of the British Indian provinces had to pass through one or both of the earlier stages before becoming Governors' Provinces under the Government of

India Act, 1919. A distinction was also made between 'major provinces' and 'minor administrations'. The first category included the Governors' Provinces, Lieutenant-Governors' Provinces, and the two largest Chief Commissionerships, Assam and the Central Provinces, invested with powers nearly as wide as those of the second category. All the other Chief Commissionerships were called 'minor administrations' and were administered directly by the Central Government. What the Government of India Act, 1935, did was to recognize three categories of component units, namely, Governors' Provinces, federating Indian States, and Chief Commissionerships.

The administrative units of British India remained virtually intact on the transfer of power. The former princely States, however, saw a revolutionary change come over them after Independence. 216 of the smaller Indian States were merged in the provinces; 61 were formed into new centrally-administered units, and 275 States were integrated to create new administrative and federating units.[19]

Proceeding on the lines already indicated by the 1935 Act, the Constitution of India recognized all three categories of States described therein and added a fourth category not included in it. The status of the first two categories, namely, Part A States (Governors' Provinces) and Part B States (federating Indian States) of Schedule I was based on the concept of federalism. Apart from the institution of a Rajpramukh functioning as the head of Part B States, the main feature that distinguished Part B States from Part A was the provision in Article 371 which vested in the central executive supervisory authority over the governments of Part B States for a specified period. The provision so made was unfederal in character, but it was not intended in principle to alter the basic relationship between these States and the Centre, which was essentially governed by a division of powers. Part C States were, however, to be administered by the Centre on a unitary basis. It consisted of two types of territories, namely, the princely States not merged in the provinces or integrated as federating units, and certain areas placed under Central control for strategic and other reasons. These were to be administered by the President through the agency of a Lieutenant-Governor or Chief Commissioner. The Government of Part C States Act, 1951 no doubt provided for Legislative Assemblies, Councils of Ministers and Councils of Advisers for Part C States. But the legislative power was limited and unevenly distributed.[20] Some were allowed a legislature of elected and nominated representatives with restricted authority and functions, while others had only an advisory council. The devolution of powers to the legislatures and governments of some of these States under the 1951 Act, however, did not detract from the legislative authority of Parliament over these States or the responsibility of the Union Government for their administration. There were also territories specified in Part D of Schedule I, which formed part of India.

The influence of history was thus clearly reflected in the organization of the States in different categories with unequal status and range of authority. The framers of the Act of 1935 and the Indian Constitution which borrowed from it. were both conscious of the absence of natural ingredients in the Indian federation which was created artificially to satisfy the demands of politics. The powers of Parliament under Articles 2 and 3 of the Constitution recognized the four-fold division of the territories. But this was to be a temporary expedient intended, though not expressly stated, to carry the arrangement to its logical conclusion in due course by abolishing the inequality of the constituent units. Powers were therefore reserved to Parliament to effect on a more rational principle a readjustment of the territories of the erstwhile provinces and princely States. The powers so given to Parliament could, however, destroy the very existence of a State. It is true that under the States Reorganization Act of 1956 the President was required to ascertain the views of the legislature of the State affected. But the Act did not enjoin that the concurrence of the State legislature concerned should be obtained or a referendum held before such parliamentary legislation was initiated. It was sufficient if Parliament passed a bill for the purpose by a simple majority, not by a two-thirds majority of members present and voting, as required for a constitutional amendment.

The 1935 Act had also prescribed territorial reorganization by ordinary legislation. It found acceptance with the Congress leadership, for it was feared that a rational redistribution of territories might not be possible with the consent of the States on account of their parochial and political bias, especially in Part B States. However, this procedural simplicity also afforded opportunity to linguistic groups to press for the creation of linguistic States.

Historically, the demand for the redistribution of British Indian provinces on a linguistic basis flowed from two main developments. The one was cultural, and the other essentially political. The cultural factor was a result of the downward filtration of a national system of education introduced by Macaulay in 1835, and the subsequent emphasis laid on vernacular education by Wood's Despatch in 1854. Together they contributed to a phenomenal growth of regional languages and the development amongst their promoters of a consciousness of being distinct cultural units. The activity of Christian Missions and the official policy of free enterprise in education after 1882 created a situation which further strengthened that consciousness. The political factor, on the other hand, proceeded initially as an expedient to meet a state of imperial financial crisis by asking the provinces to mobilize their own tax resources and satisfy their local needs. It was this policy which promoted the growth of provincial finance, involving, in turn, a devolution of administrative authority under dyarchy in 1921 and a constitutional division of powers under provincial autonomy in 1937.

Since both the cultural and political considerations were interrelated, they were sought to be met as a matter of local importance without prejudice, however, to imperial interests which could not but take into account considerations of geographical unity, administrative convenience, strategic importance, internal security and financial viability, etc.[21] Right from the partition of Bengal in 1905 to the emergence of Orissa on a linguistic and cultural basis in 1936 there was a growing realization in official circles that the steady progress of vernacular languages would in course of time draw into the arena of public life men who would not be able to conduct the business of legislation in English. The individuality of the provinces was therefore sought to be developed by considerations of linguistic homogeneity[22] as a natural basis for regional development, which, in addition, might also serve an imperial interest by limiting the scope of Indian politics to local and provincial boundaries.

The Indian National Congress also encouraged provincialism with vigour. Doubtless, it viewed provincial autonomy as a step towards control over the Government of India. But its demand for linguistic provinces was more marked and clamorous: unlike the governing class of the British bureaucracy in India the composition of the competing Congress leadership was multi-regional and multi-cultural, immediately subject to local pressure in the Congress provinces for its own organizational purposes. In 1908, for instance, it favoured the formation of a separate province of Bihar on linguistic grounds. In 1917 it favoured the creation of two more provinces, Sind and Andhra, on the same principle. This was deliberate departure from its normal organizational pattern which had thus far adopted the boundaries of existing administrative provinces. By a resolution passed in July 1938 at Wardha, its Working Committee assured the delegations from Andhra, Karnatak and Kerala that linguistic redistribution of the provinces would be undertaken as soon as the Congress had the power to do so. Similar assurances were held out for the creation of Maharashtra in its election manifesto of 1945-6.

The Partition of India and the most serious problem of national unity that emerged forced the Congress to have a second look at the old pledges on linguistic provinces. In a remark before the Constituent Assembly on 27 November 1947 Jawaharlal Nehru emphasized that it was first necessary to ensure the security and stability of the country, not the redistribution of provinces on a linguistic basis. The Linguistic Provinces Commission (Dar Commission) appointed on the recommendation of the Drafting Committee of the Constituent Assembly held a similar view. Like the British, the Dar Commission wanted the power of the Centre to remain intact and not weakened by new centres of political influence emerging in response to linguistic demands which were by no means unrelated to a desire for the exercise of local patronage and promotion of economic interest.

In December 1948 the Jaipur Session of the Congress appointed a Commission to review the recommendations of the Dar Commission. It consisted of Jawaharlal Nehru, Vallabhabhai Patel and Pattabhi Sitaramayya and endorsed the views of the Commission. It reiterated that the primary concern of the country should be the security, unity and economic prosperity of India, not the principle of linguistic provinces which could be applied only after careful thought, lest it encourage disruptive tendencies.

In April 1949, the Congress Working Committee adopted the report of the Committee. The election manifesto issued by the party in 1951 also pointed out that, while the wishes of the people on linguistic states would be respected, there were other more important matters which no government could afford to ignore. The Congress, however, agreed to the formation of Andhra on the ground that its Tamilnad Committee and the Madras Government had both supported the proposal. Even so, delay in implementation occurred on account of some disputed areas and it was not until the death of Potti Sriramulu, who laid down his life for a separate State, that the Government created the State in 1953. A beginning had been made in the reorganization of States under Articles 2 and 3 of the Constitution.

The task of examining 'objectively and dispassionately' the question of reorganizing the States was soon entrusted to a Commission. It was required to make its recommendations by 30 June 1955, a date which was later extended by a few months to 30 September. It is not within the scope of this work to review the entire field of investigation the Commission attempted. For our immediate aim is merely to show that the Centre could at will create new States or readjust their boundaries, and that, consistent with the object of its institution, the Commission too evolved a pattern of reorganization on a principle designed to accommodate linguistic demands within the broad framework of national unity.

Before the submission of the Commission's Report, there existed in all 29 States, including Andhra. These consisted of Part A, B and C States. Part D areas were centrally administered territories not classified as States and their status remained undisturbed by the Commission. The highlight of its recommendations was the elimination, on a rational principle, of the existing distinction between Part A and B States and the disappearace of Part C States. Delhi and Manipur, which were earlier included in Part C States, were now to be centrally administered territories, and the remaining 27 States were reduced to the following 16: Andhra, Assam, Bihar, Bombay, Hyderabad, Jammu and Kashmir, Karnatak, Kerala, Madhya Pradesh, Orissa, Punjab, Rajasthan, Uttar Pradesh, Vidarbha, West Bengal.

The States Reorganization Act, 1956, however, made certain alterations. It retained Jammu and Kashmir as a Part B State, without any change in its status. Hyderabad and Vidarbha (a Marathi-speaking area) were both rejected as reorganized constituent units. In addition, the Part C States were continued.[23] The formation of new States and territorial changes effected under the Act were as follow:

PART A

State	Broad Territories
1. Andhra Pradesh	Transfer of territory from Hyderabad to Andhra and alteration of name.
2. Assam	The earlier Province of Assam, the Khasi States and the tribal areas,[24] excluding territories specified in the Schedule to the Assam (Alteration of Boundaries) Act, 1951.
3. Bihar	The existing area of Bihar.
4. Bombay	New State of Bombay including most of its existing territories plus the Kutch, Saurashtra and certain Marathi-speaking districts earlier included in Hyderabad and Madhya Pradesh.

5. Kerala	Transfer of some territory from Travancore-Cochin, a former Part B State, to Madras, and formation of a new State of Kerala consisting of the remaining territory of Travancore-Cochin plus parts of Malabar and South Kanara districts.
6. Madhya Pradesh	Comprising the existing State of Madhya Pradesh except the districts transferred to the new State of Bombay; the territories of the existing States of Bhopal and Vindhya Pradesh (former Part C States); the territories of the existing Part B State of Madhya Bharat, and part of Kotah district in Rajasthan.
7. Madras	Former Province of Madras minus the territories transferred to Andhra in 1953; the territories transferred to Madras from the State of Travancore-Cochin under the States Reorganization Act.
8. Mysore	Comprising the existing State of Mysore and Coorg; the districts of Belgaum, Gulbarga and South Kanara with certain exceptions in each case. Coorg formed a separate district.
9. Orissa	Comprising the existing area of Orissa.
10. Punjab	Punjab was formed into a new Part A State comprising the territories of the existing State of Punjab and the territories of Patiala and East Punjab States Union.
11. Rajasthan	Comprising the existing State, except a part of Kotah district; Ajmer became a district. Certain portions earlier included in Bombay and Madhya Bharat were formed into Sirohi and Jhalawar districts in the new State.
12. Uttar Pradesh	Former Province known as the United Provinces.
13. West Bengal	The existing State of West Bengal and the territory of Chandernagore as defined by the Chandernagore (Merger) Act, 1954.

PART B

1. Jammu and Kashmir[25]	Consisting of the territory which immediately before the commencement of the Constitution constituted the old State of Jammu and Kashmir.

PART C[26]

1. Delhi	Former Chief Commissioner's Province of Delhi.
2. Himachal Pradesh	Comprising Himachal Pradesh and Bilaspur under the Himachal Pradesh and Bilaspur (New

	State) Act, 1954. It remained under a Lieutenant-Governor.
3. Manipur	The territory earlier administered as a Chief Commissioner's Province under the name of Manipur.
4. Tripura	The territory earlier administered as a Chief Commissioner's Province under the name of Tripura.
5. The Laccadive, Minicoy and Amindivi Islands	A New Part C State was formed comprising the Laccadive and Minicoy Islands in Malabar district and the Amindivi Islands in South Kanara district. These ceased to form part of Madras after the establishment of new State.

By a simple Act of Parliament the Centre thus formed a number of new States by transferring territory from one State to another, by altering boundaries, or by increasing or diminishing their area as well as by altering the name. Many of the erstwhile Part C States like Ajmer, Bhopal, Bilaspur, Coorg, Vindhya Pradesh and Kutch disappeared altogether and their territories amalgamated with the neighbouring States either newly formed or existing from before. Of the Part B States, Hyderabad become completely non-existent. PEPSU was merged in Punjab and Saurashtra in Bombay. The very territorial integrity of a State thus depended upon the will of the Centre. The federal principle of the division of power was naturally divested of its significance. Though federal in form, the Constitution remained essentially unitary in spirit.

The task of the States Reorganization Commission had been to strike a balance between local demands and national requirements. The arrangement made under the Act of 1956 was, however, weighted more in favour of tradition than change. Apart from the continuance of linguistic minorities in most States, the two newly formed States of Bombay and Punjab remained essentially bilingual. The tribal areas of Assam, too, remained tagged to the people of the planes (the Brahmaputra and Surma Valleys), the dominant element in the administration of Assam. The increasing consciousness of language-based and job-motivated distinct cultural entities naturally pressed hard for local and regional autonomy involving further reorganization of the States. Certain territories were, for instance, transferred from Andhra Pradesh to Madras and *vice versa* under the Andhra Pradesh and Madras (Alteration of Boundaries) Act, 1959. A similar transfer took place between Rajasthan and Madhya Pradesh (Transfer of Territories) Act, 1959.[27] Under the Bombay Reorganization

Act, 1960 Gujarat was formed into a new State by a transfer of certain territories formerly included in the State of Bombay. The residuary State of Bombay thus came to be known as Maharashtra. With the formation of Gujarat on 1 May 1960 a separate High Court for that State was established on the same day. The High Court of Bombay thus became the High Court for Maharashtra. The Aquired Territories (Merger) Act, 1960 which came into effect on 17 January 1960, provided for the merger into the States of Assam, Punjab and West Bengal certain territories acquired through agreements between India and Pakistan. Under the State of Nagaland Act, 1962, a new State of Nagaland came to be formed on 1 December 1963, with a common High Court for the State of Assam and the State of Nagaland. The new State so formed consisted of three districts, Kohima district, Mokokchung, and Tuensang. These were earlier part of the Naga Hills Tuensang Tribal Area included in Assam. Together they constituted a single parliamentary constituency.

Like the division of the State of Bombay into two linguistic States, the reorganization of Punjab on the basis of Punjabi and Hindi speaking areas was no less controversial.

The Punjab Reorganization Act, which came into force on 1 November 1966, formed the new State of Haryana comprising certain territories of the existing State of Punjab. These included the districts of Hissar, Rohtak, Gurgaon, Karnal and Mahendragarh as well as certain tahsils and parts of the district of Ambala, which were formed into two separate districts of Jind and Ambala. Chandigarh became a Union territory, ceasing to form part of the existing State of Punjab, which lost further by a transfer of some of its other territories to the Union territory of Himachal Pradesh. The territories so transferred included the districts of Simla, Kangra, Kulu and Lahaul and Spiti. These were in addition to the transfer of certain *kanungo* circles and tahsils of the districts of Hoshiarpur and Gurdaspur, tahsils which were merged partly in Simla and partly in Kangra. The residuary territories of the earlier State of Punjab were formed into the Punjabi-speaking State of Punjab. There was to be a common High Court for Punjab and Haryana and for the Union territory of Chandigarh, to be called the High Court of Punjab and Haryana.

Changes effected by ordinary Acts of Parliament related also to certain readjustments of boundaries and alterations of name. The Andhra Pradesh and Mysore (Transfer of Territory) Act, 1968, for instance, made certain alterations in the arrangements arrived at in 1953, 1956 and 1959. Certain territory was transferred from the

State of Mysore to Andhra Pradesh and included in Anantapur district of the latter State. A few boundary changes were likewise effected between Bihar and Uttar Pradesh as a result of change in the course of the Ghaghara in the district of Ballia in Uttar Pradesh and Ganga in the districts of Saran and Shahabad in Bihar. This was done under the Bihar and Uttar Pradesh (Alteration of Boundaries) Act, 1968 which came into force on 10 June 1970. The Madras State (Alteration of Name) Act, 1968 changed the name of 'Madras'. It became known as 'Tamil Nadu' with effect from 14 January 1969. Two years later, the Union territory of Himachal Pradesh acquired the status of a Governor's State under the State of Himachal Pradesh Act, 1970 which came into effect on 25 January 1971.

On 30 September 1971, Parliament passed the North-Eastern Areas (Reorganization) Act. It provided for the establishment of the States of Manipur and Tripura as well as for the formation of the State of Meghalaya and the Union Territories of Mizoram and Arunachal Pradesh. The Act came into force on 21 January 1972. The three States of Manipur, Tripura and Meghalaya as well as the two Union territories of Mizoram and Arunachal Pradesh thus ceased to be part of the existing State of Assam. Instead of the High Court of Assam and Nagaland, a common High Court was established for the States of Assam, Nagaland, Manipur, Tripura and Meghalaya, to be called the Gauhati High Court. They were all also placed under a common Governor.

As a result of agitation and 'revolutionary' developments in the sensitive border region of India against the ruling king of Sikkim, the Government of India proceeded in April 1975 to recognize by an Act of Parliament the formation of Sikkim as a new State. With the inclusion of Sikkim, the number of States functioning under the Constitution of India comes to 22; and there are, in addition, nine Union Territories, centrally administered on unitary principles.

Considerations of language in the reorganization of States thus played a more important role after 1956. This, however, does not mean that the Government of India subordinated its security interests and considerations of India's unity and stability. Indeed, these were taken care of before the enactment of the 1956 Act itself. After the Cabinet had considered the Report of the States Reorganization Commission, Govind Ballabh Pant, Minister for Home Affairs, held on 20 and 21 January 1956 informal discussions with the Chief Ministers of States who were in Delhi for a meeting of the National

Development Council.[28] They discussed three issues arising from the Commission's Report. The first two were directly connected with the Report, while the third found no mention in it. It emerged at the instance of Prime Minister Nehru as an important question which was also related to provisions made in the Constitution to solve problems of inter-State as well as Union-State relations. These three issues were: (i) the problem of safeguards for the linguistic minorities in reorganized States; (ii) administrative and other matters connected with the allotment of all-India service personnel in the States; and (iii) a tentative scheme for the establishment of zonal councils by invoking Article 263[29] of the Constitution and treating the Councils as part of the whole scheme for the reorganization of States.

The Conference approved of the suggestions made by the Commission to safeguard the rights of linguistic minorities through educational institutions established and managed by them under Articles 29, 30 and 347 of the Constitution. The State Governors were considered to be the most suitable central agency for enforcing the safeguards that might from time to time be adopted for linguistic minorities, scheduled castes and scheduled tribes. The declared object of the Government was to promote educational integration by a recognition of their legitimate demand for cultural autonomy.

As regards administrative integration through the government services, the Commission had made three recommendations. First, as a general rule fifty per cent of the new entrants in the all-India services should be from outside the State concerned. Secondly, some more all-India services, such as the Indian Service of Engineers, the Indian Forest Service and the Indian Medical and Health service should be constituted, the object being to satisfy the felt need for an all-India outlook in officers dealing with problems of concern to more than one State. Thirdly, at least one-third of the number of Judges in the High Court of a State should consist of persons recruited from outside that State.

The first proposal was acceptable to the majority of the States. However, Bombay, U.P. and West Bengal did not entirely agree on the ground that it was becoming increasingly necessary for officers to be fully familiar with the language and customs of the people under their administrative charge. It was therefore suggested that under the existing working rule, only one officer not belonging to a State be allotted every year to it and that an increase in the number of 'outsiders' might be considered after five years. The informal Confer-

ence of Chief Ministers, of course, resolved to accept the principles of
the Commission's recommendation. But no Chief Minister was in
favour of rigid rules being established. The Conference merely said
that the principles on which the Commission's proposal was based,
should be kept in view. The result was that, while under the existing
rules States like U.P., Punjab, Madras and West Bengal which
usually had a surplus of successful candidates from within their
States, got only one 'outsider' allotted, certain other States like Assam
and Orissa got over fifty per cent of their officers from outside. The
increasing decline of English as a common link language perhaps led
to dependence on regional languages. As for the creation of the
proposed new all-India services, the States did not agree. The Commission's proposal had therefore to be confined for a time to the
creation of certain Central Services to man posts at the Centre or in
the centrally administered areas. The States were in general suspicious of central control in matters of recruitment and management of
services.

In its recommendation concerning the appointment of Judges in
the High Courts the Commission's view was that it would inspire
confidence and help arrest parochial trends if at least some men with
professional standing and ability were appointed on an all-India
basis. This was in line with the old practice where one-third of the
total number of Judges in a High Court used to be members of the
Indian Civil Service. The Chief Ministers' Conference, however,
thought it premature to frame and adopt any rules on this subject.
The Conference merely suggested that the Commission's proposal be
brought to the notice of the Chief Justices of India and of each new
State, so that they might keep this principle in view while making
appointments.

On the second day of the Conference the Home Minister mentioned the decision of the Cabinet to establish five zonal councils, one
each for the Northern, Central, Eastern, Western and Southern
Zones. The Minister explained that these Councils would have advisory and deliberative functions only. They were not to have executive
powers unless in particular cases the State Governments concerned
decided by agreement to entrust certain executive functions to them.
There was general agreement among the Chief Ministers that these
councils should be established. They also endorsed details of the
scheme circulated and consensus was likewise reached that it was not
necessary to involve the provisions of Article 263 for the purpose kept

in view. Considering the importance of the proposal and the expectations of the Government about the future development of these zonal councils, it was felt desirable that provision for the constitution of these councils should be made in the States Reorganization Bill itself. This was accordingly done. The five zonal councils were established under the States Reorganization Act, 1956 without any reference to the provisions of the Constitution.

As an advisory body, each Zonal Council might discuss any matter in which some or all of the States on it, or the Union, have a common interest; it could advise the Central Government and the government of each State concerned as to the action to be taken on such matters. A Zonal Council might in particular discuss and make recommendations regarding matters of common interest in the field of economic and social planning, or any matter concerning border disputes, linguistic minorities, inter-State transport, or matters arising out of the reorganization of States under the Act.

The establishment of Zonal Councils was thus envisaged as a regional agency of Central control over the States reorganized on linguistic principles. This control was to be exercised through a Union Minister nominated by the President. The person so nominated was the Minister for Home Affairs who was to function as the Chairman of the Council consisting of the Chief Ministers of each State included in the zone and two other Ministers of each such State to be nominated by the Governor. They were to be aided by their respective Chief Secretaries and other officers attached to development departments.

To ensure national unity the Chief Ministers' Conference also discussed the expediency of having common Governors, common High Courts and common Public Service Commissions for two or more States. The response on this matter was not encouraging, except for the States of the North-eastern areas. Even so, the Conference agreed on enabling clauses being provided in order to meet specific situations as and when necessary.

Agencies Promoting Federal Democracy

The principle that went into the making of the Constitution was thus the supremacy of the Centre designed to preserve unity and ensure uniformity within the broad framework of a dual polity. The Constituent Assembly attempted to weave this principle into the pattern of relationships between the Union and the States in terms of legislative, executive and judicial functions. It is true that, since the Union had to depend on the States' machinery in exercising its executive power, there existed a clear need for cooperation between the Centre and the States as well as among the States themselves. But the extraordinary and unusual provisions of the Indian Constitution imparted to the Centre an authority repugnant to the principles of democratic federalism. Conditioned as it was by the socio-political forces of history, the Indian Constitution could not free itself from the authoritarian trends embodied in the 1935 Act which the founding fathers accepted as its basis. The element of cooperation of course existed, but at a subordinate level. The dominance of the Congress Party and the periodic conferences held centrally in Delhi at both political and administrative levels tended additionally to promote authoritarian trends already encouraged by the operation of the Planning Commission and the financial dependence of the States on the Centre.

The Election Commission. In spite of its unitary bias, the Constitution does provide certain mechanisms which serve as the basic foundation of democracy in India, however. The Election Commission, for instance, constitutes an independent agency for the superintendence, control and conduct of elections to the offices of President and Vice-President as well as to Parliament and the State legislatures. It is invested with the planning and working of the entire election machinery, functioning under the laws enacted by Parliament and even State legislatures in certain cases. Its freedom from the influence of political parties creates confidence in the electoral process of democracy.

Comptroller and Auditor-General. The institution of Comptroller and Auditor-General is another independent agency, comparable in importance to the higher judiciary. He is required to prepare annually and submit to the President a general financial statement, the Combined Finance and Revenue Accounts of the Union and of all the States, including their balances and liabilities. His role is to ensure parliamentary control of Indian finance through his powers to audit all expenditure from the revenues of the Union and the States, excluding the accounts relating to Defence and Railways. The professional vigour applied to the audit of expenditure helps in the proper functioning of democratic institutions in accordance with a national pattern which the office is intended to establish. Cases are on record where even top political executives are cautioned and obliged to fall in line with the requirements of audit and financial propriety. Like the higher judiciary, the Comptroller and Auditor-General enforces the rule of law in financial matters, which, in turn, conduces to democracy in the same way as the judiciary.

The Public Service Commission. The Public Service Commissions of the Union and the States, on the other hand, are designed to discharge an equally important function. Their emphasis on the quality of recruitment and disciplinary control is aimed at securing the best talent that can be made available for the public services. As no democracy can function effectively without an efficient system of public administration, the Constitution laid down that the Commissions should consist of able and independent members capable of ensuring integrity and high standards in the selection of administrative personnel.

The All-India Services. With the same purpose, Parliament was invested with powers to create one or more all-India services under the control of the Union Government to ensure unformity of standards in administration.[30] These services are common to the Union and the States and are a unique feature of the Indian federal set-up, a product again of historical circumstances. Though intended historically to function as instruments of the Centre, the founding fathers were guided additionally by considerations of using service personnel as a real liaison between the Centre and the States.

The Role of the Judiciary. An independent and impartial judiciary based on the rule of law is by far the most important reinforcement of democracy, an agency which applies the law without fear or favour to all classes and conditions of people. The need for supporting the rule of law becomes all the more imperative in a federal system of government where the distribution of powers is demarcated by a written Constitution between the Union and its constituent units, calling for an impartial authority to adjudicate on the limits of their respective powers whenever conflicts arise between the two or between the units themselves. It is the duty of such an authority to protect the supremacy of the Constitution itself by acting as an interpreter of the scheme of distribution of powers.

The system of judicial administration which had developed in India since the days of Cornwallis (1786-93) was based on the rule of law, which in effect signified freedom of the judiciary from the influence of the executive and the legislative authority in matters of administering and interpreting the law. Cases occurred where the system lent itself to denial of justice, which suggested the expediency of a resort to executive discretion as the best mode of making justice available to the needy. But the Government of India resisted this and the principles of the Cornwallis Code remained unaffected. The supremacy of the higher judiciary was left unscathed.

Organizationally, however, the legal uniformity which the British introduced as an essential condition for India's political unity, imparted to the judicial structure an integrated character, all courts being competent to enforce the laws enacted either by the central legislature or a provincial assembly. The Constituent Assembly adopted the model which the British had already created. The Supreme Court of India became the apex of the structure, the final court of appeal in all matters, whether arising from State or Union laws.

The integrated structure of the judiciary preserved the erstwhile supremacy of the Centre. For even under the Indian Constitution the Union executive remains vested with authority to appoint the Union as well as the higher State judiciary. But this does not mean sacrifice of independence. The Constitution enjoins that the appointment of Judges of High Courts is to be made after consultation with the Chief Justice of India and the Chief Justice of the State concerned. The State Government is, on the other hand, required to consult its own High Court in the selection of its subordinate judiciary. Moreover, the Judges of the Supreme Court or of the State High Courts are not to be removed except on certain specific grounds, and after an address by each House of Parliament supported by a specified majority. However, the independence of the higher judiciary is not an absolute concept. It is subject to the final control of the Union Government, the object being to ensure the functioning of a system unaffected by local influences or pressures from regional governments.

An important object of the Supreme Court is to preserve, through its power of judicial review, the structure of democracy enshrined in the Constitution. The occasion for such review arises from three main premises, where the Supreme Court is invested with the exercise of original jurisdiction. The first is the necessity of adjudicating on the constitutional limits of the powers of legislation exercisable by the Union and State legislatures. The second is to ascertain the extent to which the laws made are void or inconsistent with the fundamental rights provided by the Constitution itself. The third arises from the

provisions of the Constitution which lay down that, for certain purposes or in the public interest, legislation affecting some fundamental rights is valid only to the extent of imposing reasonable
restrictions on the exercise of those rights. The question of reasonableness must, in terms of the purposes of legislation, be a matter of
determination by the courts. In one of its observations the Supreme
Court recognizes this position: 'The determination by the legislature
of what constitutes a reasonable restriction is not final or conclusive; it
is subject to supervision by this court'.[31]

The position so held by the Supreme Court was maintained in
Golak Nath's case against the 17th Amendment of the Constitution
enacted in 1964. The amendment of Article 368 validated as many as
forty-four State and Central Acts intended to promote land reforms,
notwithstanding the infraction of fundamental rights by them. The
interpretation which the Court put on the Article, though by a slender
majority of six to five, was nonetheless epoch-making. It barred
Parliament's right to amend the Constitution in the matter of taking
away or abridging fundamental rights, which included the right to
property also.

The question posed by the decision of the Supreme Court was
whether the Constitution was to be a mere printed finality or a
dynamic process representing the social, economic and political
tendencies of the times. The issue represented a conflict between
status and change: subsequent developments showed that the die was
cast in favour of change. The Constitution (Twenty-fourth Amendment) Act, 1971, countered the effect of the Supreme Court decision
in Golak Nath's case by investing Parliament with a complete power
to amend Part III of the Constitution dealing with fundamental
rights. It laid down that the President could not refuse assent to a Bill
passed on this subject by both Houses of Parliament. The amendment
made it clear that Article 13(2) of the Constitution was not to apply to
an amendment of the Constitution made under Article 368.

The Constitution (Twenty-fifth Amendment) Act, 1971 which
sought to remove difficulties arising from the interpretation of the
term 'compensation' to be given to the owners of property acquired
was even more radical. It omitted the word 'compensation' from
Article 31(2) and replaced it by the word 'amount'. It inserted in
addition a new Article, 31C, to give effect to the policy of the State
towards securing the Directive Principles laid down in Article 39(b)
or (c). Any law enacted to promote that objective was not deemed to
be void on the ground that it infringed a fundamental right conferred

by Articles 14, 19 or 31. If the law so enacted contained a declaration that it was to give effect to the Directive Principles, it could not be called in question in any court.

This was followed in quick succession by the Constitution (Twenty-sixth Amendment) Act, 1971, terminating the Privy Purses and Privileges of the Rulers of the former Indian States. The amendment deleted the constitutional provisions which guaranteed those purses and privileges.

When Keshvanand Bharati questioned the constitutionality of the Twenty-fifth Amendment Act, the Supreme Court delivered a further judgment on the subject on 24 April 1973. As in Golak Nath's case, the decision was reached by a narrow majority. It was recognized that Golak Nath's case had been wrongly decided and the Court overruled its earlier decision—a victory for the Union Government which believed in the unrestricted power of Parliament to amend the Constitution. However, notwithstanding the amendment of Article 368 by the Constitution (Twenty-fourth Amendment) Act, the majority held that Parliament could not 'alter the basic structure or framework of the Constitution'. And since the majority judgement did not spell out what constituted 'the basic structure or framework of the Constitution', every important amendment was bound to raise a legal debate on the subject.

As far as the Constitution (Twenty-fifth Amendment) Act itself was concerned, the majority of the judges generally confirmed its validity. They recognized, for instance, that Parliament and not the Court was the final judge of compensation payable for any property acquired from a subject. The majority judgement also accepted the position that legislation which gave effect to policy in the Directive Principles in clauses (b) or (c) of Article 39, would be deemed to be void on the ground that it was inconsistent with or took away or abridged any of the Fundamental Rights conferred by Articles 14, 19 or 31. This accepted the contention of the Union Government and recognized the supremacy of the Directive Principles over Fundamental Rights. But the majority of the Court rejected that part of the Twenty-fifth Amendment Act which prevented it from examining whether legislation gave effect to the Directive Principles in accordance with a declaration made under the Act by a legislature in that regard.

The majority of Judges thus conformed to the Government view substantially. But they did not concede the point that Parliament had unrestricted powers to amend the Constitution. The ruling party strongly reacted against this and, contrary to established convention, the Government appointed a junior Judge of the Supreme Court to succeed the retiring Chief Justice, thereby superseding three experienced and competent senior Judges of the Court. This evoked general protest in the country among educated elites. The Government did not hesitate to make it clear in Parliament that, in appointing the Chief Justice, it would choose a person known to be a supporter of the Government view . 'We are entitled', the Government spokesman emphasized, 'surely, to look into the philosophy of a Judge. We are entitled to look into his outlook. We are entitled to come to the conclusion that the philosophy of this Judge is forward-looking and of that Judge backward-looking and to decide that we will take the forward-looking Judge. Surely that much freedom should be given to us.'

This virtual confrontation between the judiciary and the Government represented two different categories of thought and behaviour patterns. Professionally trained in the principles of a free judiciary on the British model, the Judges were guided in their decisions by the abstract and sophisticated nuances of the law and Constitution. They were of course not unaware of social and political developments. They did not, for instance, fail to realize the necessity of reviewing their own decision in the light of new facts or realities. Like their British counterparts, they were not blind supporters of continuity and did not believe that adherence to the rule of law signified a complete negation of progress. The fact that they overruled their earlier view in Golak Nath's case established beyond doubt the reasonableness of their attitude towards social change. But not being politicians, they wanted this change to be within what they considered to be the basic structure or framework of the Constitution, so that there should not be an erosion of public confidence in the administration of justice.

Motivated by considerations of retaining power, the ruling party in the Government was, on the contrary, anxious to fulfil the promises made in the Fifth General Election held in 1971. The radicalism of its political posture was therefore understandable. The Prime Minister, for instance, announced at the time her determination immediately to remove poverty. Though obviously a vote-catching slogan, it was also a response to the realities of rural life. The three constitutional amendments which later became the bone of contention between the Government and the Supreme Court, were a political necessity to the ruling party in the Government. Indeed, the politics of poverty in the Indian situation suggested the expediency of tilting in favour of socialistic action against private property, action which in Golak Nath's case had earlier been adjudged *ultra vires* of the Constitution.

There could be no meeting point between the Supreme Court and the Government unless each resiled from its position to an extent and in a manner consistent with an appreciation for the difficulties of the other. It is here that the Government failed. In spite of the resilience shown by the Court, the Government proceeded to appoint a junior Judge to the office of Chief Justice and justified its action on the floor of Parliament in language which showed inadequate restraint or respect for the recognized norms of political behaviour.

The authoritarian trends already in evidence became all the more pronounced in the wake of the Fifth General Election. The Indian Constitution had given powers to the Centre to alter State boundaries; the provisions for universal and single Indian citizenship; the overriding legislative powers of the Centre in the concurrent field; the residuary power of legislation vested in the Union; the common pools of taxation; the power of the Centre to give direction to States in the execution of its policy, and, above all, the powers vested in the Centre in emergencies to divest State units of all or most of their functions, were all evidence of the bias already created by the Constitution in favour of the Centre. The States were in effect being reduced to subservience with ever increasing dependence on the High Command in New Delhi for direction. However, it was the Supreme Court's power of judicial review that still operated as a check on the executive Government. Here, too, public confidence was badly shaken by the Government's attitude.

Declared Objectives of the Constitution

Apart from the upholding of Fundamental rights laid down in Part III of the Constitution, the declared objectives of the Indian polity are contained in the Preamble and the 'Directive Principles of State Policy.'

The Preamble. The Preamble emerged from the 'Objective Resolution' moved in the Constituent Assembly by Jawaharlal Nehru on 13 December 1946. It was discussed a number of times and suitably modified later in the light of the transfer of power on 15 August 1947.[32] In its final form the Preamble declared that the sovereignty of India vested in 'the people of India' who were said to have 'resolved to constitute it into a Sovereign Democratic Republic.' The Constitution was thus declared to have been adopted and enacted by the people themselves, and was considered sovereign in the same sense as 'the people.' However, since the Constitution itself provided for a parliamentary form of government with powers vested in Parliament to make amendments under a procedure established by law, the sovereign attributes of Parliament cannot altogether be ruled out. These attributes impart to the Constitution a dynamic character without divesting it of its sovereign quality or destroying its basic structure or framework. The fusion of parliamentary government and a federal constitution has none the less created confusion about the location of sovereignty in absolute terms.

The 'Sovereign Democratic Republic' constituted under the terms of the Preamble was intended to secure social, economic and political justice. It was, in addition, designed to promote liberty of thought, expression, belief, faith and worship as well as equality of status and opportunity. The dignity of the individual and the unity of the nation were also included among the objectives the Republic was expected to achieve.

The Directive Principles. The rights given to citizens under the Constitution are of two kinds. The first category comprises the Fundamental Rights, while the second embodies the Directive Principles of State Policy. The one is justiceable, while the other is not. Briefly speaking, the fundamental rights are the rights to equality,[33] freedom,[34] freedom of religion,[35] cultural and educational rights,[36] the rights to property,[37] constitutional remedies,[38] and the right against exploitation.[39] These are guaranteed to the people and are not to be varied at will by the changing power-politics of parties.

The Directive Principles are intended for the general guidance of legislatures and governments in India. The application of these principles in legislation and administration is the concern of the State and is not cognizable by any Court.

Besides the promotion of internal and international peace and security, the Directive Principles cover the whole range of political, economic and social well-being of the State and the citizen. The State is, for instance, required to strive to create a social order in which 'justice, social, economic and political shall inform all the institutions of the national life'. In particular, it must direct its policy towards securing to every citizen, 'the right to an adequate means of livelihood', and organizing a distributive system that prevents the concentration of the ownership and control of the material resources of the community, and its essential commodities in a few individuals at the cost of the common good. The policy of the State is likewise to work for 'equal pay for equal work for both men and women'; and ensure that 'citizens shall not be forced by economic necessity to enter avocations unsuited to their age and strength', and that 'childhood and youth are protected against exploitation and against moral and material abandonment'. Within the limits of its resources the State has in addition to make 'effective provision for securing the right to work, to education and to public assistance in case of unemployment, old age, sickness, disablement and other cases of undeserved want'. The provision for social security by the State is likewise to extend to the improvement of nutrition and the living standards of the people, to the promotion of the educational and economic interests of the weaker sections of the people, and, in particular, of the Scheduled Castes, and to the elimination of communal discord.

The conclusion that flows from this review of the nature of the Government of India is that, while it is broadly parliamentary and federal in its formal constitution and based on democratic principles, there are infrastructural and peculiar features which conduce to over-centralization and obstruct the downward filtration of democracy. This does not deny the fact that the Constitution from time to time responded favourably to local urges. The formation of linguistic States to satisfy local and regional demands is a case in point. But in these, too, the distribution of developmental benefits remain confined to the properties and elite classes. For, as we shall see later, the entire framework of the political and administrative institutions envisaged by the Constitution was designed to preserve more or less a bourgeois social and economic order, very similar to that envisaged by the Act of 1935.

The degree of centralization in fact increased in the post-Independence period. This was because of two peculiar developments, the Partition of the subcontinent and the enforcement of economic planning. Partition was accepted as an opportunity for the establishment of a strong Central Government, even stronger than the structure provided by the 1935 Act under which the Provinces enjoyed greater autonomy within the limits assigned by the Act. The British Government saw that the Governors, although invested with special responsibilities, functioned as heads of state and did not interfere with their Council of Ministers.[40] The States created under the Constitution of the Republic of India became subject to the Centre for their very existence as constitutional entities.

But a more important effect of Partition was that it left the Congress party as practically the sole, viable party in the country. The Muslim League, which in pre-Independence days had acted as a balancing factor even if as a communal organization, became suddenly non-existent as a political force. Several other parties of course emerged after Independence in 1947,[41] but it was the Congress which took over power from the British in India. Though a representative organization of the people, during the struggle for freedom it had become highly centralized under its High Command. From the district Committees through the provincial Congress Committees to the All-India Congress Committee, Congressmen were guided from the apex organization, the Working Committee, which in turn looked for advice to a few leaders on top. It was they who controlled the Congress Ministries in the provinces during 1937-9. This structure remained unchanged after Independence in spite of promises of decentralization. Power remained concentrated in the leadership at the top, the States being reduced in stature and status. The All-India Parliamentary Board, for instance, made the choice of candidates for State legislatures in 1957; and when the General Elections were over, the formation of Ministries was not left to the legislative party of the State concerned. Even after the formation of Ministries, Chief Ministers and Ministers were often summoned to Delhi to settle differences. The result was an ever-increasing concentration of power at the Centre and a corresponding reduction in the importance and status of the States at both organizational and governmental levels.

The Planning Commission was set up in March 1950. Since it had no statutory authority the States were in law not bound by its decisions. In practice, however, there were two main factors which obliged them to fall in line. First, the fact that the Congress was in power at the Centre and the States almost throughout the first two decades of Independence, either through its own Ministries or Presidential rule.[42] Secondly, the financing of Plans by the Centre meant that no State would refuse to come in except at the cost of losing the massive financial assistance which the Centre alone could give. As the operational field of the Commission covered the entire sphere of administration in the Union and the States, no State could escape the authority and influence of the Centre in the conduct of its own plan policy and administration. The extra-legal machinery of the National Development Council, which the planning Commission evolved to secure the cooperation and coordination of the States, further weakened the federal fabric envisaged by the Constitution. And as the scope of planning was extended to cover even literature, art and sport, the power of the purse tended to impart to the Centre a character which could in a sense be described as bordering on totalitarian or elective dictatorship.

CHAPTER II

The President, State Governors and Central Ministers

An attempt will be made here to deal with the three main functionaries associated with the exercise of executive authority at the political level: the President, the State Governors and the Ministers at the Centre who form an integral part of the Cabinet and are the supreme controllers of the All-India and Central Services. The discussion will emphasize not so much their constitutional positions as their actual operation, especially the manner in which they laid claim to the same earnings and privileges enjoyed earlier by their British counterparts. The object is not to cast any reflection on the political élites, many of whom had reached the portals of power after great sacrifice, but to understand their behaviour after the transfer of power, when the bureaucracy came to be identified as a separate class of administrative élites functioning under the influence and control of political elements.

The President

Between 1950 and 1977 there were four Presidents who held office in regular succession: Rajendra Prasad, Sarvepalli Radhakrishnan, Zakir Husain and Varahagiri Venkata Giri.

The President is elected for a term of five years by an Electoral College consisting of the elected members of both House of Parliament as well as the elected members of Legislative Assemblies of the States. This election is held in accordance with the system of proportional representation by means of the single transferable vote. In the combined vote of the Central and the State legislatures the Central legislature has been weighted to give it parity with the combined vote of the State legislatures.

Rajendra Prasad

After the departure of Lord Mountbatten, C. Rajagopalachari became the first Indian Governor-General of the country. He remained in office till 24 January 1950, when, by a unanimous vote of the Constituent Assembly, Dr Rajendra Prasad was selected President. Since his election under the new Constitution was to be held by an Electoral College consisting of the elected representatives of both houses of Parliament and the Legislative Assemblies of the States, nomination had to be made by the Constituent Assembly for an interim period until a President was duly elected. He accordingly took office as interim President on 26 January 1950, when the new Constitution came into force. Efforts had earlier been made to see that Rajagopalachari became the first President of the Republic of India, but the Assembly favoured the nomination of Rajendra Prasad, who had won respect and admiration for his able and impartial conduct of its proceedings over the years. After the first General Election he was sworn in as President on 13 May 1952. He was re-elected for a second term on 13 May 1957.[1] Two days after Radhakrishnan took over as second President on 13 May 1963, Rajendra Prasad left Rashtrapati Bhavan for good and travelled in the special presidential train to Patna.

Rajendra Prasad held the office of President for well over twelve years. The convention established during this period shows that it is not a post of authority. Though vested formally under the Constitution with the executive authority of the Union, the President is not to use it without the aid and advice of his Council of Ministers, the real executive. Prior to the Constitution (44th Amendment) Act, 1976, there was of course no specific provision in the Constitution that the President always act on the advice of his Ministers. This omission lead to considerable difference of opinion between him and the Prime Minister, Jawaharlal Nehru.

Soon after becoming President Rajendra Prasad raised the question of his powers in a letter of 27 March 1950 to the Advocate-General. He did not accept the opinion of the Advocate-General, who compared his position to that of the Queen of England. Prasad's argument was that as he was an elected President, the people of India would naturally believe he had a hand in the administration of the country. He expressed this view in a letter to his secretariat on 22 January 1951—an expression of his sense of obligation to the electorate and designed to serve as a guideline to his successor.

Two cases illustrate in particular the controversy between the President as Head of State and the Prime Minister as head of the Government. The first related to the Hindu Code Bill in 1951. From the writings of his Military Secretary it appears that Prasad was already exercised over the powers and privileges of his office and felt that his authority was being encroached upon in various ways. He was planning to have the controversy finally resolved after the General Election of 1952,[2] but in the meantime the question of the Hindu Code Bill emerged. The President suggested that consideration of the Bill be postponed on account of strong public opinion against the legislation. As a general principle, he even expressed a desire to act solely on his own judgement while sending messages to Parliament and returning Bills for reconsideration.[3] Rather than make the Hindu Code Bill into an election issue by pushing through the legislature, the Government decided to postpone it till after the General Elections. The second controversy raised a general question about the powers of the President. In December 1960, when Prasad was addressing the Indian Law Institute in New Delhi, he called upon the Institute to examine the President's powers in a scientific manner and see how far they were comparable to those of the British Crown.[4]

On the controversy raised by Prasad, Nehru sought the opinion of jurists and constitutional experts. M.C. Setalvad and B.N. Rau held that the Constitution was based on the concept of sovereignty of 'the people', to be exercised by the Cabinet responsible to Parliament which represented 'the people'. This sovereignty could be ensured only if the President acted in all matters with 'the aid and advice' of his Council of Ministers. If he were to be free to act independently of this advice, the sovereignty of the people and of Parliament would be infringed, for under the Constitution no presidential act could be discussed in Parliament. They held that such curtailment of the powers of Parliament could not be effected except by an express provision in the Constitution. This view had in fact been expressed by Dr Prasad himself in an earlier debate in the Constituent Assembly. 'Although there is no specific provision in the Constitution itself making it binding on the President to accept the advice of his Ministers', he had observed, 'it is hoped that the convention under which in England the King always acted on the advice of his ministers would be established in this country also, and that the President would become a constitutional President in all matters.'[5] That perhaps was why the framers of the Constitution deliberately omitted such expressions as 'in his discretion' and 'in his individual judge-ment', which under the 1935 Act, had formed part of the special responsibilities and powers of the Governor-General. If the President were to be invested with discretionary powers, it would upset the whole parliamentary structure envisaged by the founding fathers. For the same reason, the indirect election of the President was devised to fit the concept of ministerial responsibility.

Intellectually well-equipped and trained in the principles of law and the Constitution, Dr Prasad was not unaware of the contrary view on the subject, which was supported by the absence of any specific Constitutional provision which made it obligatory for the President to accept the advice of his Ministers in all matters and under all circumstances. The omission of such a provision led even Patanjali Shastri, former Chief Justice of India, to hold that the President was not always bound to act on the advice of his Ministers. It was argued that, since the President alone was by the oath of his office invested with the responsibility of preventing any infringement of the Con-stitution by the Cabinet, and since he would render himself liable to removal from office by impeachment for any violation of the Constitu-tion, it was but legitimate for him to exercise his discretion. In *The President under the Indian Constitution* K.M. Munshi has even gone to the extent of investing the President with a number of supra-Ministerial powers in a situation where a Ministry cannot be relied upon for advice. These powers are (1) dismissal of a Prime Minister who does not enjoy the confidence and leadership of his party; (2) dismissal of a Ministry which has lost the confidence of Parliament; (3) dissolution of the House of the People (Lok Sabha) when it appears to the President to have lost the confidence of the people, and (4) the exercise of power as the Supreme Commander in an emer-gency when the Ministry has failed to defend the country.[6]

No occasion had however arisen for the exercise of what Munshi called 'supra-Ministerial powers'. The office of the President re-mained a glorified rubber stamp of the executive government, the Cabinet. His well-clad Military Secretary and *aides-de-camp*, or, for that matter, the splendour of Rashtrapati Bhavan itself could not add weight or lustre to his office when the Constitution itself had made it politically ineffectual. Prasad knew this very well and had no real pretensions to the contrary.

And yet the seriousness with which he posed at the Law Institute the question of the relationship between the President and his Council of Ministers is clear. Dr Prasad had in fact never been reconciled to the manner in which the provisions relating to his powers were being interpreted. He remained concerned on the subject and made no secret of his unhappiness in meetings with Ministers and M.Ps. Though personally a dedicated Gandhian, he would not shed the ceremonial pomp and pageantry that was attached to the presidency after the departure of the Viceroys. For example, while going to Hyderabad on one of his tours, Dr Prasad declined to accept the advice of the Prime Minister to stay in the city itself, and not in Faluknama Palace, which had been specially built by the Nizam for the exclusive use of touring Viceroys.[7]

Later, from 1955–6 onwards, the question of the powers and privileges of President Prasad acquired new significance, becoming related to his emoluments: these had been reduced by an Act as well as by the Prime Minister's interference in the management of the President's household expenditure. It was precisely at this time that Dr Prasad chose to worry about his obligations to the family which had earlier been taken care of by his brother, Mahendra Prasad. Writing to his Private Secretary, Gyanwati Darbar, he recalled the early days of his practice at the Bar and referred to the financial position of the family which had deteriorated after the death of his brother.

There used to be a time when I did not know anything about our family affairs. They were looked after by my brother who was so good and considerate that he would not let anything causing anxiety be communicated to me. Not only did I not do anything for the family; he looked after me also . . . . Now I am supposed to be drawing the highest salary that anyone in Government service in India can draw, although by voluntary cuts I have reduced it to half, thus making it one of the highest, though not absolutely the highest, salary in India. Yet I have to think of the family and its affairs which include, of course, its financial position. Personally, the previous position was far happier than the present . . . .[8]

For the first five years of his presidency the financial position of Dr Prasad was fairly good. Under Part A of the Second Schedule read with Article 59(3)[9] of the Constitution, the President was entitled to emoluments of Rs 10,000 per month,[10] in addition to 'such allowances as were payable to the Governor-General of the Dominion of India immediately before the Commencement of the Constitution'. One of these allowances was the sumptuary allowance of Rs 45,000 per annum.

Towards the middle of 1954 the President voluntarily surrendered in writing a sum of Rs 4,000 out of his monthly salary of Rs 10,000.

The amount surrendered was specifically exempted from income-tax and super-tax and excluded from total income under the provisions of the Voluntary Surrender of Salaries (Exemption From Tax) Act, 1950. The President, however, surrendered no portion of the sumptuary allowance of Rs 45,000 per annum all of which was exempt from income-tax and super-tax under the provisions of section 4(3) (vi) of the Indian Income-Tax Act of 1922. The trouble arose when the 1922 Act was amended in 1955 after which all entertainment allowances became subject to tax, regardless of the specific purpose for which they were granted to the recipient. The President was thus required to pay tax on the sumptuary allowance drawn on or after 1 April 1955.

In view of this additional liability attached to the sumptuary allowance, the President expressed a desire to forego a part of it, as in the case of his regular salary. A legal difficulty, however, arose. It was argued that any allowance drawn by the President under Part A of the Second Schedule[11] was due to him as a matter of right. The surrender by him of a part of the sumptuary allowance would not render that part exempt from income-tax, for tax was payable on salary allowed or due, whether actually paid or not. The voluntary relinquishment of a part of the amount legally due did not make it 'not due'.[12] The President was thus left with no alternative but to give up the whole of the sumptuary allowance, leaving the Government to look after the guests; for the amount that would have been left to the President after deducting tax would only have been about Rs 700 per month.[13]

This complete surrender of the official sumptuary allowance of Rs 45,000 a year was by itself a serious blow to the emoluments of the President. His private entertainment too did not remain free. By about the middle of 1954 Nehru suggested that the Government Hospitality Organization, which had been in existence for nearly five years as part of the Prime Minister's Secretariat, could easily look after Dr Prasad's personal entertainment, especially when it was supposed to be so small as to be hardly mentioned in the House Circular issued to the Press everyday. The President was naturally averse to his private entertainment being transferred to the Hospitality Organization and managed by his Military Secretary. He considered this an attempt to interfere with matters of personal choice and discretion. 'In a democratic republic', he cautioned his Military Secretary, 'the Head of State has a distinctive status which should not be confused with that of the Head of Government. It was precisely for this reason that I decided to call the Government House by the new name "President's House" (Rashtrapati Bhavan)'.[14] Dr Prasad asked his Military Secretary not to remain associated with the Hospitality Organization. He also discussed the matter with the Prime Minister himself, pointing out that, out of considerations of economy, he had already decided to draw a reduced salary. But the Prime Minister saw no reason to relent. Through the Military Secretary of the President the Hospitality Organization took over the Management of his private entertainment also. 'There is far too much interference in the affairs of this House', Dr Prasad complained.[15] But he could not help it.

The utilization of gifts received by the President was another bone of contention. A private company, for instance, had presented an expensive gift to him and the Prime Minister came to know of it through press reports. A controversy arose between the two. For while Dr Prasad considered the gift to have been given to him in his personal capacity for his exclusive use, Nehru treated it as State property which could not be disposed of privately. All Ministers, diplomatic representatives and other dignitaries were required to notify and surrender all valuable gifts received in the course of performance of official duties. The Military Secretary was therefore asked to apply the same rules to the President, who was to surrender all the gifts received in the discharge of official duties. The Military Secretary was in fact directed to prepare an inventory of gifts received and to display them for a time in the state rooms of Rashtrapati Bhavan.

This brief survey of the relationship between the President and the Prime Minister lends itself to some significant conclusions. For instance, the omission of any specific constitutional provision for the President to act only on the advice of the Council of Ministers was indeed meaningful. It signified a desire on the part of the Constituent Assembly to provide for checks and balances in the functioning of the Executive Government, the President being required to be normally guided by the advice of Ministers, and the Cabinet being obliged in certain situations to seek the cooperation of the President acting as a counterweight to executive despotism. The goal of checks and balances, however, depended for its success on two main conditions: Presidents of talent, honesty and firmness of character of an order at least equal, if not superior, to that of the Prime Minister; and Presidents of national stature, rooted by virtue of public service both in the country and Parliament, but free from the influence of the political party in power. The presidency suffered from handicaps in terms of both. It is true that as far as service to the nation and a spirit of sacrifice were concerned, Dr Prasad was second to none. His academic attainments, too, had few parallels, and he was, indeed, twice elected as President despite Nehru. But he was no match for Nehru in terms of dynamism, vigour, firmness and breadth of mind.

Sarvepalli Radhakrishnan

Though an intellectual and scholar of international standing, Dr Radhakrishnan was no politician. He had played no direct role in India's struggle for freedom, and as an Oxford don, had watched it from far beyond India's shores. Both as a teacher and writer he kept himself aloof from the turmoil of politics in the period between the two World Wars and leading to Independence in 1947. He became free India's first Ambassador to Moscow and then Vice-President of the country, an office he held from 1952 to 1962, when he acceded to the Presidency with the backing of the Prime Minister.

Though not a politician by profession, Dr Radhakrishnan had the advantage of being advised by Rajagopalachari, who was both a scholar and politician. During his visits to Madras the new President would invariably call on Rajagopalachari to pay his respects and discuss both domestic and foreign policies for hours on end. A statesman of outstanding calibre, Rajagopalachari had become critical of Nehru's policies both at home and in world affairs. His influence on President Radhakrishnan seems evident in the latter's public criticism of the Government for its inability to check rising prices of essential commodities or remove corruption from Government offices.[16]

Constitutionally, it is remarkable that the President had even allowed a deputation to wait upon him on 13 July 1963 and to present to him a memorandum containing allegations of corruption against Sardar Partap Singh Kairon,[17] the Chief Minister of the Punjab. The deputation consisted of Master Tara Singh and twenty-two others, while the memorandum was signed by Devi Lal and twenty-six others who claimed to be representatives of the non-Communist opposition parties. The reason for approaching the President was said to be the partisan attitude of the Prime Minister, who was not prepared to entertain any complaint against Kairon. The President asked for a public inquiry. Though not yet convinced of the existence of a *prima facie* case against Kairon, the Prime Minister agreed. Under the

Commission of Inquiry Act, 1952 a Commission was appointed on 1 November 1963. It consisted of Sudhi Ranjan Das, formerly Chief Justice of India, who submitted his report on 11 June 1964.

The Das Commission reported that Sardar Pratap Singh Kairon had abused his authority in a number of cases in the interest of his sons and that, although he himself did not commit the alleged irregularities or illegalities, he was certainly privy to them. And yet, according to the report, when the same allegations were previously inquired into by the Congress High Command, their conclusion was 'that there [was] no basis at all for any corruption'.

The appointment of the Das Commission illustrated that the President could discharge a useful function in the day-to-day administration of the country. This of course does not demonstrate the supremacy of the Presidency over the office of Prime Minister, for no Commission would have been appointed had the latter refused. After the General Election of 1967, for instance, 93 M.L.A.'s of the Samyukta Dal approached Dr Radhakrishnan when the Governor of Rajasthan did not invite their leader to form the Government there. But the President took no steps to revoke the Proclamation he had issued on the advice of the Union Government suspending the Constitution of Rajasthan, for the Congress Government at the Centre would not permit him to do that.

In spite of Rajagopalachari's recommendation, Dr Radhakrishnan was not allowed to continue for a second term. On 10 April 1967 the Congress Parliamentary Board unanimously approved the nomination of Dr Zakir Husain, the Vice-President, who was elected President on 9 May 1967.

Zakir Husain

Dr Zakir Husain was Vice-Chancellor of Aligarh Muslim University from 1948 to 1956. During this period he became a member of the Rajya Sabha in 1952 for a five-year term. He was then appointed Governor of Bihar, and elected Vice-President of India in 1962. As President he did not complete his full term because of his sudden demise on 3 May 1969.

The position of the Presidency under Dr Zakir Husain perhaps deteriorated during his tenure. There were two main reasons for this: first, the election of the two earlier Presidents was a foregone conclusion and free of controversy or serious opposition. It was not so with Dr Zakir Husain's election. Secondly, the Congress Party had suffered serious reverses in the 1967 General Election. After the death of Jawaharal Nehru and Lal Bahadur Shastri the Prime Ministership itself had been slightly shaky.

Indira Gandhi was therefore anxious 'to regain some lost position by installing a President of the Republic who would be sympathetic to the Government's point of view and willing to cooperate with the Prime Minister and her Cabinet'.[18] Zakir Husain was thus a Congress candidate of the 'ruling clique around the Prime Minister'.[19]

The Congress Party was divided in its choice of presidential candidates. The Party President, K. Kamraj, preferred Dr Radhakrishnan to continue for a second term. The Prime Minister, however, seemed opposed to his continuance. The opposition, too, did not have a unanimous choice: the Swatantra Party, the Samyukta Socialist Party and the Praja Socialist Party favoured Jaya Prakash Narayan, but the Jan Sangh opposed his candidature. Finally, the Opposition agreed to the nomination of Koka Subha Rao, then Chief Justice of India, for President and Nawab Ali Yawar Jung, Vice-Chancellor of Aligarh Muslim University, for Vice-President.

The singleness of purpose with which Mrs Gandhi worked to secure the nomination of Zakir Husain did not go in vain. At the meeting of the Congress Parliamentary Board on 5 April 1967, she mobilized the support of such leaders as Jagjivan Ram, Y.B. Chavan, Fakhruddin Ali Ahmed and Atulya Ghosh. She could not win over to her side Morarji Desai and S.K. Patil who remained with Kamraj. Dr Radhakrishnan, however, issued in the meantime a statement withdrawing from the contest; and this created a situation which brought success to the ceaseless efforts of the Prime Minister. Dr Zakir Husain was declared elected.

When combined, the manner in which Dr Zakir Husain was elected and his position as a member of a minority community had their disadvantages. It was indeed difficult for him to rise above suspicion merely by a resort to an impartial and detached view of issues involved in any situation. The Opposition parties and a cross section of the Congress looked upon him as the Prime Minister's choice, ever ready to execute her will. Such reactions, even if not well-founded, could hardly raise the dignity of the high office to which Dr Zakir Husain was elected in 1967.

V.V. Giri

After the General Election of 1967, V. V. Giri was elected

Vice-President as the nominee of the Congress Party. He became acting President on the death of Dr Zakir Husain and was elected President on 20 August 1969.

Unlike both Radhakrishnan and Zakir Husain, Giri had had an active political career before becoming Vice-President. On his return from Dublin where he had been called to the Irish Bar, he was enrolled in 1916 as an Advocate of the Madras High Court. But he renounced the profession and participated in Gandhi's satyagraha against the Rowlatt Act, leading to the non-cooperation movement which followed in 1920. After his release from jail in 1922, however, Giri moved from national politics to trade unionism. He took up the cause of railway workers and became President of the B.N. Railway Indian Labour Union. He extended the scope of his activity to the organization of trade unions in other Railways also. The result was the formation of the All-India Railwaymen's Federation in 1924. Two years later, in 1926, Giri was elected President of the All-India Trade Union Congress. He represented the workers of India at the International Labour Conference in Geneva in 1927. In 1935, he entered the Central Legislature, acting also as the Congress spokesman on labour matters. When the Congress formed its Ministry in Madras in 1937, Giri came to hold under C. Rajagopalchari the importent portfolios of Labour, Industry, Cooperation and Harijan Uplift. After the resignation of the Congress Ministries in November 1939, he was arrested and sentenced to imprisonment for fifteen months. He was later released but arrested again during the 'Quit India' movement. He came out of prison in 1945 and again became a Minister in Madras in 1946. In 1947, Giri was appointed Indian High Commissioner in Ceylon. In 1952, he successfully contested a Parliamentary seat and became Minister for Labour at the Centre. On his defeat in the General Election of 1957 he was appointed Governor of Uttar Pradesh. Later, as Governor, he moved consecutively from U.P. to Kerala and then to Mysore before becoming Vice-President in 1967.

Giri contested the presidential election of 1969 as an independent candidate, believing that the country needed a really 'independent and strong President who could see things straight and do justice well without fear or favour'.[20] Perhaps he meant that he would be 'an active partner' in the conduct of the country's administration, not 'a sleeping partner'[21] of the kind the Presidency had been reduced to. But his performance hardly gave any evidence of independence. Himself a Congressman, Giri had been known as the type of liberal labour leader popular with the Congress leadership. He naturally owed his victory in the presidential election to the tacit support of the ruling group in the Congress Party. He had in fact been obliged to the Party and its Government at the Centre for his consecutive appointments as Governor in three States, despite his defeat at the polls in 1957. Moreover, a show of genuine independence in relation to the Executive Government would hardly have brought Giri the rewards, emoluments and privileges of the presidential office.

General Remarks

Consistent with the constitutional goal of parliamentary government the President was required to act on the advice of his Council of Ministers, which the Constituent Assembly intially wanted to be binding on him. But as India declared itself to be a republic with an elected President, his relatioship with the Cabinet on certain matters like the presidential message to Parliament on legislative bills, or the question of its dissolution, was left to be determined by conventions. The manner in which the desired conventions were established, however, depended upon the personal equations of the President and the Prime Minister. Apart from lacking patronage, the President would not be able to enforce a balanced growth of conventions if his character, competence, political standing in Parliament and hold on public opinion were not equal, if not superior, to those of the Prime Minister. The Presidency in India as a matter of course was assigned to individuals who could not match the incumbent Prime Ministers in terms of political standing and firmness of character. Constitutional clashes in certain matters requiring settlement by convention were thus sought to be obviated by the appointment of convenient choices.

State Governors

The office of the Governor of a Province during British days was designed to fulfil a two-fold purpose, the security of the Empire and the promotion of provincial interests. From a study of the proceedings of the Imperial Legislative Council after 1854 it appears that althogh provinces were then no more than mere agents of the Central Government, their representatives in the Council zealously advocated the cause of their respective provinces. On the establishment of dyarchy there was a shift in emphasis, the Governors being relatively more concerned with the 'reserved' and the 'central' subjects of imperial interest than with those included in the 'transferred' field, the immediate concern of popular ministries. This trend became more pronounced with the introduction of provincial autonomy under the 1935 Act, when the Governors came to be invested with the exercise of 'discretion' in matters excluded from the domain of the Council of Ministers, and of 'individual judgement' in the discharge of 'special responsibilities' where they could reject the advice of the Ministers and act on their own. For purposes of central direction, control and supervision, their dependence on the Governor-General thus increased correspondingly with the growth of provincial autonomy: this occurred within the framework of an essentially unitary Constitution. With the division of powers on a federal principle the Constituent Assembly proceeded to further tighten control over State Governors in the name of national security.

Constitutional Position and Role

Article 153 of the Constitution provides that there shall be a Governor for each State, or for two or more States. He holds office during 'the pleasure of the President', normally for a term of five years unless he resigns. The State Government has thus no hand either in his appontment or in his removal, and he is an agent of the Centre in the State. And yet, since the state by virtue of its federal constitution forms a distinct entity in its own right, the Governor cannot but function as a formal head of the State to which he is appointed, his loyalty to the ruling party at the Centre remaining, however, undivided.

The executive power of the State is vested in the Governor and is to be exercised by him either directly or through officers subordinate to him in accordance with the Constitution, which provides for 'a Council of Ministers with the Chief Minister at the head to aid and advise the Governor in the exercise of his functions, except in so far as he is by or under this Constitution required to exercise his functions or any of them in his discretion'. It is further laid down that 'the Chief Minister shall be appointed by the Governor and the other Ministers shall be appointed by the Governor on the advice of the Chief Ministers', who 'shall hold office during the pleasure of the Governor'. The Constitution, however, proceeds in the same breath to lay down that 'the Council of Ministers shall be collectively responsible to the Legislative Assembly of the State'.

The use of the term 'pleasure' was borrowed from the Constitution of England where Ministers were said to hold office during the 'pleasure' of the Crown, even when the principle of collective responsibility to Parliament had come to be universally recognized. Under parliamentary democracy the 'pleasure' of the Crown was determined by the 'confidence' of Parliament in the Ministry, and was not absolute or unrestricted. In India, too, the original intention of the Constitution-makers was similar. 'Pleasure' and 'confidence' were recognized as identifiable terms and it was held that the loss of 'confidence' in the Ministry could alone lead to the withdrawal of 'pleasure' by the Governor.

However, the exercise of 'pleasure' by the Governor in the context of the Indian Constitution was not backed by any principle of legitimacy which the British Crown had possessed. It is a provision made by the Constitution which, in the absence of healthy conventions, is subject to being interpreted as a power of the Governor which can be exercised in his 'discretion'. This is specially so since the Constitution does not empower the State Legislative Assembly to dismiss or remove any Council of Ministers. It is the Governor of the State who is exclusively empowered to appoint or remove Ministers. If a Council of Ministers refuses to relinquish office on a vote of no-confidence, the Governor can remove it by withdrawing his 'pleasure'. But since the fact of confidence or no-confidence is to be ascertained by the Governor himself in his discretion, he may use his 'pleasure' to unseat a ministry by leaving the test of confidence not to a vote in the Assembly but to other conditions which may provide grounds for President's Rule under Article 356 of the Constitution. These conditions may be ministerial crises arising from defections and counter-defections; the resignation of a Chief Minister signifying ministerial instability; political instability supposedly proceeding from inefficiency, corruption and maladministration; instability caused by there being no presiding officer of the Assembly; a conflict between the Government and the Assembly, and so on.[22]

In a caste-based and plural society like that of India, political behaviour is bound to be influenced by a variegated pattern of loyalties causing instability in the functioning of political institutions. In the absence of a stable Opposition, constant shifts of loyalty often tend to dislocate the infrastructure of the ruling Congress Party itself. If the Governor does not remain politically neutral and wishes to promote the prospects of the government of a particular party, he finds plenty of scope in the Indian situation for the exercise of his discretion. For a clear verdict on the question of majority support in an Assembly is often a rarity. In many cases a Ministry has been reluctant to face the House because of uncertainties arising from constant floor-crossing. And as there is no fixed principle or instrument of instruction, the discretion of the Governor is exercised in various ways, not only depending on the exigency of a situation but also political expediency.[23] A Committee of Governors, too, has not approached the problem with understanding when it reiterated the Governor's right to dismiss a ministry in his discretion as soon as there was an adverse vote in the Assembly or, in its absence, on his own assessment.[24] It was not realized that the power to exercise discretion could be used to encourage ministerial instability.

In the absence of formal guidelines, Governors can, if they so choose, misuse their prerogative under Article 356 of the Constitution. In practice, they have actually shown favours to the Congress Party, as in the formation of Congress or Congress-supported Ministries in Madras in 1952; in Andhra in 1954 (P.S.P. with Congress support); in Rajasthan and Madhya Pradesh in 1962; and over the B.P. Mandal (Soshit Dal) Government in Bihar in 1968. They likewise obstructed the formation of governments by parties in opposition at the Centre, for instance in Orissa in 1958; in Kerala in 1965; in Rajasthan in 1967; and in U.P. in 1968.

In 1959 the Centre even went to the extent of manoeuvring the dismissal of the Communist Ministry in Kerala and had it replaced by President's Rule on the alleged grounds of riots, strikes and demonstrations leading to what it called lawlessness. The Communist Government commanded a majority in the Assembly and the Governor, B. Ramakrishna Rao, a former Chief Minister of Hyderabad, had expressed himself against the imposition of President's Rule. Even so, a popular Ministry had to go, as the Congress President thought this best. In 1964 another Communist Government in Kerala shared a similar fate. Though commanding an undisputed majority in the Assembly, the Minister for Home Affairs, G.L. Nanda, had the Ministry dismissed because popular agitation against the Government was supposed to have created the impression that it had lost the confidence of the electorate. It was not defeated on the floor of the House; there were of course defections and counter-defections from and to the Government which took time to settle down before the Assembly could be summoned to prove the test of confidence. The Governor, V. Vishwanathan, however, concluded from this delay that the Ministry had lost the confidence of the House and that he was thus justified in withdrawing his 'pleasure'. The experiences of 1959 and 1964 later provoked Namboodiripad to remark that 'the political history of the State of Kerala is replete with instances of how the Rajpramukh and the Governor had been used to prevent the formation of non-Congress governments, to topple them whenever they are formed and to facilitate the formation and perpetuation of Congress government'.[25]

The manner in which the State Governors functioned led the Administrative Reforms Commission to suggest the need to establish fixed norms to regulate the exercise of discretion, but the Centre rejected the suggestion. It argued that to lay down any rigid procedure for the guidance of Governors might not be consistent with their powers of discretion. Fixed norms were considered unnecessary on the grounds that they were inherent in the Governors' pledge to 'preserve, protect and defend the Constitution and the law'. But, as the *Statesman* aptly pointed out in its editorial of 9 June 1975, the demand for 'formal guidelines' for Governors 'has arisen only because the Centre has often appeared to encourage Governors to ignore the rights and powers of the State Assembly'.[26]

Though supposed to remain free from party politics under the terms of their appointment, some Governors have openly canvassed for a particular party. 'I know of one Governor', writes Sri Prakasa (a former Governor), 'who thought he could continue to be a member of the All-India Congress Committee even as Governor. I know of other Governors who used to go to their States and undertake political tours. In all such cases, the President—even the very mild, gentle and gracious Dr Rajendra Prasad—had to intervene.'[27]

The political involvements of Ajit Prasad Jain when Governor of Kerala make a strange story. Early in January 1965, he was offered that Governorship, which he assumed after the proclamation of President's Rule at the end of March. He became interested in the election of the Prime Minister when Lal Bahadur Shastri suddenly passed away and actively convassed for Mrs Gandhi against Morarji Desai. Realizing the implications of his conduct he then sent in his resignation on 17 January 1966. It took time for the Home Ministry to have the resignation accepted and a successor appointed. In between, Jain went to Delhi and participated in the election of the new Prime Minister, even as he continued to be Governor. It was only some time later that he was relieved of his office. Mrs Gandhi would have in any event won without Jain's support, but, as he himself admitted, he 'wanted to be a part of a major political decision'.[28]

There have been two other developments in the post-Independence period which militate against the dignity of the gubernatorial office. One is that, instead of sending honest and able former Ministers as State Governors, the Executive Government has often elevated those defeated at the polls, or those in no way distinguished for talent or service in public life. A person so elevated becomes entitled to emoluments and perquisites that even success at the polls would never fetch. The second development is a direct operative link established by slow degrees between the High Command of the ruling party in Delhi and its Ministries in the States. Instead of seeking the guidance of their Governor on the spot, State Ministers have started making frequent pilgrimages to Delhi for all kinds of advice. Governors are not informed as to who is being considered for inclusion in a state Cabinet. Even the choice of the leader of a Congress Legislature Party in a State began steadily to be made at the Centre over the head of its Governor. This practice has increasingly grown over the years, regardless of the earlier conventions under which the major part of negotiations and even correspondence passed through the Governor who, during the British days also reported privately to the Governor-General as to how the individual members of his Council of Ministers functioned and reacted.

Governors drawn from the Civil Service are apt even in the changed situation to use the firmness and independence of judgement that was characteristic of earlier days, regardless of the consequences that might follow. An interesting case is that of Dharma Vira, who had acquitted himself with credit as Cabinet Secretary under Jawaharlal Nehru, and later as Governor of Punjab and then of West Bengal. In 1969 he proceeded as Governor of Mysore.

In Mysore, Dharma Vira got on well with the young and energetic Chief Minister, Veerendra Patil, who belonged to the Congress (O) Party, with Nijalingappa as its political father. Together they contributed to the development of the State in various fields. This situation, however, did not last long, for a section of the Ministry was inclined to join the Indira group of the Congress, while others determined to remain with Nijalingappa. A state of instability ensued when suddenly Mrs Gandhi dissolved Parliament and announced fresh elections.

The result of the elections came as an utter surprise to the Congress

(O). Mrs Gandhi's Congress won all the 25 parliamentary seats, a victory which accelerated the process of defection. Veerendra Patil failed to ensure a stable majority, while the ruling Congress declined at the instance of the High Command to form its own Ministry. The Governor recommended the imposition of President's Rule, and the Centre agreed.

It was with the imposition of President's Rule that the Governor's troubles actually started. His training in the Civil Service did not permit him to impair the good relations he had developed with the outgoing Ministry, especially with the Chief Minister, Veerendra Patil. The newly elected MPs and MLAs, on the contrary, wanted the Governor to turn his face against members of the fallen Ministry, which he did not do. Prejudice and suspicion resulted and this was aggravated by the Governor's refusal to oblige the newly elected politicians who were interested in forwarding their own and other individual cases. Writing about them he says:

Once an M.P. came to see me on an urgent mission accompanied by a lawyer, with the request that a criminal case which was pending before a law court for defalcation of monies of a trust be withdrawn. When I told him that it was impossible, he was quite incensed and told me that I did not realize that he was an M.P., elected by the people. Another M.P. sought an urgent interview with me. At that time his area was suffering from acute drought conditions. I expected that he would discuss the relief arrangements with me. But that was not so. He brought out a case of transfer of a minor official and did not utter a word about drought.[29]

The firmness of the Governor and his political neutrality were both viewed as arrogance.

Another source of trouble was the huge overdraft with the Reserve Bank, which the State by itself could not repay. The Mysore Government represented its case to the Centre and the State was promised special accommodation of the order of Rs 105 crores. Later, the Union Minister of Finance expressed his inability to meet a substantial portion of the promised accommodation. When this news leaked out the Governor gave vent to disappointment in a statement which the Centre interpreted as a defiance of its authority. He was called by the President and put on the mat. The President, as Dharma Vira writes, was satisfied with the explanation given, but advised him to meet the Prime Minister also. He accordingly sought an interview with the Prime Minister before returning to Bangalore by 25 January to attend the Republic Day celebrations. When it became evident after repeated inquiries that the Prime Minister was unlikely to see him as requested, Dharma Vira wrote a personal letter to the Prime Minister explaining the incident and left for Bangalore as planned. Dharma Vira writes: 'My letter was delivered to the Prime Minister in the night of the 24th and had she desired to meet me I could have been asked in time to stay on. This, however, was not done and my departure without waiting for the Prime Minister's reply was made a further cause of displeasure.'[30]

As the Governor of a State Dharma Vira took care to see that its interests were not jeopardized. He felt it his moral duty to safeguard those interests 'regardless of the consequences'. But he failed to realize that he was a mere nominee of the Centre and that the State had no hand in that nomination. As an honest and able civil servant, however, he felt humiliated at the treatment meted out to him. He raises in his *memoirs* the question of propriety: 'How long is a senior and busy functionary expected to await even the Prime Minister's pleasure? Is the Prime Minister entitled to treat high dignitaries such as a Governor with scant courtesy, and force him to cool his heels in Delhi for days on end?' He calls such behaviour 'shabby treatment'[31] and points out that answers to his questions have to be found if the Governor is to fulfil the original object of his institution.

Emoluments, Allowances and Privileges

Though a nominee of the Centre, the Governor in a federal constitution is expected to justify his position as the Head of his State also. The case of Dharma Vira's Governorship of Mysore is an illustration of the consequences that follow the endeavours of a Governor to prove worthy of his salt in being loyal to his State.

Her experience as Governor of Maharashtra made Mrs Vijaya Lakshmi Pandit resign and remark that the Governorship was a useless institution: the only thing which could induce a person to accept it was the salary offered. Mrs Pandit's remark is an exaggeration, for the institution certainly has some useful and essential functions to discharge. But it fails to fulfil them adequately as the Governors, by and large, have to remain subservient to the ruling party and government at the Centre, even though the Constitution envisages and calls for political neutrality and independence on their part in satisfying local needs. This anomalous situation flows from Central control exercised on a unitary principle over federalism. What induces Governors in general to sacrifice their independence is the lure of emoluments, allowances and privileges which India's political masters inherited from the British and have since perpetuated with inadequate modification.

Under the British there were variations in the salaries of Governors. Those of Madras, Bombay, Bengal and the Unied Provinces, for instance, were under the 1935 Act paid an annual salary of Rs 120,000, while those of the Punjab and Bihar Rs 100,000. The Governor of the Central Provinces and Berar came next in status with Rs 72,000. Those who stood at the bottom were the Governors of Assam, the North-West Frontier Province, Orissa and Sind, who received Rs 66,000,[32] which was payable to Governors of all the Part A. regions.[33]

The leave allowances of the Governors of British Provinces were laid down by the Government of India (Governors' Allowances and Privileges) Order of 18 December 1936. The Order sanctioned the following monthly rates:

Governors of Madras, Bengal, Bombay, the United Provinces, the Pubjab and Bihar	Rs 4,000
Governors of the Central Provinces and Berar	Rs 3.000
Governors of other Provinces	Rs 2,750

The rate of leave allowance payable to a Governor under the Government of India (Governors' Allowances and Privileges) Order, 1950[34] was fixed at Rs 2,750 per month on a uniform basis. After the promulgation of the Constitution this Order was kept in force by virtue of Article 158(3) of the Constitution read with its Second Schedule, which entitled the Governor on leave to an allowance in lieu of salary, the acting Governor being in that case entitled to the Governor's salary. In matters other than salary and leave allowance, the President and Governors were declared by the Second Schedule to be entitled to the same allowances and privileges extended to the Governor-General and corresponding Governors before the commencement of the Constitution. Throughout his term of office each British Governor was, for instance, entitled to use free of cost his official residence and railway saloons, rivercrafts, aircraft and cars. No charge was to fall on him personally for the maintenance of any of these; he was exempt from the payment of local rates and taxes, and electricity, gas and water costs. He was also to be paid from time to time an allowance equal to his actual expenses in renewing the furnishing of his official residences, including the staff quarters and other buildings, appurtenances and gardens. To enable the Governor to discharge his duties 'conveniently and with dignity' provision was made for sumptuary allowances, staff and household establishments for a Military Secretary and ADC, a band, body guard; and a contract allowance was available for miscellaneous expenses.

All these allowances and privileges were continued by the Order of 1950, which came into force on 1 January that year. The relative maximum figures of the sums sanctioned in 1936 and 1950 for the renewal of the furnishings of official residences is given in the table below:[35]

	Maximum Allowances for Renewal of Furnishings of Official Residence (in Rs)	
	1936	1950
Madras	14,000	70,000
Bombay	23,000	1.13,000
Bengal	20,500	87,000
		(West Bengal)
U.P.	4,000	93,000
Punjab	3,000	10,000
		(East Punjab)
Bihar	4,500	50,900
C.P. and Berar	2,900	30,500
Assam	1,000	40,000
Orissa	—	46,000

Despite inflation, it appears that after the transfer of power there was an enormous increase in the costs of renewing furnishings for the official residences of Indian Governors. As regards the Governors' freedom from customs duties, the 1950 Order lifted bodily the terms of the 1936 Order. It said:

No customs duties shall be levied in India on the following articles if imported or purchased out of bond by Governors on appointment or during their tenure of office:

(a) Articles for the personal use or consumption of the Governor or any member of his family;

(b) Food, drink and tobacco for consumption by members of the Governor's household or by his guests, whether official or not;

(c) Articles for the furnishing of any of the Governor's official residences;

(d) Motor-cars provided for the Governor's use.

The provisions so made by the 1936 Order were adopted in 1950 for the Indian Governors. They were later incorporated likewise by the States Reorganization (Governors' Allowance and Privileges) Order, 1957. A comparative view of the amounts charged on account of the Governors' allowances under the rules of 1936 and 1950 is given in the tables on pages 63-5.

In addition to the renewal of furnishings, sumptuary and other allowances, including the cost on staff establishment, another item of heavy expenditure was the maintenance and repair of official residences of Governors. The tables on pages 64-5 give the expenditure sanctioned under the Order of 1950. The figures represent a norm that was hardly adhered to in practice. Expenditure under this head often exceeded the limits prescribed and was incurred even without the prior approval of the President who expected to keep a check on it.

Like the cost of 'maintenance', expenditure on railway saloons, too, often exceeded the limits laid down by the Order of 1950. With the reorganization of States in 1956 some new States came into being and some others were reorganized. Section 73 of the States Reorganization Act, 1956, provided that until provision was made by Parliament under clause (3) of Article 158 of the Constitution, the allowances and privileges of the Governor of Andhra Pradesh or Madras or each of the new States were to be such as the President should determine. It was under this provision that the States Reorganization (Governors' Allowances and Privileges) Order, 1957, was issued on 1 March 1957. The Order provided for the regulation of the allowances of the Governors of the reorganized States, viz., Andhra Pradesh, Bombay, Kerala, Madras, Madhya Pradesh, Mysore, Punjab and Rajasthan. And when the former Bombay State was reconstituted into Maharashtra and Gujarat, another Order was issued in 1960. However, as the Order of 1957 seemed to imply that the President was to determine only the allowances and privileges of the Governors of the reorganized States, it was presumed that these allowances were in addition to, and not in lieu of, their salary. That Order was later amended along with the Order of 1960, and express provision was made in 1966 that the leave allowance of a Governor was in lieu of his salary as provided in paragraph 3 of the Third Schedule to the Government of India Act, 1935.

The necessity for such an amendment arose in August 1965 from an unusual situation in the Punjab where the Governor, Hafiz Mohammad Ibrahim, took leave of absence on account of illness but

Minimum Yearly Amounts (in Rupees) Charged on the Revenues of the Provinces in Respect of Certain Allowances and Privileges of Governors under the Government of India (Governors' Allowances and Privileges) Order, 1936

	Orissa	Madras	Bombay	Bengal	United Provinces	Punjab	Bihar	Central Provinces & Berar	Assam	N.W. Frontier Province	Sind
1. Sumptuary Allowance	6,000	18,000	25,000	25,000	15,000	12,000	6,000	6,000	6,000	6,000	8,000
2. Staff and Household—											
(a) Military Secy. (or A.D.C.) and his establishment	40,000	1,12,000	1,36,000	1,12,000	1,16,000	88,000	75,000	61,000	63,000	68,000	59,000
(b) Band	—	43,000	45,000	50,000	—	—	—	—	—	—	—
(c) Bodyguard	12,000	1,26,000	78,000	1,00,000	—	—	—	—	—	—	—
(d) Surgeon and his establishment	—	36,000	33,600	34,800	—	—	—	—	—	—	—
(e) Maintenance and repairs of furnishings of official residences	8,000	21,500	25,000	34,000	14,500	10,500	13,000	9,800	4,000	5,000	4,000
3. Contract Allowance, i.e., allowances for misc. expenses	10,500	92,000	1,08,000	1,00,000	23,700	21,700	21,700	16,600	14,100	14,100	7,800
4. Tour Expenses including motor cars	35,000	1,13,000	65,000	1,22,000	1,25,000	60,000	26,000	55,000	18,000	—	30,000

Source: F. No. 19/65/65—Public 1, p. 12.

Maximum Yearly Amounts (in Rupees) Charged on the Revenues of the
Provinces in Respect of Certain Allowances and Privileges of Governors under
the Government of India (Governors' Allowances and Privileges) Order, 1950

Province	Sumptuary Allowance	Military Secy. (or A.D.C.) and his establishment	Entertainment allowance	STAFF AND HOUSEHOLD		Contract allowance, i.e. an allowance for misc. expenses including maintenance of motor cars	Tour Expenses	Total
				Surgeon and his establishment	Maintenance & repairs of furnishings of official residences			
(1)	(2)	(3)	(4)	(5)	(6)	(7)	(8)	(9)
Madras	22,500	1,20,000	5,000	17,000	25,000	1,50,000	1,53,000	4,92,500
Bombay	22,500	1,05,300	5,000	20,000	25,000	1,28,000	50,000	3,55,800
West Bengal	22,500	1,25,000	5,000	17,000	25,000	1,30,000	46,000	3,70,500
U.P.	19,000	90,000	5,000	—	15,000	50,000	1,16,000	2,95,000
East Punjab	9,000	80,000	2,500	—	7,000	39,400	42,000	1,79,900
Bihar	7,500	80,000	2,500	—	14,000	32,000	58,000	1,94,000
C.P. & Berar	7,500	76,250	2,500	—	10,000	28,300	31000	1,55,550
Assam	7,500	70,000	2,500	—	5,000	30,000	55,000	1,70,000
Orissa	7,500	55,000	2,500	—	10,000	31,400	47,000	1,53,400

Sources: F. No. 19/65/65—Public (1), p. 21, also F. No. 19/5/56—Public (1)

Expenditure in Respect of Official Residences of Governors Sanctioned under the 1950 Order (Maintenance)

Province (1)	Improvement (2)	Gardens (3)	Electricity (4)	Water (5)	Taxes (6)	Repairs (7)	Total (8)
	Rs	Rs	Rs	Rs	Rs	Rs	Rs
Madras	50,000	64,000	55,000	17,000	46,000	1,03,000	3,35,000
Bombay	42,500	38,400	50,000	39,000	34,500	3,19,500	5,23,900
West Bengal	16,000	80,000	45,000	1,50,000		2,99,000	5,90,000
United Provinces	30,000	45,000	20,000	15,000	35,000	80,000	2,25,000
East Punjab	10,000	15,000	16,500	9,700	5,100	23,700	80,000
Bihar	25,000	23,000	14,000	9,500	32,000	62,000	1,65,500
C.P. & Berar	10,000	26,000	4,000		1,000	29,000	70,000
Assam	15,000	13,100	11,200			15,700	55,000
Orissa	6,500	9,900	19,500	6,400	4,500	25,500	72,300

Included expenditure on garderns and water.
Source—F. No. 19/65/65–Public (1), p. 23.

remained in Government House at Chandigarh for treatmemt. Ujjal Singh, who was appointed acting Governor, was at the same time entitled to use the Governor's residence without payment of rent.

Separate rent-free accommodation could, of course, be provided for the acting Governor who was entitled to the same emoluments, allowances and privileges as the Governor. The question that arose was whether the Governor on leave of absence was entitled to full emoluments, or only to leave allowance, or both. The Law Ministry favoured both, but its views came as a surprise to the Home Minister. The latter argued that, since the States Reorganization (Governors' Allowances and Privileges) Order, 1957, was based on the Order of 1936, the intention underlying the former should be made conformable to that of the latter. The Law Ministry accepted the proposal and the Order of 1957 was amended accordingly in 1966. It was now specifically laid down that during a period of leave a Governor would be entitled only to a leave allowance at the rate of Rs 2,750 per mensem in lieu of his salary.

No change was, however, effected in respect of the maximum yearly amounts for maintenance and repairs or for staff establishment and other charges shown in the tables in pages 67 and 68.

The Craze for Luxury and Lavish Expenditure

As already noted, the Governors took little or no care to keep their expenditure within the prescribed limits. They often sought special sanction from the President who had little alternative but to accept a *fait accompli*. For example, the personal staff of a Governor was meant to consist of a Military Secretary or an A.D.C., but not both. In practice, however, the Governors of most States had both, a situation that later led to an amendment of the Order of 1950.

The amount sanctioned for the annual repairs and maintenance charges of the official railway saloons of the Governor of U.P. amounted to Rs 4,400, but the expenditure incurred came to Rs 18,400 in 1959–60 and Rs 48,134 in 1960–1: the President had to specially sanction the excess expenditure.[36]

The Governors also indulged their preference for luxurious foreign cars and even exceeded the limits within which British Governors managed. From a semi-official letter of 2 November 1946 which U.A. Godbole, Secretary to the Governor-General, addressed to the Governors' Secretaries for their guidance, it appears that the Governors of the erstwhile Presidencies of Madras, Bombay and Bengal were

Maximum Yearly Amounts (in Rupees) Charged on the Consolidated Fund of States in Respect of Certain Matters under the 1957 Order

State (1)	Sumptuary Allowance (2)	Military Secy. (or ADC) and his establishment (3)	Entertainment Allowance (4)	Surgeon & his establishment (5)	Maintenance and repairs of furnishings of official (6)	Contract Allowance, misc., including motor-car (7)	Tour Expenses (8)	Total (9)
Andhra Pradesh	18,000	1,04,000	5,000	–	12,000	54,000	80,000	2,73,000
Bombay	30,000	1,15,000	5,000	25,000	50,000	1,50,000	1,25,000	5,00,000
Kerala	9,000	80,000	3,000	–	10,000	35,000	30,000	1,67,000
Madras	20,000	1,00,000	5,000	20,000	25,000	1,00,000	50,000	3,20,000
Madhya Pradesh	12,000	90,000	4,000	–	10,000	50,000	50,000	2,16,000
Mysore	10,000	80,000	5,000	–	10,000	1,00,000	50,000	2,55,000
Punjab	10,000	80,000	3,000	–	10,000	50,000	50,000	2,03,000
Rajasthan	12,000	80,000	3,000	–	10,000	50,000	50,000	2,05,000

Source: F. No. 19/65/65-Public (I), p. 29.

Maximum Yearly Amounts (in Rupees) in Respect of Official Residences of Governors—Maintenance and Repairs under the 1957 Order

State	Improvement	Gardens	Electricity	Water	Taxes	Repairs	Total
(1)	(2)	(3)	(4)	(5)	(6)	(7)	(8)
Andhra Pradesh	10,000	10,000	36,000	10,000	14,000	40,000	1,20,000
Bombay	60,000	50,000	68,000	50,000	45,000	3,77,000	6,50,000
Kerala	20,000	20,000	15,000	7,000		38,000	1,00,000
Madras	50,000	64,000	55,000	17,000	46,000	1,03,000	3,35,000
Madhya Pradesh	10,000	26,000*	10,000	*	1,000	29,000	76,000
Mysore	50,000	50,000	–	50,000	–	50,000	2,00,000
Punjab	12,000	26,000	18,000	12,000	6,000	26,000	1,00,000
Rajasthan							80,000

Source: F. No. 19/65/65-Public (I), p. 30.

entitled to the use of four cars, namely two limousines, one saloon and one utility car. The Governors of the erstwhile non-Presidencies, on the other hand, were entitled to only three, one in each of the three categories. Under the advice of the Secretary of State it was made clear to the Governors that the pre-war amounts were not to be revised and that cases of replacement were to continue to be dealt with on an ad-hoc basis: when a Governor wished to have a car replaceed, he had to seek the Secretary of State's approval.[37]

In the post-Independence period the old distinction between the Presidency and the non-Presidency Governors ceased to exist. The result was that the old schedule of three cars rose to four in a number of States. The old imperial preference for imported cars continued with Indian Governors also. Of the four cars purchased for the Governor of Madras, for instance, three were imported in 1953. In 1959, he wanted to have one replaced, but by then the foreign exchange position was tight and the Commerce Ministry had stopped giving import licences even for the components of big cars. Arrangement was, however, made by the Goverment of India to make available from old stock a Studebaker assembled in India: this the Governor refused. But when he wanted to have a third big car in place of a small one, the Government of India sanctioned the purchase of a Plymouth, which was supplied free of excise duty worth Rs 3,000, for the Governor was classed amongst the dignitaries who were exempted from such payment.[38]

In principle it was for official use only that Governors were given the privilege of importing cars without payment of customs duty. Cases, however, occurred where some used this privilege for private purposes also. In January 1951, for example, the Governor of Bombay, Raja Maharaj Singh, wished to buy a foreign car from his private means without being required to pay any customs duty. The matter went to the Prime Minister and President for consideration. Legally, the provisions of the Order of 1950 were wide enough to be interpreted in favour of Maharaj Singh. Morally, however, the use of the concession seemed likely to arouse public criticism. The position was accordingly explained to the Governors in a circular letter of 30 March 1951 from H. V. R. Iengar, then Home Secretary.

This instance was nevertheless followed in 1956 by the Governor of Punjab (C. P. N. Singh), the Governor of U.P. (K. M. Munshi) and the Governor of Bombay (Hare Krushna Mehtab). Of the three, the first two were due to demit office within a year or two. The Governor of Bombay had nearly four more years to go. While Singh's proposal was for an Austin A 96 Westminster car, Munshi's preference was for a Mercedes Benz. Mehtab, on the other hand, wanted to import two Land Rovers from his private purse—one for his own use and the other for his brother.

The vast paraphernalia of Raj Bhavan maintained after the imperial fashion became yet another item of lavish expenditure. Even a newly started Government House, for instance, at Jaipur involved a sum of Rs 1,84,750 for alterations and additional suites of rooms in the Guest House as well as a big Banquet Hall for receptions. Another sum of Rs 1,50,000 was provided to complete the furnishings with elegant furniture, new carpets, chandeliers and refrigeration. An additional sum of Rs 20,000 was made available from savings, and yet the furnishings remained incomplete, requiring another Rs 15,000 for completion. It was explained that some of the articles purchased initially when the Raj Bhavan was started in November 1956 were worn out and unserviceable in 1960. It was therefore suggested that they should be replaced before the projected visit of Queen Elizabeth II of England. It was here that the Government put its foot down and regretted that the amount of Rs 15,000 sought could not be sanctioned. It was nonetheless conceded that if the expenditure was considered unavoidable, the bills might be kept pending and the excess expenditure met from the savings of subsequent years.[39]

The position of the Governor of Pubjab was even worse. In a Note of 11 October 1960 a Joint Secretary in the Home Ministry regretted that 'the Military Secretary to the Governor of Punjab has not been keeping proper accounts in respect of maintenance and repairs of furnishings of official residences in the Raj Bhavan in that State. They have committed certain irregularities which have been questioned by the audit.' This happened in spite of the fact that during 1957–9 two special orders of the President had already been issued to regulate and regularize the excess expenditure incurred without prior sanction. The total amount allotted under the 1957 Order for the maintenance and repairs of furnishings was Rs 10,000. But the expenditure actually incurred was of the order of Rs 1,29,002 in 1958-9 and Rs 1,40,128 in 1959–60. The Military Secretary was, therefore, directed 'to keep proper accounts and also to see that the accounts provided for the maintenance, etc. are not exceeded as has been done during the last four years since 1957'.[40] The Government, however, was left with no alternative but to regularize the irregularities already committed.

Ministers of Government

It is not our object here to deal with the constitutional position of Ministers or their relations with Secretaries to the Government, but to throw light on the manner in which Ministers of Government hastened, on the transfer of power, to grant themselves salaries, allowances and perquisites that are reminiscent of their imperialist predecessors.

The erstwhile Members of the Executive Council came to form a Council of Ministers on 15 August 1947. The Salaries of Ministers Act passed soon after by the Constituent Assembly recognized only one grade of Ministers: Ministers of the Dominion of India who were all Members of the Cabinet. Under the Salaries of Ministers Act each Minister was to be paid a salary of Rs 3,000 per month as well as a monthly sumptuary allowance of Rs 500. He was in addition entitled, without payment of rent, to the use of a fully furnished residence in New Delhi, including the staff quarters, other buildings and gardens attached to it. Similar provisions were made for another fully furnished residence in Simla for the summer season each year. No Minister was to bear any part of the maintenance costs of either residence, which included the payment of local rates and taxes as well as the provision of electricity and water.

With increase in the load of work at the Centre, there arose a necessity for assisting Cabinet Ministers in the discharge of their duties. It was decided to appoint Ministers of State and Deputy Ministers in certain ministries. The three persons who were appointed Ministers of State were Mohan Lal Saxena (Rehabilitation) on 8 June 1948; K. Santhanam (Transport) on 1 October 1948; and R. R. Diwakar (Information and Broadcasting) on 7 December 1948. The two Deputy Ministers who were appointed during October–December 1948 were Khurshed Lal and Dr B. V. Kesker.

These appointments were made by executive order, without reference to any Act of the Legislature. The scope of executive action, however, did not remain limited to ministerial appointments, for it was extended to their salaries, allowances and privileges also. The Ministers of State so appointed were, for instance, granted a monthly salary of Rs 3,000 each, as against a Deputy Minister who was allowed Rs 2,000. These terms were regularized under the Salaries of Ministers (Amendment) Act, 1950 though a Cabinet Minister alone was declared entitled to a sumptuary allowance of Rs 500. A confidential letter from V. Narahari Rao, then Comptroller and Auditor-General, to the Minister for Law (B. R. Ambedkar) on 7 November 1949 reveals more about allowances, however; for it indicates how Ministers, especially in the provinces, contrived to allow themselves 'concessions which were unknown even in past regimes'.

The point which Rao emphasized in his D. O. to Ambedkar was that not only 'salaries and allowances' but all the 'privileges and advantages enjoyed by Ministers having a monetary significance should be regulated by an Act of the appropriate Legislature'. Provisions for the salaries of Ministers were of course covered by sections 10(3) and 51(3) of the Government of India Act, 1935 and their adaptation in the Provisional Constitutional Order, 1947. But the privileges and advantages that were being enjoyed by Ministers were outside the provisions so made. They related to such facilities as railway saloons or reserved accommodation and the conditions governing them, cars, rent-free houses, free medical treatment for members of the family, car advances, etc. These items were regulated in the provinces by rules made by the Executive Government, not by any Act of an appropriate legislature. Under these rules Ministers of a provincial government, for example, could take members of their family and other non-officials in railway accommodation reserved at the expense of the government, without buying tickets for them. The Accountant-General of the province concerned could not persuade the government concerned to amend the rules. In another case, as the Comptroller and Auditor-General pointed out, an advance of Rs 11,164 had been drawn for the purchase of a car on 2 February 1949. But as the Minister had to demit office on 13 April an extension of three months was therefore given for the refund of the outstanding balance of the advance.

While drawing the attention of Dr Ambedkar to the irregularities of Ministers in the provinces, the Comptroller and Auditor-General pointed out that in the past when there was an Executive Council, even a car advance required the sanction of the Secretary of State; for the principle then was that no authority however high should be in a position to sanction for itself any concession or profit or advantage. He thus suggested that the sections in the Draft Constitution dealing with the salaries and allowances of Ministers should include a provision that all privileges of monetary significance should also be dealt with by the appropriate legislature, not by the Executive Government.[41]

In a letter of 23 December 1949 addressed to Dr John Matthai, then Finance Minister, Rao not only reiterated his protest against what was happening in the provinces, but also raised doubts about the validity of rules framed by the Government of India for the chartering of aircraft by Central Ministers. His objection was directed specially against a provision permitting a Minister to take, free of charge, any other person with him in the plane, provided the Minister concerned certified that 'it is necessary for the purpose of his visit on Government duty to take the person with him'. The provision so made differed little from that enabling a Minister of a provincial government to take with him non-officials in the railway accommodation reserved at government expense.[42] The Comptroller and Auditor-General in fact considered both were subject to abuse and also wrote to Sardar Vallabhbhai Patel to see that the taxpayers' money was not misused by ministerial discretion.[43] The reason for appealing to the Home Minister was that his subordinate officials were tending to extend the scope of ministerial 'allowances' beyond the existing rules.

Rao particularly called for a constitutional provision to validate the use of privileges enjoyed by Ministers. Paragraph 5 of the Second Schedule to the Constitution did precisely this. It provided that the Ministers of the Union would be entitled to such 'salaries and allowances' as were payable to them as 'Ministers for the Dominion of India immediately before the commencement of this Constitution'. And since it was held by the Law Ministry that the term 'allowance' covered all such privileges as Ministers enjoyed before the Constitution, they were declared by an executive order to be entitled to railway saloons, medical facilities, advances for cars, etc.[44] Rao, who wanted to have additional privileges specifically mentioned in order to avoid legal uncertainties, did not fully succeed against the politicians who preferred to leave such matters vague and undefined.

But this did not put an end to the trouble. A representation was, for instance, made for further concessions. Under the privileges enjoyed by a Cabinet Minister before the commencement of the Constitution in respect of his railway saloon, he could travel in it 'and take ten servants'. If members of his family travelled along with him, he had to purchase first-class tickets for them. His private secretary could, however, travel in the saloon on a second-class ticket. Formerly, the wives of Executive Councillors were permitted to travel with their husbands. But when Zafrullah Khan arrived with two wives, the Government of the day decided that tickets should be bought for wives too.[45]

After the introduction of the Constitiution four armed policemen were 'for security reasons' also required to travel in the train with a Minister, an erstwhile 'freedom-fighter'. The guards were 'supposed to run up at every place when the train (stopped) and stand on guard in front of the saloon'.[46] This information is contained in a letter of 22 January 1951 from the Commerce Minister, Sri Prakasa, to Rajagopalachari, then Home Minister, for favour of further concessions. He wanted railway saloons to be allowed to stay but did not want to pay for members of his family travelling with him. 'I do think', he wrote, 'it is hard for Ministers to have to pay for members of their families specially when they are such as are completely dependent on them and may also need to travel with them.' He therefore suggested that 'a Minister travelling in a saloon should be permitted to take three persons of his family with him free, or in the alternative with Intermediate or at best Second-Class tickets',[47] but not first-class. Rajagopalachari did not concede the request.

Sri Prakasa had made this proposal even earlier to Vallabhbhai Patel who was in principle opposed to the use of railway saloons by Ministers. As for the railway concessions proposed, Patel had made it clear that it would lead to the abuse of the privilege. A rule had in fact been established in 1948 that, except for Cabinet Ministers, Ministers of State. Deputy Ministers or a Secretary to the Government should ordinarily travel in a first-class coupe unless work required travelling in a first-class four-berth compartment. However, this rule did not remain operative for long. The Ministers of State began subsequently to be allowed to requisition a four-berth compartment or even a saloon at their discretion.[48]

The basic reason for these demands for increasing Ministerial concessions and privileges proceeded from the absence of due regard for the principle of legislative authority as the primary sanction for rule-making by the executive. The Ministers of the Government made rules to grant themselves such advantages as they alone determined. It was precisely against such practices that the Comptroller and Auditor-General, Narahari Rao, had raised his voice of protest. However, a rule-oriented Comptroller and Auditor-General could do little beyond making comments in his audit report, which he did not fail to do.[49]

Irregularities were naturally committed even by Cabinet

Ministers. In one case, the *Indian News Chronicle* of 26 June 1951 reported that the Auditor-General had made some observations regarding 'the irregularities practised by certain Ministers during air travels'. They involved two separate sums of Rs 1.015 and Rs 822 due from two Ministers and a third, heavy sum of Rs 51,562 against the chartering of planes by another Cabinet Minister over a period of seven months. This expenditure arose from Cabinet Ministers allowing people to travel with them in chartered planes without paying as the rules required. The recovery of the first two sums was waived by executive action, which was admitted by the Government when questions were put in Parliament. The reply given by the Government spokeman in the third case was that it was not possible to ascertain the total sum due, as 'the list of non-entitled persons was not available with the Air Companies concerned and no records were maintained by the Ministry' involved in the matter.[50] The name of the Minister was not disclosed for reasons of public interest. But the rules had been relaxed by the Government to save his skin.

The lack of a strict adherence to rules also caused wide variations over travelling allowances. These variations were made clear in a statement prepared at the instance of the Prime Minister who, in view of a question in Parliament, called for fuller details of the figures given in answer for each Minister. The statement is given on pages 76–7.

The statement reveals that while the monthly expenditure of the Prime Minister on travel was only of the order of one hundred rupees, that of Mehtab amounted to Rs 1,967, nearly twenty times as much. So was the case of B.V. Keskar, only a Deputy Minister, whose expenditure works out to the rate of Rs 1,292 per month. He was comparable to M. Thirumala Rao, another Deputy Minister, who drew Rs 4,911 in four months.

The travel bills of Cabinet Ministers, however, were on the whole fair and moderate. It was said of the Prime Minister, Jawaharlal Nehru, that he had not drawn till February 1951 any daily allowance. Until July 1950, 'tips were also paid by the Prime Minister out of his own pocket'. It was only in July 1950 that the Government in consultation with the Finance Ministry authorized payment of tips on behalf of the Prime Minister during his official travels.[51]

The need to enact fresh legislative measures governing the salaries and allowances of Union Ministers, however, arose immediately from the changes introduced in their designations in May 1952. From a letter of Narahari Rao dated 18 May to N.R. Pillai, Cabinet Secret-

Statement showing Amount of Travelling Allowance Drawn by the Honourable Ministers during the Year 1950–51 (up to the 18th February 1951)

S. No.	Name	Railway fare	Daily allowance	Air fare	Cost of hiring Defence Services etc. plane	Railway saloon charges	Car fare	Actual expenses	Total cols. 3-9	Total amt. as reported by AGCR	Period for which drawn
(1)	(2)	(3)	(4)	(5)	(6)	(7)	(8)	(9)	(10)	(11)	(12)
	Cabinet ministers										
1.	The Hon. the Prime Minister			333-00				665-00	998-10-0	998-10-0	11/49-9/50
2.	The Hon. Shri Sardar Patel		1537-8-0	1825-0-0				575-2-0	3934-10-0	3934-10-0	4/50-1/51
3.	The Hon. Dr. B.R. Ambedkar		1537-8-0	1825-0-0				575-2-0	3934-10-0	3934-10-0	4/50-1/51
4.	The Hon. Shri Jagjiwan Ram		862-8-0	4800-11-0		128-14-0		1179-10-0	8127-11-0	8127-11-0	3/50-1/51
5.	The Hon. Sardar Baldev Singh		840-0-0						840-0-0	840-0-0	1/50-11/50
6.	The Hon. Shri Maulana A.K. Azad		225-0-0		172-0-0			50-0-0	447-0-0	447-0-0	2/50-1/51
7.	The Hon. Shri N. V. Gadgil	438-8-0	948-12-0	2190-8-0		108-8-0		301-14-0	4031-10-0	4031-10-0	10/48-1/51
8.	The Hon. Rajkumari Amrit Kaur		660-0-0	6385-0-0		756-0-0		242-4-0	8043-4-0	8043-4-0	12/49-12/50
9.	The Hon. Shri R. A. Kidwai		641-4-0	10635-12-0		388-4-0		145-0-0	11169-0-0	11169-0-0	6/48-11/50
10.	The Hon. Shri N. G. Ayyangar		810-0-0	1854-0-0				173-7-0	2668-11-0	2668-11-0	10/47-6/50
11.	The Hon. Shri Prakasa		810-0-0	697-0-0				189-6-0	1696-6-0	1696-6-0	6/50-11/50
12.	The Hon. Shri C. D. Deshmukh		210-0-0	633-0-0				104-0-0	947-0-0	947-0-0	6/50-1/51
13.	The Hon. Shri H. K. Mahtab	52-1-0	1290-0-0	10676-0-0				1809-1-0	13767-2-0		5/50-12/50
14.	The Hon. Shri K. M. Munshi		975-0-0	4143-2-0				312-0-0	4430-2-0	4430-2-0	5/50-12/50
15.	The Hon. Shri C. Rajagopalachari			557-0-0				267-0-0	824-0-0	824-0-0	7/50–12/50
16.	The Hon. Dr. S. P. Mukherjee	181-2-0						633-13-0	814-15-0	814-15-0	4/50
17.	The Hon. Dr. John Mathai	431-0-0	90-0-0	16-12-0				824-10-0	1362-6-0	1362-6-0	4/50-11/50
18.	The Hon. Shri Jairamdas Daulat Ram	362-0-0	150-0-0	34-0-0		950-8-0		15-0-0	1511-8-0	1511-8-0	6/49-4/50
19.	The Hon. Shri K. C. Neogy	451-4-0						236-6-0	687-10-0	687-10-0	4/50

Ministers of State							
20.	The Hon. Shri Mohal Lal Saxena		879-0-0		76-4-0	3381-4-0	3459-4-0	5/49-5/50
21.	The Hon. Shri K. Santhanam	780-0-0	1241-0-0		76-7-0	3981-7-0	3981-7-0	9/49-1/51
22.	The Hon. Shri Satyanarain Sinha	660-0-0	744-0-0		467-10-0	1871-10-0	1869-10-0	5/50-10/50
23.	The Hon. Shri A. P. Jain	7-13-0	1620-0-0		390-10-0	4009-15-9	3009-15-9	6/50-12/50
24.	The Hon. Shri R. R. Diwakar	16-0-0	825-0-0		89-14-0	4671-14-0	4671-14-0	1/50-1/51
25.	The Hon. Shri C. C. Biswas			2426-0-0	1884-0-0			
Deputy Ministers							
26.	The Hon. Shri Khurshed Lal		590-0-0		1633-0-0	5641-4-0	5631-4-0	12/49-12/50
27.	The Hon. Shri B. V. Keshar	416-0-0	431-4-0		423-0-0	10338-2-0	10338-2-0	5/49-1/51
28.	The Hon. Shri D. P. Karmarkar		227-8-0			1332-4-0	1332-4-0	8/50-11/51
29.	The Hon. Shri S. N. Buragohain	211-4-0	235-0-0		384-9-0	37-5-0	3893-5-0	9/50-1/51
30.	The Hon. Shri M. Thirumala Rao	1170-13-0	345-0-0		941-10-0	4911-1-0	4911-1-0	8/50-12/50
31.	The Hon. Shri Himatsinha	107-13-0	107-8-0		12-8-0	1355-0-0	1355-0-0	10/50-1/51

Source: File No 15/54/51-Public I.

ary, it appears that, as against the three existing designations[52] of Ministers regularized under the 1950 Act, there were to be the following changes:

1. Senior Ministers, who were described as 'Ministers of Cabinet rank who are Members of the Cabinet'.

2. 'Ministers of Cabinet rank who are not Members of the Cabinet', and

3. Deputy Ministers.

A further distinction was made concerning the second category of Ministers who, if appointed to assist a member of the Cabinet, were to be described as 'Ministers of State' for that Ministry in order to be distinguished from the Senior Minister in charge of the Ministry. It was, however, made clear that such a Minister of State was not to constitute a separate class of Ministers and that his position was in all respects to be identical with that of other Ministers of Cabinet rank who were not Members of the Cabinet.[53] The position of the second category of Ministers was thus left extremely vague. It created legal difficulties in the payment of salaries. If treated as Ministers of Cabinet rank, they could also be entitled to the salaries of Cabinet Minsters under the Salaries of Ministers Act, 1947. On the other hand, since it was stated they were not Cabinet Ministers, they could not get the salary of a Cabinet Minister sanctioned under the Act. As for paying them the salary of a Minister of State under the Salaries of Ministers (Amendment) Act, 1950, this could not be done legally because the Ministers were not so described except in cases where they assisted a Senior Minister. The Comptroller and Auditor-General therefore made it clear that it was not in order to talk of Ministers of Cabinet rank when Ministers were not members of the Cabinet.

The difficulty was perhaps political, which caused legal vagueness. It arose from the fact that a Minister of State under the 1950 Act received a Cabinet Minister's salary of Rs 3000 without being entitled to the status of a Minister of Cabinet rank. If, on the other hand, he was to remain merely as a Minister of State without Cabinet rank, he was not to be allowed to draw the salary of a member of the Cabinet. Considerations of political expediency appear to have led the Government to call him a Minister of Cabinet rank without being a Cabinet Minister. In a vote of 19 May 1952, the Prime Minister in fact removed the confusion by saying that Ministers of Cabinet rank who were not members of the Cabinet, were always to be treated as Ministers of State for the purposes of salaries.[54] But this executive order of the Prime Minister was not accepted as sufficient by the Finance Secretary, for the provisions of an Act could not be modified in this manner.

There was thus no alternative but to enact new legislation by repealing the Act of 1947. This was done by the Salaries and Allowances of Ministers Act, 1952, passed on 12 August. The word 'Allowances' was added to the title of the Act, and a number of them specifically mentioned. They included sumptuary allowances; travelling and daily allowances by land, sea or air; free medical treatment to a Minister and members of his family; and advances for the purchase of cars. Features not mentioned but enjoyed so far under executive orders were declared as deemed to have been sanctioned by the Central Government by virtue of the rule-making powers vested in it under the Act.

As regards ministerial designations, the Act made no reference to 'Ministers of Cabinet rank who were not Members of the Cabinet'. It merely defined the term 'Minister' as a member of the Council of Ministers, by whatever name called, and included the Deputy Minister also. Each Minister, other than a Deputy Minister, was to be paid under the Act a salary of Rs 2,250 per mensem. A Deputy Minister, on the other hand, was to be given a monthly salary of Rs 1,850. The Central Government was in addition authorized by the Act to provide for the grant of a sumptuary allowance not exceeding Rs 500 per mensem to any Minister other than a Deputy Minister. Such rules might also provide for the grant of allowance to different Ministers at different rates. This obviously meant a difference in status among the first two categories of Ministers in terms of allowances and membership of the Cabinet, though not of salary. On the basis of a demi-official letter of 21 August 1952 from the Cabinet Secretariat the following provision was *inter alia* made in the rules framed regarding the allowances of Cabinet Ministers: 'There shall be granted, with effect from the 12th August, 1952, to every Minister other than the Prime Minister who is a Member of the Cabinet a sumptuary allowance of Rs. 500/-p.m.'[55]

The phrase 'other than the Prime Minister' was added as the then Prime Minister did not accept any sumptuary allowance. He paid for himself, for members of his family and personal guests. And as far as expenditure on his official guests and foreign dignitaries was concerned, it formed part of official entertainment arranged by the Government Hospitality Organizations.[56]

The 1952 Act further provided that each Minister was to remain entitled, as before, to the use of a 'fully furnished residence' during his term of office, and for a period of fifteen days immediately thereafter. The Central Government was authorized to make rules to carry out the purpose of this Act, but the rules made had to be laid before both Houses of Parliament.

The principle for which the Comptroller and Auditor-General had been fighting thus stood vindicated. Executive orders were superceded by legislative enactments and respect for law was enforced. The Cabinet Secretary and Finance Secretary lent their full support to Narahari Rao, while the Prime Minister too had shown his resilience in support of law and legislative authority.

At the instance of the Comptroller and Auditor-General, a certain measure of uniformity was introduced in 1955 in respect of rules regulating the drawal of mileage allowance by State Ministries for journeys performed by Ministers in cars provided by the Government. In an aide-memoire addressed to the Prime Minister it was pointed out that the mileage drawn by Ministers in the States was 'over-generous' in a number of cases, 'inviting criticism both in official and non-official circles.[57] In Assam, for instance, a car was provided by the State to each Minister who was also given an allowance of Rs 200 per mensem. He also drew full road mileage at rates admissible to government servants for journeys performed in their own cars. Since the capital cost for the purchase and the recurring cost for the maintenance of the car were both met by the State, the drawing of full mileage by Ministers had attracted adverse comment over the years. In a letter of 12 May 1955, the Prime Minister brought this to the notice of the Home Minister, Govind Ballabh Pant, who wrote to all the Chief Secretaries by name, asking them to follow the example of Rajasthan where Ministers had the use of an official car at the headquarters, subject to a ceiling on petrol allowance. If this allowance was exceeded, the cost of additional petrol was borne by the Minister. For journeys outside headquarters, the entire cost of petrol was met by the Government, the Minister in that case receiving only a daily allowance. The action taken by State Governments and the rules framed in this behalf were accordingly sent to the Home Ministry.[58] But the fact remained that most State Ministers generally showed little scruple over travelling allowances.

In a case where the Prime Minister was himself interested, the Comptroller and Auditor-General had, however, no choice but to yield, subject of course to the rules being suitably changed. The case was that of Abul Kalam Azad, Education Minister, who asked for an advance of Rs 15,000 to be repaid in five years for the purchase of a car. This clashed with the rules already framed by the Home Ministry, under which the maximum amount which could be drawn as an advance by a Minister was Rs 12,000, and recoverable from the Minister's salary in not more than 48 instalments.

There was another difficulty in meeting Azad's request, for a similar request from the Minister for Rehabilitation over repayment had already been rejected. The then Home Secretary had objected to it on the ground that 'it would be improper to depart from these [statutory] rules in particular cases merely by executive orders.' And when the 'matter was considered at a very high [ministerial] level', it was decided that there was 'no case for making discretionary provision under the Rules', because 'Ministers and Deputy Ministers' were after all 'birds of passage' and 'even 48 instalments [were] rather a long period.'[59]

And yet both the conditions were sought to be met by an amendment of the rules in question. Azad wrote to Nehru who in a letter of 10 May 1957 advised T.T. Krishnamachari, Finance Minister, to have the rules amended so as to permit advances up to Rs 15,000 repayable in 60 instalments over a period of five years. The Home Ministry was asked to 'concur and take urgent action so as to enable the Minister for Educaton to draw the advance, as desired by him in his letter to the Prime Minister'.[60] The Ministry which had earlier emphasized strict adherence to established rules, now relented and immediately expressed its concurrence in a Note of 14 May. Since the rules were framed in consultation with the Comptroller and Auditor-General, it was he who issued the revised rules.[61]

With the passage of time, new advantages came to be added to the list of privileges enjoyed by Ministers. In May 1956, Ram Niwas Mirdha, Minister for Agriculture in Rajasthan, proceeded to China on a cultural delegation and the question arose whether Mirdha should be considered to be on duty as a Minister and allowed to draw his salary and allowances during his vist. The matter was referred to the Government of India who decided that as the Constitution provided for the salaries and allowances of Ministers without any reference to matters like conditions of service, leave of absence, etc., all Ministers, whether of the Union or the States, should be deemed to continue in office until deprived of ministership, regardless of whether they were present or absent from their place of work.[62] They were to be paid even when on holiday and when they did no work.[63]

Another addition to the privileges of Ministers related to the scale of rent-free furniture supplied to them by executive orders since January 1953, apart from the scale prescribed by the Salaries and Allowances of Ministers Act, 1952. This includea certain electrical appliances, such as special table lamps, standard lamps, electric heaters and radiators, table fans, refrigerators, electric boilers, pedestal fans, etc. In a Note of 4 May 1956, the Comptroller and Auditor-General raised objections to the free supply of these items which, according to him, could not be provided thus unless the 1952 Act itself was amended to cover these items. The Accommodation Branch of the Ministry of Works, Housing and Supply, however, explained that these amenities were being supplied rent-free because certain Ministers were of the view that a 'fully furnished residence' should 'include these items also'.[64] The Home and Law Ministries also lent support to this interpretation, and did not consider it necessary to amend the 1952 Act. Arguments and counter-arguments went on for a while on the interpretation of the terms 'fully furnished residence' until the Comproller and Auditor-General decided to drop his objections.[65]

The Ministers' Residence Rules of 1962 codified in detail all the allowances and privileges enjoyed by Ministers. All Cabinet Ministers other than the Prime Minister, for instance, were granted a sumptuary allowance of Rs 500 per mensem. Although a Minister of State, Satya Narayan Singha, was given the sumptuary allowance of a Cabinet Minister, B.V. Keskar, S.K. Dey and Mehr Chand Khanna were three other Ministers of State who were granted only Rs 250 each. The daily travelling allowance of a Minister was fixed at Rs 30, while that of a Deputy Minister at Rs 15. For travel by railway on work a Minister might reserve a standard-gauge saloon or an inspection carriage in case a saloon was not available. If the railway authorites were not able to attach his reserved carriage to a mail train, he could specify a specific train at the expense of the Government. The Prime Minister could reserve place in one standard-gauge or one meter-gauge train. The rules provided for a number of other concessions, such as free accommodation in the reserved carriage for one relative and two servants, free carriage of all luggage and freight charges. The Minister was also entitled to incidentals admissible to government servants. Similar concessions were available to travel by road, sea or air.

A Minister and members of his family were entitled to free medical attendance and treatment on the scale and conditions applicable to members of the All-India Services. These facilities were extended to him while he was also on work outside India. As for advances for the purchase of cars, the maximum amount for the purpose was fixed at Rs 15,000 or the actual price of the car, whichever happened to be less. The recovery of an advance granted together with interest thereon was to be made from the salary of the Minister in not more than sixty equal monthly instalments. This was in line with the amended rule made earlier to accommodate the Minister of Education, Abul Kalam Azad. Necessary forms of agreement had to be entered into before an advance was granted. There were other concessions which Ministers enjoyed free of charge, and all these were defined and reduced to writing.

In its meeting of 13 June 1957 the Cabinet announced that members of the Council of Ministers had agreed to a ten per cent cut in salaries and allowances, the latter, as referred to in the Cabinet decision, being restricted to 'sumptuary allowance' only. However, no uniform effect was given to the cut proposed. It was reported that different Ministers gave effect to the cut from different months. In the case of Sardar Surjit Singh Majithia and K. Raghuramiah, for instance, no deduction had been made till the end of August, three months after the June announcement, and no information was received from them even after August.[66] In some cases deductions were made only in pay, while in the others, both in pay and sumptuary allowance.

The salaries of Ministers remaining constant since 1952, it was their allowances and perquisites that were subjected to public criticism. In 1963, Dahyabhai V. Patel, for instance, raised this question in the Rajya Sabha and asked the Home Minister to state the different perquisites available to Ministers and the cost of these over the previous two years. The Government answered by placing on the table of the House copies of the Salaries and Allowances of Ministers Act, 1952 and the rules made in 1957 and 1962. When the subject came up for debate on 19 December 1963, R.M. Hazarnavis, a Minister in the Home Ministry, tried to dodge the question by saying that it was not possible to evaluate the cost of all the perquisites, especially those relating to medical treatment. Even charges for electricity, water, furniture and other perquisites, he said, could not be accurately ascertained; for these differed 'from house to house, from Minister to Minister, from period to period'.[67]

Under Starred Question No. 87 for 13 February 1964 in the Rajya Sabha, Bhupesh Gupta asked the Minister for Home Affairs to state the total expenditure, including salary, allowances and perquisites, etc., of each Minister and Deputy Ministers for the year 1962. The information supplied in response did not include in the first instance salaries or sumptuary allowances, which were submitted separately. The list of perquisites included rent for residences, rent for furniture, water charges, electricity, and charges for electrical appliances. These were all provided free and calculated for audit purposes at moderate rates. The monthly rent of the portion occupied by the Prime Minister and his family at Teen Murti House, for example, amounted only to Rs 515, while the rent of furniture and water charges came to Rs 224 and Rs 18 respectively. What cost the Prime Minister most was electricity and electrical appliances. The following statement shows the total expenditure incurred by the Government on the perquisites of Union Ministers for the financial year 1962–3.[68]

	Amount	Remarks
Jawaharlal Nehru	Rs 47,490.98	Figure includes electricity charges of Rs.30496.98, covering the entire house, including road lights, boundary lights, etc.
Morarji Desai	Rs 18935.56	
Jagjivan Ram	Rs 18307.68	
Gulzarilal Nanda	Rs 15690.00	
T.T. Krishnamachari	Rs 10082.00	The figure is for Aug. 1962 to March 1963.
Lal Bahadur Shastri	Rs 17484.00	Electricity charges for March 1963 (Rs 118.55) were paid by him in cash.
Swaran Singh	Rs 14492.00	
K.C. Reddy	Rs 18529.22	
V.K. Krishna Menon	Rs 6672.62	The figure is for April 1962 to Nov. 1963; Menon ceased to be a Minister on 9.11.1962.

S.K. Patil	Rs 19781.08	
Hafiz Mohammad Ibrahim	Rs 20706.44	
A.K. Sen	Rs 17200.00	
Y.B. Chavan	Rs 4507.00	The figure is for Nov. 1962 to March 1963
K.D. Malaviya	Rs 13769.00	
B. Gopala Reddi	Rs 16095.75	
C. Subramaniam	Rs 14277.00	The figure is for 23 May 1962 to March 1963.
K.L. Shrimali	Rs 11503.70	
Humayun Kabir	Rs 13412.00	
Satya Narayan Singh	Rs 18790.00	
Mehr Chand Khanna	Rs 9687.00	The figure is for June 1962 to March 63.
Manubhai Shah	Rs 11035.00	
Nityanand Kanungo	Rs 13481.00	
Raj Bahadur	Rs 11545.00	
S.K. Dey	Rs 11964.00	
Sushila Nayar	Rs 4748.00	
B.N. Datar	Rs 11716.00	The figure is for April 1962 to Feb. 63. The Minister expired on 1.3.1963.
J.L. Hathi	Rs 8962.00	
Mrs L.N. Menon	Rs 6850.00	
K. Raghuramaiah	Rs 12745.00	
O.V. Alagesan	Rs 10061.00	The figure is for 22 June 1962 to March 1963.
Ram Subhag Singh	Rs 12752.00	The figure is for 26 May 1962 to March 1963.
B.R. Bhagat	Rs 7957.00	
M.M. Das	Rs 6072.00	
Shah Nawaz Khan	Rs 8533.00	
A.M. Thomas	Rs 9083.00	

R.M. Hazarnavis	Rs 8387.00	
S.V. Ramaswamy	Rs 7896.00	
Ahmed Mohiuddin	Rs 9948.00	
Tarkeshwari Sinha	Rs 7742.00	
P.S. Naskar	Rs 9846.00	
B.S. Murthy	Rs 10225.00	
Mrs T.S. Soundaram Ramachandran	Rs 8958	The figure is for 3 May 1962 to March 1963.
D.R. Chavan	Rs 7655.00	The figure is for June 1962 to March 1963.
C.R. Pattabhi Raman	Rs 8726.00	The figure is for 25 May 62 to March 1963.
M. Chandrasekhar	7925.00	The figure is for May 1962 to March 1963.
Jaganath Rao	Rs 7498.00	The figure is for 23 June 1962 to March 1963.
Sham Nath		Stays in a private house.
D.S. Raju	Rs 6582.00	The figure is for July 1962 to March, 1963.
Dinesh Singh	Rs 6846.00	The figure is for August 1962 to March 1963.
Bibudhendra Misra	Rs 8995.00	The figure is for 24 May 1962 to March 1963
B. Bhagavati	Rs 6825.00	The figure is for June 1962 to March 1963
Shyam Dhar Misra	Rs 7511.00	The figure is for June 1962 to March 1963.
Prakash Chandra Sethi	Rs 5297.00	The figure is for August 1962 to March 1963.

NOTE: The value of perquisites such as rent-free residential accommodation and free water and electricity was liable to income-tax in accordance with the provisions of the law.

The travelling and daily allowances, however, constituted by far the heaviest items of expenditure by the Ministers. The following

figures give an idea of their range and extent during the financial year
1962–3:

Amount	No. of Ministers
Between Rs 45,000 and 50,000	2
Between Rs 40,000 and 45,000	0
Between Rs 35,000 and 40,000	1
Between Rs 30,000 and 35,000	1
Between Rs 25,000 and 30,000	1
Between Rs 20,000 and 25,000	5
Between Rs15,000 and 20,000	5
Between Rs 10,000 and 15,000	9
Between Rs 5,000 and 10,000	16
Below Rs 5,000	9
Figures not given for	4
Total number of Ministers	53

The highest amount in the above classification was drawn by
Jagjivan Ram, and the lowest amount by V. K. Krishna Menon. The
former spent Rs 46,171.25, while the latter only Rs 140.50. Those who
came near Jagjivan Ram were S. K. Patil, Rs 45,159 and K. D.
Malaviya, Rs 37,919. The figures of salary, sumptuary allowance,
travelling and daily allowances for all the 53 Ministers were given
in a statement submitted by the Home Ministry in response to
Bhupesh Gupta's question in the Rajya Sabha.[69]

The statement excludes the costs of maintaining gardens and the
provision for medical attendance and treatment, the latter being
considered specially difficult to evaluate. The rising expenses of
Ministers, however, were a matter of concern to the Government.
While replying to the questions raised by Bhupesh Gupta, therefore,
the official spokesman gave assurances that steps were being taken to
reduce the cost of perquisites. It was pointed out that instructions had
already been issued to Ministers to keep expenses to a minimum.
With effect from 1 April 1963, it was added, the Ministers had decided
to impose upon themselves a voluntary ceiling of Rs 200 per mensem
for the consumption of electricity and water at their residences. There
was, however, nothing to ensure the effectiveness of that self-imposed
ordinance.

As regards travelling and daily allowances, where the costs usually happened to be considerable, there is evidence of irregularities in some cases. While chartering a plane for travel from Delhi to Bhubaneshwar, for instance, Ajit Prasad Jain, a Central Minister for Food and Agriculture, took little or no care to observe the rules which required making a prior written request to the Defence Minister for use of an Indian Air Force communication flight. He did not even submit the names of those who travelled with him. The bills submitted for payment of Rs 5,887 included the costs for seven breakfast boxes each way for the people who travelled to see the flood-affected areas of Orissa.

A Home Ministry Note of 7 May 1956 pointed out that this was 'another case from the Ministry of F. & Agri. wherein procedure about the chartering of aeroplanes [had] not been followed'. The 'relaxation of rules about chartering aeroplanes' was, therefore, required to be sanctioned by the Finance Ministry. In a Note of 12 June 1956, the Finance Ministry in turn recalled how the Minister had earlier chartered a helicopter without following the normal procedure. The Ministry added that it had then 'agreed to regularize the position but requested the F. & A. Ministry to ensure that the instructions contained in the Rules for chartering planes were followed in future.'[70] However, after the completion of some formalities required by the rules the sanction of the President was finally obtained for payment of the necessary sum. Far from taking disciplinary action against Jain, the Government later oppointed him a Governor.

A peculiar case of misuse of Government money for party purposes occurred during a session of the All-India Congress Committee held at Raipur in Madhya Pradesh between 28 and 30 October 1960. The Central Ministers who attended included Jawaharlal Nehru, Govind Ballabh Pant, Gulzarilal Nanda, S. K. Patil, Jagjivan Ram, Lal Bahadur Shastri, K. D. Malaviya, Punjabrao Deshmukh, Dr B. Gopala Reddi, Dr P. Subbaroyan, and S. N. Mishra.[71]

Several months had passed before reports appeared in the press that the Chief Minister of Madhya Pradesh had made a statement in the local Assembly that about Rs 22,000 were spent on entertaining guests at the time of the A.I.C.C. session. This led Dahyabhai Patel to raise a question in the Rajya Sabha on 9 March 1961. In answer, the Minister in the Home Ministry, B. N. Datar, feigned ignorance about the matter on the absurd ground that he had not gone to Raipur. He however, assured the House that the information was being collected and would be laid on the table of the House in due course. The replies

later received from different sources were varied and mutually conflicting. M. L. Bazaz, Private Secretary to the Prime Minister, for
instance, pointed out that Nehru visited Raipur on 27 October 1960
and returned to Delhi on 31 October. He travelled both ways by the
I.A.F. aircraft and stayed at Rajkumar College, Raipur. But his
Secretariat, as Bazaz said, had no information as to whether expenses
at Raipur were borne by the State Government, by the A.I.C.C., or by
the College. 'It is likely', Bazaz added, 'that the expenses were borne
by the All-India Congress Committee'. The Private Secretary of K.
D. Malaviya, on the other hand, pointed out that his Minister's visit
to Raipur was 'private, at his own expense'. The visits of all the
Central Ministers to Raipur were admitted, but statements as to how
their expenses were met differed from Minister to Minister. Some
maintained that these were borne by the reception committee of the
A.I.C.C., while others held that they had made their own private
arrangements. There was also a third category of Ministers who were
declared to have been treated either as guests of the College or of
the State Government. A common feature, however, was that none
had claimed any travelling allowance from the Government of India
for attending the Raipur session of the Congress. In the letter sent to
the Government of India the Madhya Pradesh Government confirmed that the Central Ministers in question were among the 56 'State
Guests' entertained during the session of the A.I.C.C. and that 'the
expenditure incurred by the State Government on their hospitality
amounted to Rs 21,988.59'.[72]

It took a few months more for the inquiry to be completed. An
official report[73] of 27 December 1961 finally brought out the whole
truth. Arrangements for the stay of the Ministers were made by the
State Government in the buildings of Rajkumar College and in tents
pitched on the College premises. Jagjivan Ram, then Minister for
Railways, and S. K. Patil, Minister for Food and Agriculture, stayed
in the guest house of the College, while Punjabrao Deshmukh was
accommodated in one of the tents. The Minister of Labour, Employment and Planning (Gulzarilal Nanda) was provided with a suite of
rooms in the bungalow of the Vice-Principal of Rajkumar College. He
chose to spend the nights with his son working in Bhilai, but during
the day he used the suite. The report added that all the expenditure on
board, lodging and transport, etc. on the guests was incurred by the
State Government. The A.I.C.C. did not contribute anything.[74]

It is clear from a study of the functioning of the Heads of States and
Ministers of the Government that, instead of taking care to maintain

the best traditions of the struggle for freedom and set an example of sacrifice and patriotic zeal in building a new India, they became immediately interested in securing for themselves a scale of emoluments, profits and privileges which their British predecessors had earlier enjoyed. There were, of course, individual exceptions. Nehru and Patel, for instance, formed a rare combination of dynamic vision and firmness of character. Together they steered the shop of state in a manner which saved the country from being engulfed by near anarchy and lawlessness caused by unprecedented communal strife in the post-Partition period. But their combination was short-lived. Patel died in 1950 and Nehru had to carry on alone.

Nehru carried on well for a time, with his emphasis on a government of talents, irrespective of party labels or provincial and group interests. His policy was to muster the best available people, subject, of course, to the overall control of the Congress High Command. His first Cabinet of 14 members sworn in on the transfer of power in 1947 already contained persons of outstanding merit and character. Even when it was reshuffled after the introduction of the Constitution during 1950–1, his Cabinet included such non-party personages as C.D. Deshmukh, John Matthai, Shyama Prasad Mukerjee, N. Gopalaswami Ayyangar and even C. Rajagopalachari who was *persona non grata* in Congress circles. It was only with the formation of linguistic States that party, provincial and group interests came to be fully reflected in the composition of the Cabinet. By 1956 only C. D. Deshmukh had been left as a non-party member of the Cabinet. No non-party man was included in the Council of Ministers appointed on 17 April 1957. Within less than a decade self-helf and patronage had come to have a firm grip over the mind of Congress Ministers and Governors of States. This transformation was hastened by the character of Indian society, where the rule of law, with its limited area of operation, had hardly taken root. Bereft of adequate social recognition, the rule of law was ever bent to subserve either executive action in the administration or the will of dominant elements of society. Perhaps partly through inexperience and partly by virtue of the power they came to wield after 1947, the Indian political élites were more inclined to act executively than in accordance with the provisions of law and rules. This perhaps explains why they did not hesitate to grant themselves monetary profits and advantages without the prior sanction of an appropriate legislature. However, they listened to reason and usually recognized the validity of resistance put up by the higher bureaucracy in support of rules and precedents. This was particularly so with Prime Minister Nehru who was generally given to correction and amenable to well-reasoned arguments, except where he was interested in a person whom he considered worthy of his protection or even of his favour.

There is also a historical reason for the prevailing kind of gubernatorial and ministerial standards of conduct. The object of the political system that developed under British rule was not mass democracy. Ever since the days of Macaulay it had a class-oriented objective and was meant for highly educated and enlightened political elites who possessed the competence to run India's representative institutions on a model which was British, not indigenous. The founding fathers who framed the Constitution of India were themselves of this class, although they were invested with the task of building a constitutional framework that might meet the demands of a full-scale democracy based on the rule of law and legislative authority and yet retain its vital link with history. The political system so established was only sustained by the Indian Civil Service, the administrative agency possessing the intellectual culture and values comparable to those of the founding fathers.

With the passage of time, however, the situation changed in respect of both the men who were later called upon to work the Constitution and their problems which called for immediate solution. While governors and ministers happened to be a motley group representing an assorted variety of political and moral cultures, their problems became more and more complex on account of rising expectations and increasing demands for social and economic change in the direction of egalitarianism. The new generation of politicians, who were a product of the downward filtration of education among the lower orders of society, brought with them their own standards of conduct to bear upon public life, standards which hardly compared well with the earlier concept of political behaviour and integrity based on cultural excellence and class distinction. The situation so emerging was a case of growing conflict between tradition and change, between a class-based limited democracy and a caste-oriented mass democracy.

It was in this socio-political context that administrative development proceeded in the post-Independence period to accelerate the process of change. But since the new and reorganized administrative agency did not prove equal to the task, the changes so effected led more to the concentration of wealth than its diffusion.

CHAPTER III

The All-India Services
1946-56

The first phase of interaction between ministers and bureaucrats was marked by a spirit of understanding and co-operation on both sides. Barring, of course, certain exceptions, both the Cabinet and the civil service possessed talent and were inspired by a patriotic zeal to save the country from the imminent danger of disintegration which the politics of partition had posed through successive waves of mass killing and communal riots. The problem that emerged was not merely of a temporary nature involving rehabilitation, although this by itself was no easy task. It involved a reorganization of the entire gamut of administration which, on account of the exodus of European and many Muslim civil servants on the transfer of power, had been seriously depleted in its higher reaches.

The understanding with which politician and bureaucrat worked in the common task of rebuilding the administration as an instrument of national security and development, flowed not only from the non-partisan character of the earlier Council of Ministers and the civil service, but also from comparable intellectual and cultural standards. Ministers like Nehru, Sardar Patel, Rajagopalachari, N. Gopalaswami Ayyanger, C.D. Deshmukh, B.R. Ambedkar and John Matthai differed little in their educational equipment and experience from top civilians operating in the actual field of administration. This comparison faded with the lapse of time. But for the first eight or nine years of Independence the political and administrative èlites functioned as a team. Both Nehru and Patel encouraged independence of judgement, and cases occurred where even the Prime Minister was successfully opposed by a Secretary over policies which the latter considered unsound in principle. It was during this first phase that the task of reorganization was first accomplished in most of its details.

Recruitment and Reorganization

Object and Method

Until the creation of a separate Department of Personnel and Administrative Reforms as part of the Cabinet Secretariat on 1 August 1970, the public services were the immediate responsibility of the Ministry of Home Affairs in the Government of India. This responsibility did not extend to purely Provincial Services which continued to be exclusively controlled by Provincial Governments. It applied to the Central Services as well as to certain All-India Services organized and maintained jointly on behalf of the Central and Provincial Governments. The day-to-day administration of the various Services remained with the individual Ministry concerned and the responsibility of the Ministry of Home Affairs was limited to the regulation of matters of general applicability to all the Services and the maintenances of common standards of recruitment, discipline and conditions of service generally. Concerning financial matters, however, this responsibility was subject to the control of the Ministry of Finance. Apart from maintaining a common standard of administrative efficiency, the control of the Home Ministry over the public Services had a second important purpose—the maintenance of stability against the forces of internal disorder. This was the primary responsibility of Provincial (now State) Governments, but it was also essential for the Central Home Ministry to keep in day-to-day touch with developments affecting security throughout the country.

Later, there appeared a third reason for the Home Ministry control. In a Note of 14 May 1949, for instance, the Prime Minister referred to 'progressive socialization' as a principle of state policy and invited the attention of the Home Ministry to 'the question of numbers' as well as 'the question of quality' of recruitment in order to enable the state to 'spread out more and more in what has been considered private domain'. If the projected goal of 'socialization' were to succeed, he added, 'a great deal of character and integrity would be needed', and 'more examinations are not quite enough'. And this quality of character, he believed, could be ensured by a system of early selection and special training similar to that provided for the Defence Services, where younger men were recruited and rigorously trained. He therefore suggested that some such training should be adopted for the Administrative Service also. Nehru did not want the existing mode of recruitment for the Administrative Service by competitive examination to be discontinued. 'Perhaps this is the most feasible method,' he commented, 'and anyhow it should continue till a better method is evolved'. All that he wanted was 'to try both methods at the same time, that is, the competitive examination and the training of younger people who might subsequently sit in the competitive examination also'.[1]

The suggestion of the Prime Minister was examined by R. A. Gopalaswami, then Officer on Special Duty, who enjoyed the status of Secretary in the Ministry of Home Affairs. He regarded Nehru's proposal as 'open to certain objections' on both theoretical and practical grounds. Sardar Patel, the Home Minister, agreed with him and accepted the validity of his arguments. His main objection was that earlier selection and special training would render prolonged and expensive training necessary, the greater part of which would be no more than a poor substitute for the general education which students acquired on their own at the universities. It was feared that the projected training for the Administrative Service on the model of the Defence Services would impart a regimented attitude and aloofness from the general public, breeding an exclusiveness which would be a serious disadvantage in a democratic state. It was further argued that

in spite of the defects that can be pointed out in respect of the general education which our universities give, it would be too ambitious to expect that the institutions built up by Government would be in a position to impart a higher standard of education or even education of a more liberal nature than is available anywhere else in the country. On the other hand, whatever may be the standard of teaching in a Government institution of this kind or the nature of subjects taught therein, such an institution would certainly suffer from the disadvantage that it would be an exclusive one meant only for the future members of the Government services. The boys under training will not have the opportunity to mix with boys of their age of different types and calibre not selected for the services.[2]

The existing system of recruitment by competitive examination was therefore considered by far the best in terms of the country's requirements for quality and character, a conclusion which had earlier been supported by the Islington Commission.

The second question which Nehru raised in his Note of 14 May 1949 related to the availability of suitable personnel likely to be required for long-term future plans in the context of the expanding activities of the Government at various levels. It appears Nehru was unaware that the problem was already being dealt with in the Home Ministry as one of its major preoccupations. This lack of information was perhaps due to a lack of co-ordination at the Cabinet level; this was later remedied by a reorganization of the Cabinet Secretariat as part of a scheme recommended by N. Gopalaswami Ayyangar, then Transport Minister.

Man-power Recruitment

The Problem

The problem of man-power recruitment was immediately connected with a very large depletion in the strength of the Indian Civil Service on the transfer of power. The strength sanctioned by the Secretary of State during the War was maintained at 1,064, the actual strength being twenty more to make up for the shortage of Europeans in the I.C.S. as no European candidate was available for recruitment on account of the War.[3] After 1943 all vacancies were reserved for 'war service' candidates and to be filled only with the prior concurrence of the Secretary of State who had earlier suspended recruitment.

The dissolution of the Secretary of State's Services, however, became imminent in the course of the Cabinet Mission's negotiations with Indian leaders and members of the Services, both British and Indian, were reduced to a state of uncertainty about their future careers. On the advice of the Government of India the Secretary of State had agreed to announce that he hoped to include in the treaty with India a provision guaranteeing security of service for those who wished to continue to serve in India and who the Government of India wished to retain. The object was to reduce to a minimum the danger of the Services being greatly depleted. But depletion began when the control of the Secretary of State over Indian administration ceased and his rule-making power transferred to the Governor-General on 14 August 1947. The transfer of power and Partition led to the retirement of a large number of European officers and the transfer of Muslims who opted for Pakistan. According to answers given to starred questions 106 and 105 on the floor of the Constituent Assembly of India on 19 November 1947. the number of European officers who retired was as shown in the first table on page 95.[4]

As regards Muslim Civilians. there were about 100 before Partition and only twelve remained in India, in the five provinces as shown in the second table on page 95.

According to a statement made in reply to questions put by Pandit M. B. Bhargava in Parliament the position of the I.C.S. officers before Partition, on 1 August 1947, and after that in 1951 was as shown in third table on page 96.[4a]

Retirement of European Officers on Partition

Madras	33
Bombay and Sind	25
Bengal	38
U.P.	48
Punjab and N.W.F. Province	51
Central Provinces and Berar	22
Bihar and Orissa	28
Assam	9
Total	254

Muslim Civilians in Office after Pautition

Bombay	2
West Bengal	1
U.P.	5
East Punjab	2
Assam	2
Total	12

Position of I.C.S. Officers before and after Partition
Before Partition on 1 August 1947

	Serving under Govt of India	Serving under Prov. Govts	Total
ICS officers	226	729	955
Muslim ICS officers	24	79	103
MuslimICS officers who opted for Pakistan	20	73	93

After Partition on 1 January 1951

	Serving under Govt of India	Serving under State Govts	Total
ICS officers	136	256	392

The position deteriorated in 1948.[5] More than 60 per cent of the total number were lost, the I.C.S. officers remaining in the country being therefore less than 400. The sudden loss of strength involved making temporary arrangements for carrying on, and of organizing recruitment to fill on a long-term basis the abnormal gap created. This organizational recruitment had necessarily to take the form of the Indian Administrative Services, deemed initially to have been constituted on 21 October 1946 by an agreement between the Government of India and seven Provincial Governments represented by the Premiers of Assam, Bihar, Bombay, Central Provinces and Berar, Madras, Orissa and the United Provinces. The decision to create an Indian Police Service was taken in pursuance of the same agreement.[6] East Punjab and West Bengal came in a little later, thus raising the total number of cadres to nine.

Temporary Arrangements to Meet the Problem

As part of its temporary arrangements the Government of India made a rapid review of the posts formerly held by I.C.S. officers at the Centre. Alternative sources of available manpower were examined. A reserve of temporary officers was constituted on contract on the basis of the selections made by the Federal Public Service Commission from among 'war service' candidates and temporary officers with administrative experience. The remaining vacancies at the centre were filled by promotion of officers in the Central Secretariat and other Services. In the provinces the gap was filled largely by officers of the respective Provincial Services in addition to a number of I.C.S. officers being withdrawn from the judiciary and appointed to executive posts.

Long-term Recruitment

The Indian Administrative Service and the Indian Police Service became central to any scheme of long-term or permanent recruitment. Modelled respectively after the Indian Civil Service and the Indian Police, these new All-India Services were designed to fulfil the country's post-Independence requirements in terms of both calibre and character. Appointment to them was made by selection of 'war service' candidates, by competitive examinations, by promotion from the Provincial Services, or by emergency recruitment from the open market. But the appointments so made were to the regular cadres created in 1946 to fill the abnormal gap later caused by the retirement of Europeans and the transfer of Muslims to Pakistan. It was a well-conceived plan to counteract the effects of depletion at superior levels in the I.C.S. and the I.P.

The draft scheme of the 'All-India Administrative Service' was finalized soon after the Agreement of 21 October 1946 and forwarded to the Provincial Governments by the Home Ministry on 12 November 1946.[7] Except for certain minor modifications the draft

remained substantially unaltered and was forwarded as a Memorandum for the information and guidance of the Provincial Governments on 15 December 1947. Since this Memorandum is one of the
earliest documents of its kind on the subject, it is given below for
general textual reference:[8]

The Central Government and the Governments of Assam, Bihar, Bombay,
the Central Provinces & Berar, East Punjab, Madras, Orissa, the United
Provinces and West Bengal have agreed to constitute a Service called the
Indian Administrative Service in accordance with the following provisions:
1. (a)The strength including both the number and character of posts, of the
Indian Administrative Service shall be as specified in the Schedule.[9] (b)The
Schedule may, if and when considered necessary, be amended by the Central
Government in consultation with the appropriate Provincial Government.
2. (a) Recruitment to the Indian Administrative Service shall be
     (i) by direct recruitment; or
     (ii) by promotion of members of a Provincial Civil Service.
  (b) Direct recruits for appointment to the Indian Administrative Service
will be selected on the results of an examination held by, or under the
authority of, the Federal Public Service Commission and appointed to the
Service by the Central Government. The regulations setting out the conditions of eligibility, nature of tests etc. will be framed by the Central Government in consultation with the participating Provincial Governments and the
Federal Public Service Commission.
  (c) A Provincial Government may declare that such number not exceeding
twenty-five per cent of the superior posts allocated to the Provincial Government in the Schedule to this Memorandum as may be specified by that
Government shall be filled by that Government by promotion of members of
the Provincial Civil Service.
  (d) The rules regulating promotion of Provincial Civil Service officers to
the Indian Administrative Service shall be framed by the Provincial Government concerned in consultation with the Federal Public Service Commission
and shall provide that no provincial Civil Service officer shall be appointed to
hold a superior post included in the Schedule for a period of more than one
year unless the Federal Public Service Commission have certified that the
officer is in every way fit to hold a superior post in the Indian Administrative
Service.
3. (a) Posts included in the Schedule to this Memorandum shall be filled by
members of the Indian Administrative Service unless—
    (i) the vacancy is not likely to last for more than three months; or
    (ii) in the opinion of the Government concerned there is no suitable officer
         of the Indian Administrative Service available to hold the post.
  (b) Every appointment of an officer who is not a member of the Indian
Administrative Service, made to a post included in the Schedule to this
memorandum otherwise than in accordance with paragraph 2, for a period
exceeding three months should be reported by the Provincial Government

concerned to the Central Government with the reasons for making such appointment.

4. Candidates selected for appointment to the Indian Administrative Service will be allotted to the participating Provinces by the Central Government in consultation with the Provincial Government concerned and, as far as possible, in compliance with the latter's wishes. Candidates will as far as possible be allotted to their Province of origin and/or domicile.

5. (a) Candidates selected for appointment to the Indian Administrative Service will be appointed to the Service on probation and will be required to undergo probation for such periods and at such places as the Central Government may determine.

(b) The Central Government will frame, in consultation with the Provincial Governments, rules to regulate the conduct, discipline and training of probationers.

6. A probationer on successful completion of his probation will be confirmed in the Indian Administrative Service. An officer belonging to the Indian Administrative Service shall be liable to serve anywhere in India either under the Central Government or under a Provincial Government. He shall submit himself to the orders of the Government under which he is serving for the time being and of the officers and authorities under whom he may. from time to time, be placed by that Government; shall devote his whole time to his duties, shall at all times obey any rules prescribed by the Central Government and the Provincial Government under whom he is serving for the time being to govern officers of the Indian Administrative Service and shall perform such duties as may be assigned to him.

7. In order to ensure that the conditions of service applicable to officers of the Indian Administrative Service are as uniform as possible, rules regulating pay and other conditions of service will be framed by the Central Government to such extent as is considered necessary. Provincial Governments will, however, be consulted before the rules are framed, and before they are amended in any manner. In respect of matters not covered by the said rules, an officer of the Indian Administrtion Service will be governed by such rules as may be framed by the Government under which he is for the time being serving and, if no such rules are framed, by the rules applicable to the Central Service/Provincial Civil Service, Class I, as the case may be.

8. The Central Government may frame, in consultation with Provincial Governments, rules to regulate the conduct of members of the Indian Administrative Service.

9. (a) The following penalties may, for good and sufficient reason and as hereinafter provided, be imposed upon members of the Indian Administrative Service, namely—

(i) Censure;

(ii) Withholding of increment or promotion including stoppage at an efficiency bar;

(iii) Reduction to a lower post of time-scale, or to a lower stage in a time-scale;

(iv) Recovery from pay of the whole or part of any pecuniary loss caused to Government by negligence or breach of orders;

    (v) Removal from the Service of the Crown which does not disqualify from future employment;

    (iv) Dismissal from the Civil Service of the Crown which disqualifies from future employment under the Central Government or Provincial **Governments, unless the Government** concerned directs to the contrary.

Explanation. The discharge of a person appointed on probation on grounds arising out of the specific conditions laid down by appointing authority, e.g., want of a vacancy, failure to acquire prescribed special qualifications or to pass prescribed tests does not amount to removal or dismissal within the meaning of this rule. But the discharge of a probationer, whether during, or at the end of the period of probation, for some specific fault or on account of his unsuitability for the service, amounts to removal or dismissal within the meaning of this rule.

    (b) An officer against whom a disciplinary enquiry is pending may be suspended by the Government under which he is serving. An officer under suspension shall be paid by the Government suspending him a subsistence allowance equal to one-third of the average monthly pay earned by him during the preceding twelve months. In addition that Government may direct payment of any compensatory allowance of which the officer was in receipt on the date of suspension to such extent and subject to such conditions as it may direct.

10. (i) No member of the Indian Administrative Service shall be removed or dismissed except by an order of the Central Government.

(ii) Before passing such an order Central Government shall consult the Provincial Government concerned and the Federal Public Service Commission, and if the Federal Public Service Commission and the Provincial Government are in agreement, shall accept their agreed opinion. Where the Federal Public Service Commission and the Provincial Government concerned disagree, the decision as to the order to be passed shall rest with the Central Government and shall be final.

11. Subject to the provisions of Rule 12, the Government under which an officer of the Indian Administrative Service is serving may imposes on him any of the penalties specified in clauses (i) to (iv) of paragraph 9(a). Before imposing any punishment, however, the Government concerned shall consult the Federal Public Service Commission and shall not depart from the Commission's advice save only for exceptional reasons to be recorded in writing.

12. In order to provide for the case of a disciplinary order which, although not one of dismissal or removal, might have the effect of dismissal or removal by compelling an officer to resign, for example, an order requiring the recovery of loss, a Provincial Government shall, before imposing, contrary to the advice of the Federal Public Service Commission, any penalty other than censure, report the case and the penalty proposed to the Central Government. If the Central Government find that the proposed penalty is not such that it might reasonably be expected to compel the resignation of the officer concerned, they will return the case to the Provincial Government for passing final orders. If, however, the Central Government find to the contrary they will deal with the case as though it were one of dismissal or removal under rule 10.

13. (i) No order imposing a penalty other than an order of censure or an order based on facts which have led to the officer's conviction in a criminal court or by a court martial shall be passed against an officer of the Indian Administrative Service unless he is informed in writing of the grounds on which it is proposed to take action and has been afforded an adequate opportunity of defending himself. The grounds on which it is proposed to take action shall be reduced to the form of a definite charge or charges which shall be communicated to the officer charged together with a statement of the allegations on which each charge is based and of any other circumstances which it is proposed to take into consideration in passing orders on the case. He shall be required within a reasonable time to put in a written statement of his defence and to state whether he desires to be heard in person. If he so desires or if the authority concerned so directs an oral enquiry shall be held. At such enquiry evidence shall be heard as to such of the allegations as are not admitted and the officer charged shall be entitled to cross examine the witnesses, to give evidence in person and to have such witnesses called as he may wish, provided that the officer conducting the enquiry may for special and sufficient reasons to be recorded in writing refuse to call a witness. The proceedings shall contain a sufficient record of the evidence and a statement of the findings and grounds thereof.

(ii) The full procedure prescribed in sub-rule (i) above need not be followed in the case of a probationer discharged in the circumstances described in the Explanation under Rule 9. In such cases it will be sufficient if the probationer is given an opportunity to show cause in writing against the discharge after being apprised of the grounds on which it is proposed to discharge him and his reply duly considered before orders are passed.

14. There shall be no appeal against any disciplinary order but the Government passing the order may revise, of its own motion or otherwise, any orders passed by it.

The principles on which the Indian Administrative Service was constituted were thus comparable to those of the Indian Civil Service. Direct recruits were to be selected on the results of competitive examinations held by the Federal Public Service Commission and appointed by the Central Government, exercising disciplinary control in consultation with the Commission and the Provincial Governments. The all-India character of the Service was maintained, although the provinces (now States) came to be allowed a much greater say in the formulation of rules governing service conditions as well as in the choice of the appointees allotted. But organized on the model of the I.C.S., the Service was designed to be efficient and free from local and communal bias, from party allegiance or political influence. The nature of the posts (included in the Schedule to the Memorandum) to be filled exclusively by members of the Indian Administrative Service followed the pattern already set by the Indian Civil Service Act

(1861) and later adopted by the Schedules annexed to the Government of India Acts, 1919 and 1935. A non-cadre person was not to hold any cadre post included in the Schedule to the Memorandum, except for a limited period. The scheduled posts classified under the provincial cadres were all top and key positions in the civil service, such as the posts of Chief Secretary; Members, Board of Revenue; Secretaries to the Government; Additional and Deputy Secretaries; Divisional and Development Commissioners; District Magistrates and Collectors; Registrars of Co-operative Societies; Commissioners of Excise; Settlement Officers; Directors of Agriculture, and so on. These were in addition to senior civil posts under the Central Government. Subject to the final report of the first Pay Commission, the scale was fixed uniformly at Rs 350-400-450-500.

Recruitment of War Service Candidates

The first batch of recruits to the Indian Administrative Service was selected from 'war service' candidates in March 1947. They were appointed as probationers along with the candidates appointed through the combined competitive examination held in 1945 for the Indian Audit and Accounts Service and some other Central Services. The All-India Administrative Service (Probationary Service and Seniority of Recruits) Rules, 1947, which the Government of India notified for general information on 24 April, applied to both categories of probationers.[10] Before proceeding to the province to which they were assigned, probationers were as a rule required to undergo training at a centre specified by the Central Government which, in any particular case, could allow the probationary period to be spent either wholly or in part in the province to which the probationer was assigned. This proviso applied specially to candidates who had taken the competitive examination in 1945.

The Rules governing the recruitment of 'war service' candidates applied only to the first batch of recruits to the Indian Administrative Service. These were based on the I.C.S. (Probationary Service) Rules, 1940, made under the Government of India Act (1935) and suitably modified to meet the special requirements of 'war service' recruits. Under Rule VI, probationers at the end of their period of probation were required to pass an examination conducted by the Federal Public Service Commission in consultation with the Central Government. The subjects of examination included Indian law, Indian history and economics, public administration, riding, Hindustani and a specialized knowledge of one of the languages of the province to which the probationer was assigned. Probationers other than those in the 'war service' category proceeded straight to the provinces concerned and reported themselves for duty. They were required to perform during their probationary period such duties as the Provincial Government concerned might decide and, at the end of that period, to pass such examinations as their Government might prescribe.

As regards the question of seniority, it was laid down that a probationer who had rendered 'war service', would be deemed 'to have been appointed in the year succeeding the year in which he entered war service whichever is later'. No probationer was, however, deemed to have been appointed later than 1947. A probationer who had no 'war service' to his credit, was, on the other hand, deemed for purposes of seniority to be appointed in 1947. A probationer was to be junior to officers of the Indian Civil Service belonging to the year to which he was allotted. The service of probationers under these Rules began from the date of beginning probation and they would draw pay from the same date.

The 'war service' probationers who were appointed to the Indian Administrative Service before 1 June 1947,[11] were attached to the Training School (Metcalfe House) at Delhi. They were required to pass an examination before they could be posted to their respective provinces. Their training was, however, interrupted. Of the total number of 54 probationers, 28 were deputed in September for duty in East Punjab to assist the Provincial Government in tackling the refugee problem, while the remaining 26 were employed on similar duties in connexion with the emergency in Delhi. In the light of the suggestions made by M. J. Desai, Principal of the Training School, both the Federal Public Service Commission and the Central Government agreed that all the probationers undergoing training in that year should be posted to their respective provinces without being required, 'as a special case', to take any written examination. It was, however, made clear that before they were confirmed in the Service their records at the School, along with the Principal's remarks, should be sent to the Federal Public Service Commission in order to enable the Commission to assess their suitability for confirmation.[12] The Commission later cleared 49 cases and kept three for review. Of the total number of probationers so considered, 43 were confirmed by the Governor-General. The confirmation of the nine other cases was either postponed for six months or delayed in the course of consultation with the Provincial Governments concerned.[13] No effect was thus given to the Rules governing the appointment of the 'war service' candidates.

The recruitment of 'war service' candidates to the I.C.S. had already begun **weakening** its fibre. However, they were initially required to undergo training and pass a written test in certain prescribed subjects, the object being to assess their competence and suitability. Even that test had to be dispensed with, although the Home Secretary, R. N. Banerji, wanted the period of probation to be extended by a few weeks to enable the probationers to take the examination before being sent to their respective provinces. Administrative compulsions perhaps demanded it, but the relaxation of rules signified a general disregard for the recognized method of testing efficiency and intellectual quality. Both these conditions of confirmation were done away with at the instance of M. J. Desai.

No 'war service' candidates were, however, recruited to the Indian Administrative Service or the Indian Police Service after 1947, for most of the available vacancies in the two Services had already been filled by the appointment of officers recruited on a much higher standard under the Emergency recruitment scheme. The question of appointment of any more 'war service' candidates was therefore treated as closed.[14] As regards the Central Services, 70 per cent of the vacancies which occurred between 29 June 1942 and 31 December 1945 were reserved in favour of 'war service' candidates. This policy was discontinued in July 1946. Concessions regarding age and educational qualifications were to be withdrawn against the vacancies arising after 31 December 1945. The Department of Defence pleaded for the continuance of the concessions, but in the face of the Home **Department's resistance these concessions could not continue** beyond 1947.[15]

The Emergency Recruitment Scheme

The object of this Scheme was to fill the gap likely to be caused by the premature retirement of European officers. This gap was sought to be removed by recruitment from two sources, the Provincial Civil Service and the open market.

The lines on which emergency recruitment should be undertaken from Provincial Civil Service officers was investigated by the Gorwala Committee[16] and considered by the Central Government. In a telegram of 3 April 1947 the Government of India accordingly advised all the Provincial Governments of the formation of *ad hoc* Committees for the induction of Provincial Service officers in to the I.A.S. cadre.[17] These Committees consisted of a representative of the Federal Public Service Commission, a member of the Public Service Commission of the province concerned and an officer of the concerned Provincial Governments. The *ad hoc* Committees were thus distinct from the selection committees earlier appointed by Provincial Governments to form select lists of P.C.S. officers for promotion to 'listed' posts in the I.C.S. or I.A.S. The object was to ensure a common standard of recruitment for superior posts, both Central and Provincial.

The *ad hoc* Committees interviewed officers in all the provinces (except West Bengal and East Punjab) and recommended a large number for appointment to the I.A.S. Objections were raised by certain Provincial Governments who viewed the appointment of the *ad hoc* Committees as an attempt of the Central Government to interfere with the exercise of patronage and Madras, for instance, held that the lists prepared by them were to be used only to fill central superior posts, not those of the provinces. The Government of Bombay, on the other hand, wanted the name of an officer of its own choice to be added to the *ad hoc* list; but on the advice of the Federal Public Service Commission the Government of India did not agree. The Government of Bihar too made proposals for the addition of some names to the *ad hoc* list, which also had to be turned down. For the *ad hoc* lists were prepared carefully on a uniform all-India basis and meant to replace the previous 'select lists' which some Provincial Governments maintained. The time and expense spent on the preparation of the *ad hoc* lists would thus be entirely wasted if the Provincial Governments were to be allowed to disregard them and utilize their own.

However, the case of the Provincial Governments could not altogether be ignored. The Memorandum regarding the constitution of the Indian Administrative Service provided that promotions of P.C.S. officers to the I.A.S. cadre were to be made by the Provincial Governments themselves in consultation with the Federal Public Service Commission, and the actual appointments were also made by them alone. In direct consultation with Gorwala, therefore, certain proposals were formulated and circulated to the provinces for their reaction to the proposed formation of what Gorwala described as the 'Emergency Cadre'. In view of provincial resistance to the lists of the *ad hoc* Committees it was suggested that fresh lists be drawn up for promotion to the Emergency Cadre. The Government of India, however, continued in the meantime to act on the basis of the *ad hoc* lists already prepared.

In these circumstances, Gorwala's proposal for an 'Emergency Cadre' was sought to be discussed further at a conference of Chief Secretaries of all the Provincial Governments, which was held on 31 March and 1 April 1948. The scheme of emergency recruitment which the Chief Secretaries recommended provided for the appointment of an *ad hoc* selecting authority known as the Special Recruitment Board. It was to consist of a senior officer of the Ministry of Home Affairs, a representative of the Constituent Assembly, and two representatives of the Federal Public Service Commission. It was specifically meant to select officers for the I.A.S. by inviting applications from suitable over-aged candidates from the open market. The Federal Public Service Commission, on the other hand, was called upon simultaneously to review under the scheme the available P.C.S. officers for the purposes of their selection. The idea was that when selections from the two separate fields had been made by the Special Recruitment Board and the Federal Public Service Commission respectively, a joint meeting of the two bodies would draw up a final list of candidates from both. This joint list was to be submitted to the Central Government to enable it to bring the provincial cadres up to the sanctioned strength.[18] The Emergency Recruitment Scheme of the Chief Secretaries thus recognized the claims of Provincial Governments to form their own select lists for the approval of the Commission and reconciled these with the quality of recruitment made on an extended scale by a centrally appointed *ad hoc* selecting agency, the Special Recruitment Board.

The channel of selection for P.C.S. officers was thus to be through recommendations of Provincial Governments, who forwarded the recommendations to the Federal Public Service Commission. They were not to apply to the Special Recruitment Board. In a letter of 1 June 1948 the Provincial Governments were, however, advised by the Government of India that, while making recommendations, they should generally use the lists earlier prepared by the *ad hoc* committee, although it was conceded that they were 'at liberty to make any additions or alterations in those lists'.[19] The main reason for excluding P.C.S. officers from applying to the Board as open-market candidates was to prevent any possibility of an officer whose case had been considered and rejected by a Provincial Government being selected by the Special Recruitment Board.

As regards the nature of recruitment, the conference of Chief Secretaries, like the Gorwala Committee, emphasized the formation of an 'Emergency Cadre' of the I.A.S. But as the result of a Cabinet decision of 19 May 1948 the recruitment was called an 'Emergency Recruitment to the Indian Administrative Service'.[20]

In pursuance of the Cabinet decision a Special Recruitment Board was set up in the Ministry of Home Affairs to undertake recruitment of candidates from the open market to the Indian Administrative and Police Services and certain gazetted posts in the Central Secretariat. It consisted of R. N. Banerjee, the Home Secretary, as its Chairman, and three other Members: Dewan Bahadur S. G. Grubb, Member, Federal Public Service Commission; N. R. Puranik, Member, Federal Public Service Commission; and A. B. Latthe, Prime Minister, Kolhapur State, and Member, Constituent Assembly of India. The Board was required to interview candidates at the various provincial centres from the second week of September 1948 to the middle of March 1949.[21]

Under its advertisement of 10 June 1948 the Special Recruitment Board invited applications for emergency recruitment to the Indian Administrative and Police Services. Candidates were required to have a first or second class degree of a recognized university and in addition (a) possess (on 30 June 1948) a minimum of five years' service in government, a university, a public body, in an Indian State or business house; or (b) have been in receipt of a monthly salary of not less than Rs 400 for not less than one year immediately preceding 30 June 1948; or (c) possess five years' experience at the Bar. The age of candidates was to be between 27 and 45 years on 1 January 1948. Appointments to the I.A.S. were restricted to persons born or domiciled in nine of the participating provinces and, in addition, to Delhi, Ajmer-Merwara, Coorg, Himachal Pradesh and Panth-Piploda. Refugees from Pakistan were also eligible. But the Indian States were still outside the purview of the scheme.

The case of the Indian Police Service stood on a slightly different footing. The Indian Police had earlier formed a Service on the model of the I.C.S. and was an All-India Service. Its European element was recruited directly in the United Kingdom, and the Indian on a regional basis in India. Promotions from the Provincial Police Service were doubtless made, but those promoted were absorbed in the

Indian Police (IP) instead of being constituted into a separate category of listed posts, as was the case with the I.C.S. When the I.P.S. was created by the Conference of Provincial Premiers in October 1946, the 'agreement' provided for recruitment by the Central Government, but on a provincial basis. The old system of recruitment thus continued and thus the advertisement of 10 June 1948 laid down that for the Indian Police Service only candidates who were resident or treated to be resident in a particular province were eligible for appointment to the cadre for that province. Women were not eligible for appointment to the I.A.S. and I.P.S. but otherwise appointments were to be made on merit. However, if a sufficient number of suitable candidates were forthcoming from the Schedule Castes, 12½ per cent of the vacancies would be filled from amongst them.

Candidates selected for appointment to the I.A.S., the I.P.S. or gazetted posts in the Central Secretariat were to remain on probation for two years. They were eligible for pay according to the scales fixed for each of these services. The initial pay of candidates selected for appointment could be fixed either in the senior or junior scale and at a higher stage than the minimum of the time scale. In fixing the initial pay, the age, experience, qualifications and the salary last drawn by candidates were taken into account.

A representation was in the meantime made by the P.C.S. (Executive) Officers Association of East Punjab. The Association feared that, since P.C.S. officers were excluded from applying to the Special Recruitment Board, the cases of some junior P.C.S. officers might go by default. All Provincial Governments had of course been asked to go by the lists prepared by the *ad hoc* committes, but the Central Government was not sure that the claims of all P.C.S. officers, down to the junior-most man, were taken into consideration. However, it was contrary to established practice to ask Provincial Governments to consider each and every officer's claims in making recommendations, for usually only officers of a certain minimum seniority were considered for the purpose. And yet the feelings of junior P.C.S. officers could not altogether be ignored; for they would undoubtedly nurse a grievance that, being in the P.C.S., they had been prevented from competing like others and taking their chance as open market candidates.[22]

Although no fresh instructions were issued to the Provincial Governments, the Special Recruitment Board was advised to meet the situation arising from the representation. The Board not only interviewed candidates from the open market, but also interviewed, on behalf of the Federal Public Service Commission, P.C.S. officers recommended by the Provincial Governments. The Board decided to hold interviews in the provinces on the grounds that this might make available the help and advice of the Provincial Governments on the spot.[23]

The work of emergency recruitment was more or less completed by the middle of 1949 as far as the former provinces were concerned. On the recommendations of the Special Recruitment Board the Government of Indian appointed 82 candidates to the I.A.S. and 39 to the I.P.S. from among the open market candidates. In addition, 85 P.C.S. officers and 40 of the Provincial Police Service were appointed to the I.A.S. and I.P.S. respectively. Before being allotted to the provinces, they were trained at the I.A.S. Training School in Delhi, and the Central Police Training College at Mount Abu.[24]

Extension of the Scheme to States

The most important development during 1949 in respect of emergency recruitment to the All-India Services was the extension of the I.A.S. and the I.P.S. to what were formerly known as the Indian States or Unions of States. This brought about the administrative integration of the country as a whole. With the amalgamation of the Indian States into Unions a number of viable States and Unions of States came into existence, comparable to the erstwhile provinces. A proposal was then made to these States to accept the I.A.S. and I.P.S. schemes on the basis already accepted by the Provincial Governments. All the States and Unions of States, with the exception of Kashmir, agreed to participate in the scheme.

The scheme provided that future recruitment to the I.A.S. and the I.P.S. would be made from the results of competitive examinations held under the Constitution by the Union Public Commission in the same manner as with the 'Provincial' cadres. However, as no all-India service cadres had earlier existed in the States, a new procedure was adopted on the analogy of the emergency recruitment undertaken by the Special Recruitment Board for the provinces. It was provided that the existing officers of the States who held posts to be included in their respective I.A.S. and the I.P.S. cadres, would be considered and interviewed, if necessary, by the Board, and that those who were considered immediately fit for appointment to the All-India Services, would be so appointed. The Special Recruitment Board would also prepare a list of officers who, though not immediately suitable for appointment to the All-India Services, were of sufficient promise to attain the requisite standard within the next five years. Such officers were to be kept on the waiting list and, if their work continued to be satisfactory, they would be appointed to the I.A.S. or the I.P.S. within five years. There was a yet a third category of officers who, though not suitable for appointment to the All-India Services even within the next five years, had already been confirmed in the posts hereafter included in these Services, or had 'accrued rights' to continue in such posts indefinitely. The officers of this category were to be retained in the posts until retirement, without being appointed to the All-India Services in question. For the remaining vacancies the Special Recruitment Board was to invite applications from open market candidates domiciled in the States concerned, the last date for the submission of applications being 15 March 1950.[25] All appointments to these cadres were made thereafter on the results of the competitive examinations held by the Union Public Service Commission.

Combined Competitive Examinations

The competitive examination for the Indian Administrative Service was combined with that for the Indian Police Service and the Central Services, Class I. The first competitive examination was held from 1 to 11 July 1947, and the second from 20 December 1948 to 4 January 1949. Because of the unsettled state of affairs the notice given of the examination was short and the publication of results delayed in the case of the first two examinations. In 1947, for instance, the notice was first published on 12 March, and 30 April was fixed as the last date for the receipt of applications. Candidates could hardly plan their studies carefully or make adequate preparation for the examination. There was, in addition, a long delay between the holding of the examination and the announcement of results, and then again between the announcement of results and the actual selection of the candidates for appointment. The results of the 1947 examination, for example, were published eight months after the last date of the examination, and those of 1948 after six and a half months.

From 1949 onwards the I.A.S. and I.P.S. examinations began to be held at regular intervals in a fixed month. At the instance of Sardar Patel, the Home Minister, steps were taken to see that the last date for the receipt of applications was fixed at about 1 July, that the examination commenced about the middle or the third week of September, that it was concluded before the first week of October, and that the results of the written and *viva voce* tests were ready by the middle or the third week of January. Only candidates who obtained a certain minimum percentage of marks in the written test were to be called for the *viva voce*. These percentages were to be kept ready by the third week of November, so that requisition to the Provincial Governments for verification of the antecedents of these candidates could issue in time to enable them to send their replies before the full results were ready. The entire formalities were in fact required to be completed with the object of making the selected candidates available for training by the beginning of February.[26]

Separate draft rules were first framed for the conduct of examinations for the I.A.S. and I.P.S. But these were amalgamated for the combined competitive examinations held first in July 1947. The idea of having separate examinations for the All-India and Central Services, Class I, was thus given up. This was a departure from the pre-1947 practice which perhaps could not cope with the demand for speed necessary for recruitment on a scale and range much larger than before.

The rules governing the combined competitive examinations[26a] in the first couple of years are of importance in terms of future development as well as a purely Indian contribution to the solution of the gigantic problem of recruitment in a state of flux. The combined competitive examinations covered under these rules as many as eleven Services. Of these, the Indian Administrative Service and the Indian Police Service were All-India Services, while the remaining nine were Central Services, Class I. These were: 1. The Indian Foreign Service; 2. The Indian Audit and Accounts Service; 3. The Military Accounts Department; 4. The Indian Railway Accounts Service; 5. The Imperial Customs Service; 6. The Income Tax Officers (Class I, Grade II) Service; 7. The Transportation (Traffic) and Commercial Departments of the Superior Revenue Establishment of State Railways; 8. The Establishment Department of State Railways; and 9. The Indian Postal Service (Class I).

The rules laid down that the combined competitive examinations were to be conducted by the Federal Public Service Commission in the subjects listed on page 112.

Candidates for the Indian Police Service were required to select two optional subjects and candidates for all the other services were to select three and not more than three. The subjects included in 25 and 26 were, on the other hand, not to be offered by candidates for the I.A.S., the I.P.S. or the Indian Foreign Service who, in addition, were not to be allowed to select more than two subjects from the History or Law groups. The subjects indicated under 14 and 15 were to be offered only by candidates going in for the Indian Foreign Service.

	Compulsory	
	Subjects	Marks
1.	English Essay	150
2.	General English	150
3.	General Knowledge	150

	Optional	
4.	Pure Mathematics	200
5.	Applied Mathematics	200
6.	Chemistry	200
7.	Physics	200
8.	Botany	200
9.	Zoology	200
10.	Geology	200
11.	English Literature	200
12.	Indian History	200
13.	British History	200
14.	World History	200
15.	International Law	200
16.	General Economics	200
17.	Political Science	200
18.	Law	200
19.	Philosophy	200
20.	Geography	200
21.	One of the following: Latin, French, Sanskrit, Arabic, Persian, Spanish, Russian, German or Chinese	200
22.	Statistics	200
23.	Advanced Accountancy and Auditing	200
24.	Mercantile Law	200
25.	Applied Mechanics	200
26.	Prime Movers	200

The Commission was empowered to fix the qualifying mark in any or all the subjects at the examination. Candidates who so qualified at the written examination were to be summoned by the Commission for a *viva voce* test at which a maximum of 300 marks were to be awarded. It was provided that no candidate would be appointed who failed to secure 105 marks at the *vive voce*.

Two important eligibility conditions which the rules laid down for admission to the combined competitive examination were the age limit and educational qualification. Except in the case of the Transportation (Traffic) and Commercial Departments of the Superior Revenue Establishment of State Railways and the Establishment Department of State Railways, where the age limit was between 21 and 25 years on 1 August 1948, the minimum and the maximum age limit in the case of candidates for any other service were fixed at 21 and 24 years on 1 August 1948. A relaxation of this rule was, however, made for candidates who were already employed at a certain level in the Accounts and Allied Services, in the Indian Postal Service, in the Central Secretariat or the office of the Federal Public Service Commission. In such cases a candidate could be admitted to the combined competitive examination if he happened to be over 24 and under 27 on 1 August 1948. The maximum age limit was in all cases to be relaxable by three years in favour of Scheduled Caste candidates.

As regards educational qualifications, the minimum prescribed for the I.A.S. or the Indian Foreign Service was a degree of one of the universities recognized by an Act of Government. This degree was to be in Arts, Science or Commerce. Any question as to whether a degree held by a candidate was suitable for admission to the examination was to be decided by the Federal Public Service Commission. A candidate for the Indian Police Service was required to hold a degree of one of the recognized universities or to have passed the Diploma Examination from Aitchison College, Lahore, Mayo College, Ajmer, Daly College, Indore, or Rajkumar College, Raipur. A candidate holding the Cambridge Higher School Certificate was to be also entitled to admission to the I.P.S.

For admission to the combined competitive examination it was, in addition, necessary for a candidate for the I.A.S. or I.P.S. to be 'a national of the Indian Dominion' by birth or 'domiciled in the Provinces of Assam, Bihar, the Central Provinces and Berar, East Punjab, Madras, Orissa, the United Provinces, or West Bengal, or in a Chief Commissioner's province'. The rules further laid down that refugees from Pakistan would also be eligible to apply for admission to the I.A.S. or I.P.S. examinations. Vacancies in the cadre of the latter, however, were to be filled only by persons domiciled in a particular province or in the adjacent Chief Commissioner's province. As for the selection of women, the rules provided for certain restrictions: for instance, a woman candidate who was married could not be selected, and women could be asked to resign in the event of marrying subsequently. Such restrictions on the appointment of women in the Indian Foreign Service were specially emphasized. It was further emphasized that a male candidate married to a foreigner would not ordinarily be appointed to the Indian Foreign Service. And in case a candidate, after appointment to this Service, proposed to marry a foreigner he was required to notify the Secretary, Ministry of External Affairs and Commonwealth Relations, of his intention to do so. The Government of India reserved the right to require him to resign if he married such a person.

The rules governing the combined competitive examinations included provisions for probation and conditions of service also. In the case of the I.A.S., for example, it was laid down that appointments would be made on probation for a period of one year, subject to extension if necessary. There were two pay scales prescribed for the I.A.S., the junior and senior. The former was Rs 350–400–450–500–540–30–600–EB–30–870–40–950 (19 years), and the latter was to be Rs 800 (6th year or under)–50–1000–60–1300–50–1800 (25 years). A probationer was required to start on the junior scale. He was permitted to count the period spent on probation towards leave, pension or increment in the time scale. An I.A.S. officer was under these rules required compulsorily to contribute towards a Provident Fund at a minimum rate of one anna and a maximum rate of $2\frac{1}{2}$ annas in the rupee. His other benefits in respect of travelling allowance, leave and medical attendance were to be governed by Central Government rules applicable to Class I officers.

The operation of these probationary and other rules which applied to the I.A.S. extend, wish certain modifications, to other Services also. A notable feature, however, was the superiority of the I.A.S. over all other Services in terms of pay scales, where the maximum of the senior scale was not allowed to exceed Rs 1150 in the case of any Central Service or the I.P.S.

Of the eleven Services for which provision was made for the combined competitive examination, the I.A.S. was in fact by far the most important in terms of emoluments and conditions as well as the standard of examination and assessment. The Indian Foreign Service came next, and then the I.P.S.

During 1947–9, serious endeavours were made to bridge the gap caused in the higher echelons of the civil service on the transfer of power. While replying to a question in the Constituent Assembly of India, Sardar Patel pointed out on 29 November 1947 that the total number of officers recruited for the I.A.S. since 15 August 1947 came to 342. Of these, 183 were from the Provincial Services of the various provinces, 39 from among 'war service' personnel, 81 selected after interview by the Federal Public Service Commission or any Special Board appointed for the purpose, and 39 after competitive examinations. Of the 183 officers from the P.C.S. category 85 were appointed under the Emergency Recruitment Scheme on the recommendations of the Federal Public Service Commission, and 98 against the normal quota of 25 per cent of the senior posts reserved for them since 15 August 1947. No separate information was said to be available regarding the number of political sufferers and refugees appointed to the I.A.S. It was, however, suggested that some candidates selected from the open market under the Emergency Recruitment Scheme and the competitive examinations might be political sufferers or displaced persons.[27] The Home Minister did not take account of the 'war service' candidates selected for appointment in March 1947.

The figure supplied on 29 November 1949 about candidates appointed on the results of the competitive examination was, however, not up to date. For, 34 such candidates were appointed on the results of the 1947 and 36 from the 1948 examination.[28] The Note for Supplementaries to the reply of the Home Minister was, however, more precise on the subject of direct recruitment to the I.A.S. from the time of its inauguration to 1949, a period of three years. The Note pointed out that the total number of applicants who applied for the I.A.S. during this period was as many as 22,219. Of these 1,195 were from amongst war service candidates; 5,226 for the competitive examinations held in 1947, 1948 and 1949,[29] and 15,798 for emergency recruitment by the Special Recruitment Board. The total number of candidates interviewed was, however, 3,840, or one for every 6.3 applicants. The table below gives the number of candidates interviewed and appointed under each of the three categories of recruitment:[30]

Categories	No. interviewed	No. appointed
1. War Service candidates	574 (by F.P.S.C.)[31]	90
2. Open Competition—successful in written papers in 1947 and 1948	952 (by F.P.S.C.)	70 (34 in 1947 and 36 in 1948)
3. Open Market	2314 (by S.R.B.)	81

Candidates who appeared at the competitive examination of 1949 had not yet been interviewed by the Federal Public Service Commission. But on the basis of the results of 1947 and 1948 it would not be off the mark to put 30 as the number appointed in 1949. The total number of direct appointments made to the I.A.S. thus came to 271. When added to the 183 drawn from the Provincial Services (85 under emergency recruitment by the S.R.B. and 98 through promotion by the F.P.S.C.), the total rose to 454. The following table shows the percentage of recruitment made to the I.A.S. through different sources:

Recruitment to the I.A.S., 1947-49

	No of appointments	Percentage
Competitive Examination	100	22.0
War Service	90	20.0
Promotion from P.C.S.	98	21.5
Emergency from P.C.S.	85	17.8
Emergency from Open Market	81	18.7
	454	100.0

The percentage of recruitment to the I.A.S. through sources other than the competitive examination was thus as high as 78. Of this, the quota of the Provincial Services was nearly half, and two-fifths of the total itself. Even so, 97 vacancies still remained to be filled in the provincial cadres, and these were included in the list recommended by the Special Recruitment Board. But no appointments had been made out of the list so recommended. The completion of recruitment work for the erstwhile Indian States, which was expected to be over by April 1950, was awaited before the announcement of a final list could be made. It was, however, recognized that most of the existing 97 vacancies in the provincial cadres would remain unfilled even after the announcement of the final selections, for most of the Provincial Governments had expressed themselves against their cadres being overburdened by the appointment of older open market recruits. They preferred to fill the remaining vacancies by increased annual recruitment spread over five years, beginning from 1949. As this view was acceptable to the Government of India too, all the vancies in the provincial cadres were not expected to be filled till 1953.[31a]

The recruitment of over-aged candidates to the I.A.S. under the Emergency Recruitment Scheme was a major factor in the dilution of quality, especially in terms of discipline and loyalty, intellectual awareness and independence of judgement. It worsened further when the scheme was extended to the princely States where patronage had formely governed appointments.

There were other factors that tended to weaken the intellectual and moral qualities of the I.A.S. Besides an emphasis laid by political bosses on executive action to the exclusion of merit, these factors included the enormous increase in the number of applicants permitted to appear at the competitive examination without prior screening on the basis of regional quotas adopted earlier, in 1922, for the 'separate' I.C.S. examination held at Allahabad; concessions extended to political sufferers[32] and refugees in terms of age relaxation and re-employment with restoration of pensionary and other rights; a liberal policy of promotion to superior posts on extra-professional considerations, and a drastic reduction in the period of training sought to be imparted to probationers at the Training School in Delhi. The programme scheduled for probationers between 1948 and 1951 in fact provided for an average of not more than six to seven months.[33] The duration of the first batch of 'Emergency Recruits' was even less, the total of working days being 57 days only.[34]

The competitive system was of course there to ensure the continuity of the I.C.S. tradition in terms of the standard of recruitment. But there were two main limitations. First, the percentage of candidates who were so admitted to the I.A.S. remained by and large small, most entering the Service through arrangements other than the competitive examination. Secondly, even though the policy of communal representation in the All-India Services which had systematically been continuing since 1925,[35] was theoretically scrapped, the claims of the Scheduled Castes could not be overlooked for social and political reasons. It was accordingly decided that where recruitment was made by open competition through the Federal Public Service Commission or open competitive tests held by any other authority, the appointments would be subject to a reservation of 12½ per cent of the vacancies being filled by direct recruitment in favour of the Scheduled Castes. This reservation diluted the application of a high standard of recruitment based strictly on merit. The Home Minister himself acknowledged this fact in a communication to a representative of the Scheduled Castes. 'None of the Scheduled Caste candidates would have been appointed to the Indian Administrative Service', Sardar Patel pointed out, 'if their cases had been considered purely on merits in competition with other candidates; nor did the initial weeding out at the interview stage, which was completed at a high standard for the other candidates, practically affect those belonging to the Scheduled Castes.'[36]

In regard to posts filled from the open market otherwise than by competitive examination, the principle of communal representation found a much wider application. It was decided that recruitment should be made approximately in proportion to the population of the various communities in India. The following percentages of reservation were accordingly fixed for such recruitment.[37] Hindus (including Jains but excluding Scheduled Castes), 60%; Scheduled Castes,[38] 62/3%, Muslims, 13⅓%; Other Communities, 10%.

These percentages applied to Services and posts for which recruitment was made on an all-India basis. In the case of Services for which recruitment was confined to a particular area or locality, the reservations were so fixed as to be approximately proportional to the population of the various communities in the area or locality concerned.

The orders regarding reservation of vacancies in favour of communities, however, did not apply to recruitment by promotion which was to be made irrespective of communal considerations. It continued to be on the basis of seniority or merit.

The heterogeneity of the Indian social system thus became clearly reflected in the making of the administrative bureaucracy. Recruitment on a principle other than by open competition was itself a surrender to subjective elements in the choice of personnel. The injecting of a communal dimension into that choice provided an ideological basis that reinforced subjectivism as an antithesis of what might be called meritocracy. And yet the inevitability of communal representation in the public services could not but be recognized, especially under a democratic system of government functioning in a status-bound and stratified society. The communal incentive to employment was considered conducive to social change as well as beneficial to the ruling party politically.

The Central Secretariat Service

Apart from recruitment to the All-India Services, more particularly to the I.A.S., the Government of India was in the first few years after Independence saddled with the problems of reorganizing what came to be known as the Central Secretariat Service as well as of creating a central cadre of the I.A.S. that might meet the extended requirements of the Central Government.

Before the outbreak of war in 1939 the Central Secretariat up to the level of Assistant and Under Secretaries was staffed by the Imperial Secretariat Service. Direct recruitment used to be made at the level of Assistants through the competitive examinations held by the Federal Public Service Commission, the minimum qualification required being a university degree. The Assistants so appointed were eligible for promotion to the posts of Superintendents, which were regarded as selection posts. The next higher post was that of Assistant Secretary. It was filled by selection from among the Superintendents. The post of Assistant Secretary was the highest post normally open to members of the Imperial Secretariat Service. The post of Under Secretary, on the other hand, was drawn generally from the I.C.S. cadre and considered to be a training post for its officers. The duties of Assistant Secretaries and Under Secretaries were not marked. Both categories of officers held charge of Secretariat branches and discharged more or less similar functions. But while Assistant Secretaries were generally entrusted with routine administrative work, that relating to matters of policy was handled by Under Secretaries.

The necessity of reorganizing the erstwhile Imperial Secretariat Service arose from a serious dilution of its quality proceeding from its enormous expansion in the course of the War, as shown below[39]

	1939	1948	Percentage of increase
Assistant/Under Secretaries	40	248	602
Superintendents	76	393	517
Assistants	493	2,306	468

Evidently, this rapid expansion meant deterioration in quality. In pre-War days Assistants were persons who had achieved distinction in an all-India competitive examination. An Assistant had to work for 12 to 15 years in that grade and prove his worth before he could look forward to promotion to the post of a Superintendent. Few Superintendents, on the other hand, could become Assistant Secretaries much before retirement. In the course of the War, however, this completely changed. The large expansion in the upper layers of the service led to rapid promotions from the lower levels. The clerical staff which had at the close of the War increased by nearly five times was 'made up of anyone who happened to be readily available to anyone

of the numerous appointing authorities'.[40] Promotion to higher posts
from here meant that far too many inexperienced people came to hold
posts for which they were not fitted. An incompetent Superintendent,
for instance, could not guide and train his Assistants. The poor
quality and inexperience of Assistants called for more men to do the
same work, and this tendency to press for increasing staff applied also
to the higher levels of the service, a tendency which led to the
progressive deterioration of quality and efficiency.

Another important consequence of increase in the size of the Secretariat staff was the steady growth of temporary hands. Of the 2,306
Assistants in 1948, for example, all except 95 were temporary, the
others being promoted to higher grades comprising, even there, considerable numbers of temporaries. This caused a sense of insecurity
and uncertainty which could not be resolved so long as the total cadre
required for the Secretariat Service remained undetermined in terms
of its permanent strength. In the meantime efficiency continued to be
a serious casualty.

The problem of reform in the post-Independence period was not
only to restore efficiency and economy, but also to meet the shortage
of I.C.S. officers who earlier used to man roughly half the posts of
Under Secretaries. In the course of the War itself, the former distinction between them and Assistant Secretaries had begun to be given
up. Such of the officers as provinces were able to spare were required
to man the higher layers in the Central Secretariat, especially on the
retirement of Europeans. The posts of Assistant and Under Secretaries in these circumstances came to be filled almost entirely by the
Central Secretariat Service, supplemented on an *ad hoc* basis from a
variety of sources. The change so brought about during the War and
its aftermath came to stay and was recognized as permanent. The
reorganization of the Central Secretariat Service had to proceed not
only on the basis that it should provide practically all the officers
required for the grade of Assistant and Under Secretaries, but also to
supply officers for the higher grade.

It was in this context that the importance of 'reinforcement' acquired much greater emphasis. This reinforcement became necessary
at the level of Superintendents, not of Assistants, where it was essential to weed out poor material and provide better training facilities.
The main object of reinforcement was to provide for a new grade of
Assistant Superintendents, a class of direct recruits, superior to the
average category of Assistants whose quality had become too diluted

to be able to supply through promotion the personnel required for the posts of Superintendents. It was felt that great leeway would have to be made up in raising the standard of Assistants to make them fit for promotion. The direct recruitment of Assistant Superintendents of a higher calibre was thus sought to be an instrument of 'reinforcement' for the grade of Superintendents, a regular system of training being provided at the same time to fit them for that grade in a relatively short period. This arrangement, however, did not exclude the selection of competent persons from among the existing incumbents.

Reorganization and reinforcement were thus interrelated. Both were designed to provide a reserve of qualified men for selection and promotion, not only for the posts of Under Secretaries but also for higher grades, including executive posts under the Central Government or even under Provincial Governments. This objective was sought to be achieved by a scheme, which was approved by the Cabinet on 22 October 1948.[41]

The scheme embraced all posts included in the Central Secretariat Service from Assistant up to Under Secretary, except those specifically excluded with the consent of the Home Ministry. It provided for a review of permanent, quasi-permanent and purely temporary posts in the Central Secretariat and its attached offices, the object being to determine the cadre strength of the Service based on its permanent and quasi-permanent posts which were likely to last for more than three years.

In its reorganized form the Central Secretariat Service was divided into four grades. The highest grade was that of Under Secretary. It comprised not only the existing posts of Under Secretaries but also those of Assistant Secretaries, the distinction between the two being, however, abolished formally on reorganization. The next lower grade was that of Superintendents holding charge of sections.[42] The third grade was that of Assistant Superintendents, who were expected to function as Senior Assistants in larger sections and as Assistants-in-Charge in smaller ones. The lowest grade in the service continued to be that of Assistants. Provision was made for direct recruitment in the grades of both Assistants and Assistant Superintendents. In the case of Assistants, 25 per cent of their posts were reserved for clerks promoted to their rank, the remaining 75 per cent being filled by direct recruitment on the results of the Ministerial Service Examination held by the Federal Public Service Commission. In the case of Assistant Superintendents, however, direct recruitment was limited to 50 per cent only. The direct recruits in this grade were to be drawn from the results of the combined competitive examinations for the I.A.S. and the Central Services, Class I. As the posts of Assistant Superintendents were Class II posts, it was agreed that candidates who secured positions immediately below those recruited for Class I posts should be appointed as Assistant Superintendents. The remaining 50 per cent of the posts were to be filled by promotion from among Assistants. The posts of Superintendents and Under Secretaries were, on the other hand, declared as selection posts, to be filled by promotion on merit from the next lower grade.

Detailed information was accordingly sought to be obtained from various Ministries about posts in the Secretariat that might be included in the cadre of the Central Secretariat Service. Lists were also prepared of candidates who were eligible for confirmation in the different grades of the service. These were considered ministry-wise by Departmental Promotion Committees[43] designed to formulate their recommendations for approval by the Federal Public Service Commission which interviewed candidates for the posts of Under Secretary, Superintendent and Assistant Superintendent. Their interviews were completed and appointments made by the middle of 1949.[44]

The grade of Assistants came to be constituted from a variety of sources. It comprised permanent displaced government servants with at least one year of service as an Assistant, and deputationists who were at least matriculates, as well as temporary Assistants who were graduates with at least five years of service in that grade before 22 October 1948. They were to be appointed without any qualifying tests. It also included Scheduled Caste employees recruited before 31 December 1947, and permanent Third and Second Division Clerks and Assistants who qualified in the open examination before 1947. These were all to be eligible for confirmation in case they had to their credit three years of service in the grade of Assistant. The Federal Public Service Commission in addition allowed several other concessions which led to the absorption of a considerable number of temporary employees in the quasi-permanent category joining the cadre of the Central Secretariat Service.

Consistent with the recommendations of the F.P.S.C., the Government of India issued the Central Civil Services (Temporary Service) Rules in 1947.[45] These provided for the grant of 'quasi-permanent' status to those who had at least three years' service in a grade and were otherwise qualified and suitable for continued retention in that grade. However, the grant of a quasi-permanent certificate was subject to the concurrence of the F.P.S.C. in cases where consultation with it was necessary in respect of direct recruitment to the grade.

The conditions of service of the quasi-permanent employees were comparable to those of permanent employees in so far as their security of tenure, allowances, leave and procedural safeguards in disciplinary matters were concerned. Provision was also made to reserve a certain proportion of permanent vacancies in future for the absorption of quasi-permanent employees. These privileges were in addition to other concessions granted to them under instructions issued by the Central Government in May 1949.[46]

The Secretariat Training School.

The school was opened in May 1948 to improve the quality of work and the efficiency of Secretariat officers. The training given included instruction in secretariat organization, office methods and procedures, rules of business, secretariat instructions, service and financial regulations. The training was to last for two or three months. The school also made provision for special and refresher courses of two weeks' duration. It continues to function even now.

The Central Secretariat Service so reorganized and trained provided, through appropriate selection and promotion at a sufficiently early stage, officers who were not too old when they reached the rank of Deputy Secretary. Arrangements were in this regard also made with the Provincial (later State) Governments for the deputation training of Class I officers selected for a higher rank. The scheme of reorganization and reinforcement thus made a distinct departure from the old Imperial Secretariat Service, where men in most cases retired before being able to reach the stage even of Assistant or Under Secretary. Promotion indeed became quicker but quality was diluted. The reorganized Secretariat Service ensured for its officers a steady rise in the hierarchy of the civil service and bridged the gap caused by the shortage of I.C.S. officers. But it is doubtful whether administrative efficiency and public morality, which were generally a function of competition-based intellectual attainment, could be ensured by promotion and a desire to absorb an army of temporaries earlier employed to meet the contingencies of war.

In response to public agitation and debates in the Constituent Assembly an Economy Committee[47] was set up in 1948 to review the growth of expenditure and recommend economy measures in the civil expenditure of the Government of India. It was presided over by Kasturbhai Lalbhai, a leading industrialist. On the basis of the Committee's unpublished report, the *Illustrated Weekly of India* noted that the budget allotment for the 'non-military departments' rose from Rs 29 crores in 1938-9 to Rs 121 crores in 1945-6 and that it was estimated to touch Rs 184 crores in 1948-9. The number of Ministries rose from 8 to 18 and their staff which totalled only 82,000 just before the War, increased to 2,65,000 in the course of a decade.[48]

Commenting on the report of the Committee, the *Indian News Chronicle* of 6 August 1949 expressed surprise over the fact that, far from proceeding to implement its recommendations for retrenchment of the staff of the various departments,[49] the Government of India did not even see its way to making them public. As said before, the stupendous increase in the size of Central Government employees remained by and large unreduced for political and humanitarian reasons. It is true that part of that increase was due to the extended responsibilities of the government and a still larger part to the defence budget. But, as the Economy Committee reported, most of the increase proceeded from a serious fall in the standards of efficiency: two or three men did what one man used to do before the War. There was, in addition, an irrational growth of Ministries and Departments. The multiplication of Ministries and the proliferation of the Secretariat afforded opportunity for extended powers of patronage in the distribution of jobs created without justification. When the Economy Committee proposed retrenchment from Secretaries down to clerks, some Ministers threatened 'to resign even if one peon [was] dismissed from their Ministries'.[50] And since these jobs held out increasing prospects of promotion, there developed an identity of interest between the political and the bureaucratic wings of administration. Writing about the manner in which the Secretariat functioned, the *Hindustan Times* of 22 August 1949 thus observed: 'A single transfer or promotion means a major upheaval. From the Assistant Secretary upwards everyone changes from the less pretentious to the more pretentious room. Even those acting or officiating for no more than a few days insist on their right to move into a bigger, better room. There is the typical example of the Deputy Secretary, who, given a chance to officiate for a week or two, refurnished the Joint Secretary's room before occupying it. The room, belonging to an older, mellower, man was comfortable but not posh. The officiating coxcomb wouldn't set foot in it until it had been redone and rearranged. "This room is not worthy of the status and dignity of a Joint Secretary," was his verdict. Signboard painters and carpenters were consequently kept busy shifting name-plates from one room to another.[51]

Thus, while Ministers viewed retrenchment as an attempt to reduce the area and power of patronage, the bureaucracy regarded it as inimical to quick promotion. The size of the Secretariat staff naturally remained top-heavy. The Prime Minister, it is true, had expressed appreciation of the Economy Committee's view that the administration could be run by a reduced number of officials. He had even made it clear that the Government could not be expected to keep people in jobs when there was no work for them.[52] But it remained a mere expression of opinion. The bureaucracy justified the retention of the inflated staff and officials on ideological grounds and the necessity of governmental interference with private enterprise and social life, a necessity which could even call for a greater army of public servants not only to administer government regulations and controls, but also to work out new controls and regulations demanding in turn more men and women to administer and supervise them. The slogan of social and economic development in the post-Independence period was used as a convenient lever to justify ministerial expansion and bureaucratic proliferation.

The Indian Civil Administrative Cadre

As the title of the cadre suggests, it consisted of both the I.C.S. and the I.A.S. It was in fact a joint cadre of the two Services, the term 'joint cadre' being in its final form dropped because of criticism that it emphasized their separateness.[53]

Like the I.C.S., the I.A.S. was in principle assigned immediatly to the separate cadres of the provinces which agreed to its formation. But as all-India Services they were both organized and maintained to meet the requirements of all the Provincial Governments and the Central Government. The I.A.S., however, was intended to serve all the purposes formerly served by the I.C.S., except the provision of officers required for the judiciary. Constitutionally, therefore, the Indian Civil Administrative Cadre was to be a provincial cadre, allotted to each of the provinces, their deputation reserve serving the Centre as and when required.

The proposal for the constitution of Joint Indian Civil and Administrative Service Cadres in the various provinces came in for consideration by the Government of India when the Bombay branch of the I.C.S. Association raised an important issue arising from the recruitment of officers to the I.A.S. under the Emergency Recruitment Scheme in the later half of 1948. Since emergency recruitment was to be made both to the junior and the senior scale, I.C.S. officers were apprehensive lest their seniority and other prospects be affected by the emergency recruits appointed to the I.A.S. between 27 and 45 years of age. A new formula had therefore to be evolved to determine the respective seniority of four categories of officers in a common roll. These were officers of the I.C.S., I.A.S., P.C.S. officers promoted to the I.A.S. in the senior scale, and officers recruited to the I.A.S. (both senior and junior scales) under the Emergency Recruitment Scheme and allowed even a higher start.[54] Parallel action had to be taken in respect of the Indian Police and the Indian Police Service also.

The Rules governing the Indian Civil Administrative Cadre (I.C.A.) and the Indian Police Cadre (I.P.C.) were finalized and notified by the Government of India in the Gazette Extraoradinary dated 25 January 1950,[55] a day before the commencement of the Constitution of India. The Notification included the Rules relating to their pay also.

The I.C.A. Rules were made by the Government. This it did under two sources of authority, sections 241 and 247 of the Government of India Act, 1935, which dealt with the recruitment and conditions of service of persons recruited by the Secretary of State, and the Memorandum (Agreement) dated 21 October 1946[56] concluded between the Government of India and the governments of nine provinces annexed to these Rules.

The Rules laid down that every I.C.A. cadre post specified in the Schedule annexed to the Agreement must be filled by an officer:

(i) who was a member of the Indian Civil Service and was not permanently allotted to the judiciary; or (ii) who was a member of the I.C.S. and permanently allotted to the judiciary, but in respect of whom the provincial government had, by order in writing, made a declaration that he would be deemed to be a cadre officer for the purpose of these Rules; or (iii) who was substantively appointed before 21 October 1946 to a 'listed' executive post; or (iv) who was a member of the I.A.S.[57]

All appointments to cadre posts were to be made by the Provincial Government concerned. But, except with the sanction of the Government of India, no cadre post was to be filled otherwise than by a cadre officer, unless in the opinion of the Provincial Government the vacancy was not likely to last for more than three months, or there was no suitable cadre officer available. If a non-cadre officer was appointed to a cadre post for more than three months the Provincial Government was required to report the fact to the Government of India together with the reasons for making such an appointment.

The Indian Police Cadre Rules, 1950, were established and the Cadre constituted in every province on a similar principle. These were promulgated on the same date and under the same authority.[58]

The Indian Administrative and Police Services (Pay) Rules, 1950 provided not only for the time-scale pay of these Services, but also the pay of the serveral superior posts belonging to the Indian Civil Administrative and Indian Police Cadres.[59] It was in addition provided that they would be permitted to earn increments in the said scale during the period of probation. The Rules so issued also fixed the pay of Commissioners and Joint Secretaries to the Government of India at Rs 2250 per month, and that of a Secretary to the Government at Rs 3000 per month. An officer belonging to the Indian Police Service who was appointed to the selection grade of that Service was to receive a pay of Rs 1250 per month. An I.P.S. officer appointed to any of the posts in the Intelligence Bureau was, on the other hand, to receive the pay specified against each such post. The Director of the Intelligence Bureau, for instance, was to draw a salary of Rs 2500 per month, while his Deputy Director was entitled to a pay admissible to an I.P.S. officer holding the post of a Deputy Inspector-General of Police, plus a special pay of Rs 200 per month. All this was done as part of the Indian Civil Administrative Cadre Rules issued under the Home Ministry Notification, dated 23 January 1950.

In a letter addressed to the Government of India on 18 April 1950, the Joint Secretary to the Government of West Bengal, M. M. Basu, questioned the legal validity of the Indian Civil Administrative Cadre Rules, which made no provision for disciplinary matters relating to the I.A.S. The Memorandum (Agreement) had doubtless had such a provision, but though a historic document, Basu rightly held it had no statutory sanction. The creation of an all-India Service like the I.A.S. was the result of executive action. Its legal sanction, it is true, was sought to be derived under Section 263 of the Government of India Act, 1935, which provided for 'an agreement' between 'the Federation and one or more Provinces' in the creation of an all-India Service.

But the terms 'Federation' and 'Provinces' did not signify exclusion of the legislative authority which, as Basu thought, was necessary for the constitution of a new All-India Service. What the Memorandum had done was merely to incorporate the points of agreement reached between the Central and Provincial Governments represented by Ministers and civil servants without any legislative mandate.

Sections 241 and 247 of the 1935 Act covered disciplinary matters in the case of All-India Services before the commencement of the Constitution on 26 January 1950. These Services were naturally governed by the Civil Service (Classification, Control and Appeal) Rules made under those sections of the Act. But the Rules so made applied only to those all-India Services specified in the schedule to these Rules. In other words, they applied to the I.C.S., which was specified, not to the I.A.S. which found no mention in the Schedule.

Paragraphs 9 to 13 of the Memorandum, which dealt with disciplinary matters in the case of I.A.S. officers, were more or less a reproduction of the Civil Service (Classification, Control and Appeal) Rules. These had no legal force; for the Central Government, which was expressly invested with powers to make necessary rules under paragraphs 7 and 8 of the Memorandum to regulate the conditions of service of I.A.S. officers, had done nothing of the kind. Also, the Indian Civil Administrative Cadre Rules promulgated in January 1950 made no mention whatsoever of the provisions contained in paragraphs 9 to 13 of the Agreement. The Agreement itself had of course been annexed to the Cadre Rules as Annexure A. But its specific clauses dealing with disciplinary matters were not directly promulgated in the form of rules made under Sections 241 and 247 of the 1935 Act. These would have acquired statutory force if only they had been so promulgated.

In another letter dated 9 June 1950, the West Bengal Government reiterated that the conditions of service of the I.A.S. and I.P.S. could not be regulated except by law enacted under Article 312 of the Constitution. The Government of India had no alternative but to recognize the force of this argument and accept the 'questionable validity' of the Agreement.[60] It proceeded to take steps to enact legislation to impart legal validity to rules governing the recruitment and conditions of service of members of the All-India Services. The All-India Services Act, 1951 (No. LXI of 1951)[61] was the result of the independence of bureaucratic judgement and action.

The Act invested the Central Government with powers to make rules, after consultation with the Governments of the States concerned, for regulation of recruitment and conditions of service of persons appointed to an All-India Service. All rules made under it were required to be laid for not less than fourteen days before Parliament as soon as possible after they were made. The rules so made were subject to such modifications, by way of repeal or amendments, as Parliament determined.[62] It was further laid down that all rules in force immediately before the commencement of the Act and applicable to an All-India Service would continue to be in force and that these would be deemed to be rules made under the Act.[63] By an All-India Service the Act meant only the I.A.S. and I.P.S. It was by the All-India Services (Amendment) Act, 1963 (No.27 of 1963) that the Central Government was empowered, by notification in the official Gazette, to constitute three more All-India Services.[64] These were the Indian Service of Engineers (Irrigation, Power, Buildings and Roads); the Indian Forest Service; and the Indian Medical and Health Service.

The question of framing various rules under the provisions of the 1951 Act was taken up early in 1952. The tentative drafts of the various rules were discussed at a Conference of Chief Secretaries of State Governments held at Delhi in April 1954. The draft rules, which were essentially comparable to the ones already in operation on the models established during 1941-2,[65] were finalized in the light of certain modifications suggested by that Conference. By December 1955, the Central Government had promulgated 18 sets of rules and 8 sets of regulations relating to the All-India Services.[66] The I.C.S. and the I.P. were borne on the cadre strength of the I.A.S. and the I.P.S. respectively. Even so, as recruitment to the former Services had ceased, it was the latter which kept on growing.[67]

The Indian Civil Administrative Cadre came to an end in 1954. According to the Indian Administrative Service and the Indian Police Service (Recruitment) Rules of that year, the I.C.S. and the I.P. officers became members of the I.A.S. and the I.P.S. respectively, subject of course to the provisions of Article 314 of the Constitution of India which provided for the protection of the existing rights of the I.C.S. The various rules governing the conditions of service of the All-India Services, which were framed under the 1951 Act, thus came to apply to members of the I.C.S. and the I.P. also.[68] This created a unified civil service structure and introduced broad uniformity in matters of disciplinary control, a uniformity which was reinforced by a corresponding change in the Cadre Rules governing the I.A.S. and the I.P.S. A 'cadre officer', for instance, now meant only a member of the I.A.S. or the I.P.S., not of the I.C.S. or the I.P., which the I.C.A. Cadre and the I.P. Cadre Rules had earlier provided in 1950 as joint cadres. The rules so established in 1954, however, followed the pattern earlier applicable to the I.C.S. and the I.P. The legitimacy they had acquired over the years in the exercise of power and privilege came to be inherited by their successor Services, the I.A.S. and the I.P.S.

Their joint authorized cadre strength thus went on increasing considerably. The I.A.S. cadres, for example, increased from 9 to 17 in 1955.[69] The authorized strength of these cadres, including the reserves for the Central Government, rose on the other hand from 868 in 1949 to 3,117 under the I.A.S. (Fixation of Cadre Strength) Regulations, 1955.[70] The authorized total of the Indian Police cadre likewise increased from 575 to 1,763 during the same period. In actual practice, however, the cadre position was not unduly strong, particularly in superior positions. The strength of the I.C.S. which was borne on the I.A.S. cadre strength and the number of I.A.S. officers themselves who held superior posts, were considered much too small to meet the requirements of the Central Government, especially during the first few years after Independence.

Central Cadre of the Indian Administrative Service

The Central Cadre of the I.A.S. consisted mainly of the I.C.S. officers borne on the cadre of the I.A.S. It was also called the Indian Civil and Administrative (Central) Cadre, organized to meet the requirements of the Government of India, just as the Indian Civil Administrative Cadre was meant to function as a provincial cadre.

The main object underlying the creation of the 'Central Cadre of the Indian Administrative Service' was to provide for the future manning of senior administrative posts of and above the rank of Deputy Secretary in the Government of India and comparable posts existing in its Attached Offices. The Cadre was also intended to provide for a panel of junior officers, such as Under Secretaries. These were to be promoted only after due training and experience.

Necessity of a Central Cadre

The immediate necessity of a Central Cadre flowed from the breakdown of the old system under which the Central Government obtained its senior officers from the provinces who after a period of fixed tenure at the Centre, reverted to their parent provincial cadres. This system worked well in a situation where the requirements of the Central Government bore a relatively small proportion of the total cadre strength of provinces. But it was bound to fail, as it did, when the provincial cadres became depleted while the requirements of the Centre increased. The I.C.S. cadre strength, for instance, was last fixed in 1939. The sanctioned strength which prior to that year had been 1,057, was fixed at 1,064 after 1939. This was inclusive of a deputation quota which had been settled at 50 a long time before the commencement of the War and was refixed at 125 in 1939, when the War began. As the following table shows, actual deputation exceeded the limits of the sanctioned quotas beyond all proportion:[71]

Year	Deputation from Provinces		
	Senior Officers	Junior Officers	Total
1939	127	42	169
1940	162	40	202
1941	173	43	216
1942	201	50	251
1943	206	49	255
1944	222	39	261

After the transfer of power, the total number of I.C.S. officers forming part of the provincial cadres was reduced considerably on account of the retirement of Europeans and the transfer of Muslims to Pakistan. It shrank to 427, of whom 85 were judges. There remained only 342 I.C.S. officers in executive posts. The sanctioned strength of the newly created I.A.S., which was 830 in 1948, was inclusive of the 342 I.C.S. officers borne on the provincial cadres of that Service. Of the total sanctioned strength of 830, 684 were to be direct recruits and 146 promotees from the Provincial Services. The number of I.A.S. officers recruited directly, however, did not exceed 131. There was thus a gap of about 200 officers in the sanctioned cadres of 830. The continued maintenance of even 125 of the Central deputation quota depended upon the effective filling up of this gap.[72] And that could not be done easily except by promotion of Provincial Service officers in excess of their fixed quota of 25 per cent. This, as already indicated, tended to dilute the quality of recruitment.

As regards the increased requirements of the Central Government for senior administrative officers, a census was made in 1948 itself by several ministries: this showed a demand for 250 posts after excluding posts outside India as well as those in India which, though of an administrative nature, could be held by technicians. Of the total of 250 posts, 161 were meant for the Secretariat and 89 for its Attached Offices. The total number of additional posts of the rank of Deputy Secretary was 121 (98 for the Secretariat and 23 outside), while those above the rank of Deputy Secretary were 129, of which 63 were Secretariat posts and 66 non-Secretariat. It was against these posts that the provinces were expected to maintain a steady supply of 125 officers only.

A situation had thus emerged which called for a systematic arrangement to provide men for senior administrative posts at the Centre together with the appropriate complement of junior posts which, for the purposes of training and reinforcement, must necessarily go with the senior administrative posts. The Central Secretariat Service in its reorganized form constituted one such complement. But there were other Central Services which needed to be similarly reinforced and trained for promotions and transfers to senior positions. The Central Cadre of the Indian Administrative Service was designed to accomplish both the objects—provision for senior administrative posts as well as their junior complements.

The Central Cadre Scheme

The draft scheme was prepared by R. A. Gopalaswami, Joint Secretary in the Home Ministry, who came to function as Special Secretary, Reorganization, in the Ministry of Transport then presided over by N. Gopalaswami Ayyangar who was also in charge of reorganization of the machinery of government. His Draft Scheme was the result of consultation with various Central Ministries and the Chief Secretaries of the Provincial Governments. He submitted it under a Note addressed to the Minister on 25 April 1949. The figures he quoted in the Draft Scheme were more or less similar to what he had cited earlier in October 1948. Even the existing position of the senior administrative posts reinforced his arguments for the creation of a Central Cadre,[73] for that position had not changed at all materially.

The Special Secretary pointed out that all posts of the categories formerly known as 'superior' posts in the provincial cadres of the I.C.S. had come to be included in the provincial cadres of the I.A.S., which was fixed at 834. Out of this total authorized strength, the number of 'superior' or 'senior' administrative posts was 457 in the provincial cadres. Of the remaining 377, 125 posts, as said before, were meant to be always on deputation under the Central Government, while 252 were treated as a consolidated reserve, including officers under training, or employed in junior administrative posts, or on leave, or deputed to posts other than the 457 provincial posts at superior levels.

Of the 834 authorized strength of the provincial cadres of the I.A.S., the direct recruits were 687 and the promotees from Provincial Services 147. There were among the direct recruits only 345 I.C.S. officers not permanently retained in the judiciary. They continued to be members of the Service to which they were originally recruited but were to hold posts in the I.A.S. cadre and be counted against the authorized strength of the direct recruitment group so long as they were available and not retained in the judiciary. The remainder of the authorized strength of direct recruits was to consist of I.A.S. officers already appointed from among the War Service candidates and on the results of the first two competitive examinations. The direct recruitment group was expected to be constituted in its full strength as a result of the Emergency Recruitment which was in progress, and the competitive examination of 1949 which was yet to be held. The promotion group of officers in the I.A.S. were still weak in strength. They consisted of the erstwhile holders of 'listed posts' as well as those promoted from the Provincial Civil Services since 1947. Unlike the I.C.S., the I.A.S. was, however, a completely unified and integrated service, comprising both promoted officers and direct recruits.

But under-manned as the I.A.S. was, it was difficult for it to maintain even 125 officers on deputation to the Centre and continuously supply replacements for officers who returned to provincial cadres on expiry of their terms of deputation. In the existing situation where the provincial cadres of the I.A.S. were not yet fully stabilized, the only alternative left to the Centre, or even to the newly organized Indian Foreign Service, was to share the available supply of I.C.S. officers who were borne on their I.A.S. cadre strength. But the provinces could not afford to spare additional hands from their already limited I.C.S. and I.A.S. stock and could not meet the extended requirements of the Centre for more and more senior officers. It was therefore necessary that a permanent provision be made to meet the residual needs of the Central Government.

In these circumstances, the Special Secretary proposed that the existing organization of the I.A.S. should be enlarged by adding a new tenth cadre known as the Central Cadre of the Indian Administrative Service. This was to be in addition to the nine Provincial Cadres already constituted under the Agreement of 1946. Just as each Provincial Cadre operated under the immediate control of a Provincial Government, the Central Cadre was to be under the immediate control of the Central Government. Just as a certain number of the available I.C.S. officers were counted against the authorized strength of each Provincial Cadre, a corresponding number would be allotted and counted against the authorized strength of the Central Cadre on the basis of what the Special Secretary called 'quasi-permanent deputation' from the Provinces, a deputation separate and distinct from the normal deputation reserve.

There were several features of the proposed quasi-permanent deputation to the Centre. It signified an additional number of officers drawn from the Provincial Cadres. Such deputation was subject to the consent of all the three parties involved, viz., the Central Government, the Provincial Government and the officers concerned. It was to be for an indefinite period, extending, if necessary, to the rest of the officer's serving life. Vacancies created in the provincial I.A.S. Cadres on account of the quasi-permanent deputation were to be filled on a substantive basis by promotion from the Provincial Service and the promotion so provided was to be in excess of the normal quota of 25 per cent. The Central Government reserved the right under the scheme to return to the Provincial Government at any time an officer so obtained on deputation provided it was prepared to take another officer from the same cadre. The object was to see that the Provincial Cadre strength and its management remained unaffected. If at any time the Provincial Governments so desired, the services of an officer on quasi-permanent deputation to the Centre could be made available to them for a term of three to five years on reverse deputation.

In addition to the proposed quasi-permanent deputation from the Provincial Cadres of the I.A.S., a part of the Central Cadre was to be maintained by permanent transfer to it of officers drawn from the financial Services[74] and the Central Secretariat Service, Class I. Unlike a Provincial Cadre of the I.A.S. which was unitary in the sense that the I.A.S. was a purely executive Service without a separate judicial branch, the Central Cadre was to be more akin to the I.C.S. which used to be divided into two separate branches, executive and judicial. For, it was proposed that the Central Cadre, too, should consist of two separate branches, one of which was to be known as the General Administrative Pool, and the other as the Special Administrative or Finance-Commerce Pool. Both were to operate as the feeder services of the Central Cadre in the same manner as the Provincial Civil Services were intended to feed the provincial Cadres of the I.A.S. All Central I.A.S. posts in the Ministries of Finance, Commerce and Industry and Supply were to be borne on the cadre of the Special Administrative Pool, while all other Central I.A.S. posts were to be borne on the General Administrative Pool. For the initial recruitment as well as the general organization of pay scales and conditions of service the two pools were to form a single unit, the Central Cadre being itself one of the units of the I.A.S. for other purpose like postings, transfers, promotions, deputation and organization of training and varied experience needed by junior officers as a precondition to their appointment to senior administrative posts, the two pools were to form two distinct and separate units. Like the I.C.S. division into executive and judicial branches in the Provincial Cadres, the Central Cadre was to be a unifed whole as also two separate entities, depending on the purpose intended.

Consistent with the organizational principles of the Scheme, the senior and the junior administrative posts proposed to be borne on the Central Cadre and the two pools thereof were duly specified. The authorized strength and composition of the Central Cadre and the two pools were required to be initially fixed at 170 in the senior grade, of whom 70 were to be members of the I.C.S. and the remaining 100 non-I.C.S. officers. The total strenth of junior-grade officers was to be one-third of the authorized total strength of the Central Cadre.[75]

General Administrative and Finance-Commerce Pools[76]

Of the two constituent pools of the Central Cadre, the Finance-Commerce Pool had already come into being as a 'special pool' of officers to serve the specialized needs of the Finance and Commerce Departments under a Finance Department Resolution of 2 February 1939. The object was to build up a body of expert officers who, apart from having general administrative experience, had become, at a fairly early stage of service, familiar with the characteristics of Indian finance and taxation as well as the principles and methods of trade and commerce.

It was laid down that recruitment to the Finance-Commerce Pool would be on merit alone from the following Services: the Indian Civil Service; Indian Audit and Accounts Service; Military Accounts Department; Imperial Customs Service; and the Income-Tax Departments.

Apart from the posts reserved for members of the I.C.S., all posts included in the Pool were open to members of the Services and Departments specified above. Appointments to these posts were made by the Governor-General in Council on the recommendations of an Establishment Committee which also made recommendations for promotion on pure merit.[77]

The posts included in the Finance-Commerce Pool were intended to form a separate cadre of officers. Every officer employed in the Pool was on confirmation given a lien on a post in the cadre, and his lien on a post in his Service or cadre of origin was suspended. The idea was that if, after a short-term deputation or transfer, officers were found suitable and not reverted earlier, they should generally be confirmed in the Finance-Commerce Pool. This mode of recruitment provided a cue for the organization of the General Administrative Pool which had not yet been constituted but was to be created as part of the Central Cadre Scheme. This mode combined the old system of procuring officers on short-term deputation with a system adopted in the organization of the Finance-Commerce Pool functioning as a separate but unified cadre of officers originally belonging to different Services.

The Finance-Commerce Pool was a highly specialized cadre consisting of three classes of officers appointed according to their ability and experience in their Service of origin and, thereafter, their appointment to the Pool. The posts listed in the Finance-Cadre Pool under the Resolution of 2 February 1939 are given below to indicate their importance:[78]

Class 'A' Posts

		Pay (Rs)
1	Secretary, Finance Department	4,000
1	Secretary, Commerce Department	4,000
1	Addl. Secretary and *ex-officio* Chairman, Central Board of Revenue	3,500

2 Members, Central Board of Revenue	3,500[79]
1 Deputy Auditor-General	3,500
1 Finance Adviser, Military Finance	3,250
1 Joint Secretary, Finance Department	3,000
1 Joint Secretary, Commerce Department	3,000
1 Indian Trade Commissioner, London	£1, 800-40-200 Representation allowance £200 per annum.[80]

Class 'B' Posts

Deputy Trade Commissioner, London.	Full pay in the senior time scale of the I.C.S.
Trade Commissioner, New York.	Full pay in the senior time scale of the I.C.S. Representation allowance £250 per annum; house rent allowance £300 per annum; local allowance £500 per annum
Trade Commissioner, Hamburg	£1,000-50-1,500 per annum; representation allowance £250 per annum; house rent allowance £150 per annum
Trade Commissioner, Milan	£1,000-50-1,500 per annum; representation allowance £250 per annum; house rent allowance £250 per annum; house rent allowance £150 per annum
Trade Commissioner, Mombassa.	Rates of pay had not been fixed
Trade Commissioner, Japan	Rs. 1,200-100-1 500 per month; representation allowance Rs 250 per month; plus monthly house rent allowance of Rs 150 and conveyance allowance of Rs 100

3 Accountants-General of equivalent posts in the Indian Audit and Accounts Service
1 Collector of Customs
4 Commissioners of Income-Tax
2 Deputy Secretaries, Finance Departments
2 Deputy Secretaries, Commerce Departments
2 Deputy Financial Advisers, Military Finance
1 Secretary, Central Board of Revenue.
1 Financial Adviser, Communications (New J.S.)
3 Post under the Central Board of Revenue (Central Excise)
10 Deputation Posts.

Class 'C' Posts

3 Assistant Commissioners, Income-Tax
2 Assistant Collectors, Customs

3 Posts, Indian Audit and Accounts Service
8 Under Secretaries, Finance and Commerce Departments
2 Assistant Financial Advisers, Military Finance
2 Assistant Financial Advisers, Communication, Finance Ministry
1 Secretary, Central Board of Revenue

The grade of pay applicable to officers of the Central Services in the Pool, holding posts in Class 'B' or on completion of 11 years or earlier service, was as follows:

11th or earlier	Rs. 1,000
12th year	1,050
13th year	1,100
14th year	1,150
15th year	1,200
16th year	1,275
17th year	1,350
18th year	1,425
19th year	1,500
20th year	1,600
21st year	1,700
22nd year	1,800
23rd year	1,900
24th year	2,000
25th year	2,050
26th year	2,100
27th year	2,150
28th year	2,200
29th year	2,250

The most important source of recruitment to the General Administrative Pool of the proposed Central Cadre was the joint Provincial Cadre of the I.C.S. and I.A.S., out of which a quasi-permanent deputation panel was first constituted. It was to consist of as many as 100 non-I.C.S. officers and 90 I.C.S. officers, of whom 20 had already been seconded permanently to the Finance-Commerce Pool.

Another important source of recruitment to the General Administrative Pool was the Central Services (Transfer) Panel, including two separate, Senior and Junior, grades. The Senior Grade Panel consisted of officers who had completed ten years' service in Class I posts and were considered suitable for permanent appointment to the Central Cadre. This category was inclusive of all non-I.C.S. officers already confirmed in the Finance-Commerce Pool. The minimum requirement for officers of the Junior Grade Panel was five years' service in Class I posts. They were expected to attain the same

standard of fitness as senior officers after suitable training and experience during their two years' probation. As regards members of the
Central Secretariat Service, provision was made for the promotion
even of Superintendents who were Class II grade officers. A period
equal to one-half of the service rendered by them was deemed to be
service rendered in a Central Service Class I post for purposes of
appointment to the General Administrative Pool.

Senior Grade and Junior Grade panels were likewise sought to be
prepared by the Special Recruitment Board from among candidates
interviewed by the Board under the Emergency Recruitment Scheme.
But, as said before, this too formed part of the I.A.S., being the main
source of recruitment on a quasi-permanent basis.

Formulated in 1949, the Central Cadre Scheme received the approval of the Government of India, subject to the concurrence of the
State Governments. The initial constitution of the Central Cadre was
taken in hand in 1950 and was expected to be completed in the course
of 1951.[81] The selection of personnel, which had been entrusted to the
Central Establishment Board, with the Chairman of the U.P.S.C. as
President, could not however be completed on schedule, although
progress was reported to have been made.[82]

In the light of experience gained since 1950, the Indian Civil
Administrative (Central) Cadre Scheme was reconsidered in April
1954 by a Conference of Chief Secretaries. While the system of
quasi-permanent deputation (the core of the Central Cadre scheme)
had proved to be a drain on the limited strength of the I.C.S. and
I.A.S. officers in the States, the manpower requirements for senior
posts under the Central Government had steadily been increasing on
account of the successive development plans. The objection of the
States was mainly to the existence of a separate 'tenth cadre' and its
'quasi-permanent deputation' under which their senior officers, especially from the I.C.S., were lost to them. They were not opposed to
deputation under the old arrangment, in which they retained their
right to recall their officers on the expiry of the period of deputation
and to send others in their place. The whole trouble in fact centred
round the use of the term 'Cadre' at the Centre, a term which tended
to destroy the concept of the I.C.S. and I.A.S. being common to the
Centre and the States. It was therefore decided that, while as many
I.A.S. officers as were available from the States should be deputed to
the Centre, there should be no 'Central Cadre' of the I.A.S.[83]

Steps were accordingly taken to enlarge the State cadres of the

I.A.S., so that a larger number could be made available for the Centre. The State Governments on their part agreed to their deputation quotas being increased. A programme of enhanced recruitment by open competition was accordingly prepared to meet the needs of the Centre. The special recruitment of 1956 came in the same context, although its immediate justification was to meet the requirements of the Second Plan.

The idea of the 'pools' which had gone into the constitution of the Central Cadre was, however, not given up. The 'General Administrative Pool' and the 'Finance-Commerce Pool' together constituted the 'Central Administrative Pool', which was divided again into the General Branch and the Economic Branch. Functionally, the Central Cadre came to be replaced by the Central Administrative Pool, which consisted of officers earmarked for service at the Centre in view of the increasing need for specialization. This applied to those who happened to be on deputation to the Centre on a tenure basis, too. They could even be retained by the Centre on lien. According to the decision taken in 1954, senior posts at the Centre were to be filled from the sources already indicated for the constitution of the Central cadre. The constitution of the Central Administrative Pool included, in addition, a fourth category of officers recruited direct on the basis of their specialized qualifications and experience outside the government.[84] Constituted thus, the Central Administrative Pool did two things: first, it built up a reserve of officers with special training and experience for economic administration; and secondly, it maintained continuity of knowledge and experience in the field of general administration. Its important feature, however, was that it made provision for lateral recruitment of people with specialized qualifications directly from the open market at higher age levels.[85]

Selecting Authority

As recommended by its Secretariat Committee, the Government of India took steps to 'overhaul' the system of recruitment to the superior posts in the Central Secretariat. Under a Home Department Memorandum of 14 June 1938 the Government of India decided to have a Selection Board to make final recommendations for the appointment of officers of and above the rank of Under Secretary, but below that of a Secretary, with the exception of the Finance and Commerce Departments where the selection of such officers was already made by an Establishment Committee. The Board consisted of three Secretaries to the Government of India, who were to be appointed by the Governor-General in his discretion, together with the Secretary of the Department concerned if he was not already represented on the Board. Secretaries were also included in the Establishment Committee. Such Secretaries as served on it for the special cadre of the Finance and Commerce Departments were not excluded from serving on the Selection Board. A Memorandum of 21 September 1940 later provided that the Home Secretary to the Government must *ex-officio* be one of the three members of the Board, which functioned as an advisory body.[86]

The Establishment officer functioned both as Secretary to the Selection Board and the Establishment Committee. An I.C.S. officer of the status of Joint Secretary in the Government of India, he maintained a short list of officers who appeared *prima facie* to be suitable for senior posts and consulted the appropriate Provincial Governments to know whether they could spare a specified officer for appointment to a particular post. He kept for the guidance of the Selection Board the record of service of the officers due to revert to their provinces and informed the Provincial Governments concerned if the Government of India wished to retain a lien on those considered suitable for further or extended employment in the Central Government. The frequency of this practice of retaining a lien increased in the course of the War, and under a Memorandum of 1 May 1942,[87] the appointment of officers retained on lien began to be made on a mere explanatory Note, with the available information circulated by the Establishment Officer to members of the Selection Board and the Secretary of the Department concerned. That is how officers who came to the Centre on deputation remained there indefinitely, a trend arising from the exigencies of the War, but tending to acquire a prescriptive legitimacy which dislocated the working of the regular tenure system.

As Secretary to the Establishment Committee for appointments to the Finance-Commerce Pool the Establishment Officer placed his proposals regarding appointments, postings, transfers and promotions of officers to posts included in the Pool. He was also responsible for the general management of the Pool. He communicated the decisions of the Committee to the concerned authority who would either gazette an appointment to the post to which the officer concerned was to be appointed, and, if necessary, obtain the orders of the Governor-General for gazette notification.[88] In addition to normal routine

duties involving record keeping and correspondence, the Establishment officer was to obtain the Establishment Committee's recommendations about the retention of suitable officers and to arrange
for the reversion of those whose performance did not entitle them to
permanent employment in the Finance-Commerce Pool at the
Centre.[89]

Like the Establishment Committee, the Selection Board was reconstituted under the orders of the Executive Council on 1 March 1946. In
its reconstituted form the Board consisted of the Chairman, Federal
Public Service Commission; the Home Secretary of the Government
of India; two other Secretaries of the Government of India, appointed
by the Governor-General; the Secretary of the department directly
concerned with the proposal under consideration; and the Secretary
to the Executive Council who, like the Chairman of the F.P.S.C., also
served on the Establishment Committee meant specifically for appointments to the Finance-Commerce Pool. Both the bodies were in
fact governed by top-ranking officials. The administrative responsibility for both as well as for the Establishment Officer and his office
came to be assumed by the Secretariat of the Executive Council,
headed by its Secretary. The Establishment Officer was expected to
transmit the recommendations of the Committee or the Board to the
Secretary of the Department concerned, who was responsible for
obtaining the orders of the Viceroy if necessary.[90]

A few days after the transfer of power the Indian Cabinet did away
with the Establishment Committee and appointed on 20 August 1947
a single Selection Board without the Chairman, F.P.S.C., or the
Cabinet Secretary who inherited the functions of the Secretary to the
Executive Council. The new Selection Board consisted of five Secretaries to the Government: those from the Home and Finance Departments were *ex-officio*, while the third and the fourth were
nominated by the Government. The Secretary of the Department
concerned with the appointment was to be co-opted for the occasion.
The *ex-officio* members between them controlled all the civil services.
While the Home Ministry was the custodian of the rights and privileges of the civil service as a whole, the Finance Ministry, in so far as
the Finance and Commerce Pool were concerned, had a great deal of
direct interest in the business of the Board which took over the
functions earlier discharged by the Establishment Committee. A
whole-time officer of the status of Joint Secretary under the administrative control of the Home Department was designated the

Establishment Officer. The seniormost secretary was to be the Chairman of the Selection Board.

The Board was to be consulted on all appointments to Secretariat posts as well as to senior non-Secretariat posts, such as the Heads of Attached Offices and Departments, when these posts were proposed to be held by an I.C.S. officer or by members of other Services from which Secretariat officers would normally be drawn. The Selection Board would, at the request of the Department, make recommendation to its Minister for all Secretariat appointments from Under Secretary upwards as well as non-Secretariat senior appointments.

However, it was laid down that the Minister concerned might himself suggest names for consideration to the Selection Board which, after all, was a subordinate body, subject to ministerial control and influence. This was a major departure from the old practice, where all proposals were made only by the Establishment Officer on the basis of records of past performance. The Selection Board was of course still empowered to recommend a panel of three names for a post. But it was subject to approval by the Minister of the Department concerned. It was only in respect of the appointment of a Secretary or Additional Secretary that a panel was recommended by the Board in consultation with the Prime Minister. The Minister was required to make his choice from amongst the panel of names approved.

The Selection Board so constituted controlled patronage in an area earlier covered by a well-regulated Establishment Committee. It did so without having any representative either of the Federal Public Service Commission, an independent body, or of the Cabinet, the highest political executive. Criticism naturally arose about the manner in which appointments were made to superior posts under the Government of India. And this criticism was not without reason. A Home Ministry Note recorded by a Joint Secretary early in October 1948 thus observed:

It has not been unknown for Ministers to interfere actively in the selection of persons for such appointments. The members of the Public Service Commission at the Centre and in the Provinces have, to my knowledge, been frequently approached even by Ministers, in connection with selection of candidates for appointment to Government service; and it is not unlikely that even members of the Selection Board have been sometimes influenced in their recommendations by extraneous considerations, though there is no doubt in my mind that such a Board is least likely to be affected by such considerations. It is, however, essential that no room should be allowed for criticism on this score.[91]

As part of his plan to introduce his Central Cadre Scheme, R. A. Gopalswami therefore suggested the appointment of a Committee of Ministers, called the Establishment Committee of Cabinet,[92] which was to be assisted and advised by a Committee of Secretaries, known as the Central Establishment Board,[93] with which a member of the Federal Public Service Commission was to be associated. The Establishment Committee of the Cabinet and the Board were to function jointly as the controlling authority, responsible for 'carrying out the initial constitution of the Central Cadre on or before 15th August 1949'.[94]

However, matters got delayed. New cadres had to be created for the reorganized Part B States, a process which could be hastened only slowly on account of political difficulties. Direct recruitment to the I.C.S. had its own limitations, arising from the Secretary of State for India being no longer its recruiting agency. Besides, outstanding persons could not be made available at will. As regards the other feeder Services, these needed to be reorganized and reinforced by direct recruitment and training. Further, provision had to be made for constitutional recognition of the I.C.S. as an All-India Service for purposes of Part B States as also the necessary basis for its future maintenance.[95]

The Scheme was in these circumstances sanctioned by the Government of India in 1950, when the initial constitution of the Central Cadre was taken in hand, and it was expected to be completed in the course of 1951.[96] The selection of personnel, which was entrusted to the Central Establishment Board, however, continued through 1952 and 1953. Presided over by the Chairman of the Union Public Service Commission, the Board held meetings during 1953-4 also and made 'further progress'; but it could not complete the selection started in 1950.

As pointed out earlier, the Central Cadre Scheme was re-examined by a Conference of Chief Secretaries in 1954 and the quasi-permanent deputation system was considered unsatisfactory. It was therefore decided that, while maximum use should be made of as many I.A.S. officers as could be made available on normal deputation itself, there should be no separate Central Cadre. Quasi-permanent deputation thus had to go, but not regular deputation from the State Cadres. The provision for officers on deputation or transfer being retained on lien at the Centre also continued and the two branches of the administrative pools, which together formed a unified Central Administrative Pool, were not touched.

Special Recruitment to the I.A.S. in 1956

The quality of the I.A.S., which had already suffered considerably on account of emergency recruitment and rapid promotions from provincial and other sources became further weakened by undue expansion to meet the requirements of development plans. The demands of the First Five-Year Plan had already led to the revision of the All-India Service Cadres, and it was argued that during the Second Plan period, not only would the State Governments need more officers for their 'developmental activities', but the additional needs of the Centre for I.A.S. officers were estimated in 1955 at 200, a number which, in view of the Ministry-wise breakdown, was ultimately expected to exceed 335.[97] Since the gap could not possibly be filled by the normal methods of recruitment or promotion it was decided to undertake another special recruitment.[98] The principle behind this decision was that, while overall responsibility for the special recruitment would be with the Union Public Service Commission, the actual selection would be made by a Board consisting of the Chairman of the U.P.S.C. or a Member nominated by him; a Member of the U.P.S.C.; a senior officer, serving or retired; and a non-official.

The special recruitment was made from the open market as well as from State Civil Services and other State Services. Every candidate for recruitment from the open market was required to pass a qualifying written test (an 'Essay' and in 'General Knowledge'), the qualifying standard being decided by the U.P.S.C. Those who qualified at the written examination were interviewed by the Selection Board. Exceptions, however, were to be made in the case of candidates belonging to the Scheduled Castes and Scheduled Tribes who, if not qualified, could still be considered 'suitable by the Board'. This discretion was also exercisable for other candidates who may not qualify in the written test but whom the Board considered otherwise suitable in terms of age and experience. The age for eligibility in all cases was fixed at 25-40 years.

Recruitment to the I.A.S. from the State Services was to follow the procedure laid down in the Indian Civil Service (Appointment by Promotion) Regulations, 1955. According to this, each State had to constitute a Selection Committee with the Chairman of the U.P.S.C. or one of its Members as Chairman. This Selection Committee would prepare a list of suitable officers of the State Civil Service and the list so prepared was to be reviewed and revised annually; if any member of a State Civil Service was proposed to be superseded in the course of that review, the Committee had to record its reasons for doing so. The list was then to be forwarded to the Commission by the State Government along with records on the concerned officers, the observations of the State Government on the recommendations of the Committee, the records of those proposed to be superseded and the reasons of the Committee for its proposed supersession. The Commission considered the list received and approved it, unless changes were considered necessary. In case some change was required, the Commission was to inform the State Government and, after taking into account the comments received, it approved the list finally, with such modifications as seemed just and proper. The list finally approved by the Commission formed the Select List of members of the State Civil Service for promotion to the I.A.S.

The 1956 Regulations for special recruitment made some modifications concerning eligibility for promotion from the State Civil Service. Under the 1955 Regulations, for instance, the minimum length of service a State Civil Service officer was required to complete before his case could be considered was eight years (whether officiating or substantive) as a Deputy Collector or any other equivalent post. This qualifying period was reduced to six years in 1956, a relaxation which further affected the standard of recruitment. In the case of political prisoners, the upper age-limit of 40 years became relaxable to 43. For this concession, a candidate 'must have taken part in the national movement and must (i) either have been actually debarred from or refused admission to a competitive examination or Government employment on account of his political activities, or, being in Government service was punished for taking part in political activities; or (ii) have been imprisoned or detained or dismissed from service on account of his political activities; or (iii) having been in any profession or business on account of his political activities'.[99] While seemingly patriotic, this Regulation injected politics into administration and tended to vitiate the impersonality of the bureaucracy.

The grant of preferential treatment to political sufferers in matters of appointments was, however, taken recourse to as a plausible alternative to pressing demands for regular financial assistance to 'freedom fighters' from public funds. For, in 1948, Sardar Patel had already decided that no such assistance should be given 'on the ground that it would create a most embarrassing precedent'. It might be given, he suggested, from the funds of the particular party concerned, but not from public funds.[100]Also, the concessions allowed to political sufferers were, under his advice, to expire on 31 December 1951.[101]

Even so, during every session of Parliament questions were raised and resolutions moved by private members for grant of relief. H. V. Kamath, for instance, gave notice of a resolution which asked the Government to provide for the maintenance of the families of political sufferers who had participated in the national movement even in the first two decades of the twentieth century. The Cabinet, while expressing full sympathy with the idea of giving assistance, resolved on 21 November 1950 not to accept the resolution. It pointed out that, though the Government might be prepared to consider individual cases of hardship, it would be 'preferable' to rely on private sources or relief funds. In the debate in Parliament on 23 November, the Prime Minister explained the position of the Cabinet by saying that it involved no breach of any promise whatsoever; for those who were enrolled as volunteers for the freedom struggle had been told that they would get no 'dividend' for the service rendered. He said, 'I want the House to realize on what level that struggle was fought; because we have forgotten everything that the struggle meant and today all of us think more in terms of dividend, of profits and loaves and fishes'.[102]It was against this background that the Central Government issued orders granting concessions in matters of employment, including restoration of pensionary benefits and re-employment facilities, to those who were deemed to have in any way suffered under British rule for political reasons. These concessions were laid on the table of the House on 12 October 1951.[103] However, they did not expire in accordance with the decision taken earlier by Sardar Patel, for the operation of that principle was extended to the 1956 scheme of special recruitment.

The Public Service Commission

The Public Service Commission (India), as it was first called, was established in 1926, with Sir Ross Barker as Chairman and four ordinary Members. It was organized on the model of the Civil Service Commissioners in Britain. The Commission came to be known as the

Federal Public Service Commission when the Government of India Act, 1935, came into force in 1937. The Act also provided for a Public Service Commission for each province or a group of two or more provinces.

The function of the Federal Public Service Commission, as of the Provincial Public Service Commissions, was to recruit government personnel impartially and advise the Government on disciplinary control and the regulation of Service matters.

In respect of the Services and posts to which discretionary appointments were made by the Secretary of State, the Governor-General or the Governor of a province could each under Section 266(3) of the Government of India Act, 1935, make regulations in their respective fields, specifying matters on which it would not be necessary for the Public Service Commissions to be consulted.[104] Subject to these regulations, however, it was necessary for the Government to consult the Federal Public Service Commission or the relevant Provincial Commission:

(a) on all matters relating to methods of recruitment to civil Services and for civil posts;

(b) on the principles to be followed in making appointments to civil Services and posts and in making promotions and transfers from one Service to another and on the suitability of candidates for such appointments, promotions or transfers;

(c) on all disciplinary matters affecting a person serving His Majesty in a civil capacity in India, including memorials or petitions relating to such matters;[105]

(d) on any claim by or in respect of a person who is serving or has served His Majesty in a civil capacity in India that any costs incurred by him in defending legal proceedings instituted against him in respect of acts done or purporting to be done in the execution of his duty should be paid out of the revenues of the Federation or, as the case may be, the Province;[106]

(e) on any claim for the award of a pension in respect of injuries sustained by a person while serving His Majesty in a civil capacity in India, and any question as to the amount of any such award,

and it shall be the duty of a Public Service Commission to advise on any matter so referred to them and on any other matter which the Governor-General in his discretion or, as the case may be, the Governor in his discretion[107] . . . may refer to them.

These provisions were bodily lifted from Section 266(3) of the 1935 Act and incorporated in the light of the new constitutional changes into article 320(3) of the Constitution which dealt with the functions of the Union Public Service Commission or a State Public Service Commission. Consistent with Section 266(4), article 320(4) of the Constitution also laid down that, in spite of provisions made for the Commission to be consulted, nothing was to compel the Government to consult the Commission regarding the manner in which communal representation was to be effected in the Services and other posts. Here, as with regulations made by the President or a Governor on the lines earlier followed by the Secretary of State, the Governor-General or a Governor, consultation with the Commission could be dispensed within circumstances specified by them. Unlike the old practice, however, the regulations made under the Constitution to exclude the consultative jurisdiction of the Commission were subject to approval by each House of Parliament or the Legislature of the State concerned. So long as Parliament did not decide on the cases to be excluded from the purview of the Commission, the regulations made by the Governor-General remained operative even after the inauguration of the new Constitution, although the U.P.S.C. did not want the retention of such limitations on its functions as it considered unsound.

The very first report of the U.P.S.C. quoted a number of cases where the Government had declined to accept its recommendations concerning cases of re-employment or appointment to superior posts, or cases where appointments were made without its knowledge. The latter category represented a general practice of what purported to be temporary appointments for a period not exceeding one year, a category under the old regulations which was deemed to be in force under article 372(1)[108] of the new Constitution too. This provision for temporary appointment was invoked 'far too indiscriminately'. As the Commission reported:

There have been far too many cases in which posts have been filled by the ppointment of Ministries' nominees on the ostensible ground that the posts were temporary. A little reflection would, however, have shown that most of these posts were not likely to be done away with after one year. In many cases the Ministries' nominees have been kept in office for a period far in excess of one year without any reference to the Commission. Such nominees of Government cannot be denied an apportunity to compete for the post when it comes to be filled regularly on a competitive basis. The experience which they gain of the duties of the post, at the cost of the tax-payer, gives them an undue advantage over candidates from the open market. This state of things is the direct consequence of Ministries and departments not making use of the provision properly and has naturally evoked severe and widespread public criticism.[109]

The situation described applied to the period that immediately followed the introduction of the Constitution on 26 January 1950. In its subsequent reports the Commission repeated without success that some statutory safeguard should be provided by Parliament to minimize the occasions when the Government might seek to depart from the advice of the Commission. For example, it suggested the adoption of a provision similar to the Superannuation Act of 1859 in Britain, under which no civil servant could draw a pension unless he produced a certificate showing that his appointment had been made with the concurrence of the Civil Service Commission.

This interaction between administration and politics over appointments to civil posts came to the surface in an interesting case which arose soon after the Interim Government assumed office on 2 September 1946. In an informal letter of 3 September addressed personally to C. Rajagopalachari, the then Minister for Industry and Supplies, one M. Rashid, a young Indian Muslim in Leeds who held a B.Com. degree from Leeds University and possessed good general and technical qualifications, offered his services to the Government and hoped that the Minister would help him. 'I would not have written in such an informal manner,' he pointed out , 'had I no hopes that the advent of India's popular leaders to Government might make a difference from the previous regime.'[110] This obviously meant that the Minister should either make the appointment himself or exercise his political influence to secure a suitable position for the applicant in his Ministry.

On 11 September, Rajagopalachari marked the letter to Jawaharlal Nehru saying, 'This sort of thing should be seen by you. We have many men asking for employment and many jobs wanting good men—some coordination is necessary so as to make it possible to use all resources'.[111] Nehru, in turn, endorsed it on 12 September to Sir Eric Coates, 'Secretary, Cabinet Secretariat'. He said: 'The young man appears to be quite competent and should presumably be welcome in some suitable Department of Government. This Department may be Commerce, Labour or Industries. He has good qualifications and experience. We should try to take advantage of competent and trained young Indians wherever they may be.'[112] This expression of opinion by a Minister who virtually functioned as the chief political executive was more or less a recommendation for appointment.

The Cabinet Secretary, however, came in the way. In his note of 19

September he pointed out that all recruitment to government service and posts in India was done by the Federal Public Service Commission after open advertisement. What the Government did was to inform the Commission of the vacancies to be filled and the qualifications of the candidates required. It was thereafter the business of the Commission to do the recruiting. 'It is not open to Government', the Cabinet Secretary emphasized, 'to select itself individuals for appointment and merely submit them to the Commission for approval. This favours the individual who may have the ear of Government and defeats open advertisement and recruitment, and it would also result in Government being flooded with applications from individuals for appointment'. Coates therefore suggested that, after Rajagopalachari had seen these notes, the papers might be transferred to the Home Department which was at the time considering the question of extending the function of the Commission to meet the existing manpower shortage.

This reply to Nehru's note was sent after Coates had spoken to C.F.V. Williams, Joint Secretary in the Home Department, who not only endorsed the views of the Cabinet Secretary, but in a separate letter gave further reasons to reinforce the argument. 'The particular questions which arise from Mr Rashid's application are whether Government are in need of a man with his qualifications; and if so, whether he is the *best man available* with such qualifications.' The first question could be ascertained by a reference to the Departments concerned. In case they needed a man of Mr Rashid's qualifications, the only course open to them was to inform the F.P.S.C. of those qualifications and ask the Commission 'to make the best possible selection by advertisement in the open market'.[113] As regards the question of recruitment in Britain, where Rashid lived, the existing amended rules provided that the Commission should be satisfied as to whether the post could not be adequately filled by recruitment in India before any attempt was made to recruit abroad. No Minister could in these circumstances help Rashid, especially when the Departments concerned reported that they did not need a person of his qualifications.

However, the delay that occurred in recruitment by the Commission was used as a cause for interference with its functioning. It was argued that, in order to overcome manpower shortage in professional as well as specialized and technical fields, it would be necessary to take special steps to improve the method of recruitment. This obviously was the immediate result of the experience gained in Rashid's case by both Rajagopalachari and Nehru. Nehru emphasized that recruitment must on no account remain limited to candidates available in India. Attempts should be made to secure the services of all competent and trained Indians, whether in India or abroad, with the least possible delay when the need arose.

The Ministry of Home Affairs, which was already familair with the problem of delay in a general way, approached it with the emphasis indicated by Nehru. It initially proposed that advertisements should be issued in India, the U.S.A. and U.K. inviting applications from Indians with technical or specialized qualifications, not with a view to appointment to any immediate posts but in order to develop a 'waiting list', from which candidates might be considered for future vacancies. The interviewing of the candidates was to be done annually by the F.P.S.C. at the time of actual appointment, for which the list was to be kept up-to-date by annual revision.

These proposals were circulated for comment to various Departments on 29 January 1947 and then again on 26 July 1949. When consulted, most Ministries favoured the compilation of the proposed list and indicated the types of technical personnel that would be required by them in due course. The F.P.S.C. agreed to undertake the work relating to the preparation and maintenance of the list, and sent the Home Ministry a note for approval which contained the outlines of a scheme which the Commission proposed to adopt in the preparation of the list. It was, however, the Minister of Industry and Supply who, though he had made somewhat similar proposals, suggested certain alternatives that militated against the established functions of the Commission. He emphasized that definite steps should be taken to absorb foreign-trained technical personnel. For this purpose he suggested the appointment of an *ad hoc* committee[114] to compile a full list of such personnel, find out the vacancies that were available and make direct appointments to them without reference to the Commission. As regards those who were still abroad, the Minister advised that a directive should be issued to the F.P.S.C. that, subject to their qualifications being suitable, they should be appointed to suitable posts even though they might not appear at an interview. If necessary, the Minister added, they could be interviewed by special boards in the U.K. or U.S.A.

The Home Minister, Sardar Patel, would not compromise the position of the F.P.S.C. by permitting the appointment of the proposed *ad hoc* committee regardless of the Commission's concurrence required under the existing rules. Besides, the Commission's scheme had already provided for a card index for every name to be entered in its 'waiting list' and for the utilization of the 'Hollerith' tabulating equipment already installed to pick out applications at the appropriate time. As for the directive proposed to be issued to the Commission to appoint suitable candidates from abroad without interview, the Home Ministry considered it uncalled for. For, the Commission and even some of the Ministries had discovered that many Government scholars who had returned to India after training abroad and competed for posts under the Central Government, were found to be definitely inferior to those trained in India.

The Home Ministry thus felt that the views expressed by the Commission were sound and the scheme proposed by it suitable. The discussions that had taken place concerning recruitment of specialized and technical personnel thus boiled down to the following conclusions:

(i) The work of preparing a list of people with technical and specialist qualifications required for various Ministries was to be entrusted to the Commission, not to any *ad hoc* committee. The Prime Minister too came finally to agree. He observed that it was desirable that the Commission alone should be charged with the task of preparing the list.

(ii) The Commission was to be 'requested ordinarily to dispense with personal interview in the cases of overseas candidates where, in their opinion, the qualifications of such candidates are outstanding'.[115] This conclusion of the Home Ministry had likewise been endorsed by Nehru in his note of 20 July 1949. 'In the case of overseas candidates', he said, 'it is far too expensive to call them to India for interview. The Commission could easily appoint a high level selection board in London or New York or any other place and this board could do the interviewing and report to the Commission'. It was of course the Commission who was to decide whether or not the interview in question should be dispensed with.

(iii) As regards State scholars, they were to compete with other candidates. But where other considerations were equal, preference was to be given to State scholars who had returned to India after training abroad. The Commission alone was to make sure that merit was preferred to patronage even in the case of Government scholars.

(iv) So far as selections for appointment to posts under the Central

Government were concerned, the function of certain Ministries assisting State scholars was to remain limited merely to bringing to the notice of the Commission the list of such scholars with a statement of their qualifications. They were not at all to influence selections.

These conclusions of the Home Ministry were treated as proposals with which the Prime Minister generally agreed.[116]They were presented to the Cabinet which signified its approval on 26 July 1949.[117]

In the controversy that flowed immediately as a side issue from the rejection by the bureaucracy of Rashid's case, the Federal Public Service Commission thus held firmly to the original object of its institution. The firmness of character shown by its Secretary, Dr R.M. Ray, was of course an important factor. But the major factor that helped the Commission maintain itself as an independent and impartial body, was Sardar Patel, the Home Minister himself, who showed a respect for independence of judgement and would on no account allow political influence to determine administrative decisions. The importance he attached to established norms and procedures, though viewed by some as an impediment to change, conduced to stability and ordered progress. Nehru, on the contrary, did not show as much respect for rules and regulations as Patel. In his address to the Services at Kurnool on 9 December 1955, for instance, he referred to 'what might be called Service Rules and Regulations' which, he taunted, ran 'into thick volumes'. These rules, he added, were 'all right' in so far as they ensure some 'certainty' under 'a certain set of circumstances'. But it was 'going rather beyond that mark, when the whole Governmental structure, you might say, turns round the Service', especially the Indian Civil Service, who acted within the limits of 'precedents' and procedural 'framework'.[118] The condition which obtained under Sardar Patel thus started changing after his death in 1950 when C. Rajagopalachari took over as Home Minister.

CHAPTER IV

Administrative Changes 1957-72

We have in the previous chapter concentrated on the reorganization and recruitment of the All-India Services, the I.A.S. and the I.P.S. constituted respectively on the model of the I.C.S. and the I.P. This reorganization and recruitment during 1946–56 were designed mainly to achieve a two-fold object. The first was to provide against the serious depletion of experienced personnel at the level of superior administrative officers. The second, on the other hand, was to make the machinery of government and administration better fitted for the task of executing development plans.

We have covered in some depth the first of the two main objectives. A resort to varied modes of recruitment removed the inadequacy of manpower in so far as the old and established activities were concerned. But planned development under public control not only meant greater expansion but had other implications too. For instance, it necessitated changes in the governmental and administrative machinery to secure a greater degree of co-ordination. It tended to affect the importance of the bureaucracy as a class of administrative elites and to raise the status of technocrats as an agency of development. It lent support to the idea that the Services should cease 'as a class apart from the people',[1] and that they should function within the framework of the 'general will' recognized by the Constitution. In fact, the issues raised by the exigencies of social and economic development were to be judged not merely from an administrative angle of routine efficiency, but from an angle where both the administrative and political processes met and interacted. In other words, the administrator had to remain aware of the social and political realities as a guide to administrative behaviour. An attempt will therefore be made in this chapter to throw light on the changes effected not only in personnel administration and the civil services in general, but also in the institutional arrangement of the governmental machinery for the transaction of official business above the level of individual Ministries.

The Decision-making Apparatus

The main institutions involved in the making of decisions in the area of political and administrative interaction have since Independence been the Council of Ministers, the Prime Minister, the Cabinet, Cabinet Committees, inter-Ministry Committees of Secretaries to the Government and the Cabinet Secretariat.

The task of recommending measures for the reorganization of the machinery of government for developmental purposes was entrusted to N. Gopalaswami Ayyangar, Minister for Transport, who had once been a Deputy Collector promoted to a listed post in the Indian Civil Service. In the completion of his task he was assisted, as we have seen, by R.A. Gopalaswami, Joint Secretary in the Ministry of Home Affairs.

In a Memorandum of 20 May 1948 prepared for the Cabinet, Ayyangar pointed out that, although the advent of independence and a federal type of parliamentary democracy had called for radical improvements in the principles and methods of administrative organization, there was general disinclination on the part of those who had grown up under the previous regime to absorb new ideas or to change established practices. He recognized that several committees had in the past also expressed concern over the deterioration in the pace and quality of governmental business transacted at the Centre and suggested the expediency of overhauling the existing organization. Their recommendations were of course not adequate to the new task of promoting public enterprise. But, even so, such useful proposals as they did make remained largely unimplemented. Ayyangar therefore brought out the basic defects of the existing structure of the government and its mode of operation, warning the Cabinet that 'unless something drastic' was done immediately there was 'grave risk of the whole administrative machinery breaking down under the impact of the ever-mounting volume of State activity'.[2]

By a resolution of 23 July 1948 the Cabinet asked Ayyangar to proceed with the further examination of the question, which he did in consultation with the several Ministries and Secretaries to the Government. Before finalizing his Draft Report he took care specially to ascertain, in the course of a personal discussion on 13 April 1949, the views of the Deputy Prime Minister, Sardar Patel, on the various points he had dealt with in his Report. The Report was accordingly amended. Ayyangar's Special Secretary, however, discussed the outline with Patel's Private Secretary, V. Shankar, before it went to the

Cabinet for consideration in November. In its final form the Report made recommendations in respect of the various institutions of decision-making which the Cabinet accepted in several cases.

Council of Ministers

The Report recommended the retention of all the three existing categories of Ministers, namely Cabinet Ministers, Ministers of State and Deputy Ministers. But its emphasis was on the removal of doubt whether or not Ministers of State and Deputy Ministers should, technically speaking, be treated as members of the Council of Ministers. For, junior Ministers in the U.K. were, in the strict sense of the term, not Ministers, but holders of offices of profit that were specially exempted by statute from disqualification for a seat in Parliament. The Report did not import this comparison to the Indian situation, but suggested that Ministers of State and Deputy Ministers should be members of the Council of Ministers, not of the Cabinet. This position, it was pointed out, should be specifically made clear in the Rules of Business and formalities of appointment.

The distinction already existed in practice. Deputy Ministers, for example, were not in charge of Ministries, but attached to individual Cabinet Ministers to perform such functions as might be assigned to them. On the other hand, a Minister of State who was in charge of a Ministry, performed the same functions and exercised the same powers as a Minister of Cabinet rank, although he was not a member of the Cabinet and attended its meetings only when specifically invited to do so. He was distinguished even otherwise from a Deputy Minister in that he was invested with specific administrative responsibility.

These functional distinctions were, however, not precisely defined, nor was the number of Ministers regulated by fixed principles or broad criteria. The existing Council of Ministers had twenty Ministers, of whom fourteen were Ministers of Cabinet rank, four Ministers of State and two Deputy Ministers. Patel had expressed himself in favour of a small Council of Ministers, with the number of Cabinet Ministers limited to eleven.

But since any attempt to define rules to regulate the size of the Council of Ministers and their respective functions was viewed as interference with the exercise of political patronage, the Cabinet decided that the Prime Minister should have 'absolute discretion' regarding the number of Cabinet Ministers or of other Ministers he wished to appoint. It also rejected the proposal to define the functions

and responsibilities of Ministers to an extent that might restrict the
freedom of action of the Prime Minister.[3] The result was that the size
of the Council of Ministers increased from 16 in 1947 to 51 in 1967,
more than a three-fold rise in a span of twenty years. In its expanded
form the Council of Ministers included 15 Cabinet Ministers, 17
Ministers of State and 19 Deputy Ministers, in addition to 4
parliamentary secretaries.[4] Commenting on the swelling of this
number the Study Team of the Administrative Reforms Commission
thus observed: 'Much of this is explained by the expansion of governmental business; some by the need to provide training opportunities
to younger men; but a good bit can be ascribed to political compulsions', a device to mobilize support and prevent defection.[5]

The Study Team therefore stressed the desirability of a convention
being established about the broad dimensions of the Council of
Ministers. As part of an accepted convention it was suggested that the
grouping of subjects into Departments and of Departments into
Ministries should be done purely from considerations of administrative efficiency, not of political expediency. The grouping so done
should 'on no account' be disturbed and new Ministries carved out
'simply to provide for political contingencies'.[6] Another restriction
that the Study Team suggested was that, within an individual
Ministry, there should not ordinarily be more than two levels of
Ministers, not counting parliamentary secretaries. This suggestion
was made in view of the fact that certain Ministries had all three
categories of Ministers, a practice which led to considerable increase
in the size of the Council of Ministers.

The Prime Minister

Being the head of the Council of Ministers, and therefore of the
Cabinet, the Constitution authorized the Prime Minister to advise the
President about the appointment of Ministers and to act as a link
between him and the administration. As the leader of the political
executive the Prime Minister was expected to provide direction in
policy formulation to ensure administrative efficiency, and to establish liaison with the people and Parliament. In view of his primary
task of providing co-ordination and leadership, it was considered
inadvisable to put any portfolio under his specific charge or, if there
was one, it should be of a kind that did not detract from his primary
responsibilities. Even so, Nehru held charge of the Ministry of Commonwealth and External Affairs, besides being chairman of the Plan-

ning Commission, the Atomic Energy Commission and a host of other bodies. Institutional arrangements were nonetheless made as developing agencies or thinking cells to give direct assistance to the Prime Minister.

The Cabinet

In his Memorandum, Ayyangar described the functioning of the Cabinet during the first year of Independence. The picture he presented suggested an utter lack of co-ordination, although the co-ordination of policy and administration formed the most important function of the Cabinet and its chief, the Prime Minister. Speaking of the manner in which the principle of collective responsibility of the entire Cabinet operated in respect of major decisions and actions of the Government, the Memorandum observed: 'At present, a considerable number of these decisions and actions are taken by individual Ministers without reference to their colleagues. Some of them are submitted to the Cabinet for *ex post facto* approval; others are not subjected even to this formality.'[7] The existing practice thus ran counter to the principle of collective responsibility, which not merely meant that other Ministers should have information and knowledge of all such decisions and actions, but also implied that they should have the opportunity to participate in the making of those decisions.

This lack of co-ordination continued even much later. It came to light in the course of a personal discussion which the special secretary had on 12 November 1949 with V. Shankar, who revealed the mind of his boss. 'There must be rigid rules,' Shankar emphasized, 'regarding the time which should be allowed for circulation of papers before matters are taken in Cabinet. While matters may be mentioned without notice and exchange of information may take place, operative decisions should not be taken on matters introduced by way of verbal mention'.[8] This clearly shows that matters were discussed and decisions taken without their being duly processed at the secretariat level. In his discussion on the subject with Patel himself, Ayyangar was given the same impression. Both in fact agreed and regretted that 'quite often matters are considered at twelve or twenty-four hours notice. Sometimes matters are mentioned in the Cabinet and decisions taken without departmental examination of these matters. All this leads to sometimes wrong or incomplete decisions and leads to confusion and difficulties'. It was therefore suggested that rigid rules of business must be laid down, that the size of the Cabinet should be limited to not more than eleven and that it must meet 'frequently' and at regular intervals.[9]

Cabinet Committees

In view of the growth and complexity of public business, therefore, the Ayyangar Committee suggested that there should be a proper division of labour and effective delegation within the Cabinet. This proposed delegation was sought to be achieved by the establishment of Committees of Cabinet to perform such functions as were devolved on them by the Cabinet. This need was widely accepted in principle. It was also in line with the actual development that had been in progress. The Ayyangar Committee recognized the importance and position of Cabinet Committees, it also rationalized their organization and established on a permanent basis the system of delegation which had already been growing as a matter of necessity.

A distinction was however drawn between Standing Committees of the Cabinet, which were of a permanent nature, and *ad hoc* Committees which were to be appointed from time to time to meet temporary needs. It was emphasized that provision should be made for adequate secretariat and sub-committee organization to lend support to the Standing Committees which were to be guided by such procedures as were laid down in the rules of business. It was proposed that the Prime Minister should be *ex-officio* member and chairman of all the Standing Committees and that there should be a vice-chairman for each, a person who would normally preside over meetings in the absence of the Prime Minister.

The number of Standing Committees recommended was four, namely the Defence Committee,[10] the Economic Committee,[11] the Administrative Organization Committee and the Parliamentary and Legal Affairs Committee.[12] In 1950, the Cabinet approved the establishment of all four Standing Committees. An Appointments Committee,[13] however, came in place of the Administrative Organization Committee,[14] which was recognized as one of the *ad hoc* Committees in addition to the Rehabilitation Committee. The Appointments Committee consisted of the Prime Minister, the Home Minister and the Minister or Ministers concerned administratively.

The Cabinet Secretariat

Before the implementation of the Ayyangar Committee's recommendations the Cabinet Secretariat was no more than a mere office of record for the Cabinet as a whole, including also a military wing. The Economic Committee formed part of this Secretariat. It was to serve the purpose of the Economic Committee, and to fulfil its immediate task of regulating the national economy the need arose to strengthen the Cabinet Secretariat by means of a supporting organization consisting, for instance, of sub-committees of the Cabinet, the inter-Ministry Committee of Secretaries[15] and an adequate secretarial staff which might be described as the economic wing of the Cabinet Secretariat.

As head of the Cabinet Secretariat in its reorganized form, the duty of the Cabinet Secretary was to secure effective co-ordination and timely action by all Departments of the Government of India in all matters in which the Cabinet as a whole or the Prime Minister were interested. A civil servant of the highest rank selected for his ability, character, seniority and administrative experience, the Cabinet Secretary was expected to command the respect and confidence of all ranks of the permanent Services. It was recommended that he, as the first member of the public Services under the Central Government, should be *ex-officio* President of the Committee of Secretaries set up to advise the Prime Minister and his Appointments Committee on selections for administrative appointments. These recommendations relating to the reorganization of the Cabinet Secretariat were accepted in 1950 and action was taken accordingly.[16]

The Cabinet Secretariat served as a link between the political and the administrative processes, respectively representing the Cabinet on one hand and the Ministries and Departments on the other. On the political side, no recommended reform was accepted which tended in effect to reduce the power of the Prime Minister to use his discretion in the appointment of Ministers or to have the exercise of his authority subjected to fixed rules of business. The result was the expansion of political managers, not the reduction necessary for speed, economy and efficiency. On the administrative side, too, the machinery became geared to expansion. although for different reasons.

Ministries and Departments

A Ministry was identified with a Minister's charge, while a Department was identified with a Secretary's charge. This was accepted by the Cabinet as the basis of distinction between Ministries and Departments.

As recommended by the Ayyangar Committee, the Government of India accepted manageability and homogeneity as two broad principles for grouping subjects into Ministries and Departments. It was on these criteria that the number of Departments was sought to be increased from 21 to 28, subject to their responsibilities being examined in each individual case.

The Tottenham Report was quoted to justify the increase of Departments on the score of manageability. For, as the Report had said, 'the proper way to organize, if we were to ensure that the higher officers had time to think and were not overburdened with case work, would be to give each Secretary a manageable charge and recognize that this might result in having more Secretaries than members'. It was thus recognized that the function of the Secretary should be to 'think and plan ahead' and not to get 'immersed in files and burdened with routine'. The Cabinet sought to achieve this objective partly by increasing the number of Departments and therefore of Secretaries, and partly by separating from their office routine functions of a house-keeping nature.

The manageable charge of a Secretary was assumed to consist of three Deputy Secretaries, each incharge of one Secretariat Division which, in turn, was to include two Branches, each Branch consisting of an Under Secretary, two Section Officers[17] and 9 Assistants. This was considered an ideal basis for carrying out the reorganization of the internal structure of a Department. For, it was supposed to provide for a clear and uninterrupted line of command from above and a similar line of responsibility from below. The interposition of an officer called Joint or Additional Secretary in a Department was considered *prima facie* an unsatisfactory arrangement because the Secretary was not formally relieved of his general or *de jure* responsibility, although the appointment of Joint or Additional Secretary was intended to relieve him of a block of work and to deal directly with the Minister in respect of that work.

Even so, this interposition was recognized as unavoidable because the Economy Committee, as the following table shows,[18] had reported

Grade of Officer	No. in 1939	No. in 1948-9	No. recommended by the Economy Committee
Under/Asst. Secretary	41	227	187
Deputy Secretary	26	99	85
Additional & Joint Secretary	12	48	39
Secretary	12	20	20

in favour of retaining the positions of Additional Secretary and Joint Secretary.

Despite an increase in the number of Departments, the appointment of Joint Secretaries thus continued to be made, especially where the subjects handled by the Secretary and the Joint Secretary were not easily separable and susceptible of independent treatment. Even in such cases, however, the work assigned to the Joint Secretary was to be clearly localized in a distinct wing within the Department, a wing containing five Deputy Secretaries and five Secretariat Divisions as the upper limit of the manageable charge of a single Secretary. It was emphasized that maximum independence should be ensured as far as the functioning and responsibility of a Joint Secretary was concerned. In order to enable the Secretary to discharge his general responsibility, however, cases submitted by a Joint Secretary to the Minister were to be routed back through the Secretary.

The idea underlying the multiplication of Departments was to ensure both manageability and organizational homogeneity. But this, in turn, created problems of co-ordination which tended seriously to offset the advantages sought to be obtained by compact, manageable charges and a clear line of responsibility. The increase in the number of Secretaries, on the other hand, called for parallel hierarchies of inexperienced officers being pressed into the service of Departments, officers who could not discharge their responsibilities independently and without supervision or guidance. The expansion of the Departments was in fact allowed to proceed without the requisite strength of qualified and trained personnel. This increased the cost of administration but reduced its quality. Two separate grades of Secretaries had thus to be introduced, although all heads of departments continued to be designated Secretaries. Consistent with the recommendations of the first Central Pay Commission, provision was made for common rates of basic pay for Grade I as well as Grade II Secretaries and Joint Secretaries, irrespective of whether or not they were I.C.S. officers. In addition to their basic pay, I.C.S. officers could, however, be entitled to draw a compensatory personal pay, the full amount of which should be equal to the difference between the higher rates of pay admissible to the pre-1931 entrants and the new post-1931 entrants functioning under the existing rules. Generally, Grade II Secretaries were of the latter category.

As regards financial control, the Cabinet appreciated the need to improve the machinery and procedure governing financial sanctions and control of expenditure. As suggested by the Ayyangar Committee, it was agreed that (a) a specialized financial organization should be attached to each Department or group of Departments, invested with a wider measure of authority for according financial sanctions, and (b) that the desirability of introducing bulk control of expenditure as against itemized control should be further examined.

The Secretariat Reorganization Scheme of N. Gopalaswami Ayyangar thus provided for two levels of co-ordination, political and administrative: the first consisted of the higher policy-making level of the Cabinet, and the second was a Committee of Secretaries. The Cabinet Secretary and his Secretariat constitutes a bridge designed to connect the two levels.

As said before, the function of the Cabinet Secretary had till 15 August 1947 been limited to maintaining Cabinet records, a function comparable to that of the Secretary to the Executive Council in the old days. Towards the end of the Second World War, however, the Secretary to the Executive Council had also started functioning as 'Co-ordination Secretary', a post held by Sir Eric Coates, until co-ordination became impossible, thanks to Congress-League differences within the Government .

When the idea of an appointment similar to that of Sir Eric Coates was revived and Sir Raghavan Pillai was earmarked for the office of the Cabinet Secretary, he was sent on deputation to London to study the reorganization of the British Cabinet Secretariat. Sir Raghavan had the advantage of further discussion with Sir Norman Brook, the British Cabinet Secretary, who, at the instance of the Indian Prime Minister, visited New Delhi on his way back from Colombo to London.

As a senior civil servant Sir Raghavan automatically took over, in February 1950, as President of the Secretaries' Committee so far held by V.P. Menon, and brought under one roof the far-flung branches of the Cabinet Secretariat including its various sections, such as a defence wing, economic affairs, statistical work and the main office.

To ensure policy and planning co-ordination in the socio-economic field at ministerial and departmental levels, the establishment of four 'Bureaus' had also been recommended by Gopalaswami Ayyangar. The Cabinet, however, expressed doubts about the soundness of grouping social and economic services into separate bureaus exercising financial and administrative autonomy. It therefore did not approve the proposals. It was suggested that the existing system of informal contacts and discussions between Ministers for the purpose of policy co-ordination should continue. And the existing system did continue in spite of its failure to achieve the desired co-ordination in the fields of social and economic development. Another of Ayyangar's important recommendations met with a similar fate. He had emphasized that an Organization and Methods Division should be established in the Home Ministry, but the Cabinet set aside the proposal by an order to have it further examined.

The Ayyangar Committee was appointed to reorganize the machinery of Government so as to effect economy and to ensure co-ordination and efficiency for the purposes of socio-economic progress, but the Cabinet and the bureaucracy both stood against retrenchment, the former for political reasons and the latter for promotional reasons. The administration could not gear itself to meet the needs of development in terms of efficiency and economy. In the course of a reply to questions raised in Parliament in March 1950, the Finance Minister (Dr John Matthai) did some plain speaking by saying, 'When we joined the Government in 1946, we did so with the idea of honestly getting away as quickly as possible from the traditional form of Government we had inherited,but ... we have landed ourselves in a position which is not in the best interests of the kind of Government we are trying to have'.[19]

Commenting on the attitude of the bureaucracy towards reform, the *Free Press Journal* reinforced the feeling expressed by Dr Matthai. It regretted that 'many of the recommendations made by Mr Gopalaswami Ayyangar have not been accepted. The war years saw the expansion of the Central Secretariat on a scale that can only be described as monstrous. After the war came independence and expansion took another pace forward. Now the war is forgotten and it is time that the country settle down to normal work. But the Secretariat refuses to go back to its pre-war normality. It is a great victory for bureaucracy about which there will be jubilation in New Delhi. But it is a victory for which the country has to pay through its nose'.[20] The process of expansion did not cease. For instance, the gazetted officers of the Home Ministry itself increased from 41 in 1948 to 124 in 1955. The non-gazetted staff during the same period registered a rise from 243 to 920, excluding Class IV employees numbering 579 on 31 December 1955. The position of the administrative officers in the Secretariat of the Home Department showed likewise a comparable rise as indicated below:[21]

	In 1948	Proposed by the Economy Committee (1948)	On 31.12.1955
Secretary	1	1	2
Joint Secretary	1	1	5
Deputy Secretary	6	5	13
Under/Asst. Secretary	9	8	27

Minister–Secretary Relationship

Under the proposals of the Ayyangar Committee the Minister formed another level where the political and the administrative processes met and interacted. The manner in which the two sides interacted not only reflected their respective quality of character but also left their imprint on the quality of administration in general.

Speaking of the relations between a Minister and the Permanent Secretary of his Ministry, the Ayyanagar Committee pointed out that it would be a positive danger to responsible domocratic government if the Secretary put his Minister in the shade and made himself more important in the eyes of the public than his political boss. 'No less a danger is the Secretary', the Committee added, 'who says "yes" to everything that falls from the lips of the Minister. The ideal bureaucratic Secretary is the man who objectively presents the case both for and against a particular policy and leaves his Minister in no doubt as to which course he would himself advise on merits. He should at the same time give every help to his Minister to take the initiative and the responsibility for decisions which he would thereafter loyally carry out'. A Minister, on the other hand, was expected to encourage his Secretary to state his advice with independence and without fear even when he knew that the advice so given ran counter to the Minister's own view. This was an ideal relationship which, as the Committee suggested, should govern the conduct of Ministers and Secretaries. It was, however, regretted that the actual functioning of both 'leaves very much to be desired'.[22]

Far from showing improvement, the situation deteriorated with the lapse of time. The Administrative Reforms Commission, for instance, took notice of this deterioration when it said:

There is a disinclination among quite a number of ministers to welcome frank and impartial advice from the Secretary or his aides and an inclination to judge him by his willingness to do what they wish him to do. Instances are not wanting of ministers preferring a convenient subordinate to a strong one and thereby making the latter not only ineffective but a sulky and unwilling worker. This has also bred a tendency on the part of an increasing number of civil servants to attempt to anticipate the minister's wishes and proffer their advice accordingly. A further development of this unhealty trend is the emergence of personal affiliations leading to an element of politicalization among the civil servants. All these cut at the root of the healthy relationship.[23]

This post-Independence development was something unknown to the pre-Independence administration when advice was frankly sought and given. A. D. Gorwala makes it clear by saying:

It was a great merit of government in this period and of government under the same Constitution even later that it neither punished frank expression of opinion from its officers nor even resented it. When, for instance, a Commissioner had, after expressing his views in writing about the transfer of a particular officer seconded for a time to another department, discussed the matter with the Governor and obtained his consent and the file had been passed down through the Secretary to the other Secretary concerned, it did not arouse resentment when the other Secretary resubmitted the file asking for further consideration and in noting said that it seemed to him that in not allowing this transfer which he had originally mooted, every interest had been considered except the public interest. Again it was quite possible for a Governor to say smiling to a Secretary who had elaborated greatly on the immorality of a course of conduct proposed to the Governor by even higher authorities than himself, 'I have read with interest your convocation address. I will pass it on. It should have its effect.' So too an adviser who had set his mind firmly upon a particular course of action would still ask for his subordinate's view, or if he did not ask, would be prepared to consider views put to him.[24]

There was yet another change that occurred. In the pre-Independence period the Government itself was a bureaucracy. Intellectually, socially and culturally, there was practically no gap between a Member of Government and a permanent civil servant. The relationship between the two was governed by rules of decorum and good manners. There was no subservience, no lack of frankness in advice. There was no reason for a senior civil servant to feel any sense of inferiority before his political chief. And though the Member of Council had the over-riding authority to make a decision, there was no question of the parmanent official being inferior to him. In fact, the latter could himself look forward to joining the Council in due course. No such thing could happen when, apart from being Indian, the political authority became separate and distinct from the bureaucracy.

The pattern of relationship between a Minister and his Secretary became in addition subject to unusual strains for historical reasons. At the time of Partition senior civil servants were I.C.S. officers who had previously formed part of the so-called 'steel frame' of British rule. Many had even carried out instructions for the suppression of the Independence movement. The Ministers who came to power after Independence had, on the other hand, the halo attaching to men who had undergone suffering in the national cause. The men at the very top, like Jawaharlal Nehru, Vallabhbhai Patel and Rajendra Prasad, had a stature which lifted them head and shoulders above everybody else. No civilian could fail to recognize their superior status in terms of both ability and character. The halo they carried with them in addition to the political authority they came to wield created a psychological gap between them and their senior civil servants. However, the set of permanent officials who proceeded to reconstruct the administration to meet the new challenges of security as well as socio-economic development had the advantage of a great fund of administrative experience and specialized knowledge, which even top leaders could ill afford to ignore. This, and the formation of a national government of talents under the stewardship of Jawaharlal Nehru, restored normalcy and brought together the political and administrative processes to interact during 1946-56 in a manner which conduced to political stability and administrative progress. The top political leaders lost no time in establishing the most harmonious relations with those who had previously been part and parcel of the British regime. But while this was true of the leaders at the top, it was not true all down the line, particularly in the States where a pattern started developing which did not augur well for the establishment of sound and stable conventions

With the passage of time the quality of Ministers did not improve, but generally declined. They happened to be men not merely without administrative experience but also without the romantic halo of political suffering. The only basis of obedience to the orders of such Ministers was their legal authority to decide, an authority not reinforced in most cases by morality or charactter. Unlike the 'old guard' who, besides being genuine patriots, were as well-educated as the Civilians themselves, the new generation of Ministers, especially in the States, were in several cases only half educated and not even bound by any fixed code of conduct. The system of appointing three grades of Ministers was of course intended to make opportunity available for the acquiring of experience. But as politics is a mutable game of uncertainty, no Minister could be sure to run his full course and finally claim to become a Cabinet Minister on the strength of the experience so acquired. This was particularly true in a society not organized on merit or competition, but divided into numerous groups on religious, regional and caste considerations. The purely structural devices of classifying Ministers into grades therefore did not prove to be of much avail.

The bureaucracy, on the other hand, remained a competitive organization, bound by rules governing recruitment and disciplinary conditions. The standard of recruitment for the All-India and Central Services was no doubt affected a little by communal representation and a certain decline in the average quality of higher education in the post-Independence period. But since personnel administration and conditions of promotion and punishment remained subject to control by the Union Public Service Commission, the higher echelons of these Services generally endeavoured to keep the traditions they had inherited from the past. They did the noting and drafting for the Ministers, who unlike their counterparts on the former Viceregal Council, generally lacked the analytical capacity necessary for national decision-making.

This decline in the standard of ministerial efficiency either encouraged functional perversion through bureaucratic overtones in policy direction, or even led to an abuse of bureaucratic initiative in subserving the interest of an individual or a group. What suffered in either case was the democratic principle of ministerial responsibility to the legislature.

An interesting case of bureaucratic initiative and ministerial lapse occurred in 1957, with H. M. Patel of the I.C.S. functioning as Principal Finance Secretary to the Government of India, and T.T. Krishnamachari, his Finance Minister. It arose from the purchase of shares of certain private companies by the Life Insurance Corporation of India at the cost of more than a crore of rupees in order to salvage the credit of Haridas Mundhra, 'a financial adventurer'[25] of doubtful integrity, who controlled these companies.

Life insurance had earlier been nationalized and the Life Insurance Corporation was set up under an Act of Parliament on 1 September 1956. It was a step in the direction of what was deemed to be a more effective mobilization of the people's savings to promote economic development, more especially to give material assistance in the implementation of the Second Five-Year Plan. As the funds of the Corporation represented the savings of millions of hard-working people in the country, there was a special obligation cast upon those who administered those funds to manage them in the best interest of the policy-holders and the interest of the development envisaged in the Second and the subsequent Plans. It was to achieve this two-fold object that provision was made for an Investment Committee whose function it was to indicate in a broad manner what type of investment the Corporation should avoid and which particular types of investment it should view with favour.

Though autonomous, the Corporation was headed by H. M. Patel as Chairman from 1 September 1956 to 5 June 1957. He was succeeded by Kamat, also of the I.C.S., who had earlier been its Deputy Chairman. As the senior officer, Patel, however, continued to advise Kamat and carried on negotiations with Mundhra till the deal was hurriedly settled and signed in a matter of days on 24 June 1957. T.T. Krishnamachari was present in Bombay at the time. No care was taken to consult the Investment Committee and the evidence produced later before the Chagla Commission of Inquiry showed that there was a 'tendency on the part of the Finance Ministry to look upon the Corporation as a wing or branch of that Ministry'.[26] Kamat was said to be merely guided by Patel. But, as the report of the Inquiry showed, 'what technically took the shape of advice was in reality an order issued by Government and that is how it was looked upon by the officials of the Corporation'.[27]

A perusal of the evidence produced before the Chagla Commission leaves hardly any doubt that it was the principal Finance Secretary who, when approached by Mundhra, started taking an interest in promoting the deal. The Minister did not figure to an extent consistent with his responsibility. He held that the Secretary only 'casually' mentioned to him the transactions that were being carried on with Mundhra. The Secretary, on the contrary, maintained that he had been acting all along with the knowledge and approval of the Minister. The findings of the Commission, however, made it clear that independently of whether or not the Minister was aware of what Patel had done on June 1957, the fact remained that when he did come to know of these transactions, he never repudiated the action Patel had already taken.[28] There was in fact acquiescence on the part of the

Minister in the role played by Patel in bringing about the transactions. The lack of repudiation on his part thus lent support to Patel's contention that the purchase of shares at the rates quoted by Mundhra had been done with the approval of the Minister himself.

In the Lok Sabha debate which took place on 16 December 1957, T.T. Krishnamachari pleaded guilty to having asked the Life Insurance Corporation to carry out the policy of blue-chips. But he made it clear that, apart from that policy, he had not imposed any other on the Corporation. The point he made was that, if the Corporation was under Patel's advice buying the shares of the companies controlled by Mundhra in pursuance of some other policy, it would be the responsibility of the officials of the Corporation, not the result of any direction given by the Government.[29]

The Chagla Commission, however, held that constitutionally the Minister was responsible for the action taken by his Secretary with regard to the Mundhra deal. He could not shelter behind his subordinates, nor could he disown their actions. It is true that this doctrine of ministerial responsibility threw a very great burden on the Minister. But it was assumed that once the policy was laid down by the Minister, his subordinates must reflect that policy and carry it out loyally and faithfully. They rendered themselves subject to punishment in the event of failure to do so, but it was the Minister who must be held responsible for the action of his subordinates. In this case, Patel admittedly acting as the Principal Secretary of the Minister, could not be fastened with the responsibility of having effected this transaction in his Secretariat capacity. The person who was thus obliged to resign[30] and go was T. T. Krishnamachari, the Minister, who, though able and astute, was found wanting in his knowledge of details.

The question of the Minister–Secretary relationship emerged significantly again in November 1966 when Gulzari Lal Nanda, then Home Minister, made complaints against his Secretary, L.P. Singh, of the I.C.S. The occasion for trouble was the question of banning anti-cow-killing processions within a two-mile radius of Parliament House. In a meeting called by the Minister on 6 November, the Home Secretary as well as the Lieutenant-Governor and the Deputy Commissioner of Delhi expressed themselves in favour of the ban. But the Minister declined to accept their advice and gave permission for the procession to move as scheduled on 7 November. The Delhi administration was asked to make the necessary arrangements to ensure the preservation of law and order. When violence broke out despite the arrangements, the police had to open fire, which resulted in some casualties. The Minister tried to defend himself by holding his Secretary responsible for what had happened. But since the permission for the procession had proceeded from Nanda himself, it was the Minister who had to resign and go, not his Secretary.

In a letter to the Prime Minister, Nanda complained of 'unreciprocated confidence' at the political level and inadequate assistance at the secretarial. 'Devoid of adequate political support at the level of my Ministry', he said, 'and denied the kind of assistance and co-operation I needed from a civil service set-up not in tune with my ideas, I was made to feel that I had no say in the making of decisions at policy-making level.'[31] His letter of complaint shows that he wanted a Secretary of his own choice. But he himself had earlier signified his approval by affixing his signature to the appointment of L. P. Singh. The other person who was among the first to sign the paper of appointment was Lal Bahadur Shastri, the then Prime Minister. What Nanda wished was to change his own earlier decision and to have another Secretary whom he might consider to be 'in tune with [his own] ideas', not with the general policy of the Government who, in this particular cases also, did not want processions to come within a two-mile radius of Parliament House. Obviously, the Minister was guided by his personal predilections and not by the impersonality of public administration which demands some degree of cultural and intellectual sophistication.

There occurred in 1969 yet another case where a central Deputy Minister felt hurt by the remarks of the Law Secretary who did not see eye to eye with him on certain procedural matters. In a discussion the Secretary even raised his voice to emphasize his point against the Deputy Minister, who then threatened to resign. In the Parliamentary debates that followed the Minister in charge of the Ministry concerned made a statement informing the House of an amicable settlement of the difference which had led his Deputy Minister to take umbrage at the remarks of the Secretary.[32] Little did the Deputy Minister realize that he had no formal authority and status to assert himself against a Secretary to the Government.

A more recent case occurred in October 1971, when K. Hanumanthaiya, then Railway Minister, and Bankim Chandra Ganguli, Chairman of the Railway Board, who enjoyed the rank of a Principal Secretary to the Government of India, clashed. Since the former had differences with the latter on a number of issues, he passed several orders which in effect changed the assignments of the Chairman of the Railway Board even without his knowledge. On 8 October 1971 the Minister went to the extent of cancelling a tour programme of Ganguli by ordering that the carriage which he had already boarded be detached from the train scheduled to leave in a few minutes. The carriage was detached but Ganguli decided to stay in it and did not move out till the Government terminated his services on 12 October. He left in a state of humiliation, but the Minister too had to be sacked in due course of time.

It must, however, be recognized that even the most dynamic and competent of Ministers has understandable limitations which restrict the sphere of direct participation in all the intricate and detailed aspects of administration. These include the complexities of a modern government, the possibility of frequent changes in the ministerial field, the frequency of visits to constituencies, parliamentary preoccupations and, above all, the technical nature of the various decisions that have to be made without a thorough knowledge of connected papers contained in original files. The Minister's dependence on his Secretary necessarily increases in a democratic set-up. And although his leadership in the entire sphere of administration is in theory recognized as all pervasive, the scope of his actual operation does not go much beyond a clear understanding and direction of policy matters, and not a knowledge of details. Thus the Maxwell Committee in 1937 laid down a principle calculated to ensure administrative efficiency within the framework of ministerial responsibility. The Committee emphasized that as collective ministerial responsibility maintained the political unity of government, so should the unity of administrative control of each Department be ensured by concentrating the responsibility to advise the Minister in one official, namely the Secretary.[33] This right of the Secretary to advise without fear or favour was later recognized in the post-Independence period also. Constitutional guarantees for that purpose were provided to protect civil servants.

The Report of the Study Team on Personnel Administration (1967), however, pointed out that there had been 'a recognizable fall in service standards for which full responsibility must be accepted by the heads of the administration'. The political executive was partly to blame for shortcomings. But the Services also had their own share of the blame. For, there could be no 'excuse for the failure on the part of a civil servant to offer frank advice on the ground that it may not be liked or appreciated'. In fact, the Study Team found 'no valid explanation for failure to exercise supervision, for the various instances of administrative slackness and for the tacit acceptance of the present state of the administrative machinery by a fraternity who had seen it in a better form in the past'.[34]

Speaking from experience at a conference organized in March 1968 by the Indian Institute of Public Administration, New Delhi, an eminent civil servant of his time like C.D. Deshmukh shared the view earlier expressed by the Study Team. While recognizing that 'with the illiterate and uninformed electorate' one must expect 'a certain kind of lack of support, failure and shortcomings on the part of those who are called upon after election to occupy and sometimes to fill posts of political decision-making', the fact remained that there was 'a very large area of administration where the Minister is neutral and many a Minister I find is mentally prepared to be guided by a good Secretary. Really he is almost too dependent on a good Secretary and, therefore, I think that Secretaries must accept the onus of responsibility for the deteriorating state of administration in this country'.[35]

The functioning of the democratic process in the Indian situation, could not, however, restore the efficiency of administration to its pre-Independence standards. The impersonality of public administration could not be ensured by a political authority which lent itself to the contaminating influences of caste and regional loyalty. A tendency naturally grew to look not to one's immediate superior for redress of grievances or for promotion but to approach the Minister direct over the heads of bureaucrats. This brought about a situation where administrative authority was eroded beyond repair.

The change in the political complexion of the Government was reflected in the decline of bureaucratic capacity for resistance. Apart from the erosion of its authority, the reduction of its ability to fight slackness proceeded from a 'progressive deterioration' in the standard of university education, which affected the erstwhile intellectual and moral qualities of recruits. The *Third Report of the Union Public Service Commission*, for instance, made it clear that, apart from 'the unevenness in the standards of the degrees of Indian Universities' the experience of the examinations year after year indicated 'that even now the number of candidates seeking to compete for these examinations is out of proportion to the total number of vacancies. Quite a large percentage of candidates appear for these examinations who really have not the educational equipment and mental calibre for success at them. The Commission's examiners have complained, in particular, that it is a great waste of time and labour to have to wade through such a large number of answer books of inferior quality'.[36] And yet no attempt was made to screen candidates to reduce their number; for it involved the fear of a loss of 'public confidence', a political consideration. As the following table shows, the number of applicants for recruitment by written examination went on increasing, thus making it more and more difficult to find able and competent examiners to assess the scripts:

Recruitment by written test

Year	No of examinations held	No of applicants	No. of candidates interviewed
1938	10	2,552	..
1943	10	2,931	..
1945	14	3,282	..
1946	12	1,629	..
1947	17	16,813	654
1950	24	19,983	1,252
1954	30	28,900	1,173
1955	30	41,662	1,191
1956	30	65,187	1,911

This enormous increase in the number of applicants admitted to examination or interview were both responsible for a steady decline in the quality of recruitment. And so was the number of promotions which went on increasing, from 209 in 1938 to 1,776 in 1956.[37] In one of its Reports the Commission of course pointed out that it selected the best available material for the services every year. But considering the fact that private industries and business offered higher scales of pay and better prospects, 'quite a number of gifted young people who can afford to take a little time over finding a career are not being attracted to these services'.[38] In fact, the number of first-class candidates entering the civil services showed in the post-Independence period a definite downward trend. And since not all the old guard were adequately equipped intellectually and morally, such of the Secretaries as rose to that office merely by virtue of seniority or sufferance, could not offer resistance to the growing administrative malaise. They generally chose a line of least resistance and gave the kind of advice the Minister wanted.

There remained, however, an element of dichotomy underlying the relationship between the political executive and his Secretary. While experience of the recent past suggested the need of policy formulation being left to the former and its implementation to the latter, considerations of sharing in the exercise of power and patronage made it difficult to lay down any hard and fast rule governing that relationship. Things continued to depend on the personal equation of the two sides, especially because it was difficult to determine where policy ended and execution began.

Expansion of Personnel

As already noted, one of the most important features of personnel administration in the post-Independence period has been the expansion of personnel to an extent not related to function or justified by its output of work.[39] The Report of the Study Team on Personnel Administration did not hesitate to comment in 1967 'that at least some of the growth in the last two decades has been unwarranted; the most important reason for this appears to have been the accretion of unnecessary and unimportant functions, duplication and centralization'.[40] It proceeded from a mistaken idea of the dominant role of the Central Government in the administration of the country.

Leaving aside the State Governments, the expansion of the Central Secretariat itself was phenomenal at all levels. There were in 1939, for instance, only 17 Secretaries, Additional Secretaries and Joint Secretaries in the Government of India. In 1966, this number rose to 196, an increase of more than eleven times. As against 12 Deputy Secretaries in 1939, there were, on the other hand, 242 in 1966, an increase of twenty times. Similarly, the number of Under Secretaries and Assistant Secretaries increased during the same period from 20 to 448, a twenty-one fold rise. 'We are unable to convince ourselves', the Study Team pointed out, 'that this increase in personnel has been entirely or even largely due to increase in functions or in the quantum of work. Whereas twenty Under Secretaries could support the entire Central Government in 1939, even small offices require more than this number now'. The State Secretaries too did not lag behind. Their expenditure tripled during 1950-62, in a period of only twelve years.[41] The overall picture of Central Government employees showed a similar rise in numbers, increasing from 17.92 lakhs in 1956 to 30.559 lakhs in

1972, including both regular and non-regular employees in both cases.[42]

The sudden and continued expansion of personnel on an *ad hoc* basis resulted in the dilution of quality which, in turn, provided ground for upward movement in the levels of responsibility. This led to increased pressure at higher levels, for men of inferior calibre promoted to higher ranks were found unequal to the load of business their responsibility involved. More men were consequently required at those levels, a development which created a vicious circle leading to continued fall in quality. The Study Team could not but admit that, besides affecting quality, this expansion 'has also created an atmosphere of high expectations in Government; in almost all Services promotion is now expected as a matter of course', a kind of 'vested right', leading to the creation of pressure groups for the expansion of promotion opportunities by upgrading posts regardless of whether or not there was need to do so.[43] This attitude of individuals or groups found 'support even at the highest political levels'.[44]

The expansion of personnel was effected more in the higher positions of the Central Secretariat than at the lower levels. From 1939 to about 1960, for instance, the highest rate of growth was at the level of Under Secretaries, and the lowest at the level of Secretaries, Additional Secretaries and Joint Secretaries. This trend was, however, reversed after that. The administration tended to become increasingly top heavy. During 1961-5, for example, the number of Secretaries and Special Secretaries increased by 33 per cent. A similar pattern was emerging in the lower group of posts, from Section Officers to Lower Division Clerks.[45]

A relatively greater expansion of personnel in the higher positions was a feature of post-Independence development in the Central Government as a whole. During 1950-65, for instance, the ratio of gazetted employees to non-gazetted increased from 1:106 to 1:60. The rate of growth of gazetted employees was nearly three times that of the non-gazetted.[46] As the table on page 178 shows, this trend continued even later.[47]

In the Secretariat, the ratio of gazetted employees to non-gazetted, however, improved from 1:6.9 in 1960 to 1:6.2 in 1965, and in the Attached and Subordinate offices from 1:79.5 to 1:65.3.[48] An analysis of the number of employees in the four classess during 1960-5 pointed in the same direction. The number of Class I employees increased by 94 per cent during this period, that of Class II by 28 per cent, and

Year	No. of gazetted employees	No. of non-gazetted employees	Ratio of gazetted to non-gazetted employees
1966	42,184	24,70,527	1:58.5
1969	49,821	25,58,962	1:51.3
1972	56,470	26,94,843	1:47.7

Class III by 30 per cent.[49] Obviously, this reflected middle-class orientation in the employment policy of the Government and was unrelated to its declared policy of building a socialistic society.

The increasing functions of the Government and diversification of its activities led to the proliferation of new organizations which, in turn, created a demand for the appointment of new personnel. Each such organizational unit, especially those operating in the newer fields, convinced itself of its own importance and developed a defence mechanism not only to justify its own existence but also to prepare a case for bigger and better staff. *The Report of the Study Team on Personnel Administration* in fact pointed out that 'once a post or a scheme passes the hurdle of Finance, it continues without any fear of disturbance and the organization or the individual can lead a comfortable life without being accountable for showing concrete results or even without continuing to perform any useful function'.[50]

The multiplication of organizations and their strengthening which resulted in much avoidable duplication, meant, in addition, upgrading positions and recruiting persons with higher qualification. This was a development which, in turn, led to what became known as an officer-oriented administration, partially proceeding from the democratic process itself where the political executive became increasingly involved in directly disposing of cases formerly dealt with at lower levels of the administrative hierarchy. The expansion of personnel in fact made co-ordination difficult and reduced the level of efficiency to a point which cried aloud for change.

Remedial Measures

The remedial measures which the Government of India adopted were mainly designed to achieve two objects: improvement in the standard of efficiency and control over the size of personnel. The first became the charge of an O & M Division, and the second of a Special

Reorganization unit whose functions were in 1964 taken over partly by the Staff Inspection Unit and partly by the Department of Administrative Reforms.

O & M Division—The need for a permanent organization to pay continuous attention to the improvement of administrative efficiency was keenly felt during the post-War years. In 1947, a Committee was set up with A.D. Gorwala as chairman to investigate the methods of recruitment and intensive training for future administrators. This Committee recommended the establishment of a Directorate of Methods, Organization and Training as an organ for improving the competence of young administrators.[51] The Government accepted in principle the need to establish a Reorganization Unit and set up one in 1948 in the Transport Ministry and placed it in charge of N. Gopalaswami Ayyangar. In his *Report on the Reorganization of the Machinery of Government* (1949) Ayyangar actually recommended the creation of an O & M Division as part of the Ministry of Home Affairs. The Economy Committee appointed by the Government of India in 1948 had also likewise recommended the establishment of a 'separate organization to exercise strict control over the procedures and personnel of all Ministries' in order to find out 'whether officers at all levels were fully discharging the functions expected of them and to suggest improvements in the organization and methods of work'.

In 1952, when the First Five-Year Plan was published, the problem of reconstructing the administration for development purposes came up for review. The Planning Commission emphasized the importance of methods as an instrument of economy and efficiency, especially in a situation where the traditional mode of transacting public business on a small scale could not cope with an unprecedented increase in the range and scope of new responsibilities involved in the execution of developmental tasks. It therefore recommended that the Central Government should have an O & M Division which might work in close co-operation with the personnel sections of the different ministries.[52] Among the tasks proposed to be assigned to this division, the Commission suggested the inclusion of such problems as simplifying office procedures, eliminating delays, record keeping in the Central Ministries, the movement of files, and an efficiency audit in organizations of different kinds. The Commission also suggested other fields of study for the projected division. These included, for instance, interdepartmental conferences, delegation of responsibilities to different grades of officials. relations between planning units and general administration, working conditions of the lower-grade employees, and the organization of a messenger service in place of the existing methods for the employment and use of peons in government offices.[53] The functional coverage which the Planning Commission thus recommended for a Central O & M Division was wide and intensive.

Subsequently in 1953, Dean Paul H. Appleby made a general survey of public administration in India. He, like the Planning Commission, emphasized the need for the 'establishment of a Central office charged with the responsibility for giving both extensive and intensive leadership in respect of structures, management and procedures'. Soon after Appleby's recommendation, the O & M Division came into existence in March 1954. It was located in the Cabinet Secretariat to have the benefit of the Prime Minister's authority, influence and co-operation. The organization was naturally conceived at the beginning as a collective and co-operative enterprise in which the main effort at improvement was to proceed from the O & M Cells in the ministries functioning under the leadership of the Central O & M Division.[54] In practice, however, the Central Division was headed initially by a part-time Director who functioned as the Establishment Officer and Joint Secretary in the Ministry of Home Affairs. The real strength of the organization, however, flowed from the O & M Cell in each ministry under its own officer, a Deputy Secretary who had other duties to perform.

Though designed originally to provide through a long-term programme of action an overall leadership in organizational and procedural matters, the O & M Division could not achieve the object of its institution. Its activity remained generally confined to certain measures of control, such as supervisory checks, compilation of statistical data regarding the disposal of work, and reporting follow-up action on decisions taken at O & M meetings from time to time. The individual departments kept under review their own performance, their own modes of business to promote speed, economy and efficiency in the disposal of their work. All that the Central O & M Division could do was to provide a specialized service by studying problems of common interest, or by conducting analytical studies, investigations and comprehensive reviews. Departmentalism indeed stood in the way of an effective central controlling agency. And since each department had yet to build up its own 'Efficiency (O & M) Unit', the internal O & M work continued to be discharged by relatively junior officers.[55] A detailed study of structures, management and procedures remained unattempted.

Organizationally, however, the failure of the O & M Division proceeded especially from a lack of job specification, which caused functional duplication. There were, for instance, two other organizations engaged on the performance of similar tasks—the Special Reorganization Unit of the Finance Ministry and the Committee on Plan Projects in the Planning Commission. There emerged later a third organization, called the Central Economy Board, intended to co-ordinate the activities of the Economy Committees set up in June 1957 in all ministries and departments to maintain efficiency, integrity and economy. In practice, therefore, the O & M Division remained preoccupied with such routine work as looking into the *Mannual of Office Procedure*, periodical reporting and review of progress, providing training for the lower grades of staff, and dealing with control charts, level jumping, monthly lists of pending cases and weekly arrears statements.[56]

Special Reorganization Unit

The Special Reorganization Unit of the Ministry of Finance was constituted in 1952 to review the staff requirements of ministries and their attached and subordinate offices and to recommend such further changes as might be considered necessary to secure efficiency and economy.[57] It was reorganized in 1956 to carry out 'work studies' with a view to evolving staffing standards. In doing so, it had to conduct method studies for the purpose of work measurement. It was for a time given *ad hoc* assignments of organizations asking for additional staff. But since January 1960 it has acted on a three-year programme of work studies covering the entire Central Secretariat and its important offices.

The main objects of these work studies were: 1. Simplification of methods intended to eliminate inessential work to impart speed in the transaction of business; 2. Work measurement on a rational basis to relate the staffing needs of organizations to workloads; and 3. Organizational analysis designed to relate changes in methods to new organizational needs.

An important responsibility of the Special Reorganization Unit was to maintain a research bureau to study the growth of expenditure and to see how far this was related to the growth of responsibility of organizations. The O & M Division was to be directly associated with the studies and investigations undertaken by the Unit. However, these studies were by and large time-consuming and it was often difficult to secure an acceptance of the recommendations the Unit made. For, it lacked sanction and the balance of convenience lay with the organization it studied. It was thus decided in 1963 that the Ministry of Finance should develop a staff inspection service to conduct quick reviews of the work of the ministries. The Staff Inspection Unit was accordingly set up in April 1964 by renaming the Special Reorganization Unit. The new Unit was invested with such functions as the review of staff requirements through inspection and *ad hoc* studies, the development of standard norms of performance, and the grading of jobs. Such other functions as organizational analysis, method study and work measurement were assigned to a separate department in the Home Ministry. This was known as the Department of Administrative Reforms and was set up in 1964.

Committee on Plan Projects

The Committee on Plan Projects was set up by the National Development Council in September 1956. The object of the Committee was to conduct field inspection; to evolve, by means of studies, suitable organization and methods to achieve economy and efficiency; to make the results of studies generally available, and to undertake such other tasks as the Development Council might from time to time propose to promote the efficient execution of projects.

The Committee was invested with the conduct of work studies as a means to rationalize loads with staffing standards, although this was a charge already assigned to the Special Reorganization Unit. The reason for duplication was that the Secretary of the National Productivity Council, who had made a study in his own field, suggested the expediency of the Commitee also being obliged to devote 'a considerable proportion of its manpower resources to conduct work study courses', so that public sector enterprises should be able to take advantage of it at both Central and State levels.[58] The declared objectives of the studies of the Committee were the efficiency of programming techniques; roadblocks to the progress of projects according to targets; efficiency of cost estimates through standard norms developed in repetitive projects; determination of the relationship between costs and benefits, and sufficiency of the programmes.

The teams associated with work studies doubtless exposed the project staff to new ideas in technical and managerial practice. But the extent to which these studies contributed to economy was a different matter. For, as one of the reports of the O & M Division pointed out, there was 'room even in the best run projects for economy in actual expenditure. It is not the systematic and intensive analysis of the existing methods in the form of work studies that could produce the desired result'. The report admitted that this could not be done except when the personnel placed in charge of studies had the requisite 'competence, length of experience and ability to understand the practical import of the problems' involving 'varied kinds of technological disciplines' and 'the diversified nature of the Plan.'[59] This was a condition for success which, in the absence of collaboration between governmental and scholarly circles in the Indian situation, existed more in exception than as a general rule. Even so, care was taken in the formation of study teams to associate members of Parliament and state legislatures as well as members of such independent professions as consulting engineers, agricultural specialists, chartered and cost accountants, and so on. Such concepts and operational ideas as the Line of Balance Technology, the use of work studies and the efficiency of space utilization were of special benefit to private industries.

Central Economy Board

The Central Economy Board set up in June 1957 consisted of the Principal Finance Secretary, Home Secretary, Secretary (Expenditure), and the Director, O & M Division. Its business was to scrutinize, through the internal Economy Committees of ministries and departments, the existing and projected activities of the Government to see whether any could be reduced, postponed or abandoned. It was also intended to assist individual ministries to effect economy and to guide and supervise the work of the Special Reorganization Unit of the Ministry of Finance.

None of these organizations, however, seemed to have fulfilled the purpose of their institution. Following a debate on the Fourth Report of the O & M Division in the Lok Sabha, the Director of the Division attempted in a study in 1959 to estimate the work done by it in the course of the previous six years. His report was considered by the Central Economy Board who invited a number of Secretaries of other ministries to participate in the discussions. An attempt was consequently made to remove duplication. As the O & M Division and the Special Reorganization Unit covered practically the same ground on various aspects of administration, it was decided in 1960 as a temporary expedient that both should be placed under the same officer to obviate duplication or the possibility of divergent advice being offered on identical functions. And since the officer concerned was also to be the Secretary, Committee of Plan Projects, the arrangement so made provided unified direction to administrative improvement and cost reduction, which were inter-related.[60]

The unified control of direction was soon followed by another arrangement, said to be intended to secure the execution of development plans. Both the Planning Commission and the O & M Division came forward with suggestions for what they called strengthening of the administration. While the Planning Commission prepared a paper on 'measures for strengthening administration and improving implementation', the O & M Division produced a paper on 'Administrative Capacity'. On the basis of these papers the Prime Minister made a statement, which was laid before the Lok Sabha on 10 August 1961 and the Rajya Sabha on 24 August 1961,[61] in which he pointed out that, although measures for the improvement of administraion had continuously been under consideration, a special review of the existing position became necessary in view of the difficulties and poor performance of the Second Plan and the projected needs of the Third Five-Year Plan. Indeed, the special recruitment of 1956 and a series a procedural changes in the technique of administration had all proceded since then from a concern to impart success to planned development.

The Prime Minister's statement laid down certain principal objectives underlying the new plan for administrative improvement. These objectives emphasized job specification and assessment by results; an extended measure of financial decentralization; a substantial increase in the responsibility and executive authority of the head of the department concerned with the implementation of programmes; a programme of executive development to improve the managerial skill of public servants by training and counselling; simplification of procedures through work studies; and a series of programmes to improve relations with the public, especially by changing the 'authority-complex' of public servants.

In the light of the suggestions made by the Planning Commission, the Prime Minister made in his statement a number of concrete proposals to give effect to those principal objectives. The operative part of the proposals lay in the creation of a high powered Committee on Administration consisting of the higher ranks of the public services whom the Commission considered bound by obligation to assist the Government in providing direction and guidance in the excution of the Third Five-Year Plan. The Committee was not intended to take over any of the functions allotted under the Rules of Business to any of the ministries or departments of the government. While responsibility for administrative improvement continued to rest with individual ministries themselves, the Committee was to supplement the existing arrangements by providing a standing machinery for locating administrative defects, facilitating decisions for their removal and speeding action on the decisions taken. The Committee was for this purpose to conduct studies in specific problems and initiate proposals for improvement in consultation with the ministries and departments concerned. Its specific responsibility, however, was to watch and assist in the implementation of decisions which might be taken by the Government from time to time to raise standards of efficiency. In place of the Central Economy Board, which was abolished, the Committee on Administration was required to resolve, when necessary, points of difference between the administrative ministries and the Special Reorganization Unit in respect of work studies carried out by the latter.[62] It was to submit periodic reports to the Cabinet.

The high-powered Committee formed in pursuance of the Prime Minister's statement consisted of the following:[63]

CHAIRMAN

1. Vishnu Sahay, I.C.S., Cabinet Secretary

MEMBERS

2. B. N. Jha, I.C.S., Secretary, Ministry of Home Affairs
3. S. S. Khera, I.C.S., Secretary, Mines & Fuel Department
4. S. Bhoothalingam, I.C.S., Secretary, Department of Expenditure, Ministry of Finance
5. S. Ranganathan I.C.S., Secretary, Ministry of Commerce and Industry
6. L. P. Singh, I.C.S., Secretary, Ministry of Commerce and Home Affairs
7. Tarlok Singh, Additional Secretary, Planning Commission

MEMBER-SECRETARY

8. Indrajit Singh, Director, O & M Division, Cabinet Secretariat, which provided secretariat assistance to the Committee.

By March 1964 the Committee had held seventeen meetings and submitted three reports to the Cabinet. But reporting did not mean improving administration. The Prime Minister, the Planning Commission and the O & M Division had all laid stress on integrity and courtesy when recommending the establishment of the Committee. But far from the situation being improved, it was officially admitted after a couple of years by G. L. Nanda, the Home Minister, that 'bribery and corruption in public services had lately increased and infiltrated even into those rungs of administraton where they were not prevalent in the past'.[64] At the annual meeting of the Indian Institute of Public Administration held in August 1963, the Prime Minister himself in his speech regretted that 'despite preventive measures, corruption in the administration existed to a large extent'.[65] As a remedial measure again, the Government of India proposed to set up an Administrative Reforms Division in the Home Ministry to immediately introduce 'commonly agreed' reforms. The Home Minister, Gulzarilal Nanda, appointed a committee of three experts for the purpose. It consisted of V. Viswanathan, Home Ministry, and Tarlok Singh, Member, Planning Commission (Administration). They were required to study the recommendations of the numerous committees and other bodies which had reported from time to time on the subject during the last sixty years, the object being to select such proposals as could be implemented straightaway.[66] A group of three senior officers had already prepared a report on administrative reforms. This constituted the basis of deliberations by the Viswanathan Committee.[67]

In his having an Administrative Reforms Division, Nanda was guided immediately by a desire to enforce implementation, which was considered more necessary than the appointment of a full-fledged Administrative Reforms Commission on the pattern of the Hoover Commission in the U.S.A., that had been suggested by Lal Bahadur Shastri, the former Home Minister. It was felt that if a new high-level commission was appointed, it might take a couple of years to complete its report and go over the ground already covered. Besides, the study of the broader aspects of administration would need to be looked into in greater detail on a long-term basis. The idea of a commission had therefore to be deferred to a later stage.

The scrutiny of selected recommendations of earlier committees and their immediate implementation without further inquiry was, however, only one of the functions envisaged for the new Department of Administrative Reforms set up in March 1964. It became invested with other functions to enable it to operate 'on a vaster area than before' and to effect 'improvement in administration on a large scale and by shift in emphasis from mere economy and routine office procedures to administrative reform in its broader sense'.[68] Consistent with its broader objective the Department was, in addition, charged with: 1. locating important problems and initiating studies in respect of them; 2. examining the organization and procedures of selected departments with the object of eliminating problems of corruption at different points of the administrative machinery; 3. examining the question of setting up machinery for the redress of grievances of citizens; 4. preparing simultaneously the ground for a comprehensive investigation of the entire administrative system.

The Department of Administrative Reforms was thus set up in the Home Ministry 'for taking action on the recommendations and conclusions made in the past by various individuals and committees appointed for suggesting reforms and measures for reorganizing Governmental machinery, and for taking initiative generally in promoting administrative improvements in the interest of efficiency, economy and integrity'. The object was also a to avoid 'unnecessary duplication', and to make available to the new Department a body of trained staff to carry on administrative analysis. The O & M Division was therefore transferred with all its staff from the Cabinet Secretariat to the Home Ministry[69] where it was headed by a wholetime Joint Secretary instead of a part-time Director. Like the O & M Division, however, the Department of Administrative Reforms also continued to function under the general guidance of the Committee on Administration which was strengthened by the inclusion of N. N. Wanchoo, Secretary, Department of Iron and Steel, and L. K. Jha, Secretary to the Prime Minister.

The tenet which the Department accepted for its guidance and approach to work was that all fundamental and far-reaching measures of reform in any field of administration 'must be preceded by a process of painstaking analysis of the entire administrative situation in that field'. The very first report of the Department in fact emphasized that administrative policies, organization and procedures must be looked into carefully and that all recommendations had to be based 'on analytical studies', which automatically became the main work of the Department. It was decided that the Department should have only a small secretariat staff for general policy and administrative work and that, for the rest, 'it should consist mainly of study teams composed of research staff of varying grades which should collect and analyse data, uncover basic issues, frame properly documented papers for discussion and decision at the appropriate levels'.[70] These studies were of course to be undertaken with the concurrence and co-operation of the departments or ministries concerned.

To supply the inadequacy of information about different administrative techniques and practices a new unit called the Administrative Intelligence Cell was created in the Department to organize the collection of such information, including developments abroad. This unit was in fact to function as a service organization for the various study teams.

Among the several studies undertaken by the Department of Administrative Reforms, that of the working of the All-India Services was specially significant. It was stated in the very first year of its establishment as by far the 'most important step towards effecting improvements in the wide and crucial field of personnel administration'.[71] The object was 'to examine questions relating to recruitment and cadre strength, career planning and patterns of deployment, training and development of individuals, and the working of the machinery for processing cases of promotions, penalties and representations and to make appropriate recommendations'. In short, the total management situation came under study in respect of certain selected States, a study which of course took time for completion. Similarly, some of the other important studies made by the Department covered such subjects as the pyramidal staffing pattern in the ministries and their attached and subordinate offices; procedures relating to sanctions of schemes and proposals; and implementation procedure recommending the establishment of an 'empowered committee' in the Department concerned with its Secretary charged with the responsibility of completing implementation within a given period of time. The Department of Administrative Reforms also carried out reviews of what the ministries and departments had been doing on selected subjects. In the course of its review of Advisory Committees, for instance, it was discovered that the number of committees had increased from a mere dozen in 1947 to 1,077 in 1964.[72] Steps were taken to reduce their number for the sake of speed and economy and even though some were actually wound up their number remained at 833.

The establishment of the new Department thus effected a shift of emphasis from economy and procedure to a wider concept of administrative reforms which brought into focus the importance of the study of problem areas as the basis for administrative action. It was with this object in view that the Department proceeded to fill the gap between the requirements and the availability of staff trained in work study and other methods. The need for training in work study courses was felt all the more with the expansion of this Department as well as of State governments. In consultation with the Indian Institute of Public Administration and other authorities, it was therefore decided to run with effect from 1965 two sets of courses, the first of eight weeks' duration in the Secretariat Training School for officials roughly at the level of Section Officers, and the second of the same duration in the Indian Institute of Public Administration for officers of the level of Under Secretaries and Deputy Secretaries. Both courses were designed to cater to the needs of the Centre as well as State governments.

As in the case of the O & M Division, the primary responsibility of improving matters continued to rest with the ministries of the Central and State governments. The Department of Administrative Reforms maintained *liaison* and co-ordination with them to secure implementation. Its studies and implementation were indeed two direct and integral parts of the Department's responsibilities. While a study team was headed by an important Member of Parliament, the device of 'empowered committees' was used as an effective instrument for implementation. Under this method the old procedure of opening separate files for each recommendation was replaced by an immediate consideration of a whole report in a series of meetings. The Annual Report of the Department for 1965–6, for instance, showed that in the case of nine completed reports this special procedure helped in securing acceptance of 539 recommendations out of a total of 625 in just about an average of 12 weeks.[73] No economy of staff could, however, be achieved. All that the Department could do was to devise a scheme of placement under which the surplus personnel of one organization, instead of being obliged to face displacement, was absorbed by the expansion of another.

The Administrative Reforms Commission

The comprehensive inquiry into the entire administrative system projected earlier on the pattern of the U. S. Hoover Commission of 1953 came to be ordered by the Government of India who, under its resolution of 5 January 1966, established for the purpose an Administrative Reforms Commission. It was headed by Morarji Desai and had five other members who, except for one civil servant, were all

Members of Parliament. When Morarji Desai took over as Deputy Prime Minister in March 1967, K. Hanumanthaiya became Chairman of the Commission. The Commission was then left with five members only.[74]

The appointment of the Commission added a new dimension to activities in the field of administrative reform; for it was required to examine the entire field of public administration in the country and to make recommendations for reform and reorganization wherever necessary. It was in fact asked to consider the need for ensuring the highest standards of efficiency and integrity in the public services, and for making public administration a fit instrument to carry out the social and economic policies of the government. The concern for administrative improvements which the Government of India had been expressing from time to time since 1947 through a series of committees,[75] acquired a new focus and urgency by the time the Administrative Reforms Commission came to be appointed. Its terms of reference covered public administration at the Centre and in the States and the important field of Centre–State relationship. The sectors of administration mentioned in the terms of reference as requiring particular attention included such aspects as the machinery of the Goverenment of India and its procedures of work, the machinery for planning at all levels, financial administration, economic administration with special emphasis on the administration of public enterprises, administration at the State level, district administration, agricultural administration and the redress of citizens' grievances. This was the first comprehensive inquiry of its kind in India.

With the establishment of the Commission, however, the separate identity of the Department of Administrative Reforms did not come to an end. It was felt that the position of the Department from which initiative for administrative improvement could flow on a continuous basis should be maintained and developed further. The Department therefore continued to function as before, although most of its working capacity remained booked for the work of the Commission.[76] The Commission set up eighteen study teams and three working groups to examine different sectors of administration. On page 191 a list of the study teams and working groups is given with the names of the Chairman or Convener in each case.[77]

The members of the teams and working groups were persons of wide experience. Even so, the organizing of studies for three of the study teams was assigned to the Department of Administrative Reforms. These were teams which examined the machinery of the Government of India and its procedures, Centre–State relations and defence matters.

STUDY TEAMS	CHAIRMEN
On the machinery of the Government of India and its procedures of work	S. G. Barve, until his demise in March 1967. C. D. Deshmukh after that
On the machinery for planning	R. R. Morarka
On Centre-State relations	M. C. Setalvad
On economic administration	C. H. Bhabha
On public sector undertakings	Ravindra Varma
On scientific departments	M. S. Thacker
On recruitment, selection, Union Public Service Commission and State Public Service Commissions and training	Lt-Gen S. P. P. Thorat (Retd)
On promotion policies, conduct rules, discipline and morale	K. N. Nagarkatti
On personnel planning, staffing of public sector undertakings and personnel management	R. K. Patil
On budgetary reform, systems of expenditure control and procedure governing financial relations between the Centre and the States	B. Venkatappiah
On reforms in accounts, the role of audit	S. Ratnam
On defence matters	Ali Yavar Jung
On State-level administration	K. Hanumanthaiya
On district administration	Takhat Mal Jain
On agricultural administration	H. M. Chennabasappa
On administrative tribunals	S.C. Lahiri
On relations between the press and the administration	K. Santhanam
On problems of redress of citizens' grievances	C. C. Chaudhuri
WORKING GROUPS	**CONVENERS**
On police administration	S. Balakrishna Shetty
On medical and public health	Lt-Gen D.N. Chakravarty
On the railways	M. A. Qadeer

As the work of the Commission proceeded, new fields of study opened up. Two more study teams, ten working groups and one task force were therefore set up by the Commission at various stages in 1967. These are listed overleaf:[78]

	STUDY TEAMS	CHAIRMAN
1.	On Union Territories' administration	R. R. Murarka
2.	On the railways	H. N. Kunzru
	WORKING GROUPS	CONVENERS
1.	On Co-operation	Chowdhry Brahm Perkash
2.	On defence production	Ravindra Varma
3.	On small-scale sector	A. C. Guha
4.	On Central direct taxes	Mahavir Tyagi
5.	On life insurance administration	Tinneti Viswanathan
6.	On Company Law administration	D. L. Mazumdar
7.	On posts and telegraphs	Ram Kishan
8.	On development control and regulatory organization	Manubhai Shah
9.	On simplification of financial rules and manuals	N. S. Pandey
10.	On Customs and Central Excise	R. M. Hajarnavis
11.	On simplifying the procedure of payments and receipts at treasuries	B. V. Narayana Reddy

Thus an important feature of administrative development in the post-Independence period was a shift of emphasis from the old and traditional method of trial and error to that of administrative analysis based on work and performance studies in depth as a precondition for administrative change. Its object was to ensure economy, speed and integrity which had been seriously affected as a result of the indiscriminate expansion of personnel taking place during the Second World War and thereafter. Whether the new techniques of administrative improvement accomplished the object of their institution remains to be ascertained. The Commission's study team on the machinery of the Government of India, however, made it clear that the growth of personnel had been grossly excessive, and in no way functionally justified its output of work. It is of interest to note that even after introduction of level jumping in an effort to speed up decision-making on files, a review or records by the O & M Division for 1961 showed a staggering figure in the number of unweeded recorded files, which totalled 42 lakhs in the Central ministries. This assessment was later confirmed by the Report of the Archival Legislation Committee which put the recorded holdings of the Central ministries at 2,10,000 linear feet or about 40 miles, and of all other government departments and agencies at 136 linear miles of shelving, the total being 11 times the size of the National Archives Repository with its 16 miles of shelves.[79]

The Study Teams of the Commission were as a rule concerned with broad issues in their respective areas. The Working Groups, on the other hand, were for the purposes of making inquiries into what might be called departmental administration. Its total of 581 recommendations covered a wide range of subjects. It is not within the scope of this work to go into all these,[80] but the views expressed by the Study Teams on the Machinery of the Government of India and Personnel Administration are, however, of relevance to our inquiry, especially in terms of their implementation.

Machinery of the Government of India

The Commission submitted its report on the Machinery of the Government of India and its Procedures of Work on 1968. It dealt with the size of the Union Cabinet and the Council of Ministers,[81] the office of Prime Minister and Deputy Prime Minister, the Cabinet Secretary and Cabinet sub-committees, Minister–Secretary relations and levels of consideration, as well as policy formulation in the Secretariat.

An important recommendation of the Commission, which the Government of India accepted, was the creation of a separate Department of Personnel under its own separate Secretary in August 1970. The Estimates Committee of the Third Lok Sabha had pointed out in its 93rd report in April 1966 that 'the ever-expanding role of the Government in a welfare state with its natural concomitant of a large civil service, calls for effective personnel control through a single agency'.[82] It therefore recommended that this single central agency should be set up under the Cabinet Secretary who would be responsible for regulating the terms and conditions of the Services as a whole, replacing the existing dual control exercised by the Home and Finance Ministries.

Under the existing system the Services wing of the Home Ministry regulated matters of general applicability to all Services in order to maintain a common standard of recruitment, discipline, conditions of service, etc. With respect to the all-India Services the Home Ministry was responsible for matters of a general nature as also for their detailed application to individual cases. The day to day administration of the Central Services was, however, looked after by the ministries concerned, although the overall control of the Indian Economic Service, the Indian Statistical Service, the Indian Management Pool and the Central Secretariat Services remained vested with the Home Ministry itself. This responsibility of personnel regulation was shared by the Establishment Division of the Finance Ministry, which had to be consulted not only on financial matters but also on service rules involving finance, for which the Ministry was primarily responsible. Then there was the Establishment Officer of the Government of India who, though placed in the Home Ministry, was directly under the Cabinet Secretary as far as appointments to key positions were concerned. There was thus no unity of control.

The Commission found itself in agreement with the recommendation of the Estimates Committee, proposing a unification of responsibility for personnel control. It recognized that the formation of an effective central personnel agency and the allocation to it of overall functions in the field of personnel administration was one of the most important reforms required in the machinery of the Government of India.

The central agency created in the form of a separate Department of Personnel incorporated the functions earlier discharged by the Services wing of the Home Ministry. These included, for instance, postings to key posts, personnel policies and planning, recruitment policy and talent hunting, career development and disciplinary control, overall aspects of training and administrative reforms, redress of Government servants' grievances, staff welfare, administrative research, vigilance and relationships with the U.P.S.C. The Department of Personnel was placed directly under the Prime Minister, with the Cabinet Secretary as its administrative head. Besides providing for unified control, this arrangement imparted to its work the required prestige and authority and gave reality to the Cabinet Secretary's position as head of the civil services. However, this did not involve him or the Prime Minister in the details of its functions, which were placed under a separate Secretary of the Department.

Considering the numerous preoccupations of the Prime Minister with other matters of state, the central personnel agency remained a part of the Home Ministry, where it was finally located. This arrangement, in addition, prevented the position of the Home Minister from being weakened, particularly in relation to the States. The delegated financial powers which the new Department of Personnel came to exercise through its own finance officer provided a degree of expert financial advice that enabled it to deal with individual personnel cases involving financial implications, such as the fixation of pay, deviation from rules within specified limits, and other matters. Only such personnel questions were now required to be referred to the Finance Ministry as raised wider issues of wage policy in regard to the public services as a whole or any of the classes thereof. Also, over-concentration of powers in the new personnel agency was avoided by the administrative ministries continuing to exercise a considerable measure of delegated power in the management of departmental cadres. As regards the Department of Administrative Reforms, it remained part of the Home Ministry under a Minister of State till February 1973, when it was transferred to the Department of Personnel which was renamed the Department of Personnel and Administrative Reforms.

Personnel Administration

The Commission appointed three Study Teams which reported on personnel administration.

The report on Personnel Administration by R. K. Patil, which is of immediate relevance to this work, was submitted in August 1967. From a number of addresses delivered and discussions held at the Conference on Personnel Administration organized by the Indian Institute of Public Administration during 5–9 March 1968, it appears that the Commission was concerned over the failure of the existing administrative machinery to act as a fit instrument for achieving the social and economic goals of development and to become responsive to the people by ensuring the highest standards of efficiency and integrity in the conduct of public business. K. Hanumanthaiya, the Chairman of the Commission, as well as others, had a dig at what they called the administrative machine 'for colonial administration', which, as they deplored, continued without any substantial change in spite of the fact that political, economic and technological developments had added new dimensions to the size and complexity of the Government. A case was therefore sought to be made in favour of some 'basic change' in the 'administrative structure' of the country and 'personnel practices', so that these might get reoriented to the goals of 'development and welfare'.[83]

The first basic issue involved in reforming personnel administration was pruning the excessive administrative growth that had taken place despite a series of remedial measures. The all-India cadre of the Administrative Service itself, for instance, had registered an increase from 803 in 1948 to 1,672 in 1957 and 2,590 in 1968.[84]

The figures quoted by the Chairman of the Commission showed that by 1968 total employment in the state sector had exceeded 95 lakhs. This included about 27 lakh employees in the Central Government alone, 37 lakhs in the State governments and another 31 lakhs in local bodies and quasi-government establishments. Central Government employees had in fact registered an increase of 43 per cent between 1957 and 1966, as against the population increase of 24.2 per cent in the same period. As said before, the Commission's Study Team on Personnel Administration regarded this growth in the two decades as 'unwarranted', proceeding, as it did, from 'the accretion of unnecessary and unimportant functions'.[85] The several agencies created to stop expansion could not achieve the object of their institution. The O & M Division, the Staff Inspection Unit or even the Department of Administrative Reforms were not to question the existence itself of an organization. They were simply to assume its existence and then proceed merely to examine whether or not its manning was reasonable. Even the Finance Ministry concerned itself with the details of a particular plan of organization rather than with the necessity or usefulness of the schemes forwarded by the Planning Commission. The result was that the various agencies set up to effect economy tended to become additional cogs in the wheel without serving any useful purpose.[86]

There were two other important aspects of personnel administration which the Administrative Reforms Commission emphasized to rid the country's administrative system of what was thought to be a 'colonial' tradition. These were (1) the basis of the existing personnel system, and (2) the staffing of higher positions. While the Commission's recommendation was in the first case influenced by the principle of the American method of 'Position Classification', the second was loaded in favour of a unified civil service as a counterweight to the Indian Administrative Service for staffing higher positions in the Central and State Secretariats. The Study Team on Personnel Administration, however, had set its face against both, for they not only ran counter to India's social and political milieu, but also involved serious financial implications. They were not accepted by the Government.

The Service structures which developed during British rule in India primarily fed the various functional departments, especially the higher administrative positions, and came to form the basis of its personnel system. A Service denoted in the Indian context a group of civil servants with common recruitment conditions, prospects and careers. It was recruited on merit to hold a group of positions requiring similar skills, which might be technical, professional or administrative. Within a Service itself, there might be more than one grade arranged vertically according to the level of responsibility and horizontally according to the level of competence required. This concept presupposed that, within a Service, positions at the same level were analogous and that any of its members in a particular grade or position could be posted to it. While constituting a Service, care was taken not only to examine its positions or grades with reference to the skills required but also to determine whether these were equivalent and interchangeable in terms of qualifications and pay scales.

The classification of the services into the four Classes and their equivalents had been done on the basis of status and the corresponding privileges attached to them. Until the Islington Commission (1912–15), public servants used to be classified into superior, subordinate and inferior services. The Islington Commission introduced two new services or two classes of one service placed in between the 'subordinate' service and the top Imperial Service. These were called Class I and Class II, assigned to a body of work which was not sufficiently important to be given to the Imperial Services recruited in England, but yet of a nature which could not be entrusted to subordinate staff. The nomenclature Class I and Class II came into use in 1926 and has continued ever since. The first Central Pay Commission, known as the Varadachariar Commission (1946–47), introduced the terms Class III and Class IV as substitutes for 'subordinate' and 'inferior' services—an expression of socialistic delicacy.

Distinctions, however, did not disappear. The Services continued to be classified on the basis of status according to service-wise classification; by categorization into four classes; by division into gazetted and non-gazetted categories, and in accordance with pay scales. None of these classified categories signified an occupational concept based on 'Position Classification'.

'Position Classification' was a method of organizing assignments for the management of personnel affairs, which was provided by the Classification Act of 1949 in the United States. Based on job analysis and evaluation, the Act recognized the principle of equal pay for substantially equal work as by far the best form of incentive, variations in rates of basic compensation being in proportion to substantial differences in the difficulty, responsibility and qualification requirements of the work performed and to the contributions of officers and employees to efficiency and economy in the service. The second principle embodied under the Act was that, in accordance with their duties, responsibilities and qualification requirements, individual positions were to be so grouped and identified by classes and grades that the resulting position classification system could be used in all phases of personnel administration. It was in fact an attempt to establish a triangular relationship between (1) the duties and responsibiliꞇes of a job, (2) its working conditions, and (3) its qualification requirements. In other words, it identified the work actually to be done, matched the skills of candidates with the skills needed for the job, and provided the basis for a rational pay structure consistent with the contribution of the worker. This was a job oriented industrial approach to public administration. It was somewhat different from the rank oriented concept of service structure, which operated in the Indian situation as a consequence of its social and historical development.

The basic principles underlying both the concepts were, however, not entirely dissimilar in that assignments were determined in both cases by considerations of skill requirements, job responsibilities and conditions of service. In the course of a concluding address to the Conference on Personnel Administration held at the Indian Institute of Public Administration C. D. Deshmukh, an eminent Civilian of his time, in fact doubted whether 'Position Classification' was different from the grade systems which had existed in India before time-scales were introduced.[87] The civil service regulations, and the fundamental rules that followed, had actually imparted to the old grade systems the quality of a ranking in the job system. A person had to grow in a position at a subordinate level in the hierarchy till there was room to fit him into any kind of higher position. The Government took recourse to the expedient of selection grades by way of compensation. Officers, for example, were not promoted as Collectors but entered the selection grade. The availability of room was of course a factor in promotion to a superior rank calling for greater responsibility. But no less important was the factor of qualification requirement, ability and experience which entitled a person to a higher position in the service.

There were, however, certain differences of detail between the two concepts. The service concept not only classified positions into classes as the Position Classification did, but further attempted to group positions within a class which could be treated as a homogeneous group, with its personnel constituting a cadre of officers each of whom could occupy any of those positions. Another point of distinction was that, while the rank-oriented service concept was like a caste hierarchy where skill and character assessment remained by and large subjective and undefinable, the most important point about Position Classification was the refinement of its measurement techniques of jobs, which were broken into constituent parts for an objective analysis of personnel management.

But since responsibility, initiative, drive, tact and the like are all abstract concepts of human character, they cannot be reduced to precise physical scales. The comments which Deshmukh made in his concluding address on personnel administration, were most appropriate; he said: 'A human being is not exactly like a brick which can be fitted, by size, shape and composition, into a particular kind of structure. Man is non-uniform; psychological needs and growing family responsibilities vary; there is unequal range of capacity for development. Many of the higher administrative jobs call for a well-developed capacity for judgment which is largely nurtured by the trial and error method'.[88] This argument lent support to the administrative principle which had developed over the years in India. It was based on the assumption that, given the basic intellectual calibre and academic attainment ascertained through competitive tests, special skills could be developed in individuals through a series of work experiences and training programmes, the wrong choices, if any, being rectified by a period of probation provided under service rules. The support of certain academic enthusiasts for a formal acceptance of the Position Classification approach as a basis of India's personnel system remained, more or less, an exercise in futility, although the service concept itself was being slowly reinforced with the use of modern techniques of administrative improvement through work studies and performance evaluation.

However, a more important problem of personnel administration was the staffing of higher positions, especially at the top policy-making level. Doubtless there existed a comparable problem at district and other levels, but the most important level was that of the Central Secretariat where the political and administrative processes met and interacted. In addition to its supportive staff, this consisted of 'consideration' levels and the policy-formulation levels, with the political executive functioning as the spearhead of the decision-making mechanism. The 'consideration' levels comprised Under Secretaries and Deputy Secretaries, while the policy-formulation levels included officers of the rank of Joint Secretaries and Secretaries. Each of these four categories of officers formed part of the higher secretariat and departmental positions for which a much wider[89] field of selection was contemplated than the somewhat simpler selections for technical and specialist departments, where the corresponding technical or specialist services usually provided personnel for the highest decision-making levels.

At the Centre, higher posts were as a rule not specifically included by name in the 'authorized strength' of any Service. Even so, I.A.S. officers manned not only 'generalist' departments and departments whose 'specialist' nature happened to be still embryonic, but also such other departments as called for administrative leadership rather than mere expertise. In fact, the staffing scheme of the Government of India was in theory governed by three broad principles according to the report of the Study Team on Personnel Administration. These were:[90]

(i) A large part of senior administrative manpower at the Centre should consist of officers with field experience of the kind that the I.A.S. provided or executive experience in various departments as in the case of the Central Services, Class I;

(ii) Another part is provided by, more or less, a permanent group consisting of selected officers of the Central Administrative Pool which is built up from substantially the same sources as in (i) but there is also a provision for the recruitment of persons with specialized qualifications directly from the open market;

(iii) A small part of the Deputy Secretary level is provided by a permanent group consisting of selection grade officers of the Central Secretariat Service. There is a fixed authorized strength of 45 in the G.S.S. cadre for this purpose.

The Study Team of which R. K. Patil was Chairman recognized that the existing staffing scheme in principle provided for the best elements being selected from all possible sources for senior management positions, including, if necessary, persons from the private sector. Conceptually, there was hardly any room for improvement. In practice, however, the situation was very much off the mark on account of the lack of perspective planning, of appropriate career development and clear appreciation of personnel requirments resulting from consideration of the interest of pressure groups. The inclusion of technical services, for instance, was rarely considered. There was no systematic approach to the inclusion of persons with specialized qualifications, even though the Central Administrative Pool had provided for lateral entry. The requirements of professionalism and expertise, though not ignored, were not adequately met. These had to go by default. For, the induction of officers of specialist services had been admissible there by virtue of their belonging to Class I, not as a consequence of any fixed policy of determining their suitability for specific positions on the basis of the experience gained in parent departments. The results was that, although the higher management posts were, in principle, not the preserve of any one service, I.A.S. officers remained in a dominant position, especially at the upper levels of policy formulation. This is clear from the table given on page 202.[91]

Another criticism of the existing pattern of staffing was that while the salaries of secretariat positions in the Gvernment happened to be considerably higher, those of field positions were relatively low. This affected the nature of the secretariat–field relationship which came to be generally viewed as a superior–subordinate one. What became important was their respective status and cadres, not their skills, which were relegated to the background or ignored. The superior–subordinate relationship of secretariat and field personnel was professionally unsound and administratively inexpedient. But it could not be otherwise in the context of the British imperial tradition and the indigenous Brahmanic social order. Both were authoritarian and status-bound.

However, this caused in a democratic set-up a distortion of perspective with respect to personnel problems at the policy formulation levels. It was in these circumstances that the idea of a unified civil service emerged as a possible way out. It was suggested by certain interest groups that at the junior Class I level, if possible, there should be one common recruitment for all the services, generalist or specialist; or, alternatively, there should be a second selection for the higher positions (Deputy Secretary and higher levels in Secretariat and enquivalent levels in departments) from all the Class I services towards the end of the first half of these officers' careers. This could be done by means of a common competitive examination or some other method.

However, opinions differed widely as to whether the proposed unified civil service should cover all the higher Central or State Government positions, or whether its scope should be limited to the Central Government only. There was no unanimity even on questions of functional coverage. Some wanted a unified civil service to cover only the higher secretariat positions, while others desired extension to all departments. There was, in addition, no clarity about the organiza-

Services	As on 1.1.1961				As on 1.12.1966			
	Secretaries & Special Secretaries	Additional Secretaries	Joint Secretaries	Deputy Secretaries	Secretaries & Special Secretaries	Additional Secretaries	Joint Secretaries	Deputy Secretaries
ICS/IAS	25	9	43	64	47	23	139	161
Indian Audit & Accounts Service	1	—	6	1	1	4	3	21
Indian Defence Accounts Service	—	1	5	4	—	1	8	6
Indian Railway Service	—	—	4	16	—	2	6	30
Indian Police Service	—	—	—	3	—	—	1	9
Indian Railway Accounts Service	—	—	2	2	1	—	1	2
State Civil Service	—	—	—	3	—	—	—	—
Central Secretariat Service	1	1	6	93	2	1	18	155
Others	9	3	18	7	10	4	19	12
Total · · ·	36	14	84	193	61	35	195	396

tional details involved in giving shape to the ideas suggested by interested groups.

The advocates of a unified civil service were guided partly by considerations of professionalism which, as they thought, should underlie personnel policies. That led them to emphasize that professional skills acquired through work in a single department should alone constitute a title to promotion to policy formulation levels in the Secretariat. This was a functional approach to personnel problems, each department being invested with a specific task to be performed by its own internal personnel agency equipped with special skills. It was a rather narrow approach which could not comprehend an overall situation. It was realized, and rightly so, that although professionalism was needed up to a point for higher Secretariat posts, the task of policy-making called for the additional important requirement of varied experience and a knowledge of administration at the 'grass-roots'. This was an important consideration that dictated the necessity of continuing the existing system of staffing through service structures which provided most of the higher level personnel, there being in practice at the same time permissive provisions for the utilization of all the manpower resources available within the Government and outside. It was a comprehensive approach to personnel policy, not exclusive to any specific service.

The emphasis of certain circles on professionalism was, however, not free from a desire to forward the sectional claims of 'specialists' who refused to recognize a 'generalist' as another kind of specialist. Their claim that all administrative ills could be cured if only the so-called 'generalists' were removed from positions of vantage and replaced by specialists created a generalist–specialist controversy without establishing whether the departments manned by specialists even at the highest levels fared better than those manned by non-specialists. The important question was not whether a specialist did better than a generalist and *vice versa*. The factors which contributed to success, as the Study Team on Personnel Administration rightly pointed out, 'have been a high level of intellectual ability, a continuing awareness of developments in the modern world, an eagerness to benefit from experience, a willingness to undertake risks, wide-ranging experience, intimate knowledge of departmental administration, and a strong determination to achieve desired results'.[92] These attributes of human behaviour in administration could not be a monopoly of a specialist or a generalist, but must be cultivated and acquired through constant reading and reflection in the course of one's career in the public service, not through the use of pressure to secure proportionate shares in higher positions on the basis of separate service or class distinctions. Based as it was on a limited view of the generalist–specialist controversy, the unified service concept could not be recognized as a viable alternative to the existing staffing system which had stood the test of time.

The I.A.S. stood not only on prestige, but rather on its own functional merit inherited from the traditions of the I.C.S. This was recognized by the States Reorganization Commission. Among its package measures suggested to ensure national integration in the context of linguistic States, the importance of the I.A.S. was specially emphasized as an antidote to the destructive centrifugal tendencies that might be encouraged by regional loyalties. In view of the standards of recruitment on a national footing, the Commission firmly held that the I.A.S. would reinforce the framework of an impartial and efficient all-India administrative system capable of subordinating counter-productive pulls to a long-term national interest.[93] It was anticipated that more all-India services would be created as a bulwark against the forces of disruption, of caste, community and language and uphold a national standard of efficiency on the pattern of the I.A.S. At a meeting of the Chief Ministers of States and Central Ministers held in August 1961, it was agreed in principle to create three new All-India Services, namely (1) the Indian Service of Engineers, (2) the Indian Forest Service, and (3) the Indian Medical and Health Service. Subsequently, the Rajya Sabha adopted on 6 December 1961 a resolution for their creation and legislation for the purpose was enacted by Parliament on 6 September 1963.[94] The Central Government after consultation with the State Governments constituted for each State or group of States an Indian Forest Service Cadre and framed rules for the same in July 1966.[95] But the other two services did not come into being despite Parliamentary legislation and the orders of the Central Government, thanks to the reluctance of some States whose participation was necessary for the creation of any all-India service.[96] Two more all-India services were likewise sought to be created by the Central Government—the Indian Educational Service and the Indian Agricultural Service, but these too met a similar fate.[97] The fact that the States viewed any progress in the creation of more all-India services as an invasion of their right to patronage establishes beyond doubt the importance of the I.A.S. and other such services as the most effective instrument of national unity and political integration.

None the less, the criticism levelled against the I.A.S, of its being chiefly in the corridors of power, was not without foundation. Although essentially a field-based Service from which the Secretariat advisers at the State and Central levels were drawn, the plan for the Central Cadre of the I.A.S. and the establishment of the Central Administrative Pool, as said before, seriously dislocated the functioning of the well-tried tenure system. Soon after Independence and for nearly 15 years the Government of India lost sight of the need for top administrators to keep in touch with the field; for the I.C.S. officers and other administrators seconded to the Pool were freed from the operation of the tenure rule and continued in the Government of India indefinitely. This, in a large measure, was the reason for the start of the criticism; for continued departure from the tenure system was a clear denial of the avowed principle that the bulk of the senior administrative position in the Central Secretariat should be manned by officers with such field experience as the I.A.S. provided. This was an error of planning which the technocrats interpreted as a deliberate attempt to exclude them from the centres of power.

Though modelled initially on the lines of the old Commerce and Finance Pool, the source of recruitment to the Central Administrative Pool was enlarged in 1950 in view of the constitution of the several new Services after Independence. The list of eligible Services for the Administrative Pool included, as said before, the I.A.S. and the other non-technical Services like the Indian Audit and Accounts Service, the Indian Income Tax service, the Indian Postal Service, etc. In 1957, a revised scheme[98] was introduced and the field of recruitment to the Pool further widened to include not only a few more non-technical Class I Services borrowed on tenure deputation from the States, the Central Services and other selection grades of the Central Secretariat Service, but also from higher technical Services and personnel of public sector undertakings; for the public sector too had by this time established its own Industrial Management Pool.[99]

Though sound in principle, the scheme of 1957 also remained inoperative due to the interference of pressure groups. The result was that no further additions were made to the Central Administrative Pool. Getting into higher positions at the Centre became an *ad hoc* practice, depending upon the pressure a Service was able to exert in favour of its candidate. Consequently about 75 per cent of the posts of Joint Secretaries and above continued to be held by members of the

I.A.S. The Estimates Committee (1965–6), while commending the idea of a Central Administrative Pool, emphasized that while the selection of officers to it should continue to be made from the All-India Services and the Central Services, it should also be made keeping in view their respective strength so that there might be a fair representation of all the Services in the higher posts of the Central Government. However, this principle of proportional representation in the distribution of jobs at the highest levels was viewed by the Government as dangerous to the interests of public administration and efficiency. It therefore rejected the recommendation and permitted the existing arrangement to continue without prejudice to any of the constituent Services.

In the controversy that followed the rejection of the recommendation of the Estimates Committee, the technocrats reiterated that they must hold Secretariat posts in order to be able to advise ministers correctly about scientific and technical matters where the generalist administrators possessed little or no competence. This controversy received fresh impetus with the release in 1968 of the Fulton Commttee Report on the Civil Services of Britain. The Committee emphasized the need to throw open Secretariat posts in Britain not only to the Home Civil Service but also to other Services which could be rendered suitable for more jobs through appropriate in-service training and career development.

However, the pattern of administration that developed in India in modern times, though in principle influenced by Britain's rule-oriented, procedural and substantive laws, remained essentially field-based. The districts which had through the ages functioned more or less as permanent units of administration in spite of political uncertainties continued to be so even under British rule. Unlike Britain, where the Secretariat jobs were the preserve of the Home Civil Service because of the restricted function of the Central Government thanks to decentralization, the I.C.S. officers in the Indian situation had to start with the executive, revenue and judicial administration in the districts. It was in the districts that they acquired an intimate knowledge of the people and their habits of mind before they worked their way up to superior positions in the Secretariat, the policy-making level of the Government. Even so, the Services associated with the administration of the Secretariat were not the preserve of the I.C.S. alone. The change-over had started taking place even before 1946 when its successor Service, the I.A.S., was first created. By 1970, the position of the I.A.S. at the Centre was as follows:[100]

Posts	Held by I.A.S.	Held by others
Secretary	32	12
Addl. Secretary	15	13
Joint Secretary	80	68
Deputy Secretary	84	186
Under Secretary	51	420

A cadre-wise break-up of Deputy Secretaries in the Central Secretariat as on 1 October 1974 showed that the number drawn from the I.A.S. had declined to nearly 25 per cent of the total. This is indicated in the table below:[101]

Sl. No.	Cadre	No. of Deputy Secretaries	Percentage of I.A.S.
1.	(i) Indian Administrative Service	126	25.4
	(ii) Indian Police Service	5	1.0
2.	*Central Service, Class I (Non-Technical)*		
	(i) Indian Revenue Service	53	10
	(ii) Indian Economic Service/ Indian Statistical Service[102]	41	8.2
	(iii) Indian Railway Traffic Service	41	6
	(iv) Indian Postal Service	11	2.2
	(v) Indian Audit and Accounts Service	20	4
	(vi) Indian Defence Accounts Service	10	2
	(vii) Indian Railway Accounts Service	11	2.2
	(viii) Military Lands & Cantonment Service	9	1.8
3.	*Central Secretariat Service* (Selection Grade)	9	1.8
4.	Others	3	6
	Grant Total	495	100

Another significant development that appears from the table is the phenomenal rise of the Central Secretariat Service in terms of both quantity and functional elevation. The former Imperial Secretariat Service in the Government of India had been designed merely to man lower positions in the Central Secretariat, seldom rising beyond the level of Assistant Secretaries. As heads of Sections and Branches their duty was to assist those operating at 'consideration' and policy-formulation levels by bringing to their notice relevant facts and precedents. The breakdown of the tenure system at the level of Under Secretary following the acute shortage of officers in the higher services led to the abolition of the distinction that earlier existed between

Assistant and Under Secretaries. When the Central Secretariat Service was formally constituted, the original purpose remained unchanged. But the old barrier was removed, so that some positions at the Under Secretary's level and a fixed number of Deputy Secretary's posts came to be included in the cadre of the Service so constituted. The result was that, while members of the Service swamped the bulk of the Under Secretary's positions, by 1974 they came to hold 35.5 per cent of the positions of Deputy Secretaries. Some were even permitted to rise to posts of Joint Secretaries.

The I.A.S. differed from the British Home Civil Service in yet another respect. The latter at its lower levels is far less involved with elected representatives. Being essentially a field service, the I.A.S. could not remain completely free from involvement with such representatives at local levels. It required a highly developed sense of political maturity and administrative skill on the part of field officers to function within the Weberian framework of administrative impersonality especially in a society still only partially accustomed to the rule of law. And since not all administrators were found equal to the task of reducing the heterogeniety of caste-bound politics to the rule-bound uniformity of administration, a tendency grew among them to seek refuge in the Central Secretariat or even in the Secretariats of their State Governments. Delhi being the most important city in respect of amenities and prospects for promotion, their tendency to gravitate to Delhi and stick to the posts there became their first choice. The State headquarters were the next favoured goal. The pioneering spirit of the early British administrators, who built up the administration of the rural districts in the most difficult and hostile surroundings, seemed to become a thing of the past, perhaps not to be restored or even remembered. The other Services soon started copying the premier Service and thus the distaste for work in the rural areas spread.

The I.A.S. was found wanting in the knowledge of law also. For, at the time of its formation in 1946, it was decided that its members would not be called upon to go in for the judicial line at any stage of their careers. This was contrary to the earlier practice, when I.C.S. probationers were required not only to acquire a knowledge of the laws and constitution of India, but also to master such basic works as Blackstone's *Commentaries*, Austin's *Jurisprudence*, Maine's *Ancient Law* and Bentham's *Theory of Legislatioin*. They were in addition called upon to attend English courts of law and submit before each half-yearly examination a full report on cases heard, the substance of the evidence given, the objections made to evidence, the argument of counsel, the view taken by the judge and the ultimate results.[103] No doubt they had the choice to opt for the judicial line at about the tenth year of service, but a basic understanding of law and the constitution was essential for all I.C.S. men, so that they might appreciate the limitations within which they were required to function and exercise their executive authority. It was here that the predecessors of the I.A.S. had an edge over it.

However, the necessity of the I.A.S. as a premier service was generally recognized. This necessity flowed from a variety of consideration. It constituted the link not only between the State and the Central Services, but also between the field administration and the higher management personnel of the Central Secretariat. It acted, in addition, as the pioneer, the improviser and an innovator by being able to organize and manage non-cadre positions in the changing environment, where the fields of specialization after being sufficiently developed are built up and identified as the services of specialists and technocrats who then take over from the generalist administrators. This is a functional necessity which further reinforced the concept of the I.A.S., a concept which did not clash with the consensus that the best man available, no matter what the sources, should be selected for the senior management positions, including, if necessary, from the private sector. The idea of a unified civil service and Position Classification which the Administrative Reforms Commission recommended for acceptance to the Government were thus both given up.

Speaking broadly, the administrative changes that took place in about the first two decades and a half after Independence, especially after March 1954, were declaredly intended to create an administrative agency for greater economy and efficiency. The need for such an agency was felt in the course of the First Five-Year Plan and its urgency realized from subsequent experience of poor performance. But the task was not easy. The craze for rapid promotion that suddenly appeared on the retirement of European officers was weakening the higher echelons of the civil services on the transfer of power. The absence of political will to reduce the already surplus staff to a size required for the normal transaction of public business not only enabled all the war-time temporaries to cling on, but found for them a place of refuge under a hastily conceived plan of what came to be known broadly as development administration, which included such nebulous activity as rural reconstruction, community development, basic education and extention service. It took nearly a decade to realize the error of the earlier obsession. Apart from changes in the institutional arrangements of the Secretariat to effect economy and efficiency, the Government of India took certain other measures to achieve the same objective. To place a check on the tendency of government departments to continuously expand, a ban was imposed in January 1960 on the creation of posts other than those required for Plan schemes and for security purposes. The ban, however, did not apply to the normal recruitment for maintaining the strength of the cadres of the various organized Services. Also, the ban so imposed could be relaxed in special cases, subject to the personal orders of the Home Minister and the Finance Minister.[104] Another step towards economy was the establishment of an Economy Committee in 1963, with the Home Minister as its Chairman. The Committee made a study of the staff strengths of 24 ministries and departments and recommended reductions covering all classes from Joint Secretaries to peons. Its recommendations were accepted. But the surplus officers were allowed to be retained until they were actually absorbed.[105] The question of redeployment of the surplus staff was later examined, and, after reviewing the existing arrangements, the Government of India decided to set up a Central (Surplus Staff) Cell. This was actually established in the Home Ministry with effect from 25 December 1966. The scheme later applied to the staff rendered surplus as a result of studies of work measurement or due to abolition and winding up of permanent and long-term organizations. On transfer to the Central Cell, however, the surplus staff continued to receive the pay and allowances in their previous scales till they were absorbed elsewhere.

A ban continued to operate on direct recruitment to all posts in ministries of the Central Government. The object was to effect speedy re-employment of surplus staff. No recruitment was made to such posts unless a certificate was obtained from the Central (Surplus Staff) Cell to the effect that the Cell had no suitable candidate to offer. Apart from Class I and Class II officers, this ban extended to all Class III posts and certain categories of promotion posts, such as the Upper Division Clerks and Head Clerks.[106]

No economy could thus be effected in the pay bills of the Government of India. Democracy, which in practice is frequently a government of pressure groups, would not permit any retrenchment and the surplus identified as a result of work studies in one department was sought to be absorbed in another.

Service conditions were, however, modified so as to make it possible for the Government to prematurely retire its servants, if necessary, at the age of 50. A recommendation to this effect was first made in a paper on 'Measures for Strengthening the Administration' which, as said before, was laid on the Table of both Houses of Parliament in August 1961. It was proposed that the Government should take powers to retire a Government servant after he had attained the age of 50 years or completed 25 years of service, if it was considered necessary to do so in the public interest. The Santhanam Committee on Prevention of Corruption later made a similar recommendation in its report. The conditions of service were accordingly amended on 17 May 1969 to provide for retirement of Class I and II Central Government servants on attaining the age of 50 and of Class III on completing 30 years of service. The amendment, in addition, conferred in all cases a corresponding right on Government servants to so retire voluntarily.[107]

The rule of the Central Government to retire its servants before their due date was, however, motivated more by considerations of disciplinary control than by a desire to effect economy in administration. In the light of the extent of administrative expansion that took place after 1947 it would not be unreasonable to hold the view that the political leadership and the bureaucracy were both averse to any reduction in the size of their staff. Parkinson's Law was allowed to operate.

CHAPTER V

The Management of the Administrative Service

The Service which will be discussed here in terms of management is the Indian Administrative Service created on 21 October 1946 as a result of an Agreement between the Government of India and a number of participating provinces.[1] This was done at a Conference of their Premiers, who met under the chairmanship of Sardar Valla-bhbhai Patel, then Home Member of the Interim Government, and decided to have a 'Central Administrative Service' which they all considered not only 'advisable but essential' for the Indian personnel system in which key posts in the administration, both central and provincial, could be manned by a body of officers of high calibre with a common training and informed by the same traditions as existed earlier in the Indian Civil Service.

These traditions had grown from the early years of British rule. They bore the stamp of the administrative reforms of such men as Hastings, Cornwallis, Wellesley and Bentinck, who built up a regular administrative hierarchy on a principle which, unlike Mughal ad-ministration, emphasized uniformity and the rule of law as the basic conditions of efficiency and integrity of conduct. But broadly speak-ing, the forces that went into the making of these reforms were those of nascent capitalism and the principle of contract that flowed from it. Together, they dictated the necessity of political action that called for a highly centralized government on the one hand and downward penetration of administrative institutions on the other. Both were necessary for the security and progress of commerce and capitalist enterprise which, in turn, led to a development of roads and railways, transport and communications, education and agriculture. Later, the growth of capitalism in Britain and the demand for a 'representative bureaucracy' in India as an efficient instrument of government led to the introduction of open competition as a mode of recruitment for a civil service that came to be invested with the promotion of free enterprise, both European and Indian. Macaulay, who had suggested a four-fold principle of limited competition in 1833, introduced a regular system of open competition in 1855. The early practice of the East India Company to have separate cadres for each of the presidencies or provinces was subsequently modified in 1878, when the concept of an All-India Civil Service was first introduced as an imperial measure to promote political integration and the interest of backward areas.

Doubtless, the concept of an all-India service was at the time an imperial concept. It required members of the I.C.S. to view India as a unified geographical entity which they were in principle bound to serve regardless of their original assignments to different provincial cadres. The idea was of course to look after the total interest of the Indian Empire and to preserve, by means of an efficient administration, its territorial integrity which later came to be of equal importance to any national government. The necessity of the concept of an all-India service, however, arose immediately from the administrative exigencies of a colonial economy operating at the grass roots in the exploitation of the country's natural resources, especially in a backward and tea-producing province like Assam, which was the first to give cause for the introduction of the new all-India concept. These administrative exigencies, which included considerations of political stability and such other functions as revenue collection and distribution of justice, called for a kind of elitist civil service which, by virtue of its higher education and training, might be action-oriented in terms of the requirements of field administration, and thought-oriented in terms of the need for policy formulation at the headquarters. In the Indian situation, such an all-India bureaucratic concept was all the more essential because the bureaucracy itself happened to be the government responsible practically both for decision-making and administrative action

On the transfer of power the political and administrative functions became separate and distinct, the former becoming a ministerial responsibility while the latter remaining bureaucratic as before. But, functionally speaking, the relevance of an elitist all-India civil service of the kind built up earlier in the imperial context did not diminish in the new situation. On the contrary, the importance of the successor service increased all the more, not only as a traditional instrument of peace, tranquility and territorial integrity, but also as a co-ordinating agency for development administration, involving, at local levels, a range and variety of social and economic activity that exceeded all previous records. The decision-making political apparatus was of course there as a substitute for the erstwhile Civilian Members of the Government. But while, as elected representatives, their approach to problems was bound to be party-oriented and partial, their tenure of office remained insecure and fleeting. Above all, ministers did not have the expertise or the knowledge and technique of field administration. The civil servant alone could bring his administrative experience to bear upon the making of policies. In fact, it formed part of the function of bureaucracy not only to assist ministers in policy-formulation by a regular supply of that knowledge, but also to see that the poicy so formulated represented the 'general will' of the electorate and not merely the partial view of the party in power. Freedom from political influence was a *sine qua non* for ideal bureaucratic functioning.

This conceptual framework of the Indian Civil Service which had developed as part of a historical process in the country, found full support with Sardar Patel. While recommending the creation of an all-India Administrative Service on 21 October 1946, he made it clear that this Service, like the I.C.S., was not to be 'at the mercy of changing parties or changing conditions in the country; the Service must not have to participate in the activities of any political party or other party'.[2]

Motivated by a desire for the exercise of local patronage and control, the Premiers of even the Congress provinces were anxious that they should be left with powers to punish officers serving under them. They were not prepared to reconcile themselves to a position where a civil servant in a Provincial Government should be permitted to look for protection to an authority other than that Government itself. This clashed with the basic concept of an all-India Service, although the Congress alone had in the past been responsible for engendering provincialism as part of its policy to have the Service completely Indianized. Athough conscious of provincial susceptibilities, Patel, however, yielded ground to none on this question of central control over disciplinary matters as a means to preserve the all-India character of the new Administrative Service. He emphasized that a centrally controlled Service could alone be efficient, impartial and free from local and communal bias, party allegiance or political influence. No locally controlled Service could act independently or put up resistance to local intrigues and politics.[3]

Summing up the reason for setting up the Indian Administrative

Service, the minute of the Conference of Provincial Premiers, who took the final decision to constitute the Service, thus said:[4]

The reason which promoted the decision in favour of an All-India Service was mutual advantage both to the Centre and the Provinces. It would facilitate liaison between the Centre and Provinces, ensure a certain uniformity in standards of administration and maintain the central administrative machinery in touch with realities. The provincial administrative machinery would on its part acquire a wider outlook and obtain the best material for the higher posts. The Home Minister emphasized that there was need for ensuring contentment and security in the Services and for seeing that the Services were free from communal or party bias.

Though modelled after the I.C.S., the I.A.S. as an all-India Service was not a matching institution. Unlike the former, the latter was of course not created by an act of legislature. It came into existence merely as a result of deliberation between the Home Member of the Government of India and the Premiers of the participating Provinces. These were later approved by the Central Cabinet and the concerned Provincial Governments. Its recognition by the Constitution and by an Act of Parliament came still later. But even otherwise the position of the new Service was different. Besides a lower scale of pay allowed to members of the I.A.S., there was no unity of control over their recruitment and conditions of service. It was to be excersied by the Home Ministry and the Finance Ministry on the basis of 'mutual advantage both to the Centre and Provinces', not of considerations governing the public service in its totality. The emphasis was on the distribution of power and patronage as between the Centre and the provinces, not on 'security in the Services' and their freedom from 'communal and party bias', two essential qualities of the Service attributed by the Conference to Sardar Patel alone, without the provincial premiers being in any way bound by that emphasis. We shall in the course of this chapter see how certain provinces, in spite of service regulations to the contrary, arrogated to themselves a degree of control over recruitment and service conditions which in principle did not belong to them. The Home Ministry used to be confronted with a series of *fait accompli* resulting in the decline of efficency and integrity of conduct.

However, when the I.A.S. was first created in 1946, its main objective, beside being a federal Service common to the Union and the provinces, was to provide personnel of high quality and calibre to man important administrative posts. The continuing validity of this objective, though questioned at times, was recognized by the Study Teams of the Administrative Reforms Commission which, in the light of the past experience of British rule, emphatically affirmed the need for all-India services.[5]

The original mechanism to achieve this objective sought to induct talent in the I.A.S. mainly by three methods. The first method was to structure the cadre in such a way that 79 to 80 per cent of the senior posts went to direct recruits and only 21 to 20 per cent to promotees from the provincial services. The senior posts were to be earmarked to the extent of 75 per cent for direct recruits under the provincial Government as its cadre schedule, and under the Central Government as the Central Deputation Quota, as well as the entire portion attributed to the deputation and leave reserves. It was hoped that the combined competitive examination of the best candidates from the universities between 21 and 24 years of age would throw up 80 per cent of the senior officers of the cadre. The second method to achieve the objective was by a recruitment policy that might control numbers through appropriate selection. The third mode designed to secure the objective was by ensuring an attractive environment of work, including high prestige, lucrative positions, good pay and attractive conditions of service. In practice, however, the mechanism originally devised for the purpose of high quality and calibre underwent severe distortions proceeding from too heavy a rate of recruitment, structural and compositional imbalance and deterioration in the environment of work.

Recruitment

As regards the annual rate of recruitment to the I.A.S., which took its toll in terms of quality, it reached enormous proportions in course of the very first two decades after Independence. The number of direct recruits increased from 33 in 1947 to 138 in 1965 and then aimed at 160 soon after. This rate of recruitment was, however, not an isolated problem. It was organically linked with the expansion of I.A.S. cadres, With an increase in cadres, recruitment was bound to be stepped up. The table on page 217 gives an idea of the magnitude of expansion in the I.A.S. cadres.

The rate of recruitment thus proceeded more or less in accordance with the increase of cadre strength, for which the States were immediately responsible. When recruitment was stepped up to meet the rising demands of the States, the quantity of recruitment, as the Study Team on Centre–State Relationship pointed out, declined to a point

Expansion in the I.A.S. Cadres

Year	Authorized cadre strength	Actual position
1950-1	897	Not given
1955-6	Not given	1,173
1957-8	—	1,561
1958-9	—	1,676
1959-60	1,862	1,722
1960-1	2,010	1,786
1961-2	2,147	1,825
1962-3	2,253	1,918
1963-4	2,278	1,982
1964-5	2,470	2,145
1965-6	2,567	2,232
1966-7	2,855	2,325
1967-8	2,882	2,545
1968-9	3,035	2,619
1969-70	3,234	2,725

where it was bound to cause concern; for it created in addition problems of promotion, deployment and balance in the cadre. A rational recruitment policy needed to take into account such relevant dimensions as the size and anticipated growth of the cadre, the anticipated number required for manning posts outside the cadre, the quality of the recruit, a balance between the composition of the service and promotional opportunities. If some of these elements happened to pull in different directions, a balance could then be maintained only in a manner best suited to the needs of the State. But sudden additions to the cadre on an *ad hoc* basis seriously interfered with the pursuit of any consistent policy. In other words, the absence of planning led to haphazard growth. In the case, for example, of Maharashtra, Punjab and U.P. there were spurts of growth between static periods, its extent fluctuating, as will be clear from the table on page 218.[6]

The growth arising from the integration of the princely states in 1949 and the reorganization of States in 1956 was to an extent unpredictable. But these events were only partially responsible for the sudden spurts in growth. It was the advent of the Five Year Plans and increased development activity that demanded more personnel and it was here that the element of personnel planning was found wanting. When it was discovered that the cadres needed considerable expansion, their inadequacy was met by a sudden and haphazard increase under a scheme of Special Recruitment in 1956. The study which the

No. of senior posts as on 1 January

Year	Maharashtra	Punjab	U.P.	Remarks
1948	47	24	102	
1948	47	24	102	After Integration of
1950	64	26	102	the princely States
1951	64	26	102	in 1949
1952	64	26	102	
1953	64	26	102	
1954	64	26	102	
1955	64	25	102	
1956	63	30	101	After Reorganization
1957	89	43	101	of States in 1956
1958	109	54	121	
1959	109	54	121	
1960	77	54	121	After bifurcation of
1961	77	71	124	Bombay into Maha-
1962	77	81	124	rashtra and Gujarat
1963	95	80	124	(1960)
1964	95	81	124	
1965	95	81	153	
1966	98	81	153	
1967	114	—	153	

Department of Administrative Reforms made of the I.A.S. cadre in Maharashtra shows that a sudden jump in 1957 from 89 to 109 was the result of administrative exigencies flowing from the needs of the Second Plan. These needs had neither been anticipated through proper planning nor spread out or phased to avoid suddenness.

And not all the increase effected in 1957 was so pressing 'as to necessitate such a large-scale abjuration of the normal principles of growth'. It soon became difficult to justify an increase at one stroke of twenty posts created in 1957, which, in turn, led to an addition of twenty-seven to the Direct Recruitment Quota. For, within a period of three years of their inclusion in the cadre, nearly 50 per cent of the total of twenty posts created were 'abolished or taken outside the cadre to be manned by officers of other services'. If the number of posts created had been less, the degree of distortion would have been proportionately reduced. The Direct Recruitment Quota had none the less to be settled at 27 on the insistence of the State Government, although the Home Minstry was in favour of a lower target.

The cadre remained static until 1962 when it increased by 18 posts leading to an expansion of 24, again all of a sudden. This was said to have been due to the appointment of a Chief Executive Officer for each of the zila parishads created by an Act of the State Legislature as a developmental measure of democratic decentralization. This could have been done in phases by a regular process of personnel planning. But it was argued that since the decisions were taken at the highest political level, there was practically no room for any decisive role for personnel planning in a field of development administration. It was further emphasized that it was not possible to postpone the scheme of zila parishads or phase it out in accordance with the availability of personnel for the purpose. However, the encadrement of the posts of Chief Executive Officer might easily have been spread out in lots. But that was not done on the ground that the officers appointed to the large majority of these posts were in any case State Civil Service officers who were borne on the select list for promotion to the I.A.S. cadre. Though sad in terms of quality, this was an interesting development of a State Government using development administration as an opportunity to extend its patronage as well as control over the cadre by means of extended encadrement of its own ex-cadre posts.[8] This unconventional method of recruitment to the I.A.S. was comparable to the 'Extension to the State Scheme' of 1949 and the 'Special Recruitment' of 1956. Together they resulted in the influx of State Civil Service officers in excess of the normal 5 per cent promotion quota, although, technically, they were all shown against the direct recruitment quota based on open competition.[9] This imbalance in the cadre structure of the I.A.S. arose likewise from the representation of the Scheduled Caste and Schedule Tribe officers whose strength had been far in excess of the promotion quota from the very beginning. Although unavoidable, the earlier resort to such *ad hoc* recruitment as War Service recruitment and Emergency Recruitment had produced similar effects by reducing the proportion of regular recruits. Cumulatively, the direct recruitment quota which was intended originally to be filled entirely by officers taken through the annual competitive examinations, came to be composed of various elements. The mixture of the senior scale of the different State Service officers appointed to the I.A.S. through these *ad hoc* methods accounted for anything from 27.6 per cent in Madras to 52 per cent in Rajasthan. To take an all-India view on the same data, the recruits admitted as a result of the open competitive examination accounted for only 43.2 per cent of the officers of the I.A.S. in the senior scale and above, instead of the original expectation of 80 per cent.[10] A conscious effect could have rectified, by means of advance planning, the earlier imbalance in the structure of the Service. But, as subsequent methods of *ad hoc* recruitment showed, development planning, instead of being dovetailed, remained divorced from personnel planning.

This was not only peculiar to Maharashtra. It happened in certain other States also, particularly in Punjab.[11] The first rise in its cadre from 35 to 43 was due mainly to the reorganization of States and the consequent merger of PEPSU with Punjab. Even so, taking 1 January 1957 as the base where the merger with PEPSU had been completed and the Second Five-Year Plan started, its cadre nearly doubled in the six years ending 1 January 1963, senior posts in the cadre under the State Government increasing from 43 to 80. On the basis of information received by the Department of Administrative Reforms, it transpired that this had happened not strictly on merit, but due to manoeuvring by different agencies at the administrative and political levels 'functioning under certain pulls and pressures'. These 'brought in extraneous considerations to bear' on matters of personnel policy and organization. The *Report* of the Department of Administrative Reforms thus commented by saying. 'This has in fact been the bane of the management of the I.A.S. cadre in the States in recent years. Cadres have been sought to be revised, or not revised, on irrelevant considerations like the benefits such a step would confer on officers of the Select List'[12] formed by the State Government for the promotion of its officers to the I.A.S. cadre, the object being to ensure an extension of its control over that cadre through its own nominees. In addition, ex-cadre posts, with duties and responsibilities identical to those of the cadre posts, were created for the same purpose in lieu of cadre posts kept in abeyance. These were then upgraded or encadred to reinforce the strength of the State Government's personnel in the I.A.S. cadre.

It is therefore not only the cadre that expanded rapidly in Punjab. The more disturbing trend was the phenomenal growth of the equivalent ex-cadre posts created during 1948–64. The number of such posts which existed during the six years including and preceding 1964, and the manner in which they were manned, is shown in the table on page 221, which gives similar figures for three earlier years selected for comparison.[13]

The beginning of the Third Five-Year Plan in 1960–1 thus witnessed a sudden increase in the number of ex-cadre posts which were either encadred or kept in abeyance for promotional purposes. This heavy increase became especially marked after 1962. It was tantamount practically to forming a parallel cadre. It indicated also a heavy and irregular diversion of cadre officers to ex-cadre posts since 1961, the beginning of the Third Plan. The creation of such a large number of ex-cadre posts upset the management of the I.A.S. cadre of the State.

Year	No. of ex-cadre posts equivalent to IAS	No. held by	
		Cadre officers	Non-cadre officers
1948	23	5	18
1949	28	8	20
1956	22	7	15
1959	27	7	20
1960	45	34	11
1961	49	41	8
1962	61	38	23
1963	75	41	34
1964	89	43	46

These posts were normally meant to be manned by deputation reserves in the cadre. The distortion created by such large-scale creation of equivalent ex-cadre posts was connected with the maintenance of over-large select lists,[14] which resulted in the effective promotion of a disproportionately heavy number of State Civil Service officers, far in excess of the quota envisaged by the I.A.S. scheme, as well as to the incorrect and irregular utilization of I.A.S. officers. The irregularity arising from over-staffing at senior levels in the Secretariat was clearly brought out in the Report of the Punjab Administrative Reforms Commission.

There were other States which in the six year period from 1957 also made additions to their respective cadres. But none of them match Punjab in terms of cadre expansion. Punjab, with an 86 per cent increase, led the next State (Orissa) by a margin of 18 per cent and other States by even more. Comparable additions in other States, for instance, were as follows:[15] Andhra Pradesh, 18 per cent; Bihar 20 per cent; Kerala 7 per cent; Madhya Pradesh 19 per cent; Madras 3 per cent; Mysore 11 per cent; Orissa 68 per cent; Rajasthan 1 per cent; Utter Pradesh 4 per cent; and West Bengal 21 per cent.

Prima facie, therefore, the additions made in the Punjab cadre were 'excessive'. But a more objectionable feature of those additions was that they 'became necessary not to meet the needs of work but to absorb personnel'.[16] The empirical studies which the Department of Administrative Reforms completed in 1968 showed that in the case of Punjab deletion and addition of cadre posts were done 'for personal reasons'. It cited an instance where a post which had been created during the Second World War was deleted from the cadre and kept outside it with a view to accommodating a non-I.A.S. officer in a substantive capacity on a permanent post in a higher scale to enable him to drew pensionary benefits against that post. The declared exigencies of development administration in such cases acted as a cover to justify the use of unconventional methods of recruitment by appointing authorities on the score of their so-called commitment to official policy. And all this happened under the chief ministership of Sardar Pratap Singh Kairon, who enjoyed the full support of Jawaharlal Nehru, the Prime Minister.

Apart from the increase in the number of ex-cadre posts, there were temporary additions to the cadre, which State Governments used as another cover for control over the I.A.S. Under the Memorandum regarding the constitution of the I.A.S., all posts included in the Cadre Schedule were to be filled by members of that Service, unless the vacancy was not likely to last for more than three months, or, in the opinion of the Government concerned, there was no suitable I.A.S. officer to hold the post. All such appointments for a period exceeding three months were required to be reported to the Central Government with reasons for making them. But in no case was a Provincial Civil Service officer to be appointed to hold a superior post included in the Schedule for a period of more than one year, unless the Federal Public Service Commission (later U.P.S.C.) certified that the officer was fit to hold a superior post in the I.A.S. And for the continuance of such posts for more than one year the approval of the Government of India was also necessary. No such posts were, however, to continue beyond a period of three years. Yet these rules were continuously violated with impunity in Uttar Pradesh where resort was taken to the creation of temporary additions in preference to ex-cadre posts. This is clear from the following table:[17]

Temporary additions in U.P.

Period for which post existed	No. of posts
Less than 1 year	45
1–3 years	64
3–5 years	37
Over 5 years	40
	186

The study of Uttar Pradesh made by the Department of Administrative Reforms brought to the surface a number of disclosures which reflected even on the Home Ministry. The State Government, for instance, continued temporary posts from year to year without the approval of the Central Government. No one seemed to bother till the Accountant-General raised objections in 1957. The result was that approval for the continuance of posts beyond one year was sought after a considerable lapse of time. Surprisingly, the approval of the Central Government was given at the level of Under Secretary, without any examination being done at the Centre of the necessity of having all these posts in the senior scale: the permission was given at this level as a routine matter and no particular importance was thus attached to the continuous violation of rules. Even so, a large number of posts (41 per cent) continued illegally beyond a period of three years. Unapproved officers in fact continued to officiate on these or regular posts. 'This', as the study pointed out, 'throws considerable light on the actual mechanics of the management of the cadre by the State Government and on the absence of proper scrutiny even in the Ministry of Home Affairs.[18]

Excessive expansion of cadre and equivalent ex-cadre posts, plus temporary additions, were thus all developments which seriously impaired the quality of recruitment. The excessive expansion of the cadre, as said before, proceeded from the absence of a proper quantitative and qualitative assessment before creating posts. Posts were created with inadequate workload or at unnecessarily high levels, when the kind of work involved could be performed by personnel of a lower category. This was specially so in Punjab, where several posts of Under Secretary were upgraded without justification, a tendency adversely commented upon even by the Punjab Administrative Reforms Commission. Another important cause for expansion was the inadequacy of specialized and technical personnel, which dictated the expendiency of including in the cadre such specialized posts as could be manned by I.A.S. officers because of the managerial and co-ordinative dimensions involved in the performance of their duties. The posts of Director of Agriculture or of Fisheries, etc. came under this category, which, in the long run, was intended to be manned by technical hands. This principle also applied to foreign postings and those of a semi-specialized character which did not necessarily have to be manned by I.A.S. officers. A more important factor in the expansion of the cadre, however, was the pressure from those awaiting promotion; for with the multiplication of senior posts, increased opportunities of promotion became naturally available. This was surprisingly recognized by certain States as a principle that influenced the expansion of the cadre.

To improve the quality of recruitment it was therefore suggested that, while the demand for certain ex-cadre posts of a specialized nature should be met by the deputation reserve of a State on a 'flexible' basis, the appointment of the 'essential cadre' of I.A.S. officers should be restricted on a fairly uniform basis to such posts as Chief Secretary, Home Secretary, Commissioners of Divisions, the Collector, Members of the Board of Revenue, Secretaries, Deputy Secretaries and certain heads of departments. And since the exigencies that needed to be met by the deputation reserve were bound to be of a flexible nature, this reserve could be increased or decreased according to the requirements of the State concerned. In addition, care had to be taken to see that only those ex-cadre posts should be equated to cadre posts which had, besides an adequate load of work, an important managerial content. On the other hand, such posts as qualified for inclusion in the cadre could not be kept in abeyance or outside the cadre beyond a maximum limit of three years. Seized with the problem of how best to improve the standards of recruitment, the Study Team on 'Centre–State Relations' later added a new dimension by recommending a special examination for first and high second class graduates as well as a review of the existing patterns of remuneration and the environment of work, which influenced potential entrants to the Service.

The mechanism of the rules governing the I.A.S. was another factor that raised certain problems affecting recruitment and cadre management. Though elaborately devised, these rules left a number of loopholes which caused confusion, for example, between 'deputation reserve' and the 'central deputation quota'. In the absence of a clearly defined purpose the central deputations, which were intended to be made exclusively from the central deputation quota, claimed at times a share in the deputation reserve designed to fulfil the needs of a State. This caused imbalance in the distribution of personnel between the Centre and the State. Similarly, there was ambiguity over the 'direct recruitment quota' and 'promotion quota'. Although the cadre schedule did mention a direct recruitment quota and the general understanding was that posts other than those in the promotion quota of the State Civil Service were normally to be filled by direct recruitment from the annual competitive examinations, there were no specific provisions in the recruitment rules to this effect. The rules did not specifically provide that direct recruits and promotees were to be recruited in the ratio of 80 per cent and 20 per cent. The result, as said before, was that the percentage of direct recruits in the cadre remained far below the schedule.

Promotions from the State Civil Service were governed by the Indian Administrative Serive (Appointment by Promotion) Regulation, 1955. This Regulation, as already mentioned, had provided for selection to be made by a Committee, which, in addition to the Chairman of the U.P.S.C., or, in his absence, any other Member of the Commission, consisted of the Chief Secretary and three or four senior civil servants belonging to the State cadre. In fact, no member of the Committee other than the Chairman or the Member of the U.P.S.C. was to be a person who was not a member of the Service. Under the Regulation, the Central Government could, of course, amend the schedule describing the composition of the Selection Committee. But it could not do this independently of the State government. It remained even unrepresented on the Committee. The select lists formed by the State governments were under the Regulation subject to review and revision by the U.P.S.C., but this too was more formal than real. Besides, there was hardly any provision to ensure timely review or revision and the U.P.S.C. could not ensure it, not being responsible executively.

The tradition of provincial autonomy in respect of 'listed posts' had indeed been reinforced by the additional concessions made by the Central Government when the I.A.S. was created.[19] These concessions and the federal nature of the Constitution that followed, whetted the appetite of the successor State governments for an extention of patronage and disciplinary control. In the formation of the select lists, therefore, it was the power of local politics that weighed, not the higher considerations of professional efficiency and uprightness of conduct. The schedule describing the composition of the selection committee in the different States thus specified categories and not officers, the object being to leave undefined the discretion to be exercised by a State government, more especially the minister concerned, who could appoint to a selection committee officers of his own choice even within a restricted category. The position of a State government became further strengthened by a Home Ministry Notification of 2 June 1969 which provided that the absence of a member, other than the Chairman or Member of the U.P.S.C., 'shall not invalidate the proceedings of the Committee if more than half the members of the Committee had attended its meetings'.[20] A State government had yet another advantage arising from the select list being treated as 'confidential'; for if the list were to be notified or circulated, it might operate as a serious check on the exercise of ministerial discretion to alter or modify it; for the Regulation provided that, while making appointments a State government must follow the order in which the names of officers appeared in the select list.

The select list was thus not an effective safeguard against the abuse of patronage through promotion. This was specially so because a State government had under the Regulation the necessary power to appoint to a cadre post a member of the State Civil Service whose name was not in the select list or listed sufficiently high in it.[21] The only condition for such appointments was that the vacancy was not likely to last for more than three months or that there was, according to the State government, no suitable cadre officer available to fill it. But, as mentioned before, the promotion so made to cadre posts continued for years even without reference to the Central Government.

Further, rule 10 of the I.A.S. Cadre Rules, 1954, had laid down that when a State government proposed to keep a cadre post vacant for a period exceeding six months, 'the State Government shall forthwith make a report to the Central Government' in respect of the reasons for the proposal, the period for which the State government proposed to keep the post vacant, and whether it was proposed to make any arrangements for the performance of the functions of the post held in abeyance, and, if so, the particulars of such arrangements.[22] And yet, as already seen, the practice of keeping cadre posts in abeyance and creating ex-cadre posts in lieu continued merely for the promotion of individuals.[23] This was a result not only of loopholes in the rules, but also of a considerable measure of discretionary authority left with the State governments originally to secure their participation in the Central scheme for an all-India Administrative Service. The vagueness of rules flowed from the need to reconcile the requirements of national unity with local desires for the exercise of patronage.

When the I.A.S. was first created, it was agreed that, subject to the final report of the first Pay Commission already appointed, the scale of pay should be fixed uniformly at Rs 350–400–450–450–500. While recruitment was to be governed by the existing Regulations for the I.C.S., the question of leave, pension and other conditions of service was to be regulated by rules applicable to the Provincial Civil Service.

The rules governing the combined competitive examinations held in 1947–8[24] fixed the time-scale of pay for I.A.S. officers under two separate scales, junior and senior. The junior scale was Rs 350–400–450–450–500–540–30–600–EB–30–870–40–950 (19 years). The senior scale, on the other hand, was fixed at Rs 800 (6th year or under)–50–1000–60–1300–50–1800 (25 years). A probationer was to start on the junior time-scale, his period of probation being counted towards leave, pension or increment.

Further changes were introduced under the Indian Administrative Service (Pay) Rules 1954. These were statutory rules made under the All-India Service Act, 1951. The time-scales of pay admissible under these rules and the dates with effect from which the time-scales were to be deemed to have come into force were as follows:[25]

Junior Scale
Rs 400–400–500–40–700–EB–30–1,000   With effect from 1 April 1960
          (18 years)

Senior Scale
(a) Time-scale: Rs 900(6th year or under)—   With effect from 1 April 1960
          50–1,000–60–1,600–50–1800 (22 years)
(b) Selection Grade: Rs 1,800–100–2,000   With effect from 1 March 1962

However, in order to safeguard the interest of I.C.S. officers, the rules provided that a member of the Service to whom another time-scale of pay was admissible under any order in force immediately before the commencement of these rules was to continue to draw pay in that scale.

In addition to the scales so introduced under the 1954 rules, three super time-scales of pay were introduced under a Home Ministry Notification dated 1 September 1964.[26] These super time-scales, which were above the selection grade, existed in 1968 when the Department of Administrative Reforms reported on the management of the I.A.S.[27] They were (i) Rs 2500–125–2750, (ii) Rs 3,000 and (iii) Rs 3,500.

Although considered technically as part of the senior scale and clubbed together with other super time-scale posts when calculating promotions, the selection grade was not attached to any specific post. It was allowed to suitable officers on a personal basis, subject to the prescribed minimum of 5 per cent and the maximum limit of 20 per cent of the senior posts in the cadre under the State government concerned.

In the beginning there was no rule governing promotion to different grades. As a result of certain judicial proceedings in the Supreme Court, however, it was found necessary to insert a rule in the I.A.S. (Recruitment) Rules, 1954. Rule 6–A, inserted under a Home Ministry Notification of 13 September 1966 thus empowered the State governments to promote at their discretion a direct recruit from the junior scale to the senior scale on the basis of his length of service, experience and performance in the junior scale.

Rule 6–A, which came into force in September 1966, thus introduced two new dimensions in terms of promotion. First, appointments of direct recruits to posts in the senior time-scale were to be made by the State government concerned; and secondly, notwithstanding considerations of the length of service, experience and prior performance, no direct recruit could be promoted to a senior scale unless the State government was satisfied that he was suitable for appointment to a post in the senior time-scale. Both the conditions of promotion, which were heavily weighted in favour of the State governments in terms of disciplinary control, tended to weaken the original all-India concept of the I.A.S.

But since the actual length of service, qualifications and standards of performance required for promotion had not been defined by Rule 6–A or any other rule, different standards and practices developed in different States resulting in highly fluctuating promotion prospects Regular recruits were promoted to senior time-scales between four years of service and seven, and promotions regulated by the pyramidal principle of earmarking a fixed percentage of posts in the States for superior grades. A corrective was supplied by the Home Ministry in 1956, when the State governments were urged to consider regular recruits with four years' service for promotion. It introduced some measure of uniformity. Even so, variations continued from State to State.

The 1968 report of the Department of Administrative Reforms on the management of the I.A.S. recognized the broad principle that it was undesirable to have wide variations from State to State in promotion prospects, and that the four-year norm was sound, although the V.T. Krishnamachari Report on District Administration had suggested a course of training according to which an I.A.S. officer would go to the districts as Collector after a period of not less than six years. It was argued that in the post-1947 period conditions had progressively changed and a larger number of senior-scale posts created in the Secretariat and departments which could be manned by young officers, for in these posts they were not directly exposed to influences and situations requiring greater experience and maturity. Promotion to those posts, on the other hand, gave officers an opportunity to develop initiative, confidence and the ability to take decisions while they had, in addition, the advantage of guidance and supervision by departmental or secretariat chiefs. The four-year norm was therefore defended as the most suitable and it was thought it would develop officers of a basically high calibre quickly by giving them responsible jobs at an early age.

This argument in favour of a four-year norm was apparently sound and logical, but it was not without compulsion that the Home Ministry introduced it in 1956 to prevent stagnation arising from the excessive and unplanned growth of the cadre, particularly following the Special Recruitment of that year which brought in over-age officers recruited from the open market and the State Services. It was this over-recruitment that dictated the expediency of early promotion for direct recruits who might otherwise have missed the opportunity because of the large-scale entry into the cadre of extraneous elements.

Even so, the four-year norm remained by and large inoperative. Studies made by the Department of Administrative Reforms showed that in Maharashtra, Mysore and Uttar Pradesh this was not followed in several cases, even though vacancies existed. But these were filled by ex-cadre officers, although the I.A.S. Rules of 1954 had specifically laid down that 'every cadre post shall be filled by a cadre officer'.[28] The State governments took advantage of their discretion under Rule 9 to make temporary appointments of non-cadre officers who officiated in cadre posts. Once appointed, they at times continued indefinitely, without the Central Government being informed. This practice which different States adopted to fill cadre posts by non-cadre officers naturally distorted the character and the structure of the Service: but on some occasions even the Home Ministry did not object. Commenting on this state of affairs the report of the Department of Administrative Reforms thus pointed out:

It is understandable that the Central Government should be reluctant to use Rule 9 and thus fetter the discretion of the State governments. But it must at the same time be borne in mind that the I.A.S. is an all-India Service and the Home Ministry, to say the least, shared with the State governments the

230   *Government and Bureaucracy in India (1947–76)*

responsibility for its correct management and indeed is the ultimate repository of it. The application of this rule is a delicate matter and a balance has to be maintained between the claims of correct management and the discretion of the States, but considering a long and almost uninterrupted history of *laissez faire* in which some States distorted management without any correction, the Ministry of Home Affairs must be considered to have been too tardy in using this rule.[29]

Promotion above the senior time-scales was in two stages, namely, to the selection grade and to posts above that to super time-scale. While the first became relevant from March 1962, the second consisted of sub-stages, each sub-stage representing a level in the top hierarchy, such as Divisional Commissioner, First Member of the Board of Revenue, and Chief Secretary.

A general feature of promotion trends was that, while at the centre a super time-scale post of Joint Secretary's rank, for instance, was reached after 17 years' service, even the selection grade in some States would not be attained before 19-21 years.[30] This was specially so in Uttar Pradesh and Maharashtra where a disproportionately heavy intake under the war service and emergency recruitments caused serious bottlenecks, slowing down the upward movement of officers to the super time-scale posts. Partly to remove these bottlenecks, the Study Team of the Administrative Reforms Commission on Centre–State Relations recommended a scheme of voluntary retirement on proportionate pension after 15 years of service. The benefits of such an arrangement, it was hoped, might accrue to both sides in certain situations. The option, for example, might be welcomed by some officers in a situation where promotions were made on merit and not on seniority. Another situation was 'afforded by bottlenecks in promotion which exist in some States and which, in view of the large recruitment undertaken, will always afflict personnel management in some State or the other'. An 'exodus', as a result of a liberalized retirement rule, would in these circumstances be more likely to be realized in cadres 'where there are such bottlenecks than where there are none and should not be considered an unhealthy development'. This scheme of voluntary retirement was thus designed to 'fight frustration and relieve congestion on the one hand and, on the other, help unsuitable officers to make their exist'. A limit of 15 years was suggested, so that the retiring officers might be able to take to an alternative profession if he so wished.[31] The principle of this recommendation 'was also indicated by the Commission's Study Team on the 'Machinery of Government.'

Executive Development and Deployment

Executive development and the deployment of officers formed part of the device by which the main objectives[32] of the I.A.S. were sought to be achieved. While the policy of recruitment tried to secure the objectives by means of an all-India competitive examination of high standards, a policy of development aimed, first, at training young officers for higher jobs by exposing them gradually to wider areas of responsibility, and secondly, at sharing their services with the Centre on a systematic basis.

The object of executive development was to promote in senior officers the necessary confidence to take decisions and the ability to appreciate complicated situations. The first attribute called for a progressive devolution of responsibility, while the second demanded a knowledge not only of men and affairs, but also of the administrative process and activity involved in the complexity of situations. In this age of technological advance it meant a degree of specialization signifying not a total technical professionalization, but a broad understanding of related functions and an adequate knowledge of the task undertaken. This concept of specialization needed to be systematically developed both at the Centre and in the States. In other words, the deputation of I.A.S. officers to the Centre ought ideally to be guided by all three principles involved in a policy of executive development, that is, the principle of commonness of the Service to the Centre and the States, the principle of the progressive devolution of responsibility and the principle of specialization, the first of these principles being primarily a function of Central deputation.

The development of decision-taking capacity through devolution of responsibility involved mainly two things: inculcation of independance and self-confidence at an early age, when the habits of mind could still be moulded, and the avoidance of situations where a raw hand would burn his fingers repeatedly to produce the opposite result. Development therefore called for a positive attempt at devolving responsibility on officers and an effort to see that this devolution was graduated. The task of graduated devolution, however, could be accomplished successfully in a cadre system only through a classification of posts in terms of the extent and nature of responsibility, and the absence of the position-classification system made this necessary in regulating any upward movement from a lower class to a higher. There was no difficulty at the junior level; for posts in the junior scale continued, according to the old tradition, to be actually training posts. All posts above the senior scale likewise presented little or no difficulty; for they were comparatively few and well classified, there being not much variation in the responsibility attaching to posts in the same grade. It was the senior-scale posts that needed to be classified carefully; for the scale itself was wide, ranging, as it did, from Rs 900 to Rs 1800 and an officer spent more time in this grade than in any other.

The classification attempted by the Department of Administrative Reforms divided senior-scale posts into four categories, identifiable in terms of the responsibility involved in each. The post of Collector formed a clear and recognizable category by itself and so did that of a Secretary to the government in a State where it was in the senior scale. However, there were (and still are) posts like deputies to certain heads of departments, Additional Collectors, Subdivisional Officers and Under Secretaries in the senior scale which did not require the same experience and decision-making capacity as a Collector. These were recognized as posts for first promotion. The second category normally consisted of Collectors, a distinct category clearly identifiable and known historically for their cumulative responsibility in the field of district administration. The third category included posts of Additional/Joint Secretaries and heads of departments other than those classed in the fourth category. Some Deputy Secretaries were also included here in some States where Secretaries were in the rank of Commissioners. Category IV, on the other hand, was made up of Secretaries and heads of major departments. There were, in addition, Central deputation posts which, in this classification, included equivalents to categories III and IV. Though part of the senior time-scale, the selection grade, as said before, remained unattached to any specific post, being open to suitable officers on merit.

An analysis of deployment practice in the States, however, showed that no clear policy was followed in respect of postings. Often, senior officers were posted to lower categories and their juniors to higher categories. For instance, select-list officers who ought to have been absorbed normally in category I posts, the first wing of the responsibility ladder, were often appointed to posts in categories II and III, with cadre officers of 15 years' seniority (and at times 16-19 years' seniority). This became particularly noticeable in cases of posts in category IV being held by officers of 8-12 years' experience when the several officers with 15-23 years' service were found in lower categories.[33]

The case of district postings included in the second category was specially noteworthy. The V.T.Krishnamachari Report had suggested that since adequate district experience was of primary importance for a young I.A.S. officer, State governments should ensure that every regular recruit after a minimum of six years' experience had an opportunity of serving as Collector for three years at least. The 1968 study of the Department of Administration Reforms, however, revealed a different story in practice. According to it, there was a general aversion to posting regular recruits to districts, non-cadre offfficers being preferred for such postings in spite of the availability of suitable officers of six years' service. As the following table shows very few Collectorships were, for example, given to regular recruits in Maharashtra.[34]

As on 1 Jan.	Total no. of posts	No. of regular recruits holding posts	No. of regular recruits eligible for posts who had not held them
1956	28	7 (inc. 5 ICS)	4
1957	43	3	7
1958	43	7	7
1959	43	7	10
1960	43	4	10
1961	26	4	9
1962	26	7	11
1963	51	9	11
1964	51	9	11
1965	51	7	8
1966	51	12	8

Thus of the total number of 456 posts in Maharashtra, only 76 or 16.6 per cent were held by regular recruits during 1956–66. This number included the Chief Executive Officers of zila parishads who formed part of Category II posts, so the regular recruits who held charge of the districts were thus far fewer. The Punjab situation was slightly better, with regular recruits holding 17.6 per cent of the 198 such charges, as shown in the table overleaf.[35]

The position improved a little when the Home Ministry stressed the desirability of giving district experience to regular recruits. Even so, on 1 January 1967 out of a total of 321 Collectors all over India, only 134 were regular recruits.[36] A majority of the regular recruits posted to districts were kept there for less than two years and some even for less than a year. Denial of a full tenure could not be explained

As on 1 Jan.	Total no. of districts	No. of regular recruits holding posts	No. of regular recruits eligible for posts who had not held them
1956	13	3	2
1957	18	6	1
1958	18	2	3
1959	18	3	2
1960	18	2	4
1961	18	2	6
1962	19	2	6
1963	19	3	4
1964	19	2	7
1965	19	4	4
1966	19	6	7

by a surfeit of cadre officers awaiting their turn, for in most cases non-cadre officers received the benefit of district experience. For instance in terms of length of stay in districts the break-up in Maharashtra on 1 January 1967 was as follows:[37]

Up to 1 year	1 (6.2%)
1 year and above, but below 2 years	17 (53.1%)
2 years and above, but below 3 years	10 (31.3%)
3 years and above	3 (9.4%)

There were, in addition, cases where eligible officers had not been posted to districts at all, either as Collectors or Chief Executive Officers; some were deputed to the Centre as Under Secretaries, though they should have first acquired district experience as part of a sound development policy. In Punjab, too, a number of eligible officers had not been allowed to hold district charges.[38] It was this faulty implementation of policy that caused instability among direct recruits, affected their independence of judgement and rendered them subject to local and political influences. The need for specialization in the generalist framework had been recognized and this shift in emphasis had become perceptible as early as the 1870's when, in view of the urgency of relief operations, there grew a demand for the magistracy as a class being relieved of judicial functions. Sir James Fitzjames Stephen, the Law Member of the Government of India, agreed in principle to the separation of executive and judicial functions in respect of the magistracy in general, but not of the Collectors who 'within their own limits' acted for all practical purposes as 'the

Government', exercising criminal jurisdiction, 'the most distinctive and most easily and generally recognized mark of sovereign power'.[39] Considering the nature of Indian society, it took decades for the projected separation of functions to take effect. Even so, civil servants, as part of their criminal judicial duties, got themselves directly involved in such welfare activity as the abolition of infanticide, sati and thuggee; the protection of the cultivating peasantry through a series of land reforms; the administration of relief against famines and epidemics; the construction of railways under public control; the development of a well-knit communications system; the promotion of rural education and local bodies; the development of irrigation sources like the Mahanadi, Godavari, Krishna anicuts, and later, the entire Ganga-Jamuna canal system. The administrators could not but play their part in the promotion of social and economic development. 'The liberalism of British politics in the nineteenth century could not be kept on leash'.[40]

The old concept of the district officer being a virtual sovereign of his district could not remain unchanged, particularly under the impact of the First World War. Speaking of the civil service of India, the Montford Report (1918), for instance, clearly pointed out: 'We are no longer seeking to govern a subject race by means of the Services, we are seeking to make the Indian people self-governing'.[41] The Reforms introduced for the first time an era of partnership and consultation emphasizing attempts to convince rather than to direct. Operationally, this new trend was limited to the provinces. But a beginning had none the less been made towards seeking popular co-operation for administrative action, a change that was necessary for developmental purposes.

The socio-economic developments that were taking place in the pre-1919 period were, broadly speaking, within the framework of free enterprise, with a minimum of state participation where necessary, but socialistic trends which followed the First World War pressed for increasing state participation. The appointment of the Industrial Commission during the War and, subsequently, of the Royal Commissions on Agriculture and Labour in the 1920's were all expressions of official concern for public control over the agencies of production. This concern was reinforced by the experiences of the Second World War. The whole attitude of the bureaucracy towards the role of the state in economic development was being modified, and the fear of communism in the post-War period obliged the government to formulate some detailed and comprehensive plans for post-War reconstruction.

The first step was the creation of an official Board of Industrial and Scientific Research, which was followed by the establishment of a Reconstruction Committee of the Viceregal Council. In June 1944, a Planning and Development Department was created under Sir Ardeshir Dalal. The so-called 'Bombay Plan' was simultaneously sponsored by some of India's most distinguished industrialists. To provide general guidance the Reconstruction Committee formulated and published in 1945 its *Second Report*, a document at once bold in conception and socialistic in character. The years 1944-6 in fact saw the publication of a series of reports on subjects of developmental importance, especially in the fields of agriculture and agricultural technology, rural credit and co-operation, public health and education, irrigation, railways and insurance. These were reflected in the formulation of the First Five-Year Plan which, structurally speaking, might be said to be an offspring of the Bombay Plan, while its contents were largely derived from the official Reconstruction Programmes of the pre-1947 Government.[42]

This gradual shift of emphasis in favour of the positive functions of the state tended to reduce the position of the Collector from a virtual custodian of sovereign power to a mere co-ordinator of official functions in his district. But since social change did not keep pace with political progress and administrative transformation, the importance of maintenance administration did not diminish to the extent demanded by development administration. The problems of law and order created by serious communal riots and campus disturbances continued more or less unabated in the Indian situation. Thus, while the need for the generalist administrator remained undiminished, the exigencies of development administration dictated the necessity of specialization, especially in the post-Independence period when the volume and variety of development activity underwent a sudden spurt. A specialist in a generalist civil service was appropriate in the conditions of Indian society.

This limited concept of specialization within the framework of a generalist civil service demanded that individual officers should be posted to jobs of a related nature, such as, for example, personnel administration, financial administration, general or regulatory administration, and development administration, covering agricultural administration, economic and technological development, social services and local bodies. It was not easy putting the concept into practice, however. It involved operational difficulties in harmonizing the principle of specialization with that of seniority on the one hand and of the progressive devolution of higher responsibility on the other. For different specialized categories offered different avenues of advancement, especially for the rank of Commissioner and above. And, if officers were to be kept within their specialized categories irrespective of seniority, injustice and hardship would occur. If this was to be avoided by a free upward movement, specialization would not become a fact. These difficulties could be partly obviated through central deputation, which might leave some mobility to a State in rationalizing promotion outlets consistent with the main object of specialization.

Central deputation and limited mobility in a State did not provide the whole answer, however. Even so, it was emphasized by the Department of Administrative Reforms that the choice of a specialized field should be offered to an officer at about the tenth year of service in accordance with his aptitude and potentiality. Some running-in period could be allowed, if necessary, to test his bent of mind, but a conscious effort had to be made to post an officer to the specialized category to which he had been allotted. A flexible device was also suggested to make specialization an operational feasibility. This related to a modification of the status of posts of Secretary and Head of department. It was pointed out that, if the post of Finance Secretary (in the rank of a Commissioner) fell vacant in a State and the next person equipped to fill it by virtue of his experience of financial matters was not ripe for promotion to this grade because two or three of his seniors might already be working in a different field, the solution was not to give the post to an unqualified senior but to appoint the specialized and qualified junior by including the post in the senior scale. To prevent adverse effects on the overall promotional opportunities of the cadre as a whole, the seniormost officer eligible in such a situation could be given the scale of Commissioner, while continuing to hold his existing post. This approach was in a sense comparable to the principle of 'parallel lines of promotion' introduced in 1873 by the Lieutenant-Governor of Bengal, Sir George Campbell, to enable officers to specialize either in the judicial or the executive branch of the I.C.S. after an initial experience of about ten years in the general line.[43] Despite the difficulties experienced in the management of promotional avenues, the principle of specialization in the generalist I.A.S. has come to be recognized as an essential feature of deployment policy.

As regards the system of Central deputation, it was intended to benefit governments both at the Centre and the States. To achieve this object two measures were adopted, one by fixing quotas for central deputation, and the other by fixing tenures for individual officers. The idea behind the first was that every State should have a fair share in giving and receiving experience, while that of the second was that this share should spread over as large a number of officers as could be accommodated. In neither case, however, did this system fulfil the purpose of its institution.

The allocation of the Central deputation quota was to be governed by definite rules. Each State under these rules was expected to depute a fixed number of officers and keep to this level when withdrawing officers who had completed their tenure by sending in their place other officers. In actual practice, however, this did not happen. This is clear from the table on page 239 which gives an idea of the extent to which the Central deputation quota was utilized as on 1 January 1966.[44]

It is seen that there was considerable imbalance in the proportion of officers drawn from the different states at the level of Deputy Secretary and above. Excepting Bihar and Uttar Pradesh, all the States had underutilized their quota. Bihar and Uttar Pradesh, on the other hand, were a case of over-utilization, and the number of officers deputed by them to the Centre was larger than the rules permitted. This was especially so in Uttar Pradesh where the over-utilization was alarmingly heavy and adversely affected cadre management. Moreover, as the quota for Central needs was fixed for each State separately and recruitment planned on that basis, any over-utilization of a particular reserve was bound to be at the cost of other constituents of the cadre. A large-scale diversion of cadre officers to the Centre in fact exposed more and more cadre posts in the States concerned to non-cadre officers. The only remedy suggested was to secure a return to the States of officers deputed in excess of the authorized strength. But this involved practical problems in situations where the over-utilization was as large as in the case of Uttar Pradesh. It caused not only personal hardship to officers who did not want to return, but administrative difficulties to the concerned State which was called upon to find suitable jobs for the reverted senior officers. The tenure principle laid down for Central deputation was

Utilization of the Central Deputation Quota

State	Sanctioned strength	*Proportionate strength	Utilization		Total	Imbalance (with ref. to)	
			Senior scale	Supertime scale		Col. 2	Col. 3
1	2	3	4	5	6	7	
Andhra Pradesh	37	33	14	12	26	+11	+7
Assam	32	20	7	7	14	+18	+6
Bihar	37	36	18	23	41	−4	−5
Delhi & H.P.	16	9	1	1	2	+14	+7
Gujarat	34	26	10	11	21	+13	+5
Jammu and Kashmir	10	4	2	—	2	+8	+2
Kerala	16	14	4	5	9	+7	+5
Madhya Pradesh	39	36	16	14	30	+9	+6
Madras	34	28	11	13	24	+10	+4
Maharashtra	39	34	15	16	31	+8	+3
Mysore	28	22	15	8	23	+5	−1
Orissa	33	27	11	13	24	+9	+3
Punjab	32	32	17	9	26	+6	+6
Rajasthan	28	26	23	2	25	+3	+1
Uttar Pradesh	61	53	41	61	102	−41	−49
West Bengal	33	29	16	11	27	+6	+2

*Proportionate strength was calculated with reference to the number of officers in position in the cadre.

thus largely followed at the middle level and not at the more senior
levels of Joint Secretary and above. At the level of Secretary, Special
Secretary and Additional Secretary, officers hardly went back to their
parent States. Commenting on the situation the Study Team of the
Administrative Reforms Commission on Centre-State relations thus
rightly pointed out: [45]

One reason why the system of forward and backward movement at the level of
Secretary to the Government of India breaks down completely is that he is
senior to, and carries emoluments higher than, any officer under a State
government. He therefore tends to develop a personal interest in staying as
long as possible in Delhi. Nor indeed in actual practice is he forced to return as
it is informally recognized that that would amount to a come down for him.
Unhealthy attitudes are therefore bred affecting morale, independence of
judgement and standards of behaviour.

The Study Team therefore suggested a way out, a flexible approach
to the Chief Secretary's post and status, so that it could be entertained, if personnel considerations so required, in a rank equivalent to
that of a Secretary to the Government of India. This, it was believed,
would enable the return of a senior officer to a State without implying
demotion. A similar principle could be followed for the post of Financial
Commissioner or Development Commissioner by allowing them to be
equated with an Additional Secretary to the Government of India. It
was hoped that this principle might make the required rotation
physically possible.

Training

Another means by which the main objectives of the I.A.S. were
sought to be secured was to subject recruits to rigorous training in a
residential institute where, through study and interaction, they might
develop insights into the manifold aspects of administrative behaviour and acquire the ability to handle with confidence both regulatory and developmental functions.

The training of I.A.S. recruits proceeded on the lines of the erstwhile I.C.S. [46] No drastic or even clearly defined break with the past
occurred on the transfer of power. What distinguished the I.A.S. from
the I.C.S., however, was that the new Service was wholly Indian in
composition and, in the absence of the 'special responsibilities'
formerly vested in the Governors, its independence of judgement,
resilience of character and permeative strength were reduced before
the forces of democracy and the egalitarian philosophy intended to

replace the oligarchic guardianship of the men who earlier ruled India. It was only in terms of administrative functions that the I.A.S. was supposed to have been designed on the model of the I.C.S., and thus the training of the new recruits followed the old pattern generally even while accommodating changing needs.

When training in England was stopped in 1940, a temporary institution located at Dehra Dun trained entrants to the I.C.S. from 1941 to 1944. With recruitment to the I.A.S. beginning with war service candidates the Indian Administrative Service Training School was established in Delhi at Metcalfe House in March 1947. This was redesignated the National Academy of Administration and moved to Mussoorie in September 1959.

The training of the first I.A.S. batch of probationers admitted to the Training School in Delhi was to be governed by the I.A.S. (Probationary Service and Seniority of Recruits) Rules issued under a Home Department Notification of 24 April 1947. These Rules were 'based on the I.C.S. (Probationary Service) Rules, 1940' and modified only to meet the special requirements of 'war service' recruits.[47] Rule 6 had laid down that probationers 'who undergo probation at a training centre shall be required, at the end of the period of probation, to obtain such marks in each subject at an examination to be conducted by the Federal Public Service Commission as the Central Government may decide in consultation with the Commision'.[48] The subjects of this examination were Indian law, Indian history, economics (with particular reference to Indian economics), public administration, riding, Hindustani, and one language of the province to which the probationer was assigned.

On the recommendation[49] of M.J. Desai of the I.C.S., the first Principal of the School, the Federal Public Service Commission agreed to dispense with the final examination of the probationers and in lieu of this, the Principal and teachers of the School were to conduct periodical tests and interviews to assess the performance of each officer. It was none the less emphasized by the Commission that at the end of the training period a full record of each candidate, including not merely his marks in the written tests but a detailed assessment of his intelligence and character, should be furnished to the Commission, together with a list indicating the order in which the Principal wished to place the candidates. The Commission was then to interview them and, on the results of the interview and their record, decide their final ranking.[50] Though Desai agreed in principle with these suggestions in respect of the ranking of the probationers, he reiterated that it would not be practicable to adopt them in so far as the first batch of recruits was concerned; for during their training they had to be employed in the performance of emergency work in East Punjab and Delhi. He therefore insisted that the probationers should be exempted from the final examination and posted to the provinces without being required to appear before the Commission. The probationers, in all 54, were thus posted to the several provinces regardless of the Rules and suggestions of the F.P.S.C.

Indeed, in the first few years of its establishment the Training School could not function with rigour or institutional formality. It was called upon to conduct short-term courses for all categories of entrants to the Service, such as war-service candidates, emergency recruits and regular recruits. Its tasks were in addition complicated by their disparity in age and experience and the urgent requirements of the States which called for trainees being deputed to handle the post-Partition situation. The special orientation courses which were sought to be organized for officers recruited from the former princely states were yet another source of headache. In these circumstances, quality became a serious casualty.

When Desai left for the Ministry of Commerce on 7 June 1948, he was succeeded by S.B. Bapat, then Joint Secretary in the Home Ministry. Desai had earlier submitted to the Home Ministry a significant Note,[51] giving details of a programme of I.A.S. training in the provinces and requiring every Provincial Government to depute one P.C.S. officer a year for training at the School in Delhi. It was felt that the presence at the School of P.C.S. officers with a knowledge and experience of practical administration would be of value to I.A.S. trainees when they visited their respective provinces for further training.

The main features of the programme suggested by Desai represented a new shift of emphasis, both pragmatic and ideological. The I.A.S. training in the provinces was to be related to a job to be done at each stage, from the village upwards, and followed by a definite test by a superior officer immediately above. The object was to undo the effect of a 'very pronounced' tendency on the part of senior officers 'during the past few years' to leave junior officers alone without taking sufficient interest in the training of new probationers. The probationer, on the other hand, was asked to note 'that the amount of respect and influence he will command from amongst his subordinates will depend not on his status in Service, but upon his capacity and knowledge and the extent to which he is able effectively to supervise and guide his subordinates'. It was hoped that the training of I.A.S. probationers from the village stage upwards would secure the required type of association with subordinates and the development of a proper attitudes. However, little did Desai realize that I.A.S. officers so trained were to function in a milieu where social relationships were governed not by contract but status assigned to caste or position.

At the Training School in Delhi the full-time teaching staff was small, consisting of a law lecturer belonging to the Central Provinces' judicial cadre, who was replaced by a refugee civil judge from Sind on 1 May 1948. The post of Reader in Economics was sanctioned and the F.P.S.C. selected a candidate who joined the staff on 19 April 1948. Besides the Principal, there was a lecturer who taught criminal and Muslim law. In addition to the regular curriculum, a series of lectures were delivered by outsiders on such subjects as Indian constitutional history, economic geography, public administration, the machinery of the Government of India, and Indian history. There were, in addition, extra-curricular lectures by visitors who were either Civilians or other officers of the government in civil or military establishments.[52] A complaint was in fact made to Sardar Patel, the Home Minister, against what was being regarded as a Civilian-dominated course for trainees at the School.[53] The Home Minister dismissed the complaint as fallacious, pointing out that the I.C.S. had received 'the best of training' and knew how to adapt to changed conditions. 'There is certainly some difference in the use to which that training was put in the past', he added, 'but I am quite satisfied that it cannot be put to the same use again and it will harm rather than profit us to dwell upon the past when we know for certain that the present is different and the future would be even more so'.[54]

An analysis of the hours spent on curricular subjects in the second term of 1948 (9 August to 11 December) shows that in its early years the School emphasized more the professional aspects than the cultivation of officers' minds through cultural training. This is clear from the figures given below:[55]

Percentage of time spent on Curricular Subjects

Law	42.5%
History	10.0%
Public Administration	15.0%
Economics	10.0%
Hindustani	12.5%
Provincial languages (per probationer)	10.0%

An experiment for professional efficiency was made in the very first year of the School when probationers were sent to their provinces for a fortnight's secretariat training. With the concurrence of the provinces the experiment was successfully repeated during the summer vacation of 1948. This later became a regular feature of I.A.S. training in the provinces, as also two or three weeks' attachment to military units. Visits to important development projects and historic places also formed part of the scheme for training.[56]

The Training School started functioning more or less on a regular basis from 1952 onwards. The training given at the School conformed to a pattern formulated in 1951, and it became a complete year's course. The professional part of the course consisted of criminal law and procedure, the law of evidence, Hindustani, regional languages and riding, while the general subjects included a broad understanding of Indian history in its cultural, political and administrative aspects; the principles of economics; and the general principles of public administration with emphasis on the organization, function and ideals of a modern civil service. The curriculum as modified in 1955 included such additional subjects as district administration, a special study of Community Projects and the Five-Year Plan. It also highlighted the importance of the special study of co-operation, food production, cottage industries, public finance and state management of industrial enterprises. This modified curriculum became the basis of the examination conducted by the Union Public Service Commission for the National Academy.

Another change that took place in 1955 was the appointment of a full-time principal for the School. He was also to function as Director of Training whose duty it was to ensure that all the States provided for adequate training programmes for their administrative services. This recommendation had been made by the Planning Commission in the First Five-Year Plan. The organization of refresher courses at the School and its development into a centre for the study of public administration generally also formed part the Commission's recommendations.[57]

The I.A.S. Staff College, Simla, was established in July 1957 to organize refresher courses as well as the training of the special recruits selected in 1956. No important refresher course was in fact organized at Simla, but new subjects were introduced at the School in Delhi in 1957. These included Gandhian philosophy as well as a course in Indian socialism.

An important development in 1958 was in the direction of integrated training programmes for the various Services. The idea was mooted as early as 1955 when Ashok Chanda, then Comptroller and Auditor-General, proposed the establishment of a common training institution to provide for both 'general' and 'special' Services, the one being applicable to all higher public servants and the other relevant to the needs of particular Services.[58] The proposal for a common training institution was accepted by the Government which worked out in 1958 all its details in terms of the Services to be included, the syllabuses, staff requirements and finances. The new institution was to be called the National Academy of Administration. In a statement made to the Lok Sabha on 15 April 1958 the Home Minister announced that 'training in foundational and fundamental subjects should be given to all those who are recruited for senior grades of service. So, instead of our Indian Administrative Training School, we propose to set up a National Academy of Training so that the Services, wherever they may function, whether as Administrative Officers or as Accountants or as Revenue Officers, might imbibe the true spirit and discharge their duties in a manner which will raise their efficiency and establish concord between them and the public completely'.[59] Consistent with this announcement, the Government decided in July 1959 to start at the I.A.S. Training School itself a four-month foundational course for probationers of the I.A.S., the Indian Foreign Service and the non-technical Class I Union Services. Late in August 1959, the School was moved to Mussoorie along with the I.A.S. Staff College, Simla, and both were merged to constitute the National Academy of Administration, officially created on 1 September 1959. It completed the first foundational course, started in Delhi, by November 1959. The next foundational course, which was started in May 1960, was of five months' duration, a norm followed subsequently as part of the actual training of probationers. The combined foundational course introduced in 1959 was a distinct departure from the I.C.S. tradition, where no I.C.S. officer ever competed with non-I.C.S. candidates or participated in training programmes with anyone outside his cadre.

The National Academy of Administration conducted three seprate, though related, training programmes. These were the foundational course, the training of I.A.S. probationers and the refresher courses or special seminars for senior personnel of all Services. The training of I.A.S. probationers was divided into two parts, namely, the common foundational course for a period of five months, and a subsequent seven month course exclusively for the I.A.S. Of the seven months, three were devoted to extensive study and the remaining four to detailed study of the subjects prescribed for the final examination conducted by the U.P.S.C. under the 1955 Regulations (which were amended in 1961). In their amended form the Regulations provided for four papers at the probationers' final examination. These papers which were of 75 marks each, consisted of Political Theory, the Constitution of India, Economic Principles and the Five-Year Plans, Law and General Administrative Knowledge. The Academy made use of the syndicate method of study where study reports or papers were discussed before the entire body of probationers and their teachers. It was designed to develop critical faculties, powers of reasoning and public disputation. Selected syndicate studies were published in the *Journal of the National Academy of Administration.*

The period of probation became two years in 1962. After the probationers' final examination was over, they reported at the States to which they were allotted, which marked the second phase of their training, a purely on-the-job training with a mixture of institutional and practical assignments. The period of training in the various States varied from ten months to two years. Briefly, it called for a knowledge of the State Secretariat and its various departments; the functioning of the Collector's office in its manifold aspects, especially treasury work, settlement and land records; an experience of the police office and its working; a knowledge of development departments, such as agriculture, co-operation, panchayats, community development and the national extension service. It also covered the subdivisional office, magisterial work and work done at the level of tahsils or talukas, the I.A.S. officers acting as Block Development Officers. However, as no specific responsibilty was given to trainees at this stage, they concentrated on preparing for their departmental examinations, which entitled them to appointment as Subdivisional Officers. After a few years' experience as Subdivisional Magistrates they were posted as Additional District Magistrates or as Under Secretaries in the State Secretariat. As said before, it took nearly six years, sometimes more, before the independent charge of a district was given to an I.A.S. officer, although the norm suggested by the Home Ministry in 1956 was four years after the probationers' final examination.

Such was the initial training of the I.A.S. officers until 1969.

Occasionally a few went abroad for a specialized course in certain fields, but so far as the general body of probationers was concerned, their formal education after the initial training was from their capacity to learn from circumstances. The change-over to the objectives of a welfare state dictated the necessity of specialization. On the French pattern, the I.A.S. probationers could specialize in such subjects as general administration, economic and financial administration and social administration: but since this risked sacrificing their general competence, the question of specialization arose only after officers had put in about ten years of service.

To keep the Services up-to-date with the subjects they were called upon to handle, the need for periodical in-service training was recognized by the Government of India. Prior to the establishment of the National Academy in 1959, for instance, the former I.A.S. Staff College at Simla conducted certain refresher courses for officers of six to ten years' standing. The Academy organized a number of refresher courses for higher training during 1961–3. Similar courses were held by the Administrative Staff College, Hyderabad; the Central Institute of Community Development, Mussoorie; the National Council of Applied Economic Research, New Delhi; the Indian School of Public Administration (now abolished), New Delhi; the Institute of Applied Manpower Research, and some other institutions.[60] Theoretical knowledge was not aimed at, and the object in all cases was to ensure improvements in administration through an exchange of ideas and experience gained by officers in a variety of conditions. The benefit of cross fertilization was sought to be imparted to participants through conferences, seminars and syndicates. The subjects covered in these discussions at the 1961 course of the Academy, for instance, included, among other topics, public administration in its practical and related aspects; the economic environment, thought, policies and institutions; the Constitution of India; law, including jurisprudence, equity, torts and contracts; and social administration with reference to the welfare state, social security and social insurance, including labour and industrial relations.[61]

Of the institutions imparting higher training to I.A.S. officers, the Administrative Staff College, in Hyderabad, was specially distinguished for its quality and standards. The mixed groups of officials undergoing training at this college have generally been those who hold key positions in their respective fields, men who are in the middle range of management but capable of rising to still higher levels of responsibility for top management. The Indian Institute of Public Administration is another institution which emerged in the 1960's as a centre of mid-career training, particularly after 1967 when its teaching programme was dropped to promote training as its principal preoccupation. The participants of the in-service training orgainized at the Institute were drawn from such Services as the State Administrative/Secretariat Services, the Central Secretariat Service, the I.A.S., the Indian Ordnance Factory Service, the Indian Audit and Accounts Service, the Indian Police Service, the Survey of India (Class I) Service, the State Forest Services and a number of other areas, including the Air Force and Engineering Service. The subjects discussed were naturally of an assorted nature, including, for instance, the techniques of administrative improvement, administrative behaviour, budgeting, development administration, decision-making, material planning and management, performance budgeting, project formulation, personnel administration, social policy and administration, introduction to computers, O & M techniques in the government, and techniques in Plan formulation at the State level.

Thus the importance of training as a means of executive development came to be generally recognized, more particularly after the Second Plan. However, the response of participants did not match the concern of the government to improve administrative efficiency for developmental purposes. An important reason for this lack of interest was that performance in such training had hardly any bearing on promotion prospects, which were often determined irrationally by extraneous considerations. But the inadequacy of able and competent persons to handle training programmes was also a cause for their ineffectiveness. This inadequacy often arose from the failure of the official machinery to pool resources available both inside and outside the government. In other words, the traditional gap between scholarship and skill did not disappear in the post-Independence period: it became in fact more marked. Though possessed of the administrative skill, the administrators as a class showed little or no evidence of scholarly interests. Though learned in their own field of specialization, the scholars, on the other hand, remained on the whole poor specimens of administrative skill. The old tradition of the scholar-administrator, which had grown over the years in the context of the nineteenth-century 'Competitionwalas' slowly became a thing of the past amidst the current din and bustle of 'development'.

There were other factors too which militated against the benefits of higher training. In some cases the courses were unrelated to felt needs and administrative realities. A training programme was at times encouraged not because there was a practical utility in it, but because the theme proposed was deemed to be ideologically popular—for example, analysing imaginary imperfections of the existing administrative arrangements often dubbed an imperialist legacy. Then again, participants were sometimes chosen by sponsoring organizations purely because they were available or easily dispensed with in their organizations. Besides, the training institutions themselves were found wanting in enforcing discipline and getting work out of the trainees. The participants functioned on the principle of *laissez-faire* and dispersed without any let or hindrance, apparently never to be heard of again. The sponsoring authorities and the training institutes both remained unconcerned about the outcome of the investment made on higher training.

As regards junior civil servants, there appeared a general lack of rigour in the training imparted to them by district officers.[62] Under the old regime senior Collectors trained probationers and took care of them as guides. But with the transfer of power, things were bound to change, as they did, in a situation where the conceptual impersonality and professionalism of the Service got mixed with inferior loyalties governing administrative behaviour. The rigour which the rules imposed earlier were relaxed through the influence of politics. Even if known for honesty and uprightness of conduct, a Collector in free India could not but bend the rules generally to subserve a dominant interest. Functionally, too, his preoccupations, especially social and political, happened to be too numerous to permit him to train probationers adequately.

The training programme for I.A.S. probationers was in these circumstances modified in 1969 in accordance with the French model, involving interspersing practical and theoretical training. The Government of India introduced the 'sandwich course' for new recruits to the I.A.S. It meant two spells of training with an interval of a year. The first spell consisted of a foundational course and professional training. As before, the foundational course was intended for I.A.S. probationers as well as for Class I Central Services, exclusive of the Central Service for which there was a separate arrangement. The purpose of this course was to impart to officers of the higher services a clear understanding of the social, economic and constitutional framework within which they were to function and contribute to the

formulation and execution of policies and programmes. Professionally, they were in addition required to acquaint themselves not only
with the machinery of government and the broad principles of public
administration, but also with such matters as the rights and obligations of the civil services, including the ethics of the profession.

After completing the foundational course in six months the probationers proceeed for a year's practical training to the States to which
they were assigned. On completion of this they were brought back to
the Academy at Mussoorie for a second spell of seven months' duration. The emphasis here was on the discussion of the administrative
problems they had come across during their practical experience in
the States. At the end of a year they appeared at an examination held
by the U.P.S.C., which marked their confirmation and the end of
their formal training.

As part of the in-service training programme a decision was taken
by the Government of India in 1970 to analyse the job requirements of
the various posts in each Service and organize the career management
of its members so that forward planning could be done to keep ready
the right type of person for a post at the right time. It was with this end
in view that the Administrative Staff College at Hyderabad had
already started the training of middle-range officers in order to fit them
for a still higher level of responsibility in their careers. A training
programme for career management had likewise been organized by
the Indian Institute of Public Administration.[63]

The Union Public Service Commission

We have in the preceding sections discussed the operational side of
the various mechanisms designed to improve the standards and
quality of the I.A.S., the main pillar of the bureaucracy in India. Here
we shall reflect on the U.P.S.C., by far the most important
mechanism devised to ensure quality in the public services as a whole.

The functions of the U.P.S.C. have been laid down in Article 320 of
the Constitution. These are more or less the same as were prescribed
by the Public Service Commission (India) established in 1926, and
the Federal Public Service Commission constituted under the Government of India Act, 1935. Its main functions according to the
Constitution are to serve as an independent and impartial agency (a)
for the selection of candidates for appointment to the public Services
by examinations, interviews and promotion; and (b) for advising the
government on disciplinary cases and service matters generally, inc-

luding the costs of legal proceedings instituted against it and claims of pensions in respect of injuries sustained while on official work.

The Federal Public Service Commission suffered from certain limitations which had a bearing on the Commission's independence. For instance, important matters like the tenure of its Members and the method of terminating their service were determined by regulations to be framed by the executive government. Members were, for example, eligible for extension in their posts. Except for the Chairman, they were, after retirement, also eligible for re-employment in government service. The new Constitution, however, did away with such provisions. It laid down that a person who held office as Member of the Commission was not to be eligible for re-appointment to that office or for any other employment either under the Government of India or of a State. A member was to hold office for a term of six years or until he attained the age of sixty-five, whichever was earlier. He could, however, vacate office by resignation or be removed for misbehaviour.

The Constitution thus remedied some of the old imperfections. But this did not mean that the Commission's independence was allowed to remain untouched. It was affected in two ways: first, by limitations put on its functions; and secondly, by conditions of service left to be determined by the President, which, in reality, meant the executive government.

Limitations on U.P.S.C.'s Functions

Under a proviso to clause 3 of Article 320 of the Constitution, the President is authorized to make regulations 'specifying the matters in which either generally, or in any particular class of case or in any particular circumstances, it shall not be necessary for a Public Service Commission to be consulted'. But since all regulations made under the proviso to clause 3 were subject to approval by Parliament, the pre-1947 list of matters to be excluded remained in force pending a final decision by Parliament. One category of cases where the Commission was not to be consulted under the old rules was, as pointed out before, what purported to be temporary appointments for periods not exceeding one year. The manner in which Ministries and Departments of the government misused this rule has already been referred to. In its annual reports the Commission kept on raising serious objections to what it called 'irregular' and '*ad hoc* appointments'. The occasion for such appointments arose from a lack of perspective planning and a proper communication to the Commission of personnel requirements. Commenting on the abuse of power by Ministries and Departments, the *Twenty-Second Report* of the Commission regretted the continuance of this practice and concluded by saying:[64]

The foregoing paragraphs also refer, as do the earlier reports of the Commission, to certain aspects of personnel management which deserve urgent attention of Government. The somewhat persistent tendency to make *ad hoc* appointments and to allow them to continue without adequate justification, the lack of adequate care in the assessment of manpower requirements, and the failure on the part of controlling authorities of certain Services to convey timely intimation regarding their requirements to the Commission, are features that tend to weaken the administrative machinery and vitiate the process of personnel recruitment. As mentioned by the Commission in their earlier reports, most of these features arise not from any absence of adequate instructions and procedures in this behalf but from sheer non-observance thereof.

The Commission made repeated complaints of instances where the number of vacancies initially reported bore no relation to the number finally required to be filled by examinations. The table given below makes it clear that in the case of some examinations held by the Commission in 1972 this disparity was very wide indeed:[65]

Examination	No. of vacancies notified	No. of vacancies finally reported
1. I.A.S.	158	455
2. Engineering Services	139	403
3. Engineering Services (Electronics)	78	241
4. Assistants' Grade Examination	44	263

Despite the Commission's protests, matters did not improve, perhaps because of pressure from below or influence from above. The case of the Director of the National Museum in Delhi is especially worthy of being quoted to illustrate the manner in which the Commission persisted in its efforts to secure observance of the rules governing recruitment. Appointed under the Department of Culture on a scale of pay of Rs 1,800–2,000, the incumbent of the post attained the age of superannuation on 15 June 1967 but was continued as Director on extension of service. In 1968 he was offered a Fellowship by the Nehru Memorial Fund, which made him ask to be relieved of his duties. The post was therefore advertised and an officer recommended for appointment by the Commission in a letter dated 7 April 1969. However, the officer so recommended was not appointed to the post, and, instead, the previous incumbent was continued in it. The post was in the meantime upgraded, with the scale of pay revised to a maximum of Rs 2,250: the former Director was then appointed to the upgraded post with effect from 1 January 1971. After he had held it for more than a year, a reference was made to the Commission for approval of his continued *ad hoc* appointment as Director up to the end of December 1972.

However, the Commission did not agree to the re-employment of the officer with effect from 1 January 1971. While explaining the reasons for disagreement, it pointed out that the irregular appointment for superannuated officers, especially when made in contravention of the procedure and instructions on the subject, could not be said to be in the public interest, particularly when such a step had followed the non-appointment of a candidate selected by the Commission in accordance with the established rules. Moreover, as the Government of India's instructions envisaged that even Technical/Scientific personnel should not be re-employed beyond the age of 62, there could be no justification whatever for the re-employment of an officer who had already attained that age.

Even so, these reasons for refusal went unheaded. The Department approached the Commission again in September 1972 to agree to the continued re-employment of the officer in the post up to 31 March 1973. It was argued that the Government was considering the recommendation of the high powered Central Museum Review Committee that the National Museum should be converted into an autonomous organization to be managed by a board outside the purview of the Commission. This argument too carried no conviction and the proposal of the Department was rejected. It was asked to forward to the Commission a requisition stating the rules of recruitment for the upgraded post for necessary action.

In December 1972, the Department informed the Commission that the recruitment rules for the upgraded post of Director, National Museum, had not yet been finalized and that a requisition for the post would be sent to the Commission only after the rules had been duly notified. Meanwhile, the Department sought the Commission's approval to the continued *ad hoc* appointed of the officer in the post up to 31 March 1973. The Commission reiterated its earlier objections and again asked for the requisition required for recruitment to the post.

The tangle went on, and only when the matter attracted the notice of the press and Parliament did the Department send the Commission the necessary requisition to fill the post by direct recruitment. The Commission was, however, requested in the same breath to reconsider its earlier advice and allow the old incumbent to continue for a few months more till it was filled through proper advertisement. The Commision considered the case carefully but found no justification for the proposal of the Department, especially when the incumbent had by then crossed 63½ years of age. The Department was therefore advised to terminate his services forthwith and make an alternative *ad hoc* arrangement [66]

As indicated before, such cases were not exceptions. They occurred every year in spite of the Commission's repeated advice to the contrary.It actually regretted in one of its concluding remarks that

in several spheres of personnel administration many of the problems arise more from non-observance of agreed policies, practices and methods of personnel management than, necessarily, from any inherent defects in them. One of the primary instruments for regulating matters connected with personnel administration are the rules of recruitment required to be framed under the proviso to Article 309 of the Constitution. Reference has been made, in the earlier Reports, to the absence of such rules for several civil posts, to delays on notification of such rules after they have been finalized in consultation with the Commission, and also to the tendency not to adhere to such rules even after they have been finalized. These are factors which vitiate proper programmes of recruitment to services and posts; they encourage *ad hoc* and irregular appointments, thwarting the employment prospects of fresh graduates from universities, technical institutions, etc. aspiring to compete for such services and posts; and tend to erode the confidence of the public servants themselves in the objective and fair implementation of agreed personnel policies as envisaged in the rules framed for the purpose.[67]

The Reports of the U.P.S.C. thus present yet another view of the manner in which the process of recruitment was distorted. Though different in approach to recruitment as an instrument of personnel administration, these Reports confirm the conclusions which the Department of Administrative Reforms had in this regard reached in its *Report on the Management of the Administrative Service (1968)*. Both confirm the decline in the standards of recruitment and imbalance in the composition of the Services. But while the Reports of the Commission attribute this decline to the management, that of the Department of Administrative Reforms holds that excessive recruitment and defects in rules and policies were no less responsible for distortion. Both,

however, recognize the absence of planning in manpower requirements as the basic cause for imbalance in the bureaucratic structure,
a defect which flowed partly from a desire for control over patronage.

Temporary appointments which caused these irregularities were
but one category of cases exempt from consultation with the Commission. There were other instances regarding which the President was to
frame regulations under the proviso to clause 3 of Article 320 of the
Constitution. It was under this proviso that the Union Public Service
Commission (Exemption from Consultation) Regulations were
framed in 1958.[68] The Schedule to the Regulations listed the services
and posts exempted from the purview of the Commission, but the list
continued to grow even after the schedule framed in 1958. The
additions made till March 1963, for instance, included as many as
eight new categories of cases[69] and thirteen others were added by 31
March 1971. The supernumerary posts of scientists, technologists,
engineers and medical specialists created by the government during
1964–5 for a period of two years in the first instance were likewise
excluded from consultation with the Commission for a temporary
period. This exclusion later applied to the posts of Lokpal and
Lokayuktas for which formal amendments were made to the Union
Public Service Commission (Exemption from Consultation) Regulations, 1958.

The list of services and posts beyond regulation by the Commission
thus continued to swell. On 27 May 1970 the government even went
to the extent of issuing an order amending the Schedule of 1958. In
spite of the Commission's view to the contrary, the order excluded
from its purview all scientifiic and technical posts in the Secretariat of
the Committee on Science and Technology.[70] The Commission emphasized that it was only with the expertise, resources and prestige of
a statutory organization set up under the Constitution and specially
charged with the responsibility for making selections for civil posts
that recruitment to such posts could be expected to be made objectively, impartially and correctly.[71] But it was a cry in the wilderness
and the government did not change its mind.

Another interesting case where quality was sacrificed to considerations of patronage related to recruitment to the grade of Section
Officers in the Central Secretariat Service. The proposals of the
Government were mainly two: first, a reduction in the direct recruitment quota to 16 per cent, as against 33⅓ per cent of the substantive
vacancies provided under the Rules governing the Central Secretariat

Service; and secondly, the provision of a quota for appointment to the grade of Section Officer of Assistants with the longest years of service, irrespective of their position in the seniority list of Assistants.

The Commission's advice was against both proposals. Its argument in respect of the first was based on the Central Secretariat Service Rules, 1962, which provided that 33⅓ per cent of the substantive vacancies (this quota was temporarily reduced to 25 per cent for five years from 1 October 1962) should be filled by direct recruitment on the results of the competitive examination held by the Commission. An adherence to the established quota was all the more necessary because the actual intake of direct recruits to the grade of Section Officers had not been commensurate even with the reduced quota of 25 per cent, the average annual intake during 1964-6 having been only eight, as against the average size of the select list for promotion being of the order of 81. The direct recruits had thus remained an insignificant portion of the total strength of Section Officers in the entire Secretariat. It was therefore emphasized that any further erosion of the percentage of direct recruits would not be conducive to the efficiency of the Central Secretariat Service.

The main argument which the Government used in support of a quota for the promotion of Assistants was that even those with more than 20 years' service as Assistants suffered over seniority and could not become Section Officers because different principles happened to determine seniority at different times. The Commission tried to meet this argument by saying that the purpose of a seniority list was to determine the order in which employees should be considered for confirmation in a particular grade or for promotion to the next higher grade and that it would not be correct to draw two groups of Assistants from the same seniority list and apply different criteria for promotion. Such a step, it added, would be a violation of recognized principles of promotion and could cause repercussions in other grades and Services. To remove the existing stagnation in the grade of Assistants the Commission even suggested the introduction of a selection grade to which Assistants with a prescribed length of service could be appointed. But the Government rejected the advice of the Commission. On 26 June 1970, the Home Ministry notified amendments to the Central Secretariat Service Rules, 1962, reducing the quota of direct recruitment to one-sixth of the substantive vacancies and providing that one-third of the persons included in the select list for promotion to the grade of Section Officers would be Assistants with the longest years of service.[72] The annual Reports of the Commission cite numerous instances of its function being rendered nugatory by a pronounced tendency on the part of certain Ministries/Departments to seek exemption in regard to large categories of posts under them.[73] But the total exclusion of scientific and technical posts from its purview was regarded by the Commission as the most serious step taken by the Government in 1970 on such matters. For, as the Commission pointed out, nearly 80 per cent of the recruitment conducted by the Commission other than the competitive examination related to scientific and technical posts, including medical appointments. Apart from its deleterious effects on the efficiency and morale of the public Services, the exclusion of these posts from the Commission's function meant an inevitable erosion of its authority. It therefore regretted that, though 'ostensibly designed to serve the cause of science and technology', the Government instituted through this step a pattern of recruitment which allowed it 'unfettered freedom' in the use of patronage. The Commission naturally considered that the amendments of the 1958 Schedule raised 'certain fundamental issues of national importance, the precise impact of which on the role and functions of the Commission, on the standared and quality of the public Services, and on the morale of the officers manning these Services need to be clearly understood in the country'.[74] The nature of the 'impact' in question is clear to scholars: interference with the independence of the Commission in the exercise of its constitutional functions has meant nothing but executive interposition and the negation of democracy.

Conditions of Service. Constitutionally, the U.P.S.C. was supposed to have been designed to function as an independent body like the Supreme Court, the High Courts and the Comptroller and Auditor General. Its independence was, however, of a more limited nature. For instance, before assuming office every person appointed a Judge of the Supreme Court, a High Court or as Comptroller and Auditor General was under the Constitution required to make or subscribe to an oath or affirmation before a competent authority. The Constitution prescribed no such oath of office for Members of the Commission. Further, the appointment of a Judge of the Supreme Court, High Court, or of the Comptroller and Auditor General was to be made by the President 'by warrant under his hand and seal'.[75] No such condition was laid down for the appointment of the Chairman and Members of U.P.S.C. Both the conditions of appointment made a difference to status and prestige. The difference was to be observed also in respect of removal from office. A Judge of the Supreme Court, for instance, was not to be removed from office except by an order of the President passed after an address by a majority in each House of Parliament and by not less than two-thirds of the members of that House present and voting. The same conditions were to apply to the removal of the Comptroller and Auditor General[76] or a Judge of a High Court.[77] The Chairman and Members of the Commission could be removed without any reference to an address by Parliament. They were made subject to removal by mere order of the President on the ground of misbehaviour established after an inquiry by the Supreme Court on reference made to it by the President.[78]

The framers of the Constitution thus acted with reservation in respect of the U.P.S.C. Though feigning to make it appear an independent body, they assigned it a position not comparable to that of the Supreme Court, the High Courts or the Comptroller and Auditor General. Nor were the conditions of service laid down immediately under Article 318(a) of the Constitution, which authorized the President to determine the number of Members of the Commission and their conditions of service. This was done in 1969 and until then the old regulations framed by the Governor-General under the Act of 1935 prevailed.

The question of framing regulations under Article 318(a) of the Constitution had been under the consideration of the Government almost since the Constitution came into force. The basic points underlying that consideration however pertained to the pay and pension of the Chairman and Members of the Commission, not of its functions.

The monthly pay allowed to the Chairman and Members of the Federal Public Service Commission under the rules made in 1926 were Rs 5,000 and Rs 3,000 respectively. These rates were revised by the Federal Public Service Commission (Conditions of Service) Regulations, 1937 and their salaries were accordingly fixed at Rs 4,000 and Rs 3,500 respectively. By an executive order of 1950 the salaries were further reduced to Rs 3,500 and Rs 3,000 a month respectively, a personal pay of Rs 500 a month being, however, admissible to officers of the I.C.S. and other officers receiving salaries on pre-1931 rates immediately before appointment to the Commission. An amendment to these regulations was notified on 2 June 1964 validating the substance of the executive decision taken in 1950. This was followed by the Regulations framed by the President in 1969 under Article 318(a) of the Constitution. The Union Public Service Commission (Members) Regulations so framed also provided for monthly salaries of Rs 3,500 and Rs 3,000 to the Chairman and Members.

The Commission raised objections against the salaries fixed in 1969. The reason was plain and simple: until August 1965 the Members were paid at the rate of Rs 3,000 a month, which was the grade until then admissible to non-I.C.S. Secretaries to the Government of India. By a Memorandum of 24 August 1965, which revised the salaries of officers at senior levels, those of Secretaries and equivalent posts carrying Rs 3,000 were raised to Rs 3,500 a month. This revision did not, however, apply to Members of the Commission who continued to draw Rs 3,000 a month. In terms of pay they were thus reduced to a position inferior to that of Secretaries. In a demi-official letter of 29 March 1966 the Home Ministry stated that the question of raising the pay of Members of the Commission to Rs, 3500 was under consideration and that after this had been settled the Government would take up the case of the Chairman. No concrete steps were, however, taken despite representations made by the Commission which, while the Union Public Service Commission (Members) Regulations, 1969 were under consideration, had *inter-alia* urged the Government to consider the following proposals:[79]

1. The emoluments of the Chairman and Members of the Commission should appropriately be placed at par with those of Chief Justice and Judges of a High Court respectively and such parity should be maintained in assigning positions in the warrant of precedence also.

2. Pensions should be admissible to all 'non-officials' Members and should not be restricted to those who had completed three years of service as Members; and additional pensions should be allowed to 'official' Members for the service rendered in the Commission, as in the case of Judges of the High Court and the Comptroller and Auditor General of India.

3. The conditions of service of Members of the Commission should be regulated by suitable legislation enacted by Parliament, as in the case of High Court Judges and the Comptroller and Auditor General, and not by the regulation-making procedure of the executive followed by the President.

But, except for the grant of pensions to non-official Members, none of these proposals made by the Commission were given effect to even after Union Public Service Commission (Members) Regulations, 1969, had been formally notified.

The question of the salary of the Chairman and Members assumed yet another dimension when the salaries of Chief Secretaries were raised to Rs 3,500 per month. The lower salary of Members of the Commission became particularly anomalous when they presided over meetings of a Selection Committee of which the Chief Secretaries of a State Government and a Secretary to the Government of India happened to be members. The anomaly was further heightened when appointments to posts of Secretaries to the Government were from persons outside the civil services, especially when such appointments were required to be made on the advice of the U.P.S.C. itself.

Consistent with the duties and responsibilities entrusted to it by the Constitution, the Commission therefore insisted that the emoluments of its Chairman and Members should not be less than those of the Chief Justice and Judges of a High Court respectively. These were comparable positions which, as the U.P.S.C. argued, had been recommended by the Lee Commission as far back as 1924, not only in terms of pay but also of the Warrant of Precedence. In support of its claim for equality with Judges of a High Court in terms of pay and status, the Commission also quoted the view of the Estimates Committee which, in its report of 8 March 1968, had emphasized the need to re-examine the question of the emoluments and other perquisites of the Chairman and Members of the Commission. The Committee had further highlighted their case for special consideration by saying that, while there existed a constitutional bar against their further employment, there was no such bar regarding employment under the Government in respect of the Chief Justice and Judges of a High Court or, for that matter, even of the Supreme Court.

The question of the rate of pension was another important matter put up for consideration. It emerged immediately from the Union Public Service Commission (Members) Regulations, 1969, which provided that non-official Members would be entitled to a pension only if they had rendered a minimum of three years' service as Member or Chairman. In the case of High Court Judges. however, there was no such minimum service prescribed for entitlement to pension. The Commission held the view that the pension of its Chairman and Members had to be considered not only in terms of the service rendered by them as Chairman and Members, which was limited by a provision[80] in the Constitution, but also by the fact that it had to be treated as compensation for the ban against future employment under the Government. It was therefore suggested that no minimum period should be prescribed to earn a pension and that the minimum monthly pension should not be less than Rs 1000. The Commission also felt that it was unfair not to provide for the earning of additional pensions by officials for the service they rendered as Chairman and Members. Its argument was reinforced by provisions which already existed in support of additional pensions for the Comptroller and Auditor General as well as for members of the judicial service who were appointed Judges of High Courts. However, the proposals of the Commission remained in a state of correspondence. They did not go beyond the limits of annual reporting. Even its *Twenty-third Report*, which covered a period from 1 April 1972 to 31 March 1973, ended with a note of disappointment over the results. It appears that the reduced status and authority of the U.P.S.C. became a factor in the frequency with which its advice was rejected by the Government in the post-1947 period. Consequently, the Commission showed a tendency to proceed, if necessary, on the lines of least resistance. On the question of the combined I.A.S. examinations, for example, it assumed a mild attitude when the upper age-limit was raised to 26 in 1972 and the number of chances taken by a candidate increased in February 1973. These were both steps which affected the quality of recruitment for the I.A.S.

The Administrative Reforms Commission had first recommended in its report on Personnel Administration[81] that the upper age-limit for admission to the competitive examination (for recruitment to the non-technical higher services) might be raised to 26 years. On the recommendation of the Department of Personnel the U.P.S.C. accepted the proposal in respect of the combined Indian Administrative Service, etc. examination. The Commission, however, agreed on the understanding that no candidate would be allowed to take more than two chances in the scheme of the examination and that the relaxed age-limit should apply for a period of two or three years and the position reviewed in the light of experience. Orders raising the upper age-limit from 24 to 26 years for admission to the Indian Administrative, etc. examination were accordingly issued by the Government on 11 April 1972, making the enhanced upper age-limit applicable from the examination of 1972 which had already been notified on 4 March 1972.[82] It appears that the Government was in a hurry to introduce the change for political reasons in a year of General Elections.

The Government soon changed its mind about the understanding over two chances in the scheme of the examination. Before the year 1972 ran out it had asked the Commission to consider the question of increasing the number of chances from two to three. It was argued that, as under the existing arrangement, the three constituent parts of the Indian Administrative Service, etc. examinations were being treated as comprising three separate and distinct examinations, it was theoretically possible for a candidate to take the examination six times during the age span of 20–26 years. In December 1972 the Government proposed that the three separate and distinct examinations for three categories of Services be treated as a single examination and that the number of chances allowed to candidates should be raised from two (for each category) to three (for the examination as a whole).

The Commission held on for a time to the existing practice of two chances for each category of the Services. It was guided by the advice of the Public Service (Qualifications for Recruitment) Committee. In recommending a time span of two as against three years for the administrative services the Committee had expressed the view 'that the mental qualities as also the personality can be best tested in one or at the most two examinations' and 'that a person who fails to come to the standard in the first two examinations may, on the basis of his experience of the examinations and having the techniques thereof, be successful in the third'. Such success, the Committee had observed, 'does not necessarily reflect the innate qualities of the candidate' Even so, the Commission agreed to the revised proposals of the Government on the basis of three separate examinations for the three categories of Services being treated as one. Candidates were to be allowed under this arrangement to take the combined competitive examination in any three years of the age span 20–26 years. No candidate was to be allowed to appear more freqently, although the age span of six years (20–26) could theoretically lend itself to six chances. The Commission accepted the Government's revised proposals on the assumption that these had been formulated after full consideration, more especially 'the legal aspects of the matter'.[83] Its acceptance was thus communicated to the Government in January 1973.

But the Government changed its view once again on the ground that some doubt had arisen about the 'legal validity' of its earlier proposal to treat the three separate examinations for the three categories of services as a single examination. The 'single examination' concept, which had earlier been said to be legally sound, came now to be declared of doubtful legal validity after the Commission's concurrence had been obtained. And this occurred within barely a month. In February 1973, the Government, without any further reference to the Commission and contrary to its own earlier proposal, decided that the Indian Administrative Service, etc. Examination,1973, should, as hitherto, be held on the basis that it comprised three separate and distinct examinations for three categories of Services and that three chances should be available for candidates to appear at each of the three separate examinations.[84]

The enhanced upper age-limit and the withdrawal of restrictions on the number of chances were in fact matters where the Government seemed to have acted in haste. The taking of a decision and it reversal in quick succession betrayed either slip-shod decision-making, or the working of pressure groups influencing administrative decisions from considerations other than administrative. The Commission, on the other hand, felt neglected and could do no more than record in its report a mild sermon: 'The Commission need hardly add,' it was noted, 'that in regard to a fundamental concept of this nature, Government should have considered the matter more fully before making a reference to the Commission instead of later differing from them after obtaining their concurrence to the proposal'.[85]

As regards the management of the I.A.S., the fact remained that the enhanced upper age-limit and the increase in the number of chances both contributed to a fall in the standards of recruitment. The Commission attributed this fall to sporadic decisions which, in turn, flowed from a lack of perspective planning and assessment of manpower requirements on the part of the controlling authorities. It did recognize that the method of competitive examinations had provided by far the most 'streamlined method' of recruitment. But *ad hoc* steps to satisfy these requirements, as the Commission regretted, resulted 'inevitably in certain adverse consequences, such as inadequate fresh intake, sporadic requirements of personnel or wide fluctuations in the number of vacancies reported from time to time, aggravation of uncertainties in the minds of prospective candidates regarding employment opportunities, imbalances in the age of members of a Service resulting in possible stagnation at certain stages, or, as commonly noticed, *ad hoc* and irregular appointments and promotions. All these factors lead in turn to impoverishment of the Services'.[86]

APPENDIX

UNION PUBLIC SERVICE COMMISSION (EXEMPTION FROM CONSULTATION) REGULATIONS, 1958

As amended up to 16 December 1958

In exercise of the powers conferred by the proviso to clause (3) of Article 320 of the Constitution and in supersession of all previous regulations on the subject, the President hereby makes the following regulations, namely:

1. These regulations may be called the Union Public Service Commission (Exemption from Consultation) Regulations, 1958.

2. It shall not be necessary to consult the Commission in regard to any of the matters mentioned in sub-clauses (a) and (b) of clause (3) of Article 320 of the Constitution in the case of the Services and posts specified in the Schedule to these Regulations.

3. Save as otherwise expressly provided in the rules governing recruitment to the civil service or civil post concerned it shall not be necessary to consult the Commission in regard to the selection for appointment

(a) to a post included in an all-India Service, of any officer who is already a member of an all-India Service;

(b) to a post included in a Central Service Class I, of any officer in the armed forces of the Union or any officer who is already a member of an all-India Service or a Central Service Class I;

(c) to a Central Service Class II, or to a post included in a Central Service Class II, of any officer who is already a member of a Central Service Class II, or Central Service Class III, or of any officer in the Armed Forces of the Union; and

(d) to a tenure post included in a Central Service Class I, or a Central Service Class II, of an officer of a State Service.

Note. In this regulation:

(i) the terms 'Central Service Class I', 'Central Service Class II' and 'Central Service Class III', shall include the corresponding Railway Services, and Defence Services (Civilian);

(ii) the term 'Officer' includes a person holding a permanent or quasi-permanent appointment, but does not include a person in temporary employment;

(iii) the term 'State Service' means service in a State appointments to which are made by the Governor;

(iv) the term 'tenure post' means a post, whether permanent or temporary, which has been classified as a tenure post in consultation with the Commission.

4. It shall not be necessary to consult the Commission in regard to the selection for temporary or officiating appointment to a post, if

(a) the person appointed is not likely to hold the post for a period of more than one year; and

264

(b) it is necessary in the public interest to make the appointment immediately and a reference to the Commission will cause undue delay.

Provided that

(i) such appointment shall be reported to the Commission as soon as it is made;

(ii) if the appointment continues beyond a period of six months, a fresh estimate as to the period for which the person appointed is likely to hold the post shall be made and reported to the Commission: and

(iii) if such estimate indicates that the person appointed is likely to hold the post for a period of more than one year from the date of appointment, the Commission shall immediately be consulted in regard to the filling of the post.

5. (1) It shall not be necessary to consult the Commission in regard to the making of any order in any disciplinary case other than

  (a) an original order by the President imposing any of the following penalties:

  (i) censure;

  (ii) withholding of increments or promotion;

  (iii) recovery from pay of the whole or part of any pecuniary loss caused to the Government by negligence or breach of orders;

  (iv) reduction to a lower Service, grade or post, or to a lower time-scale or to a lower stage in a time-scale;

  (v) compulsory retirement;

  (vi) removal from service;

  (vii) dismissal from service;

  (b) an order by the President on an appeal against an order imposing any of the said penalties made by a subordinate authority;

  (c) an order by the President over-ruling or modifying, after consideration of any petition or memorial or otherwise, an order imposing any of the said penalties made by the President or by a subordinate authority.

(2) It shall not be necessary to consult the Commission in regard to any disciplinary matter affecting a person belonging to a Defence Service (Civilian).

(3) It shall not be necessary to consult the Commission in regard to any order made under the Central Civil Services (Safeguarding of National Security) Rules, 1953 or the Railway Services (Safeguarding of National Security) Rules, 1954.

SCHEDULE

(1) Posts in respect of which the authority to **appoint is specifically** conferred on the President by the Constitution.

(2) Posts of Chairman or members of any Board, Tribunal, Commission, Committee or other similar authority created by or under the provisions of a statute.

(3) Posts of Chairman or Members of any Board, Tribunal, Commission, Committee or other similar body appointed by or under the authority of a

resolution of either House or Parliament or by a resolution of Government for the purpose of conducting any investigation or inquiry into or for advising Government on specified matters.

(4) Posts of Heads of Diplomatic, Consular, and other similar Indian Missions in countries (e.g., Ambassadors, High Commissioners, Ministers, Commissioners, Consuls-General, Representatives, Agents).

(5) Posts on the personal staff attached to holders of posts mentioned in items (1) to (4) above.

(6) Posts in the Secretariats of the Lok Sabha and the Rajya Sabha.

(7) All technical and administrative posts in or under the Atomic Energy Commission.

(8) Judicial Commissioners and Additional Judicial Commissioners, District Judges and Additional District Judges in Union Territories.

(9) Subordinate Judges and Munsifs in the Union Territories of Manipur, Tripura and Himachal Pradesh.

(10) All Class III and Class IV Services and posts, save as otherwise expressly provided in the relevant rules or orders governing recruitment thereto.

(11) Any Service or post concerned with the administration of the North-East Frontier Agency.

(12) Any Service or post or class of posts in respect of which the Commission has agreed that it shall not be necessary for it to be consulted.

CHAPTER VI

Standards of
Administrative Morality

An important conclusion that emerges from an analysis of administrative developments after 1947 is that several changes were introduced to ensure in the transaction of public business speed, integrity and efficiency which had declined as a result of excessive and disfunctional expansion. Surprisingly, however, the poor quality of staff recruited during the War was not reduced in keeping with actual requirements, and, in fact, was allowed not only to continue, but increase through promotional and other avenues in the post-Independence period. The extended scope of social and economic activities provided justification for what the government did in the name of development administration. But in the absence of anything like a planned personnel policy, there was nothing to check bureaucratic expansion. The increasing share of public participation in developmental activity without a corresponding will to plan its requisite personnel gave rise to numerous problems, one of which was a deepening crisis in administrative morality. The object of this chapter is to discuss this crisis in a historical setting.

Historical Perspective

The early administration of the East India Company in Bengal began with corruption which flowed from a variety of circumstances, more especially from a union of civil and commercial functions exercised by the Company's covenanted servants in the first few years after the grant of the diwani in 1765.[1] In 1772, however, the Company took over the administration of the diwani provinces directly through the agency of its own officers called Collectors who, under the

Regulating Act (1773), became purely civil functionaries. The distinction which the Act brought about between the Company's civil and commercial functions called for a separate personnel classification which established the superiority of the civil service over other services. For its new covenant not only demanded sacrificing private trade, but also forbade the acceptance of gifts or presents from 'the natives of India', a practice which was common in earlier days. The Company's civil service became a public service theoretically, though its conceptual content remained rudimentary until Cornwallis enriched it against all opposition. In the meantime, the India Act of 1784 not only forbade the acceptance of presents or indulgence in corrupt bargains, but made these as well as any act of insubordination punishable as misdemeanours.

The commercial and political functions of the Company, it is true, remained united at the level of its government in India, which carried on both commerce and civil administration through separate agencies. But that too did not continue for much longer. While the Charter Act of 1813 ordered a clear separation of its commercial and territorial accounts, the Government of India Act (1833) transformed its very character from a trading organization into an administrative corporation. The process of transformation was initiated by Wellesley (1798-1805) who viewed the dominion of India as a 'sacred trust', worthy of being governed by a civil service capable of 'an inexhaustible supply of useful knowledge, cultivated talents and disciplined morals'.[2] Indeed, the early experiments of British rule show that clean civil administration could not have been possible except by divesting it of profit-motivated trading operations. This was realized by the British Parliament whose enactments helped the Company's Indian government enforce discipline as well as integrity of character in the performance of public duties.

Apart from fixing a rate of salary in keeping with the required degree of responsibility, the British rulers introduced two other important measures designed to promote administrative morality. These were the rule of law and the system of open competition as a mode of recruitment.

The introduction of the rule of law and the formation of the Cornwallis Code (1793) established for the first time a definitive legal and rational principle for the guidance of the civil service. While the Code laid the foundation for the growth of procedural law and administrative uniformity for inspectional purposes, the rule of law contributed to the growth of the legal profession.[3] Together they constituted a framework of specified powers within which a civil servant was called upon to function and administer. The object was to impose administrative discipline and curb licence which flowed from extravagance and the search for affluence through commercial avenues, a hangover of the past where there had been no check on illicit gain through trade, gift and bribery.

Originally, the object of an emphasis on procedure was to reduce the evils arising from the exercise of discretion on the part of Indian judges who were used to trying the same case a number of times, giving mutually contradictory judgements in favour of or against a party according to the rewards offered by each side. Later, its aim was to protect suitors against the chicanery of the inferior court officials who duped untrained European judges and led them into errors for personal gain. Emphasis was then laid on finer rules of procedure to reduce the area within which even a European judge could use discretion. The increasing perfection of procedural law, however, did not improve the matter. On the contrary, it tended to vitiate the course of justice itself, with the help of lawyers who turned procedural sophistication into a weapon to put their adversaries at a disadvantage.

Speaking from his own experience as the Lieutenant-Governor of Bengal, Sir George Campbell pointed out in a letter addressed to the Government of India on 15 July 1873 that the rich and litigious class of zamindars and moneylenders was raising lawyers to a dominant position in Indian society and causing the ruination of the cultivating community by transfer of land effected in satisfaction of bonded debts. Justice was being confused with law and the existing system of supervision by a High Court was of no help to those who stood to suffer. The rule of law and procedural perfection had, in fact, become a cause for the denial of justice to them. He therefore suggested that all appeals to High Courts should be stopped and substituted by executive revision. For he believed that in a society unevenly balanced in terms of the distribution of social and economic power it was difficult to ensure justice except by an executive revision of judicial decrees. This view had earlier been expressed by Holt Mackenzie.[4]

Campbell's proposal was turned down on the recommendation of A. C. Lyall, the Secretary to the Government of India. He pointed out that executive control over the judiciary 'would set up arbitrary will in the place of law; it would substitute a rapid conjecture for methodical examination; it would multiply the elements of chance which must always exist in law-suits; and it would rapidly destroy the very notion of fixed and sovereign law paramount over all individual will and power, which, at least ever since the Regulations of 1793, it has been the steady policy of the British Government to inculcate on the people of India'.[5] Indeed, the rule of law, as originally conceived, had been recognized as an important device to check arbitrary proceedings and restrict the area of discretion as a means to ensure integrity in the discharge of public duties.

The system of open competition introduced in 1855 in accordance with the recommendations of the Macaulay Committee replaced the old system of patronage under which the nominees of the Company's Directors or their friends were admitted to Haileybury for training before being sent out to India as covenanted civil servants. Though the conditions of nomination to Haileybury were such that the quality of the service was on the whole not allowed to suffer, the scope of selection was limited and could not hope to maintain the highest standards in the long run. The Macaulary Committee made it clear that the standard of morality in the public service was related to the quality of intellectual competition. In other words, a decline in the intellectual standard of the test was bound to be reflected in a decline of moral quality. Experience established the validity of this principle in respect of the I.C.S. When the upper age limit was reduced to 19, there was a sudden fall in the number of candidates from Oxford and Cambridge. A gradual lowering of intellectual standards followed, producing a corresponding deterioration in the behavioural pattern of civil servants.[6] The upper age limit was raised again in 1892, which effected some improvement, even though political agitations later dissuaded the best graduates from British universities from joining the I.C.S. Even so, the competitive system and other institutional arrangements which had remained operative over the years on the strength of Parliamentary enactments and official policies, worked well. They provided, on the whole, for a clean administration in spite of the stresses and strains caused by a variety of forces, both external and internal.

However, the integrity of the public service which British rule sought to ensure applied chiefly to the I.C.S., not to the lower grades of government servants. The latter remained by and large accustomed to practicing bribery and corruption. This was a hangover of medieval times, when offices were bought and sold or held as hereditary possession, in recognition of any service rendered to a controlling authority. Officers of the government were similarly entitled to perquisites or even a share in fees and fines imposed as part of judicial determinations. There were no definite laws or rules and the few authorities that existed for the collection of revenue or the administration of justice acted mostly at their discretion. So long as officials were loyal to the existing regime, they were free to do as they liked. They could amass wealth for themselves and advance their material interest without let or hindrance, either from society or higher authorities. Cases occurred where a man drawing a mere pittance rose to affluence and spent lakhs over domestic ceremonies.[7] These traits were absorbed into the ranks of the Company's 'monthly writers', who later came to form part of the uncovenanted services, including such functionaries as tahsildars, talukdars, mamlatdars, sub-deputy collectors and a number of subordinate officers on the judicial side. It was from the uncovenanted servants that subordinate cadres of deputy collectors and deputy magistrates were created respectively in 1833 and 1843. The uncovenanted employees, however, remained long neglected, without definite conditions of service being laid down to regulate their conduct or their terms of employment. It was only in 1892 that the Provincial Civil Service was constituted out of the upper layers of the uncovenanted service: only then did the Government of India introduce certain conditions to control the quality of recruitment and some P.C.S. officers under the new rules were sought to be promoted to 'listed' posts reserved for members of the I.C.S.

Traditionally, therefore, the provincial Services, which were invested with the execution of details under the supervision of I.C.S. officers, did not have anything like clean records of performance. Their past was a history of bribery and corruption. With the prospects of promotion created in 1892, however, care was taken to provide against the abuse of power that might occur in the event of a provincial service man being raised to the office of Collector and District Magistrate or to any other office of a higher rank. In addition to the I.C.S., a number of other all India Services were created between 1892 and 1906. Their members were all recruited in England and posted to different provinces, where they set a higher standard of performance and also acted as watch-dogs for the government in terms not only of honesty and integrity, but also of an all-India perspective. These objectives were defeated and historical perspectives lost sight of when, as a result of political agitation for Indianization, the Lee Commission had to recommend their abolition in 1924. This affected both efficiency and integrity. For it led to the expansion and strengthening of the provincial services, which were prone, by tradition, to political subservience, and to seek wealth and riches. In respect of recruitment and disciplinary control they were not even subject strictly to any public service commission until the Government of India Act (1935) ordered the establishment of such commissions for each province or groups of provinces.

In the meantime, the rule of law and the rules governing the conduct of public officials brought under the category of corruption cases which, given the country's customs, could very well have passed as perquisites. In its modern connotation, corruption thus became prevalent in the provincial services, more especially in such departments as revenue, the police, excise and public works. Provincial Civil Service men, however, worked generally under an I.C.S. officer, who supervised the execution of administrative orders. He commanded obedience by virtue of his integrity, power and thorough training in public administration. Each Collector was virtually a little governor, and the Executive Councillors at both central and provincial levels were all I.C.S. men. They were known generally for their keenness on the job and it was their first-hand grip of detail that made them both feared and respected. The P.C.S., functioning directly under them was therefore comparatively clean. With the introduction of provincial autonomy the situation started changing in the 1920's. Cases began to occur[8] where, by virtue of new rules introduced in 1922, certain P.C.S. officers stole a march over European Civilians in respect of promotion. These cases tended to inject into administrative fields a political dimension which weakened the role that the supervisory administrative agency once played in enforcing integrity.

However, the limited scope of state activity, the economic depression that occurred around 1929-30 and the general lack of fluid resources within the framework of free enterprise set limits to opportunities for individuals to corrupt or get corrupted. The Second World War removed most of these barriers to corruption. It involved an annual expenditure of hundreds of crores of rupees over war supplies and contracts which created unprecedented opportunities for the acquisition of wealth by doubtful means. It set into motion a network of controls and a permit system which opened opportunities to officials for bribery, corruption and favouritism. And since the whole object was to win the War by any means, the importance of propriety lost much of its weight. The War was won, but the moral fabric of society and administration was shaken to its very foundations.

Causes of the Growth of Corruption

Of the causes that contributed to the growth of corruption, the incapacity of society to resist this evil has been by far the most important. It ran parallel to the administrative system built up in modern times. For the rule of law and open competition, which went into the making of modern administration, had no place in traditional Indian society. A person appointed to a subordinate rank in a modern administration can move to a higher rank in due course according to the quality of his performance. But no such promotional avenues existed in the traditional caste order.

In view of this polar gap between the principles governing administrative and social institutions no liaison could be established between the two. Macaulay thought that the western-educated middle class could provide a link, but a couple of serious difficulties stood in the way. First, the benefits of English education remained restricted to the upper layers of society, for the most part brahmanic in social terms. This tended to provide continuity rather than social change. Secondly, the dominant group of the educated elites so created used the traditional principles of Hindu social organization as a basis for anti-western agitation and to fight for political power. Though politically conducive to progress, the struggle for freedom was essentially motivated by an attitude of social reaction. No effective public opinion could therefore grow as a social force against corruption in a stratified society where affluence was considered a divine favour, education a privilege of certain classes, and the loyalty of groups subject to caste affiliations, not to considerations of ideology or interest.

When the new Government took over in 1946, it found that the administrative machinery had become considerably weakened by the war-time neglect. The situation worsened on account of the departure of a large number of experienced officers, necessitating rapid promotions even of those with little or no merit. The dilution of experience and ability was caused likewise by the recruitment of a large number of officers in various grades to handle the expanded activities of the Government in new fields involving expenditure of the order of

Rs 1,000 crores a year. These were developments which afforded to unscrupulous elements in the public service and politics unprecedented opportunities for acquiring wealth by dubious means. A sudden spurt in government spending encouraged inflationary tendencies which caused a decline in real incomes, particularly amongst the salaried classes, most of whom were in government service. Though a fall in the standard of living is no justification for a fall in the standard of integrity, the fact remains that economic necessity did, in certain cases, encourage those who had the opportunities, to succumb to temptation.

On assuming office in 1946 the new Government took a number of steps to deal with the problems of corruption. The Delhi Special Police Establishment, for instance, was organized on a permanent footing under the Delhi Special Police Establishment Act, 1946. The Prevention of Corruption Act became law on 11 March 1947. A committee was set up in 1947 with Bakshi Tek Chand as its chairman. This committee was to review the working of the Prevention of Corruption Act, 1947, and recommend improvements in the laws and machinery designed to enforce them. The committee was also to assess the performance of the Special Police Establishment and suggest organizational improvements to combat corruption. The Government even made over to it four inquiry cases in which ministers themselves were involved. Some ministers in Rajasthan and Vindhya Pradesh were actually prosecuted in 1949-50. A Railway Corruption Inquiry Committee was appointed in October 1953, with Acharya Kripalani as its chairman. This was followed by the establishment of an Administrative Vigilance Division as part of the Ministry of Home Affairs in August 1955. The appointment of the Vivian Bose Commission in December 1956 was yet another step taken to prevent corruption. Some leading industrialists were prosecuted during 1950-60. The Government, which had been constituted on non-party lines in the first decade after Independence, thus exhibited considerable interest and energy in an attempt to cleanse the administration of the country.

These measures, however, could not accomplish the object of their institution. The sudden expansion of the economic activities of the Government put into operation a large number of regulations, control mechanisms, licences and permits. These involved a corresponding multiplication of the administrative processes, which extended considerably the scope of administrative action. The operational scope, for instance, of the community development projects and the national extension scheme became so vast that officers at all levels could freely exercise a great deal of discretion outside the four walls of law and propriety, without the injured citizen being in a position to obtain any effective redress. The union of power and discretion vested at different levels in the execution of development schemes was bound to produce corruption, as it did, in the context of scarcity and pressure to spend public money in a given period of time.

The situation created by a spurt in the economic functions of the Government in fact increased corruption. It caused delay if functions remained centralized and corruption in case these were decentralized. Delay encouraged the growth of what the Santhanam Committee described as 'speed money', paid in matters relating to the grant of licences and permits, etc. As the Committee reported, 'It was stated by a Secretary [to the Government] that even after an order had been passed the fact of the passing of such order itself is kept back till the unfortunate applicant has paid appropriate gratification to the subordinate concerned'.[9] 'Speed money' was thus a serious cause of delay. Decentralization, on the other hand, meant delegation of authority to subordinate officers with a degree of discretion which, besides being responsible for extravagance and peculation, was also used to delay and extort money from needy people.

In addition to what has been said above, the two contributory and immediate factors which the Santhanam Committee emphasized were (i) an unwillingness to deal drastically with corrupt and inefficient public servants; and (ii) the protection given to the Services in India under Article 311 of the Constitution. 'It was distressing', the Committee observed, 'to hear heads of departments confess that, even where they were morally convinced that one of the officials working under them was corrupt, they were unable to do anything because of the difficulties in obtaining formal proof, finding or conviction. They could not even make an adverse entry in the confidential roll without their being required to justify such an entry with proof when it was challenged after its communication to the Government servant concerned'.[10]

There were further factors which contributed to the growth of corruption and still continue to do so: the influence wielded on the higher bureaucracy by the industrial and commercial classes, and the interests of ministers, legislators and party officials. The ranks of these classes had emerged in strength in the course of the Second

World War and later accumulated large amounts of unaccounted money by various methods, especially by obtaining licences in the names of bogus firms and individuals, by trafficking in licences and permits, by manupulation of accounts to avoid taxes, by under-valuation of transactions in immovable property, and by employing other questionable means. They spent huge sums on entertainment and maintained an army of contact-men whose business it was to make a careful study of the character, tastes and weaknesses of officials with whom they had to deal, so that they could exploit those weaknesses and get things done quickly. The Santhanam Committee thus observed that possession of 'large amounts of unaccounted money by various persons including those belonging to the industrial and commercial classes is a major impediment in the purification of public life. If anti-corruption activities are to be successful, it must be recognized that it is as important to fight these unscrupulous agencies of corruption as to eliminate corruption in the public services. In fact they go together'.[11]

Administrative integrity began to worsen more strikingly from 1956 onwards, when the administration became subject to a purely party government after the exclusion of C. D. Deshmukh. The Industrial Policy Resolution of 30 April 1956,[12] which emphasized in the meantime a socialist pattern of society as the objective of social and economic policy, laid down that the State must assume direct responsibility for the future development of industries over a wide area. The Resolution so classified industries as to give the State exclusive responsibility over all industries of basic and strategic im-portance, including those affecting public utility services. The confid-ence of millowners and manufacturers was shaken by the Govern-ment's expressed desire to progressively take over such industries which, for the time, were left under the private sector. Whatever the goal or intention of the Industrial Policy Resolution, it certainly created a situation where the leaders of industry became alarmed by what they considered an ideological overtone in it. Their central organization declined co-operation with official attempts to fight corruption amongst big business. The Santhanam Committee thus regretted 'that while a number of Trade Associations and State Chambers of Commerce readily accepted our invitation to help us with their views and advice, the Federation of Indian Chambers of Commerce, which could have given powerful support to the fight against corruption, would not even accept our invitation to meet us'.[13]

The Second Plan, which proceeded on the lines indicated in the Industrial Policy Resolution of 1956, saw corruption growing into an organized force. By 1960 the number of cases investigated by the Delhi Police Establishment alone increased almost two-fold in about ten years.[14] In these circumstances the Cabinet Secretariat prepared its *Papers on Measures for the Strengthening of Administration* in 1961. But by the time these papers were prepared with the assistance of the Planning Commission and the O & M Division, the problem of corruption had come to assume serious proportions, already engaging the attention of the press, Parliament and the public. From 1 April 1956 to 31 December 1962 complaints and vigilance cases of corruption had registered nearly a five-fold increase.[15]

By the time the Santhanam Committee was appointed in September 1962, corruption had increased to an extent where people had started losing faith in the integrity of public administration itself, not excluding even its decision-making political apparatus.

It was expected that in the governance of the country, the followers of Gandhi would set a standard of integrity that might justify popular expectations in both political and administrative fields. But, as the Committee 'frankly admitted', this 'hope has not been realised in full measure'. However, the Committee also noted that 'a good percentage of our public servants', 'maintain and function in accordance with strict standards of integrity'. It was hoped that 'this solid and hard core of honest public servants' could serve as a base for doing 'a thorough cleansing of our public life'.[16]

Measures Suggested for Eradication of Corruption

The Committee's approach to remedial measures was legalistic and took a somewhat restricted view of a highly complex problem which called for deeper socio-political analysis. In addition to suggestions concerning such departments as came into direct contact with people, the Committee's recommendations dealt merely with the rules of conduct and disciplinary matters pertaining to government servants. The object was to rationalize the framework of these rules in a manner that might improve the administrative morality of the public services.

Conduct Rules. The Committee found that the existing rules governing the conduct of public servants were more or less unchanged from those existing prior to the commencement of the Constitution. It was therefore emphasized that the rules pertaining to integrity should be uniform and that certain other changes should be made to plug loopholes in the conduct rules. The changes so made cast a specific responsibility and duty on superior officers to keep a watchful eye on the integrity of their subordinates. Every government servant was, however, to take full responsibility for his own actions and orders except when acting under the direction of his official superior. It was felt that this exception was necessary in the light of experience gained during the Mundhra Affair, where officers involved in the judicial proceedings tried to shield themselves under the plea that they had acted under the direction or advice of their superiors.

The rules relating to raising subscriptions, acceptance of gifts, engaging in speculation, private trade or employment after retirement remained more or less unchanged. No government servant was to ask for or accept contributions to, or associate himself with the raising of, any funds or collections although the Government could permit such collection for a specific purpose. The question of the receipt of gifts, on the other hand, was made clearer and liberalized slightly. While the definition of gifts included free transport, lodging and other services or any other pecuniary advantages when provided by any person other than a near relative or personal friend having no official dealings, government servants were permitted to accept occasional lifts or meals or casual hospitality for public purposes. This was done with a view to preventing undue interference and pin-pricks in private life. More important than this, however, was the rule relating to submission of property returns. The existing provision for annual immovable property returns had become out of date in view of the modern tendency to hold assets otherwise than as immovable property. The Santhanam Committee therefore recommended that government servants should submit periodically a complete statement of their assets and liabilities instead of the annual immovable property statements which had in the past served no useful purpose. The new periodical returns were to include statements relating to the value of movable property, except articles of daily use like clothes, utensils, crockery and books, but not excluding jewellery and other movable assets. The periodical reports were designed not only to serve as a check against corruption, but also to see that they served the purpose for which they were obtained. Indeed, the Committee felt that in order to enable the government to ascertain whether any of its officials was in possession of assets disproportionate to his known sources of income, or whether he was running into debt, it would be necessary that the official furnish a complete statement of his assets and liabilities periodically. The government, however, was to have the power to exempt from this rule any specified categories of government servants. It was, for instance, not considered necessary to obtain such returns from Class IV officers or some categories of those in Class III.

Disciplinary Rules. The English Common Law under which all servants of the Crown held office during the pleasure of the Crown and were subject to dismissal without any reasons being assigned for such dismissal, came to apply to the services of the East India Company under Section 74 of the Government of India Act, 1833. It made these services subject to the pleasure of the Crown and, except in cases where the appointment was made directly by the Crown, also subject to the pleasure of the Court of Directors. Under the Government of India Act, 1858, the Secretary of State for India came to be invested with all the powers which the ·Directors exercised before. The doctrine of pleasure continued to be operative in the Indian situation until Section 96 B of the Government of India Act, 1919, seemed apparently to have circumscribed that doctrine by providing that every person in the civil services of the Crown in India held office during His Majesty's pleasure 'subject to the provisions of this Act and the rules made thereunder'. It was, however, held by the Privy Council that the proviso so made was not to have the effect of limiting the doctrine of pleasure. The enactment which actually limited that doctrine was the Government of India Act, 1935. Section 240 of this Act did two things. First, it reproduced Section 96B of the 1919 Act in sub-section (1) which said: 'Except as expressly provided by this Act, every person who is a member of a civil service of the Crown in India, or holds any civil post under the Crown in India, holds office during His Majesty's pleasure'. Secondly, it added a new sub-section by which additional protection was given to the civil servant. It provided that no civil servant 'shall be dismissed from the service of His Majesty by any authority subordinate to that by which he was appointed'.[17] This security of service was reinforced by another provision which laid down that no such civil servant 'shall be dismissed or reduced in rank until he has been given a reasonable opportunity of showing cause against the action proposed to be taken against him'.[18]

The doctrine of pleasure was thus circumscribed by the Government of India Act, 1935, which in its anxiety to protect civil servants against political influence saw no alternative but to introduce additional safeguards against ministerial action. These, for the same purpose, also formed part of the 'special responsibilities' of the Governor-General and the Governors of Provinces. The Interim Government that took office in 1946 accepted the principle of this arrangement which continued until the Constitution of India came into force in 1950. Its introduction was, however, marked by no substantial change. Article 309 dealt with the rule-making power of the President and Governors; Article 310, on the other hand, provided that civil servants held office during the pleasure of the President or the Governor of a State as the case might be. Instead of making any radical change in the constitution of the civil service, Article 311 not only retained the provisions of Section 240 of the 1935 Act, but reinforced them to make the civil service still more secure.

Article 311 reiterated the old principle by providing that 'no person who is a member of a civil service of a Union or an all-India service or a civil service of a State or holds a civil post under the Union or a State shall be dismissed or removed by an authority subordinate to that by which he was appointed'.[19] It further laid down that no such person was to be dismissed, removed or reduced in rank 'except after an inquiry in which he has been informed of the charges against him and given a reasonable opportunity of being heard in respect of those charges and where it is proposed, after such inquiry, to impose on him any such penalty, until he has been given a reasonable opportunity of making representation on the penalty proposed, but only on the basis of the evidence adduced during such inquiry'.[20] A reasonable opportunity of being heard was thus to be made available to the accused on two occasions: first in the course of an inquiry and, secondly, before the imposition of the penalty proposed after the inquiry. No such security existed under Section 240 (3) of the Government of India Act, 1935, which had provided for only one such opportunity.

The clause dealing with the disciplinary provisions of dismissal, removal or reduction in rank was, however, not to apply

(a) where a person is dismissed or removed or reduced in rank on the ground of conduct which has led to his conviction on a criminal charge; or

(b) where the authority empowered to dismiss or remove a person or to reduce him in rank is satisfied that for some reason, to be recorded by that authority in writing, it is not reasonably practicable to hold such inquiry; or

(c) where the President or the Governor, as the case may be, is satisfied that in the interest of the security of the State it is not expedient to hold such inquiry.[21]

The constitutional protection given to officials under Article 311 was by itself sufficient to make disciplinary proceedings difficult. Its judicial interpretation made these proceedings all the more involved. It was held by the Supreme Court that the opportunity provided could be considered reasonable only if it gave the government servant the chance to deny his guilt and establish his innocence by cross-examining the witnesses produced against him, by examining himself or other witnesses in support of his defence, and by making representations as to why the punishment proposed as a result of inquiry should not be inflicted on him. The judicial interpretations of the term 'reasonable opportunity' in fact imposed several restrictions on the manner of inquiry; and even if the inquiring officer happened to conform to prescribed norms, the delinquent official could advance a plea that he had already prejudged the issues and that he was not amenable to consider the matter objectively and dispassionately.

Securing the punishment of a delinquent officer under Article 311(2) of the Constitution was thus more difficult than doing so under Section 240(3) of the 1935 Act which was itself sufficiently involved. A case where an I.C.S. officer was sought to be punished under that section illustrates the degree of security which government servants had come to enjoy after the doctrine of pleasure was limited in the Indian situation. I.M. Lall, who had joined the I.C.S. in 1922 as a member of the Punjab cadre,[22] had disciplinary proceedings started against him in July 1937 on the basis of a couple of charges. The first charge was nepotism, where he had been accused of having shown undue favour to his wife's relative, Sunder Das, whom he confirmed in his job over others without regard to rules. The second was victimization, for Lall had recorded adverse entries in the character rolls of those who represented against his alleged acts of nepotism. In July 1939, he was ordered to proceed on leave and he was later removed from the I.C.S. by an order of the Secretary of State for India with effect from 4 June 1940.

Lall took recourse to judicial proceedings. He brought a suit against the Secretary of State for India on 20 July 1942. He contended that the requirements of Section 240(3) of the 1935 Act, which demanded that a reasonable opportunity be given to the accused to show cause against the action proposed to be taken, had not been complied with. He therefore sought a judicial declaration that his removal from service was wrongful and that the order of removal was void and insufficient for the termination of his services. The suit was decreed by the Punjab High Court at Lahore on 27 March 1944. The Court gave Lall the declaration in the terms asked for. The Secretary of State appealed against that decision to the Federal Court, who dismissed the appeal on 4 May 1945, upholding the decision of the High Court that the order of removal was void and inoperative. The Secretary of State then appealed to the Privy Council by special leave. Here too the appeal was lost. The Privy Council's judgement, delivered on 18 March 1948, declared that the order of dismissal was void and inoperative and that he remained a member of the I.C.S. at the date of the suit, which was 20 July 1942. The Council, however, held that he had no right to recover arrears of pay by legal proceedings. As a result of this decision, Lall returned to the I.C.S.

As regards the consequential matters that needed to be settled, the Home Ministry expressed itself against continuing Lall in service after the transfer of power. It was suggested that, since the new Government of India could refuse to entertain a member of the Secretary of State's Services after 14 August 1947, Lall's employment could be terminated thereafter. He could in that case be entitled only to a compensation amounting to £3,500 and a pension of £1,000 per annum admissible under the rules. The Government thought that the charges against Lall were precise and definite. He could remain in service subject only to the disciplinary proceedings already started against him being continued. But that involved serious difficulties. For, although the charges levelled against Lall were precise and definite, it was not easy to form a provisional decision as to whether or what punishment was called for, so that Lall could accordingly appeal under Section 240(3) of the Government of India Act, 1935. The difficulties of technical compliance with the requirements of law led the Home Ministry to suggest the termination of Lall's service. However, the Home Minister, Sardar Vallabhbhai Patel, ruled out any question of reviving departmental proceedings. 'The only honourable course open to Government', he advised, 'is to reinstate him in the service to which he has been adjudged to belong, even though it involves decision on certain awkward questions.' In view of Lall's seniority in the I.C.S. he was entitled to a judgeship of a High Court. But having been out of touch with judicial work for a number of years, he had already 'expressed a desire to continue to take interset and deal with labour matters'. Patel therefore suggested that 'the best course would be to continue him in service with attendant benefits and to utilize his service on deputation at the Centre in connection with labour matters.'[23] Lall was accordingly re-instated and put in charge of labour.

A close reading of the papers connected with the disciplinary proceedings of I.M. Lall lends itself to two main conclusions. First, the statutory provision of Section 240(3) of the 1935 Act, which was further reinforced by Article 311(2) of the new Constitution of India, made it extremely difficult for the government to punish any act of corruption; for a resort to judicial proceedings against a decision of the executive in administrative matters invested a court of law with an interpretative authority that tended to make it almost a rival state. Secondly, the top echelons of the bureaucracy realized the difficulties involved in reviving departmental proceedings against Lall after the transfer of power. Thus they wanted to get rid of him before that on the basis of the announcements already made by the Viceroy. But political influence was brought to bear upon Sardar Patel who ordered reinstatement. The Santhanam Committee was indeed right in saying that it was 'a matter of profound concern that in the past there has been a certain amount of complacency with the situation'[24] which demanded the enforcement of anti-corruption measures without any let or hindrance.

The Constitution (Fifteenth Amendment) Act, 1963, amended Article 311 of the Constitution. But it did not improve matters. The Committee therefore suggested that it would not be an unreasonable classification to treat disciplinary proceedings involving charges of bribery, corruption and lack of integrity as a separate category and to provide for a simplified procedure limiting the jurisdiction of courts by a suitable constitutional amendment. Parliament would then by law regulate all matters relating to the maintenance of integrity and honesty in the services and posts under the Union and States.

In its interim report submitted on 23 August 1963 the Santhanam Committee made a number of other important recommendations to improve the situation. It suggested, for instance, that there should be only one set of Discipline and Appeal Rules for all government servants and that the President should have the powers to impose any of the prescribed penalities and institute disciplinary proceedings against any government servant, including members of the All-India Services. It was emphasized that disciplinary rules must remain operative even after an official retired. The penalties of withholding or withdrawing in full or in part the pension which could be imposed in respect of the Death-cum-Retirement Benefits Rules of 1958, were part of the Discipline and Appeal Rules. Apart from the government's power to compulsorily retire a government servant after 25 years of service or at 50 years of age, the Committee made two other important suggestions. The requirement of the accused officer submitting a written statement of defence after the framing of charges was to be dispensed with; and so was to be the case in respect of a memorial or an appeal that was required to be submitted through the authority which passed the order of punishment.

Ministers' Conduct. The Santhanam Committee referred to the general consensus of opinion which held that a new tradition of integrity could not be established if the ministers of the Central and State Governments failed to set an example. The Committee therefore recommended certain steps which it considered necessary in the interest of the future of public life in the country.

A code of conduct for ministers was, for example, suggested on the lines recommended for public servants. It included provisions relating to the acquisition of property, acceptance of gifts and disclosure of assets and liabilities. This code was to have the sanction of Parliament. The Prime Minister and the Chief Ministers were, on the other hand, to consider themselves responsible for enforcing it. It was emphasized that specific allegations against a minister should be promptly investigated by an agency commanding respect. If a formal allegation was made by any 10 members of Parliament or a Legislature, and if the allegation so made was addressed in writing through the Speakers or Chairmen to the Prime Minister or Chief Minister, the latter should consider themselves obliged by convention to refer the allegation for immediate investigation by an *ad hoc* Committee selected by the President out of a national panel consisting of three people, one of whom should have held or should be holding a high judicial office. This Committee was to ascertain whether there was a *prima facie* case. If so, it might direct the Central Bureau of Investigation to investigate and report, or it might suggest inquiries through another agency. In the latter case the Committee was to be given the necessary facilities without being hampered by any claim of privilege. In the light of its inquiry the Committee could advise that a regular case be registered with a view to prosecuting the minister concerned, or a commission of inquiry be appointed under the Commission of Inquiry Act, 1952. Independantly of the mode of inquiry, the Santhanam Committee stressed the point that, if a minister was found guilty of any act of corruption, he should be dismissed and declared ineligible for ministership or for elective office under necessary legislation to be enacted for the purpose.

The Prime Minister or Chief Ministers were also expected to take note of allegations made either in the press or which otherwise came to their notice. Apart from referring cases to the *ad hoc* Committee, the old method of filing a criminal suit was considered desirable in all other situations. It was advised that ministers against whom allegations were made should, as a rule, institute legal proceedings by filing a complaint against criminal defamation and should be given legitimate assistance to clear their conduct. In instances where ministers were unwilling to do so, the Prime Minister or the concerned Chief Minister was to consider himself obliged by convention, unless there was irrefutable proof of integrity of the minister concerned, to advise the President or Governor to withdraw his pleasure. The minister would thus have to relinquish office unless he himself chose to resign.

Since ministers in a democracy are subject to influence by M.P.s and state legislators, it was regretted by the Committee that some of these members used their position to obtain permits, licences and easier access to ministers and higher officials for industrialists and businessmen. It is through them that corrupt individuals, vested interests and pressure groups achieved their ends either executively or through legislative enactments. The Santhanam Committee therefore recommended that there should also be a code of conduct for legislators. It felt that they should not undertake, from considerations of financial gain or personal advantage, to promote the interests of, or obtain favours for, any private party either in the legislature or with the Government. It suggested that this code of conduct should be framed by a special committee of Parliament and legislatures, to be nominated by the Speakers and Chairmen. Such nominations were in addition to be approved formally by resolutions of appropriate legislative authority. Infringement was thus to be treated as a breach of privilege, to be looked into by the Committee of Privileges.

A far more baneful influence was, however, the conduct of political parties. The Santhanam Committee pointed out that nothing less than a total ban on donations by companies to political parties could clear the atmosphere of corruption. It was pointedly advised that all political parties should keep proper account of their receipts and expenditure and that they should publish them annually, duly audited with a statement giving details of all receipts. In case a political party failed to do this, it should be debarred from recognition by the Election Commission.

While recommending anti-corruption measures, the Committee did not ignore the importance of public opinion, for it clearly pointed out that those found guilty of corruption should not only feel that they would lose their jobs but also feel socially degraded. Little did the Committee realize that the fear of degradation is generally non-existent in a society where the phenomenon of accumulated wealth by itself imparts legitimacy to a title to social prestige, irrespective of the means by which that wealth has been acquired.

Institutional Arrangements to Check Corruption

Administrative Vigilance Division. In a Note of 8 August 1955 the then Home Minister (Govind Ballabh Pant) regretted that, despite the recommendations of many committees and some steps already taken to check corruption in the public services, the results achieved could not be regarded as satisfactory. The explanation he gave for 'comparative failure' was that 'the Central Government is an unwieldly machine functioning through numerous departments and agencies spread over a vast area and employing hundreds of thousands of persons in all grades and types of posts'. And yet there had in the past been no provision for a 'centralized drive, direction and co-ordination'.[25] While recognizing that each ministry and department was responsible within its own sphere for the prevention and punishment of corruption, Pant emphasized the necessity of having a central agency to co-ordinate the efforts of the various ministries and departments to provide direction, drive and assistance wherever needed. A Central Administrative Vigilance Division was accordingly created in the Home Ministry with a Director at its head and adequate staff to assist him.[26] Subject to the overall direction and control of the Home Secretary, the Director was to supervise the working of the Special Police Establishment in the conduct of investigations. He was expected to maintain close liaison with the Secretaries and Vigilance officers of the ministries and departments to eliminate delay and impart speed in the detection and punishment of persons involved in corruption.

In the initial stages, however, the Director, Organization and Methods Division, was also invested with the overall charge of the Administrative Vigilance Division. It was similarly considered desirable in many ministries to combine in a single officer the duties of Vigilance Officer and O & M Officer.

Central Bureau of Investigation. The Central Bureau of Investigation, established under a Government of India Resolution dated 1 April 1963,[27] was designed to extend the scope of the functions earlier assigned to the Delhi Special Police Establishment already created under the Delhi Special Police Establishment Act, 1946. It was felt that the Delhi Special Police Establishment alone would not be able to cope with the problems raised by economic changes and a growing administration. A bigger organization with extended functions was needed to keep a strict surveillance over the huge investments in industry and development projects.

The crimes investigated by the Delhi Special Police Establishment included specially important cases under the Defence of India Act and Rules, such as hoarding, blackmarketing and profiteering in essential commodities. The functions of the Central Bureau of Investigation included, in addition, the collection of intelligence relating to certain specific types of crimes; participation in the work of the National Central Bureau connected with the International Criminal Police Organization; the maintenance of crime statistics and dissemination of information relating to crime and criminals; the study of specialized crimes of particular interest to the Government of India or crimes with all-India or inter-State ramifications or of particular importance from the social point of view; the conduct of police research; and the coordination of laws relating to crime. As a first step in this direction, when the Government of India set up the Central Bureau of Investigation at Delhi, it had six Divisions, one of which absorbed the Delhi Special Police Establishment. The six Divisions were as follows: 1. Investigation and Anti-Corruption Division (Delhi Special Police Establishment); 2. Technical; 3. Crime Records and Statistics Division; 4. Research; 5. Legal and General; 6. Administration Division.

A seventh Division, the 'Economic Offences Division', was added on 1 July 1964.[28] The strength of the Central Bureau of Investigation increased from 144 gazetted officers and 1,288 non-gazetted officers in April 1963 to 257 gazetted and 1,755 non-gazetted officers in November 1964. Its role became significantly different from that of a normal police agency. Apart from investigating specific cases of corruption, it also started collecting information relating to corruption on a systematic and organized basis. It further undertook special drives to cleanse departments where corruption was known to be prevalent and assisted sensitive departments in improving their vigilance arrangements and planning preventive measures.

The Economic Offences Division was intended to deal exclusively with economic offences and had zonal offices in Delhi, Bombay, Calcutta and Madras. Apart from the cases it took up on its own initiative, this Division investigated such economic offences as might be entrusted to it either by the Finance Ministery or by the Director, Central Bureau of Investigation. The categories and types of cases dealt with by the Division included those under the Customs Act, the General Excise Act, the Income Tax Act, the Opium and Dangerous Drugs Act, the Company Law Act and the Gold Control Rules.

During 1963 the Special Police Establishment of the C.B.I. investigated 1,356 fresh cases of bribery, corruption, misappropriation and other dishonest practices involving public servants. The corresponding figure for 1962 was 1,134, and such cases had more than doubled since 1956.[29]

The Central Vigilance Commission. This organization resulted from one of the recommendations of the Santhanam Committee. The Commission was a reorganized form of the Administrative Vigilance Division which had been functioning since 1955.

The existing Administrative Vigilance Division in the Home Ministry and vigilance officers in all the ministries and departments were mainly intended to investigate and punish corruption and misuse of authority by individual members of the civil services. While this was indispensable, the Santhanam Committee felt that the problem of maintaining integrity in administration could not be viewed in isolation from the general administrative processes which often led to injustices, oppression or an abuse of authority. It realized that it was necessary to take into account 'the root causes, of which the most important is the wide discretionary power which has to be exercised by the executive in carrying on the complicated work of modern administration', which involved ever-increasing subordinate legislation arising from a considerable extension in the functions of the State.

This general approach led to a search for a high-level central agency to which an aggrieved citizen might resort for the redress of his grievances. The Committee's answer was a Central Vigilance Commission. It came to this conclusion after studying arrangements in some other countries: in Sweden and Denmark, for instance, the institution of Ombudsman is responsible for examining complaints of maladministration or unfair administrative action proceeding from corrupt motives, spite, laziness or inefficiency. The Committee likewise took into consideration the office of the Parliamentary Commissioner created in New Zealand, the administrative courts in France intended to provide a cheap and quick remedy for redress of grievances against administrative decisions, and the Procurator-General in Soviet Russia whose regional and area assistants serve as links between the citizen and the administration for the removal of grievances.

The Santhanam Committee recognized that in the discharge of his duties the Central Vigilance Commissioner should be independent of the government and not answerable to any minister, even though administratively placed under the Home Ministry. To preserve that independence the Committee also emphasized that, though for a time attached to the Home Ministry, steps should be taken to put the Commission on a statutory basis, so that in terms of appointment and disciplinary control the Commissioner might become equal in status to the Comptroller and Auditor General, the Election Commissioner, or the Chairman or Members of the Union Public Service Commission. In suggesting a broadening of the scope of the existing arrangement to include investigation into public complaints against administrative action or inaction, the Committee recommended this be done in two ways: first, by reorganizing the Administrative Vigilance Division on a broad basis without undermining the general principle that the secretaries and heads of departments were primarily responsible for the integrity and efficiency of their departments; and secondly, by establishing through the Central Bureau of Investigation a link between the vigilance organizations, the secretaries/heads of departments and the Delhi Special Police Establishment which came to form part of the Central Bureau of Intelligence itself. Indeed, the scheme of a Central Vigilance Commission in its final and approved form had to provide that the Central Bureau of Investigation would forward to the Home Ministry through the Commission the final report on all cases investigated by the Bureau in which it considered that prosecution should be launched, subject of course to a sanction in the name of the President wherever required under law. The Vigilance Commissioner was thus to function in between the secretaries and heads of departments on the one hand and the Central Bureau of Investigation on the other.

The Santhanam Committee had in fact not been sure of the Government reaction to its recommendation for the establishment of a Central Vigilance Commission. This led the Committee to make a supplementary recommendation regarding the powers of the Central Vigilance Commissioner to the effect that he be given by suitable legislation the powers that would be exercised by a Commssion of Inquiry appointed under the Commission of Inquiry Act, 1952. In a statement laid before the Lok Sabha and Rajya Sabha on 12 December 1963, however, the Government made it clear that the Vigilance Commission 'would normally get inquiries or investigations made by the Central Bureau of Investigation, [or by] the Commissioners for Departmental Inquiries or the departmental authorities, and that in any exceptional case where the Commission wishes to make an inquiry itself the Government can appoint a Commission of Inquiry under the Commission of Inquiry Act'.[30] In other words, the Commission could not but function within the given bureaucratic framework of secretaries and heads of departments, for under the Prevention of Corruption Act, 1957, no inquiry or prosecution could be started without the prior permission of the appointing authority. The powers exercised by secretaries and heads of departments over the years remained unaffected.

The suggested role of the Central Vigilance Commission as a grievance authority was likewise whittled down. The Government considered that this problem was big enough to require a separate agency and felt the Commission would be over-burdened if the responsibility were to be placed upon it in addition to the immediate function of dealing with the problem of corruption. The Government therefore decided that action should be taken only on such recommendations of the Santhanam Committee as related to prevention of corruption and maintenance of integrity in the public services. And since the question of evolving a machinery for dealing with the grievances of citizens was being separately[31] examined, the Vigilance Commission was not allowed to have its proposed Directorate of General Complaints and Redress.

As regards the Committee's recommendation that the Central Vigilance Commissioner hold office for a term of six years or till the age of 65, whichever was earlier, the Government decided that the best person available, irrespective of his age, should be appointed the first Vigilance Commissioner, the conditions of service regarding age and tenure for future appointments being left open to the discretion of the Government. However, it was suggested that the first Vigilance Commissioner should be a person who had held one of the highest judicial offices in the country or who had a high standing in public life.

The Central Vigilance Commission was given a status and a role which, though not statutory, were broadly comparable to those of the Union Public Service Commission. The Central Vigilance Commissioner was appointed by the President under his hand and seal. He was to have the status of a Secretary to the Government, though in the exercise of his powers and functions he was not to be subordinate to any ministry or department. There was to be a Chief Vigilance Officer of the rank of Deputy Secretary in each ministry and department and Vigilance Officers in all subordinate and attached offices acting under the guidance of their Chief Vigilance Officer. Besides being the link between the Central Vigilance Commission and a ministry and department, the Chief Vigilance Officer and Vigilance Officers continued, as under the existing arrangement, to function as special assistants to secretaries or the heads of departments whose unified and traditional administrative control thus remained unchallenged within their departmental limits. The minister's responsibilities and accountability to Parliament, as well as his control over a ministry, remained similarly unaffected. The Central Vigilance Commissioner was not to make any inquiry into the conduct of a minister or his secretary. As the Committee itself suggested, inquiries into ministerial corruption were to be made by an *ad hoc* committee drawn from a national panel appointed by the President in consultation with the Prime Minister.

Constitutionally and legally, the functions of the Central Vigilance Commission were advisory, like those of the Union Public Service Commission. But the nature of its functions and the fact that its reports were required to be placed before Parliament imparted to it some added importance in the fight against administrative corruption.

However, the Government Servants' Conduct Rules were revised more or less on the lines suggested by the Santhanam Committee.

Every government servant holding a supervisory post was, for instance, required to ensure the integrity of his subordinates. All government servants acting under the direction of their official superior were called upon to obtain the direction in writing and, where it was not practicable to do so, they were to obtain without much delay written confirmation of the oral direction already given. Government servants were specially enjoined not to use their position or influence directly or indirectly to secure employment for members of their families in private undertakings. Emphasis was likewise laid on the submission of a periodical return of assets and liabilities, with full particulars of movable and immovable assets as well as debts and other liabilities incurred by officials directly or indirectly. The rules relating to 'gifts' were modified so as to cover free transport, board, lodging or any pecuniary advantage provided by a person other than a near relative or personal friend without official dealings with the government servant. Restrictions were similarly imposed on hospitality, more especially lavish or frequent hospitality from an individual or commercial organization. These and certain other changes were introduced in the Central Civil Services (Conduct) Rules, 1964, issued in a Home Ministry Notification of 30 November 1964.[32]

Revisions of the Discipline and Appeal Rules were also considered broadly on the recommendations made by the Santhanam Committee. Amendments were made to the law and procedure relating to corruption on the lines suggested by the Committee. The Anti-Corruption Laws (Amendment) Act accordingly received the assent of the President on 18 December 1964.[33] The recommendation of the Committee regarding amendment of Article 311 of the Constitution, however, remained in a state of consideration.

As regards the code of conduct for ministers, its importance was recognized by the Government in terms of maintaining the highest standard of integrity and probity at the political level. A Code of Conduct for ministers was actually worked out and approved by the Cabinet, which made it public on 29 October 1964.[34] A copy of the Code was soon placed on the Table of the Lok Sabha on 18 November and of the Rajya Sabha on 20 November. It was also suggested to Chief Ministers of the states that they might adopt the Code for their own Cabinets.

But when it came to the question of projected inquiries into ministerial conduct, trouble arose. While discussing the Santhanam Committee's report on corruption at the political level the Cabinet was strongly against the approach adopted by the Committee. 'Particularly strong was the objection to the Committee's recommendation that the commissions of inquiry should be set up wherever there were allegations against a state minister by 10 MLAs and against a Central Minister by 10 MPs'.[35] In fact, 'One senior minister', as the *Statesman* added, 'is reported to have remarked that the Committee's suggestion for the formation of an all-India panel of jurists to provide members for the proposed inquiry commissions would amount to setting up a parallel Supreme Court which would perpetually be in session. Several other ministers are said to have emphasized that the Committee's suggestion would open the floodgates of malicious complaints and charges, and that not all the safeguards suggested by the Home Ministry would save the country's political climate from being thoroughly poisoned.' The Mundhra inquiry, set up at the instance of Feroze Gandhi, was quoted to justify rejection of the Committee's recommendation for inquiry into ministerial conduct.[36]

In recommending inquiry into ministerial conduct the Santhanam Committee was guided by a conviction that 'the general belief about the failure of integrity amongst ministers is as damaging as actual failure'. This widespread belief, as the Committee felt, had 'unfortunately' been 'reinforced by the conduct of a few ministers as also by the embarrassing revelations of considerable fortunes in money and estate left by deceased Congressmen once ruling in seats of authority'.[37] The Committee in fact regretted that 'complaints against the highly placed in public life were not dealt with in the manner that they should have been dealt with if public confidence had to be maintained. Weakness in this respect created cynicism and the growth of the belief that while Governments were against corruption they were not against corrupt individuals, if such individuals had the requisite amount of power, influence and protection'.[38] An important example was that of Sardar Pratap Singh Kairon, the Chief Minister of Punjab, who was said to have the protection of no less a person than Prime Minister Jawaharalal Nehru himself.[39] To restore public confidence in the integrity of ministers it was therefore considered reasonable that they should be as amenable to the scrutiny of governmental probes as ordinary officials operating at less exalted levels. For, as one newspaper pointed out, the 'public services, though terminologically confined to officials, extend [no less] to ministers, the more so since these individuals are most vociferous in declaring their sacrifices in the public service'.[40]

The Code of Conduct for ministers which the Cabinet finally worked out, naturally differed considerably from the Santhanam Committee's recommendations on the subject. The authority to inquire into allegations against ministers was left with the Prime Minister at the Centre, and with the Chief Minister of the state concerned and the Union Home Minister when charges were levelled against state ministers. Inquiries into ministerial conduct thus remained subject to the determination of party bosses whose primary concern was bound to be political rather than moral.

Patriot described the finally approved Code of Conduct for Minister as 'an admission of moral collapse within the Congress of which any political party should be ashamed'. Ministers were, for instance, expected to 'disclose the total approximate value of shares and debentures, case holdings, jewellery and immovable property', but such disclosures could be made after the impediments involved had been passed on to obliging relatives and friends. Another important potential restriction imposed on ministers prevented them from starting or joining any firm or business. This was of no significance, for, as the newspaper rightly commented, 'no minister while he is in office normally does this. What can be done and is not prevented by the Code is the starting of business by friends or relatives who benefit because of the position of the minister. Suspicion that many people in office are anxiously interested in some business or the other is widely current and the Code by itself will not remove that suspicion'.

The Santhanam Committee viewed the collection of funds by political parties as highly pernicious and destructive of public morality. The Code of Conduct, however, permitted even ministers to associate themselves with the collection of funds for 'a registered society or a charitable body, an institution recognized by a public authority and a political party'.[41] Instead of a 'total ban on all donations' to political parties, the Code permitted ministers to collect funds which they used for political purposes, including electioneering, an important source of corruption. The Code did not endorse the Committee's proposal that ministers subjected to allegations in the press should as a rule institute defamation suits, unless the matter was before some inquiry committee. This was a practice generally adopted in the case of officials during the British raj, when reluctance to initiate such legal action was deemed officially to be tantamount to admission of guilt.

Machinery for Redress of Grievances. Writing about the functioning of the official system under British rule, the Montford Report said: 'in every district, and portion of district—that is to say, in many parts of the country, within not more than twelve or fifteen miles of every single inhabitant—there is a district representative of the Government, to whom complaints on every conceivable subject can be addressed, and through whom the Government can act'.[42] With the introduction of democracy, however, the public was taught to bring its troubles to the notice of an elected representative. The fate of the ordinary citizen none the less remained unchanged. Despite the utmost vigilance and energy a district officer could not prevent petty corruption and oppression from disfiguring his official business, but elected representatives cared more for politics and political power than the purity of public conduct.

Apart from the measures taken since 1946, vigilance authorities, including ultimately the Central Vigilance Commission, were set up to deal not only with corruption and lack of integrity on the part of Central Government servants, but also with such grievances as were related to corruption or lack of integrity. Grievances might, however, arise from an exercise of discretion even where there was honest and efficient administration. For instance, orders passed in accordance with the relevant law and rules might not be just and equitable but be harsh and cause irritation. In Britain such matters were taken to ministers through the Members of Parliament. This was so in India too, though the number of cases which might reach ministers through parliamentarians or a local legislature were only a fraction of the genuine grievances of citizens. A resort to appeals to higher officers in the bureaucratic hierarchy could still be thought of as an alternative to a separate 'grievance man'. But officers could not deliver the goods for two main reasons. In the first place, the Indian official himself could not normally rise above the petty loyalties of race, religion, region or caste in the distribution of justice; and, secondly, even if he was able to act impartially, democracy, which encourages inferior loyalties in the Indian social context, renders his efforts for the most part nugatory. In these circumstances the Home Minister, G.L. Nanda, expressed his anxiety that effective arrangements should be made as early as possible for receiving and dealing with the grievances of citizens against the administration.[43] While discussing the Santhanam Report senior officers thought that the situation in India was too complex to be remedied by a nostrun. The problem had to be approached from many sides and a variety of measures taken to achieve success. These involved changes in organization, in method as well as in the procedure of work, which were all being examined by the Department of Administrative Reforms already set up in the Home Ministery in March 1964. It was suggested that one cause of grievance could in the meantime be removed by setting up, on the model of Britain, Licence Justices to advice the Government regarding the grant of licences, permits, quotas, etc. This recommendation had in fact already been made by an *ad hoc* committee of the Cabinet. At the request of the Home Minister, the Planning Commission had also started making a general survey of the levels at which discretion was being used for the issue of licences, permits and quotas, the object being to eliminate causes of grievance in these matters of special interest to industry and big business. Another suggestion which the meeting of senior officers made was that a cell should be created in each ministry, department and major office to furnish information to citizens in order to help them in their legitimate dealings with the Government and to attend to any complaints of delay, iniquitous orders, etc. that they might have. Some ministries and departments had already introduced such measures, but the senior officers wanted a general plan.

As regards the appointment of an Ombudsman, the important argument adduced against the proposal was that this institution had so far been tried only in small and developed countries where a single individual with standing in national life could, with a small staff, deal with a relatively small number of complaints. It was argued that the Central Vigilance Commissioner and the State Vigilance Commissioners were in a sense Ombudsmen, except that their jurisdiction was limited to matters involving corruption or lack of integrity on the part of public servants. The case of administrative tribunals was similarly shown to have little or no relevance to the Indian situation. It was pointed out that in the field of revenue administration and industrial relations such courts did exist. The 'whole judicial tradition [in the country] is against a system of two parallel hierarchies of courts as in France',[44] it was further emphasized.

The meeting of senior officers of the Government of India argued that the demands of the existing situation could be met if the decision to set up cells for furnishing information was put through vigorously in the entire field of administration and a Commissioner for the redress of citizens' grievances was appointed as a sort of complement to the Central Vigilance Commissioner. It was, however, suggested that the function of the Additional Commissioner to be so appointed should be limited to ensuring that arrangements were made in each ministry, department and office for receiving and dealing with citizens' grievances and that the arrangements so made worked efficiently. His business would be to inspect these units, advise those put in charge, and communicate his observations to the heads of department or to the secretary as he might deem fit. He would also inform the minister concerned about the manner in which the arrangement in the departments actually operated and might also prepare for Parliament an annual report on the lines already indicated by the Director of the Administrative Vigilance Division. He would be expected to keep the Home Ministry fully informed, but, in essence, he would be no more than a mere inspector and supervisor under each minister, providing a common service from his base in the Home Ministry. The Commission could, in the normal course, wield a great deal of influence, but he was not to exercise any powers unless authorized by the minister concerned, who generally acted in the light of the advice given to him by the secretary or the head of a department.

As already noted, the Central Vigilance Commission was appointed, but not the projected grievance commissioner. The Vigilance Commissioner functioned with the assistance of the vigilance authorities and grievance cells located in the ministries and departments. The latter surrendered no part of their immediate administrative authority, or their final control over administration, which they exercised subject to the constitutional responsibilities of their ministers for the work of their departments. Senior officers were in fact unanimous in maintaining that no public grievance machinery within the Government should be allowed to function as a body higher than the ministries or on a footing comparable to that of a Judge. The Home Minister too agreed. The traditional structure of departments and the indivisible control of secretaries over them did not permit a grievance commissioner to reduce their authority or to weaken ministerial responsibility. This old bureaucratic structures constituted the bottlenecks, and even as late as 1974–5, for instance, the Central Vigilance Commission deplored the 'gross delay' of various ministries, departments and public undertakings in implementing its advice for action against corrupt officials.

In its annual report for 1974-5 the Vigilance Commission indicated a number of cases where the reluctance to punish corruption was 'not due to procedural handicaps but extraneous considerations.' For, as the report said, 'some disciplinary authorities are still guided by the notion that giving protection to the private careers of individual officers is more important than the obvious public interest in ensuring and maintaining a high standard of public service. The report even quoted two specific cases, one in a nationalized bank and another in a government department, where efforts had been made to protect corrupt officers. In the case of the bank the impugned officer was charge-sheeted on 12 counts, and the inquiry officer had recommended his dismissal from service. But the disciplinary action committee of the bank toned down the recommendation to ensure that the officer concerned suffered no monetary loss. The Vigilance Commissioner regretted this kind of attitude on the part of ministries and departments: it led to an increase in the number of cases in 1974-5—744 against 632 in the previous year.[45] Of these 744 cases, 21 were on the basis of reports from the Central Bureau of Intelligence which recommended prosecution, 245 were from the report of the Central Bureau of Investigation recommending regular departmental action, 208 references were from ministries and departments, and 270 were general complaints of corruption against public servants. The Vigilance Commission also received directly 1,030 general complaints of which 701 involved corruption, 11 misconduct other than corruption and 215 related to matters concerning State Governments.[46]

As regards the creation of a separate machinery for the redress of public grievances, the Department of Administrative Reforms furnished material and secretarial support to a committee of MPs appointed by the Special Consultative Group on administrative reforms to go into this question. In the meantime, it also did the spade work for the appointment in February 1966 of an Additional Secretary who was to deal with public grievances as part of the Home Ministry. He was to oversee the working of the cells in the various ministries and departments.[47] In the evolution of the projected machinery, the Additional Secretary was to assist the Administrative Reforms Commission set up a month earlier than his own appointment.

In its interim report submitted on 20 October 1966 the Administrative Reforms Commission made various recommendations. After considering these, the Government decided to create a statutory machinery to inquire into complaints of injustice arising from mal-administration or complaints of corruption in the Central Government. The machinery so recommended was to be headed by a *Lokpal* who was to look into grievances and allegations arising out of the administrative acts of central ministers and secretaries. He was also to coordinate the working of two other functionaries envisaged in the machinery, who were to have the status suggested by the Commission for *Lokayuktas*. While one of them was primarily to have the authority to go into grievances, the other was to inquire into allegations in relation to central government servants lower than secretaries. Grievances and allegations relating to state ministers and secretaries which were recommended for inclusion in the Lokpal's jurisdiction by the Administrative Reforms Commission were to be left out for a time. Necessary legislation was to be introduced in Parliament but no legislation has so far been enacted.

A conference of Chief Secretaries held in New Delhi on 8-9 May 1976 again recommended a resort to the existing administrative structure as a source of relief. It decided that all heads of departments and district-level officers should devote at least one hour every day to redress the grievances of the public. Arrangements were to be made for this purpose at village, district and state levels. The conference proposed that carefully selected and trained officials should be given public contact posts and that the decision-making levels should be reduced to minimize the delay that lead to corruption.[48]

The institutions of the Lokpal and Lokayukta were designed to provide the ultimate set-up for such redress as had not previously been available through the normal channels of government departments. But these were by no means intended to absolve the departmental machinery of its obligations to remove citizens' grievances. The Administrative Reforms Commission made it clear that the administration itself 'must play the major role in reducing the area of grievances and providing remedies wherever necessary and feasible'. The Commission had in view the cells and vigilance authorities already functioning in ministries and departments: 'A large number of cases which arise at lower levels of administration,' it pointed out, 'should in fact adequately be dealt with by this in-built departmental machinery. When the machinery functions effectively, the number of cases which will have to go to an authority outside the machinery or the department should be comparatively small.' The Commission was perhaps aware of the potential danger of a clash between the departmental machinery and the statutory authority which was being proposed and thus concluded when saying, 'We would in these circumstances strongly advocate that the responsibility of the departments to deal adequately with public grievances must be squarely faced by them.'[49]

And yet the Commission recommended in the same breath that the Lokpal and Lokayukta should be demonstrably independent of the executive government, that their status should compare with the highest judicial functionaries in the country, that they should have powers to call for all relevant information required in the discharge of their duties, and that they should not expect any benefit or pecuniary advantage from the executive government.

The Lokpal was to be appointed by the President on the advice of the Prime Minister who, before giving such advice, was required to consult the Chief Justice of India and the Leader of the Opposition. He was to have the same status and the same scale of salary as the Chief Justice of India. He could be removed from office in the manner prescribed in the Constitution for the removal of a Judge of the Supreme Court. The Commission also recommended that the Lokpal should have powers to investigate any administrative act done by or with the approval of a minister or secretary at the centre or in a state if the complaint was made by a person or corporation affected by it. He could also in his discretion inquire into complaints of maladministration or favouritism and initiate investigation into administrative acts which might come to his notice without a complaint being made by anyone.

The office of the Lokpal so conceived was a response to the current tendency which demanded the establishment of an independent authority outside the departmental machinery. In view of the recommendations of the Santhanam Committee the desire to set up such an authority was quite understandable. However, the Commission proposed the Lokpal, without making an adequate study of its implications. A detailed re-examination of the existing administrative structure was needed, but the government was neither able nor willing to do this. The existing arrangement for administrative vigilance thus continued without any statutory body like an Ombudsman coming into being. In the absence of an effective check on ministerial corruption, several cases of political corruption came to light, such as the Aminchand, Serajjudin and Mundhra scandals.[50] Similarly, the case against the Chief Minister of Punjab, Sardar Pratap Singh Kairon, aroused considerable public interest. In response to persistent allegations of corruption against Kairon, Nehru, the Prime Minister, finally had to appoint on 1 November 1963 a Commission of Inquiry. It consisted, in fact, solely of S. R. Das, formerly Chief Justice of India. The inquiry was held in New Delhi and the report submitted on 11 June 1964. On publication of the report Kairon submitted his resignation and that of his Council of Ministers on 14 June. The Das Commission held that, although Kairon was not directly involved in a number of shady transactions, he had abused his authority in several cases, more especially in the purchase of certain lands and other property which brought substantial benefits to his sons.

On his resignation, Kairon was succeeded by Ram Kishan as Chief Minister of Punjab. New facts came to light as a result of questions raised in Rajya Sabha debates in September 1964. These related to the expenditure incurred on the Das Commission by the Central Government and the Government of Punjab. The answer given by the Home Ministry showed that, while the Central Government had spent Rs 37,141.41, excluding Rs 25,400 for the printing of the report, the expenditure of the state government was Rs 1,72,111.17, of which Rs 1,26,166.63 was spent by it in defending Sardar Pratap Singh Kairon.

It was then naturally asked why such a heavy amount was spent on the defence of a person who had been declared guilty of grave misuse of office. The Punjab Government had in fact decided that, since the allegations overwhelmingly related to the official acts of Kairon, he should be defended officially, although he might also defend himself privately against allegations which were purely of a private nature. This decision had been taken by the Home and Finance Ministers of Punjab, not the entire Council of Ministers, and a strong feeling arose among the public against what the Punjab Government had done to defend Kairon. His successor also held that the decision to defend Kairon was not correct, and, in fact, sought the advice of the Government of India on whether the decision was legal, and whether it was feasible to review it or recover from Kairon the amount spent on his defence.

In a Note of 22 September 1964, the Home Secretary, L. P. Singh, pointed out that there was perhaps 'no provision for the recovery of a grant' once made. 'In the Punjab case,' he argued, 'the first question is whether what was done was proper. But the more important question is whether, even assuming that it was improper, there are any powers under the law under which the amount spent can in whole or in part be recovered from Sardar Partap Singh Kairon.'[51] In a Note of 29 September, the Law Secretary also doubted that it would be legally feasible to require Kairon to reimburse the expenditure for the simple reason that he might contend, not without force, that he acted upon the Government decision.[52] Even the Law Minister did not think that there was any valid claim for reimbursement. A reply was accordingly sent to the Punjab Chief Minister, but in a secret interview with the Home Minister, Nanda, on 14 October 1964 he obtained a decision broadly in favour of recovering the expenses incurred on the defence of Kairon. The Home Minister felt that, even if no legal means were available for the recovery of the money spent, the Comptroller and Auditor General should examine the matter thoroughly. A Note from his Ministry now added: 'If he [the Comptroller and Auditor General] says that the expenditure had been improperly incurred, one more condemnation will be added to the list of unfavourable verdicts on Sardar Partap Singh even though no financial consequences would follow.'[53]

In fact, the office of the Comptroller and Auditor General did not approve of the Punjab Government's defence of Kairon (who had in the meantime been assassinated). The Director of Audit and Accounts pointed out that

The question of the State Government meeting the cost of defence of the late ex-Chief Minister should have been cosidered only after the conclusion of the inquiry against him and that, too, when the proceedings would have concluded in his favour. Whether the impugned acts can be deemed to be official acts or whether a Minister has acted malafide or is guilty of misconduct or abuse of offical authority, can be decided only after the conclusion of inquiry. In fact on some of the charges the Commission's findings lead to the conclusion that the action that was taken could not be said to be in the discharge of offical duties of the late Shri Kairon.

The office of the Comptroller and Auditor General therefore held that sanctioning the expenditure from the public exchequer 'on the plea that the inquiry was into the official acts of ex-Chief Minister amounted to anticipation of the findings of the Commission and was, thus, irregular'. It was added that under the provisions of the Punjab Ministers' Salaries Act, 1947, the expenditure so incurred would need to be regularized by an act of the state legislature, even if it was accepted that the inquiry was about the official transactions of Kairon.[54]

On the assassination of Kairon the question of the recovery of money was naturally set aside. The attitude of the Home Minister too became slightly subdued. In a letter of 4 March 1965 he wrote to the Chief Minister of Punjab: 'We obtained the advice of Law Ministry and informed you that the decision of the State Government to incur expenditure on the defence of the former Chief Minister was not unconstitutional and it was not feasible to require Shri Kairon to reimburse the legal expenses at this stage. You however again desired that we should get the whole question re-examined. We were obtaining the views of the Comptroller and Auditor General of India. In view however of the recent tragic assassination of Shri Kairon this question does not now need any further examination.'[55] In consultation with its own Law Department the Government of Punjab also decided that no legislation was necessary to regularize the matter.

The Kairon case was thus dropped. But a close perusal of the papers connected with it leaves no doubt that, while he was misusing his influence and the authority of his government to promote the private interests of his family, the central government took hardly any steps to prevent him from doing so until the President himself intervened to have the Commission of Inquiry appointed. The Punjab situation was allowed to drift even otherwise. As the Home Secretary suggested in his Note, provisions did exist for the grant of advances for legal and financial assistance to government servants involved in legal proceedings. Though recoverable, this advance, too, was to be made when the defence of the government and the government servant involved happened to be substantially the same and there was no conflict of interest between the two. But instead of an advance, the entire cost of Kairon's defence was sought to be met out of the Consolidated Fund, and that, too, at a time when the results of the inquiry were still unknown. The office of the Comptroller and Auditor General was justified in observing that the grant should not have been allowed before the conclusion of the inquiry, but Government of India remained largely a silent spectator. After Nehru's death and at Ram Kishan's instance the Home Ministry re-opened the question of reimbursement; but earlier it had raised no objection when the Home and Finance Ministers of Punjab decided to meet the cost of Kairon's defence without even a formal sanction from the Council of Ministers. Public administration in the Indian situation had developed a tendency to become personalized. The Weberian impersonality of rules remained more a misnomer than a reality. The reason for a deviation from the 'ideal type' was, however, socio-political rather than simply bureaucratic.

Sadachar Samiti. The organization of *Samyukta Sadachar Samiti* or Joint Good Conduct Committee was the result of what the *Observer* called 'a wild idea' of the Home Minister himself.[56] It was described as a people's court held in a big marquee set up in his garden under a banyan tree, with Gulzarilal Nanda at one end. In his declared war on corruption, which he promised to root out in a year's time, Nanda invited anyone with experience of official misbehaviour to call round at his house in New Delhi and tell him about it.

Among others, the Sadachar Samiti consisted of Bhimsen Sachar, general secretary of the Samiti; A. N. Bhandari, a former Chief Justice of the Punjab High Court; Surinder Saini, junior Vice-President of the New Delhi Municipal Committee; and Brijkishan Chandiwala, an affluent man who was once Gandhi's secretary. The cases were heard at tables ranged round the open sides of the tent and the Samiti intended to hear complaints every day from 8.30 in the morning until such time as all the complaints were duly registered. Nanda, however, was to hear complaints and register grievances only for an hour, from 8.30 to 9.30 in the morning.

Nanda's people's court was called *Diwan-i-Aam* by a staff reporter of the *Statesman.* Seven people, including a teenager and a policeman, submitted complaints to him at his residence on the first day of his audience: the reporter, who attended the Union Home Minister's *Diwan-i-Aam*, made out a summary of the several complaints heard on the occasion. A teenager from Daryaganj, for instance, alleged that his father had been murdered in January 1963, but the case was not being pursued by the police. He wanted the Home Minister to order an investigation. The policeman, on the other hand, alleged that he had been unjustly dismissed and wanted the Minister to get him reinstated. An industrialist sought the Home Minister's help to get his stocks of goods released, for he was not being allowed to sell them, even though the goods in question had been imported a year earlier. In yet another case a young man told the Home Minister that his father was being prosecuted because he had sold sugar at Rs 1.24 per kg instead of Rs 1.23.

This mode of hearing complaints, though in keeping with the age-old style of the grand Mughals, had little or no relevance to modern administration which had developed in India in the course of a couple of centuries. However, it did no harm; for while the members of the Committee were to serve without payment from the public exchequer, their business was merely to process the complaints and forward them to the appropriate departments. The only danger was the possibility of their exploiting the influence which they could build through their association with the Home Minister. But since this arrangement was not to last long, it did no harm even on that score.

Public Enterprise. The public sector enterprise in the immediate post-Independence period was conceived as a means of transforming India from an agricultural and colonial economy to an advanced industrial one. The Industrial Policy Resolution of 1948 was an expression of this idea. The development of the private sector could not altogether be ruled out. But the public sector was emphasized not only because it could undertake massive projects in the development of the economy where profits happened to be low and the period of gestation long, but also because it was intended to promote balanced development and obviate the danger of corruption through 'vigilant governmental intervention at strategic points'. In other words, the whole object of public control was to shape the economy according to the projections of the planners and the social preferences of the government, an egalitarian aim which called for public motivation in the promotion of planned economic development.

The Industries (Development and Regulation) Act, 1951, was accordingly passed as the main instrument of carrying out the industrial policy laid down in 1948 and modified subsequently in 1956 through Schedules which specified the operational spheres of the public and private sectors. It was designed to (a) regulate industrial development in accordance with planned priorities; (b) avoid concentration of ownership and control of industries; (c) ensure regional balance in the dispersal of industries, especially to undeveloped regions; (d) prevent undue competition between large-scale industries and small cottage industries; and (e) make sure that the limited foreign exchange resources of the country were utilized fully and properly.

In practice, however, the action of the Government did not conform to the declared objectives of the Act. For the Central Government had taken powers under the Act itself to exempt any industrial undertaking or any scheduled industry or class of scheduled industries listed under the Industrial Policy Resulution of 1956 from the operation of all or any of the provisions of the Act. By a Notification of 26 February 1960 the Government accordingly announced that all industrial undertakings in the scheduled industries employing less than 100 workers with fixed assets of less than Rs 10 lakhs in value were exempted from the licensing provisions of the Act. By a subsequent Notification dated 13 February 1964, all undertakings with the exception of coal, textiles, leather, matches, vanaspati, oil seed crushing and roller flour milling units with fixed assets of less than Rs 25 lakhs in value were also exempted from the licensing provisions of the Act. It was argued that the relaxation was intended to encourage industies using indigenous capital, equipment and raw material. Though required to get themselves registered, the registration of such industries was automatic and intended merely for statistical purposes.

A further liberalization of industrial licensing was done by a Notification dated 13 May 1966 which exempted eleven industries from the licensing provisions of the Act, irrespective of the investment involved. These included iron and steal castings and forgings, electric motors (not exceeding 10 H.P), pulp, power alcohol, solvent extracted oils, glue and gelatine, sheet and plate glass, optical glass, fire bricks, portland cement and plywood. By a Resolution of 7 July 1966 two more industries, paper and newsprint and hand tools, were also 'decontrolled'. This was soon followed on 14 November by 29 more industries being similarly exempted from licensing requirements. The reason given was that the industries so freed had an export potential and did not involve a substantial import of components or raw material. It was also thought that they did not hamper the growth of cottage industries. Freedom was likewise granted on certain conditions to both the engineering and non-engineering industries to diversify production by the manufacture of new articles without the licence required under the Act of 1951.

These progressive exemptions from the normal provisions of the Act were clear indication of the Government's wish to promote the interests of private enterprise. The former commitment of the Indian National Congress to prevent the concentration of economic power, which went back to the historic Karachi Resolution of 1931, was in fact slackened in the post-Independence period to secure the co-operation of the big business houses. This slackening began in the course of the Second Plan period and acquired momentum during the Third Plan which witnessed the Chinese invasion in 1962 and the Indo-Pakistan war in 1965.

The Prime Minister soon realized the loss of direction in the pursuit of his Government's economic policy. He asked: 'Where has the wealth created since independence gone?'[57] The Government appointed in 1960 the Mahalanobis Committee to find an answer to this question by a review of the trends in the economy during the First and the Second Plan periods. The Committee confirmed a widely shared view that the policy of planned economic growth had, in part at least, contributed to the concentration of wealth by making licensing facilities and other aids available to big business in India. Its conclusion was that 'the concentration of economic power in the private sector is more than what could be justified on functional ground'.[58]

The Mahalanobis Committee's view was subsequently confirmed by the Monopolies Inquiry Commission (MIC) appointed by the Government in April 1964. The Commission pointed out that planned development had itself become a 'potent factor for further concentration'; for 'big business was at an advantage in securing licenses for starting new industries or for expanding the existing capacity'. This led to the growth of monopolists who had also the advantage over small people in obtaining loans and other assistance from banks and other financial institutions. Moreover, the licensing procedures were so devised as to restrict the entry of newcomers to an industry. The Commission considered it a necessary evil, though R. C. Dutt, its dissenting member, attributed the evil to the existence and operation of economic power in the hands of a few families.

The study conducted by Dr R. K. Hazari in 1967 indicated that during the Second and Third Plan periods a few industrial houses obtained most of the industrial licenses. During this period the Birla group emerged as the second biggest industrial house in the country in terms of the magnitude of its assets. The other groups that came into the limelight, included Mafatlal, Shri Ram and Soorajmull-Nagarmull, who made maximum use of the opportunities provided by the licensing system. The study highlighted the manner in which the licensing system operated and showed how certain big houses booked targetted capacity by pre-emption and thus prevented the entry of new entrepreneurs. Their monopoly naturally continued. The Industrial Licensing Policy Inquiry Committee (ILPIC), which was to report whether the growth of monopolies flowed from the economics of scale or from the use of political influence, not only established the conclusions already arrived at by Hazari, but gave a detailed account of the manner in which a few large concerns had influenced decisions of the government.

The Study Team of the Administrative Reforms Commission on Economic Administration reviewed the working of the Licensing Act of 1951 and analysed the causes which led to the failure of its objectives. It pointed out that while the licensing powers under the Act could be exercised to ensure that an undue number of licenses to set up industrial units was not granted to big groups, the subsequent transfer of ownership and control in their favour could not be regulated by the Act. For, historically,[59] business enterprise at higher levels in the Indian situation was, and still is, a close-knit family concern conducted on the principle of legal, financial and administrative interlocking. The Managing Agency system, which for over a century had lent support to administrative and financial interlocking as a form of industrial management, was of course abolished in 1956. But it reappeared from the backdoor in the form of consultancy agencies, sole selling agencies, purchase agencies and the like. These contributed to the growth of corruption in diluting efforts to prevent dispersal either in terms of regional balance or social benefit.

There was yet another source of corruption that flowed from the working of the licensing system. After an industrial license was issued, the licensee was under the rules required to submit a progress report till the licensed capacity was installed and he was ready to commence production. In the event of delay on his part, the license could be revoked by the licensing authority. Case studies undertaken by the Department of Administrative Reforms, however, showed that action against defaulters was seldom taken and extensions of time were given as a matter of routine. As a result, the possibility of licensed capacity remained frozen with defaulting parties at the cost of more enterprising potential applicants. The Study Team on Economic Administration (1967) attributed this irregularity to the fact that at the time of the grant of a license nothing was committed by the Government except a part of the national capacity available in an industry. Even after the national capacity was fully booked, much discretion could be exercised by officials, and this discretion, which remained unregulated, bred corruption. The licensing system, which had been designed originally to fulfil social and economic objectives, could not, in these circumstances, accomplish the object of its institution.

The public sector, on the other hand, suffered from slow and authoritarian bureaucratic ways. It could not deliver the goods because of over-centralization in decision making. Its rigid and rule-bound accountability to government and Parliament caused considerable delay and inhibited initiative. Its whole emphasis was procedure-oriented and not result-oriented.

The number of public sector enterprises increased from five in 1951 to over a hundred in 1973, their total investment rising in the same period from Rs 29 crores to Rs 4,600 crores, with a total accumulated loss of Rs 492 crores.[60] The failure of the public sector to show results was mainly due to the continuance of the old administrative structure where decisions were made by non-technical civil servants within the framework of secretariat rules and procedures imvolving several layers of authority, such as the Cabinet, the Planning Commission, the Ministry of Finance, the administrative ministry and department, the managing agent and the directors of the industry concerned.

The importance of the public sector in promoting quick industrialization and ensuring equitable distribution of the fruits of development on the principle of social justice has been recognized the world over, especially in underdeveloped countries. But the most crucial problem was that of proper organization and effective management. It is here that the public sector had to evolve alternatives, which, within the framework of bureaucracy and rule-bound administration might achieve the social and economic objectives of the State with an efficiency and economy not inconsistent with business principles.

Even before Independence the public sector had evolved three main types of organization, which continued with a shift of declared emphasis under the Industrial Policy Resolutions of 1948 and 1956. These were (i) departmental management,[61] (ii) public corporations, and (iii) a company form of management. Of the three, the company form of management came to be recognized from experience as by far the most acceptable form for the public sector in the field of industrial and commercial enterprise. Corporations, too, functioned more or less as companies designed to manage a number of producing units, such as Hindustan Steel Ltd. managing three steel plants in the public sector or the National Coal Development Corporation looking after all the state collieries. All the companies meant for the management of the public sector were to be set up under the Indian Companies Act, 1956, with their own Boards of Directors and managing agents. The company form of management was considered by far the most convenient because even when compared to a government-controlled corporation these enjoyed a much greater degree of freedom from the rules governing the personnel, budget, accounting, audit and procedures applicable to government departments and agencies.

It was through this company form of management that the government hoped to attract foreign and indigenous private capital into the areas exclusively reserved for the public sector. When a financial crisis deepened after the border conflict with China and war with Pakistan, the Government announced the partial delicensing of industries and invited, with majority participation, foreign private capital to enter the fertilizer industry, which was so far reserved for expansion under the public sector. While the public announcements of the Government decried the concentration of economic power, its invitation to private capital to collaborate with it as majority partners in the core industries drove in the opposite direction. In the joint sector so organized, public money came under private operation.

The economic policy of the Government of India has thus suffered from a lack of consistency. Capitalism has been allowed to grow under the cover of socialism, a feature that brings money to politicians and the political parties for a variety of purposes. The corruption so generated at the political level has found its way down the bureaucratic hierarchy, where the exercise of discretion at executive and subordinate levels has had to be accompanied by what the Santhanam Committee called the 'speed money' paid to avoid delay.

The Working of Vigilance Arrangements

As already noted the vigilance arrangments of the Government of India consisted of the Central Bureau of Investigation (CBI), the Central Vigilance Commission (CVC), and the Vigilance Branches of ministries and departments.

The CBI investigates for the most part cases against Central Government servants. The investigation of crimes, robberies, riots or economic offences does not generally form part of its work. Its organization is inclusive of the Special Police Establishment (SPE). In the course of five years from its establishment in 1963 the strength of the CBI increased considerably in terms of both size and expenditure.[62] While the total staff increased by 88 per cent, from 1,432 to 2,690, the strength of police personnel of different categories rose from 984 to

1,888. The posts of Deputy Director/DIG and above increased, on the other hand, from 3 in 1963 to 15 in 1968.

The CBI thus kept on expanding fast, its main role being limited to drawing up more and more cases for departmental action. The original object of the CBI was to deal with complex cases at the higher levels of the bureaucracy. It was, for that purpose, given powers to call for information from various sources which could not otherwise be made available to the normal departmental machinery. The idea underlying the investigation of important cases was to deter those engaged in corrupt practices. But in the early years of its establishment the CBI took up far too many minor cases, perhaps to fill up a certain quota for statistical purposes. This occurred particularly thanks to an increase in the number of petty officials of the rank of Inspectors and below who raked up too many petty cases which affected the reputation of the organization. Later, however, the CBI began to take up, by and large, only those cases where the prospect of prosecution was sound and strong. The time taken with prosecution cases none the less continued to be unduly long. It caused harassment to the guilty and the innocent alike. For the number of persons found guilty of grave lapses was only 2.7 per cent of the complaints received in 1966-7, 2.4 per cent in 1967-8 and 1.3 per cent in 1968-9. But all those who were accused had to remain in a state of suspense until they were finally cleared. The percentage only of minor punishment, especially of warnings, was by far the highest for the CBI as well as for the CVC.[63]

The other wing of the vigilance organization, the CVC was empowered to inquire into any transaction in which a public servant was suspected or alleged to have acted in a corrupt manner. The CVC was also to advise the Government to change any procedure or practice which, in its opinion, afforded scope or facility for corruption.

In a circular letter issued on 13 April 1964, the Home Ministry laid down procedural instructions designed to give effect to its Resolution of 11 February which had created the CVC. According to these instructions, the CVC could entrust the matter for inquiry to the administrative ministry or deparment concerned.[64] There the vigilance officer reported his findings along with relevant records to the CVC for such action as it deemed fit to take. Alternatively, the CVC could ask the CBI to make an inquiry. The CVC was then to advise the ministry or department about the action to be taken and the Director, CBI could also be asked to register a case and investigate it.

The CVC was thus intended to exercise an effective check on the

CBI and the vigilance branches of ministries and departments. Like the CBI, however, the CVC also observed no time limit in the disposal of cases. This delay flowed specially from too many consultations with different agencies about the responsibility for investigation, about the processing of cases and the taking of final decisions. There often arose, in addition, a conflict of jurisdiction between the heads of deparments and the vigilance authorities, the former abdicating at times their initiative and responsibility. They felt that the vigilance hierarchies set up in the departments tended to erode and diffuse the responsibility of the heads of departments in such matters as related to the integrity and efficiency of administration. Preoccupied with too many petty cases, the CVC, on the other hand, did not have any positive responsibility or accountability.

The Report of the Estimates Committee (1968-9) thus made it clear that neither the CBI nor the CVC could fully accomplish the object of their institution, which was to punish the guilty quickly and protect the innocent from harassment. This view of the vigilance arrangements was supported by Justice Wanchoo, the Chief Justice of India, who came to this conclusion as a result of his inquiry into railway accidents.

The Wanchoo Committee held that the effect of the vigilance set-up was to weaken the initiative and disposition of departments to take the right decision and it encouraged a general shirking of responsibility as well as a tendency to pass the buck upwards or sideways. The existing practice of referring cases involving gazetted officers to the CVC not only caused considerable delay during which the officer concerned had to be kept under suspense, but also affected his career, his efficiency and morale. The working of the vigilance organization thus created a general sense of insecurity and, even where an officer was not actually involved in any case, he did not use his discretionary authority to initiate action, but endeavoured, whenever possible, either to pass on the responsibility to a colleague, or his superior, or at least to share his responsibility with others. The Wanchoo Committee also doubted the integrity of the sources which supplied information leading to investigation. The system of informers, it was held, often made a mockery of the official directive that no notice should be taken of anonymous complaints. Though credited in certain isolated cases with the achievement of some good results, the vigilance organization was on the whole held by the Committee to have failed to ensure honesty and efficiency in public administration.

However, the CVC alone was not to blame for this failure. In its drive against corruption it was found right at the start that undue delays occurred even in cases where the facts had already been investigated by the SPE and material for proving charges had been made available to the ministries. The reason often was that the ministries and departments did not at times spare any officer to conduct oral inquiries which involved complicated questions of fact or called for the examination of a number of witness as well as numerous documents. The departmental officers had also had their normal work to perform and were unable to give over-riding priority to inquiries. To expedite the disposal of oral inquiries, therefore, the Home Ministry appointed Officers on Special Duty on the staff of the Administrative Vigilance Division. Later, these officers were redesignated as Commissioners for Departmental Inquiries. On the recommendation of the Santhanan Committee they were placed directly under the control of the CVC.[65] But, as already noted, the function of the CVC was not based on statutory sanction. It was purely advisory, and the ministries or departments were not bound to accept its advice. The *Ninth Annual Report of the Central Vigilance Commission* (1 April 1972 to 31 March 1973) thus stated:

Unfortunately, however, the Commission was still constrained to discharge its responsibilities without any statutory basis, as the Lokpal and Lokayuktas Bill, designed *inter alia* to place the functions of the Commission on a statutory footing, though introduced years ago, has not yet become part of the law of the land.[66]

The CVC had to function under another legal handicap.[67] For instance, a case occurred where a gazetted officer was alleged to have accepted a number of gifts from the representatives of a business house who also entertained him in hotels and restaurants in an attempt to obtain information regarding matters pertaining to their company which were under consideration with the government. A regular departmental inquiry was held by a Commissioner for Departmental Inquiries. The officer held that the charges against the accused could not be proved because material prosecution witnesses in the case did not appear for examination and the inquiry officer lacked the power to compel the attendance of materal witnesses. One of the witnesses who had actually been produced and examined by the prosecution, did not appear for cross-examination by the defence, presumably on the instigation of the impugned officer. Since his attendance could not be legally enforced, the Commission had no option but to advise the acceptance of the findings of the Inquiry Officer, which meant the exoneration of the accused gazetted officer.

In order to invest the inquiring officers with requisite legal powers to compel the attendance of witnesses and the production of documents in departmental inquiries, necessary legislation was enacted in May 1972 through the Departmental Inquiries (Enforcement of Attendance and Production of Documents) Act. It however took time before the draft rules under the Act were finalized.

The Commission had in fact to rely on the goodwill and cooperation of the ministries and departments as well as public undertakings and nationalized banks to which its jurisdiction extended under the terms of its appointment. There was, however, scope for more co-operation to be extended to the Commission by the various disciplinary authorities. There occurred cases where attempts were made even to cover delinquency. For, as the *Report* pointed out, 'While deliberate attempts to shield delinquent officers may not have been frequent, there have been regrettably large numbers of instances in which disciplinary authorities seem to have failed to recognize that prompt, decisive and deterrent action can only make for improvement rather than deterioration in administrative efficiency and integrity'.[68]

This leniency towards delinquent officers had, however, its roots in society itself. The Commission was therefore justified in emphasizing 'that the battle against corruption cannot be won unless a social climate can be created in which corruption is universally recognized as a social evil in all spheres of public life—in business and in politics, as much as in the public service—and is visited with social approbrium in addition to legal penalties. Integrity is indivisible, and the problem of corruption cannot be dealt with satisfactorily on a compartmental basis'.[69]

The Officers Involved and Punishments Given

The kinds of officers generally found involved in acts of corruption were not members of the all-India Services recruited on the basis of open competition. There were cases where a Deputy Secretary and a few Under Secretaries to the government were proceeded against departmentally for the imposition of major penalty.[70] But they were of the Central Secretariat Service, promoted to higher ranks from subordinate or inferior positions.

A perusal of the *Annual Reports of the Central Vigilance Commission* shows that the officers punished for corruption were either of the Central Services like the Railways, Posts and Telegraphs, Income Tax, Accounts and Excise, or those who held such technical and other situations as the posts of engineers, controllers of stores and purchase, inspectors, principals of schools, educational officers, personnel and administrative officers, doctors, marketing officers, police officers of middle and lower ranks, deputy directors of food, airport officers and senior scientific officers. An analysis of vigilance cases in fact makes it clear that corruption was closely related to the exercise of patronage, especially in a status-bound society where caste and regional considerations had a clear edge over merit. The Union Public Service Commission had of course been intended to cast its weight on the side of intellectual excellence. But, as already pointed out, considerations of 'social justice' and the *ad hoc* appointments frequently made and invested with prescriptive legitimacy were both antithetical to the original object of that institution. The situation worsened further when the functions of the CVC were later reduced by the withdrawal of technical and scientific posts from its jurisdiction, a measure which extended the area of patronage exerciseable by the Council of Scientific and Industrial Research.[71] It was only in respect of the all-India Services that the old standards of recruitment were supposed to have been allowed to continue. In spite of their limitations, it is the higher echelons of these Services that sustain the body politic and constitute the kernel for resistance to corruption.

On the question of punishment the advice of the CVC extended for the most part to gazetted officers. The table on page 316 indicates the nature of punishment imposed by the disciplinary authorities on the advice tendered by the Commission during 1964-7.[72]

None of the 9 gazetted officers who were dismissed or removed from service belonged to the Administrative Service. They were[73] a Deputy Chairman of the Dock Labour Board, three Income-tax officers, an Executive Engineer, two Assistant Engineers, a Deputy Director of Food, and a Station Superintendent.

The cases of compulsory retirement, on the other hand, included an Assistant Garrison Engineer and an Assistant Engineer. Those who were reduced in rank or pay were an Income-tax officer, an educational officer, a marketing officer, a superintendent of a regional passport office, a local purchase officer and a block development officer. They were in fact all technical personnel in their respective functional departments and working at the middle and lower levels of administration.

S. No.	Nature of Punishment	Status			Total
		Gazetted	Non-Gazetted	Public Under-taking employees	
1	2	3	4	5	6
1.	Dismissal from service	5	7	1	13
2.	Removal from service	4	—	—	4
3.	Cut in pension	—	1	—	1
4.	Compulsory retirement	2	—	—	2
5.	Reduction to a lower time scale of pay, grade, post or service	2	—	—	2
6.	Reduction to a lower stage in the time scale of pay	5	5	—	10
7.	Recovery of loss	1	1	—	2
8.	Withholding of increments	14	1	1	16
9.	Withholding of promotion	1		1	2
10.	Censure	48	2	5	55
11.	Lapses brought to notice, communication of Governments' displeasure, issue of warning/caution	159	29	11	199
		241	46	19	306

It was the technical personnel in functional departments, especially at executive and subordinate levels, that remained for the most part contaminated. Even the Council of Scientific and Industrial Research was reported to be no exception. The CVC noticed that the Council acted in contravention of its own 'Rules & Procedures' to favour particular candidates. For instance, Selection Committees were not constituted in accordance with the provisions of the CSIR bye-laws. Selections were also made by Selection Committees which were not constitued for the posts for which selections were made. Posts were even filled up without being advertised and there were cases where the advertisements themselves were tailored to suit a particular individual or individuals. Even those who did not apply for posts were selected. No care was taken to verify entries in the confidential character rolls, nor did the officers responsible for recruitment dissociate themselves from the Selection Committee when their near relations themsleves happened to be candidates. Added to these irregularities, were the *ad hoc* appointments which were continued for long periods, in some cases even 'for years together'.[74] At the instance of the CVC, however, the Director-General of the CSIR issued a circular to the Directors of Regional Laboratories/Institutes asking them to avoid such irregularities.

Another interesting case of corruption, which was reported by the Union Public Service Commission, was that of a high-ranking officer, the Director of an institution under the Ministry of Defence, who participated in a UPSC Selection Board when his brother-in-law appeared as a candidate. He had also 'approached' a professor of a particular university to sponsor the name of his relation. The UPSC viewed this conduct as highly irregular, amounting to 'thinly-disguised nepotism', deserving censure.[75] A case like this is unfortunately not rare in the Indian situation.

There may be in the public mind an exaggerated notion about the extent of corruption. But the fact remains that, with the commencement of the Second Plan period, the atmosphere began to get vitiated by the abuse of power under party rule, of corruption in all walks of life. An all-round inefficiency which had been growing over the years as a result of unprecedented expansion in the machinery of government assumed serious proportions with the growth of monopolies. The myth of corruption might of course have become greater than the fact of corruption. But the myth so created was no less damaging to the social fabric than the actual extent of corruption.

The vigilance arrangements of the Government of India were intended to stem the tide of corruption. But their operation did not extend beyond the limits of the Central Governments employees and the Union territories. And there too the absence of quick and impartial enquiry was at the root of their incapacity to deliver the goods. The excessive time taken in the process of investigation eroded efficiency and proved destructive of the morale of the public services in respect of both the guilty and the innocent.

CHAPTER VII

Some General Reflections

Conceptual Foundations

The organization of modern government and bureaucracy in India proceeded from the British colonial pattern, a pattern that was informed by western ideas and institutions, but adapted to local conditions not with a view to assimilation but to implantation and imposition. Though socially peripheral, its effect in terms of political and administrative penetration was quite sustained and even conducive to a renaissance in urban centres. Structurally, the bureaucratic set-up introduced and developed under British rule thus continued despite the change in the political complexion of the state in 1947.

The Weberian Concept—This bureaucratic continuity was in keeping with the Weberian concept of organizational sociology, a concept which applied to all modern organizatins, independently of whether they were social, economic or political. Weber held that bureaucracy was an integral part of every planned and organized group activity called administration, and that it was not restricted to any particular system, colonial or capitalist, socialist or communist. It formed as much a part of scientific, technological or even religious organizations as of so-called general administration. It would not in fact be possible to do away with bureaucracy in the transaction of human business in any organized field of activity.

Starting from this general principle of organizational sociology, Weber analysed bureaucracy as an administrative organization and then proceeded to deal specifically with his pure or rational type of bureaucracy called the 'ideal type'. This consisted of an impersonal and legal body of salaried and professional administrators, appointed on selection by open competition, employed on a full-time basis and organized hierarchically in deparments in accordance with rules governing the terms and conditions of service. The formal constitution of the bureaucracy that developed in India contained these basic ingredients of Weber's rational or ideal type.

Though modified in several respects by recent researches, the Weberian model has over the years remained a sound synthesis of two important dimensions of bureaucracy, namely, organizational or technical and political or pejorative. Weber united both in a single frame of reference. From his analysis of the rational type he went on to deal with politics and society with special reference to democracy. Unlike the supporters of the elitist concept of organizational sociology, who held that bureaucracy and democracy were mutually exclusive categories, he attempted to show that this was not so. He regarded both as mutually inclusive; for, according to him, no pejorative element attached to bureaucracy. His argument was that, since the specific nature of modern administration and the control of the apparatus of the modern state were conceptually distinct, bureaucracy and democracy could very well co-exist. He even suggested the use of a number of checks to make their co-existence both formal and real. Weber in fact treated bureaucracy as an independent unit of analysis. He supplied a conceptual basis for the political 'neutrality' of civil servants, a neutrality that flowed from the evolution of the modern state as an organized political expression of society as a whole, not from the old notion of officials being the King's servants and bound to him by personal loyalty.

Even so, the political issue remained unresolved. The validity of the Weberian model continued to be questioned. The issue was not that bureaucracy was dispensable. The question was one of emphasis. Should that emphasis be laid on the technical or organizational aspect of administration, on the bureaucratic machine and the rules regulating that machine to ensure economy, speed and efficiency, or should it be on bureaucracy as a social class of power elites controlling society either for its own sake, or for the sake of an ideology, or a combination of both? If the emphasis is on the technique of administration, the nature of controversy, if any, remains professional and for the most part limited. But in case the focus is shifted to an analysis of power and its class complex, bureaucracy gets immediately involved in a maze of controversy in a pejorative sense. It divides government and society into groups based on religion, language, profession, economic interest and so on, each vying for a share in power, which not only gives status and prestige but also opens out prospects for better living standards.

According to Weber, the source of authority for both the administrative bureaucracy and political leadership was the modern state. They were two separate and distinct units of analysis, functioning as the two wheels of a cart joined together by a mechanism in the nature of an axle to ensure co-ordinate movement or progress. He envisaged co-operation, not confrontation, between appointed officials and elected executives. They were both to serve the state from the positions respectively assigned to them in the machinery of government, the bureaucracy functioning as the instrument of the state independently of any change in the political complexion of government. The bureaucrat was to be loyal to the Constitution expressing the 'general will', not to any political party representing only certain sections of that will. In other words, he was to be politically neutral. This was Weber's concept of rational bureaucracy.

The British—The principle of political neutrality had already come to form part of the British civil service, a principle which later became operative in the Indian situation also. Before the eighteenth century there existed in England no distinction between administrative and political functions. The King's civil servants exercised both the functions by holding administrative offices as well as seats in Parliament where they supported the King with zeal and fervour. In the first half of the seventeeth century, however, some servants of the Stuart kings, especially those in the law courts and in the departments, were being recognized as public servants of the Crown and distinguished specifically from the private servants of the sovereign. The idea of loyalty to the emerging concept of the state, or the public good, as distinct from service to the King, was slowly engaging men's minds. Pym and his followers in Parliament were in fact thinking in those terms when, in the course of the Civil War, they emphasized that they were not fighting against the King, but against the evil counsellors who misguided him. But since the religious foundation of monarchy was still strong and the person of the monarch was still considered inviolate, it was not possible to treat the King's servants as public servants unless he himself had to a considerable extent been depersonalized and in some degree also depoliticized. The civil servants of the Stuarts naturally continued to be deemed as the King's own servants and lending support to their masters in both administration and Parliament.

It was to ensure its political independence that Parliament enacted after the Glorious Revolution of 1688-9 a series of measures exclud-

ing certain office-holders from the House of Commons, and ultimately disenfranchising the bulk of the civil service by the time Queen
Anne took over. This principle of exclusion applied to government
contractors in 1782 and to the clergymen of the established church in
1801. By the turn of the nineteenth century the permanent separation
of the administrative staff from the political branch of the British
Government thus became fairly well recognized. And although it was
not until the Reforms Act of 1832 that the old aristocratic complexion
of Parliament started changing in favour of the middle class, it did not
take long before the royal system of 'patronage' also came to be
replaced by a competitive system under the Northcote-Trevelyan
Report of 1853. The King's servants had become public servants loyal
to the state and its constitution, not personally to the King who had
become an office, abstract and impersonal.

The civil service so evolved was politically neutral in two main
respects. The first was the formulation of policies and their implementation, the former being recognized as the concern of ministers, and
the latter as the legitimate sphere of civil servants. The second postu-
late of 'neutrality' was that by virtue of his training and tradition a
civil servant could be brought up to be an 'apolitical' being, whose
business it was to implement policies laid down for him without
allowing such implementation to be in any way influenced by his
own political views. Both features of civil service neutrality were
considered essential to the functioning of parliamentary democracy,
where the complexion of the political party in power was subject to
periodic change. They were the natural consequence of the gradual
separation of administration from politics effected over the years to
ensure the sovereignty of law.

The political neutrality of a British civil servant which flowed from
the growth of democracy and parliamentary government was, however, not inconsistent with what we call 'commitment'. To him 'political neutrality' and 'commitment' were not mutually exclusive terms.
He was certainly politically neutral in terms of civil service regulations and was ever ready to implement the policies laid down by any
ruling party. But he was staunchly committed to the state and its
constitution which reflected the dominant middle-class value system
of British society, a value system which was in harmony with the
social origins of the British civil servant and reinforced by the entire
educational processes to which he remained subjected. Because of the
cultural cross-fertilization brought about by the evenness of social
and economic development, there grew between the civil servant and

his political masters a spirit of sharing not only of the value system but a broad understanding of national interest and social progress. Britain in fact developed a representative bureaucracy.[1]

The Indian Situation—The Indian Civil Service, however, had to function in a totally different environment, where the mass of Indian society was divided into diverse races, creeds and castes in a manner unrelated to anything in the nature of the rule of law, which the British established to regulate the conduct of their political and administrative institutions in India. In the words of Lord Dufferin, who drew a graphic social picture of India, this society was

composed of a large number of distinct nationalities, professing various religions, practising diverse rites, speaking different languages, while many of them are still further separated from one another by discordant prejudices, by conflicting source of usages, and even antagonistic material interests. But perhaps the most patent characteristic of our Indian cosmos is its division into two mighty political communities as distant from each other as the poles asunder in their religious faith, their historical antecedents, their social organization, their natural aptitudes; on the one hand the Hindus numbering 190 millions, with their polytheistic beliefs, their temples adorned with images and idols, their veneration for the sacred cow, their elaborate caste distinctions, and their habits of submission to successive conquerors—on the other hand, the Mahomedans, a nation of 50 millions, with their monotheism, their iconoclastic fanaticism, their animal sacrifices, their social equality, and their remembrance of the days when, enthroned at Delhi, they reigned supreme from the Himalayas to Cape Comorin.[2]

Dufferin went on to mention other communities almost as widely differentiated from one another as were Hindus from Muhammadans. But the point he emphasized most was the serious gaps in social and economic development:

Again, amongst those numerous communities may be found at one and the same moment all the various stages of civilization through which mankind has passed from the prehistoric ages to the present day. At one end of the scale we have the naked savage hillman, with his stone weapons, his head-hunting, his polyandrous habits, and his childish superstitions; and at the other, the Europeanized native gentleman, with his English costume, his advanced democratic ideas, his Western philosophy, and his literary culture; while between the two lies layer upon layer, or in close juxtaposition, wandering communities with their flocks of goats and moving tents; collections of undisciplined warriors, with their blood feuds, their clan organization, and loose tribal government; feudal chiefs and barons with their retainers, their senorial jurisdiction, and their medieval notions; and modernized country gentlemen and enterprising merchants and manufacturers, with their well-managed estates and prosperous enterprises.[3]

The heterogeneity of India's social composition representing at the same moment the various stages of civilization in a colonial situation thus did not fit the 'ideal type' of the Weberian model, a model fashioned after a highly developed, homogeneous and less varied democratic society. To devise a system of administration which might represent the highest common denominator in the Indian context was in fact no easy task. It was doubtful whether the 'Europeanized native gentleman' who formed part of the middle class educated elites, could at all deliver the goods. Writing to Northbrook on the subject of extended elite representation in the Council, Dufferin thus said in a letter of 16 October 1886:

> If it could be done, of course it would be an excellent thing; but the more I see of these people the less sanguine I am of reaching a conclusion which will both work advantageously for the country at large and satisfy native aspirations. There would be great difficulty in getting hold of the best men, and then, when we have got them, they represent after all only an infinitesimal section of the people and the interests of a minute minority in reference to a great proportion of the subjects with which legislation deals. All the efforts of the Government of India are principally directed towards the improvement of the condition of the masses. We should be very apt to find ourselves thwarted and opposed by constituencies whose qualifications are simply wealth and education. For instance, all our recent legislation (especially on tenancy and rural debt) would have been carried with infinitely more difficulty if more natives had been present in the Council.[4]

Bureaucratic despotism was therefore provided as the answer to the administrative problem posed by Indian society. It was considered conducive to both social justice and imperial interest. The nationalist struggle for political freedom doubtless rendered the bureaucracy subject to the control of the elected executive. But since corresponding social change had not accompanied the march of political progress, the administrative system which the British had built up to suit the needs of Indian society and their imperial objectives continued in the post-Independence period also. Experience dictated the necessity of reinforcing executive dominance even in the erstwhile 'Regulation Provinces' where, unlike the 'Non-Regulation Provinces', executive and judicial functions were not united except in a limited way. The Government of India was even obliged to declare on 26 June 1975 a state of Emergency under which all judicial protection provided by the Constitution had to be withdrawn in the interest of national security.

Politically, the Weberian view of bureaucracy and democracy did not apply to the Indian situation for the greater part of British rule. Democracy was of course introduced in the provinces under the Constitution Act of 1935. Civil servants became subject to ministerial control. But the presence of imperialism made this control more formal than real. The Secretaries to Government reported to their Governors, and the Governors in their turn to the Viceroy, over the heads of ministers. In fact, the officials and ministers did not function within the limits of their respective administrative and political assignments. There was at times an overlapping of jurisdiction on both sides. While the former had in mind their imperial strength to reinforce independence in the conduct of administration, the latter attempted to make use of ministerial position to promote political interests.[5] They quarrelled: they did not co-exist. The British Government in India remained a bureaucracy until the formation of the Interim Government in September 1946 when the balance tilted in favour of democracy for the first time.

But the democracy that emerged from the transfer of power in India produced a different result from that in Western countries. For, unlike the West where democracy had grown from below as a result of the atomization of individuals proceeding immediately from socio-economic changes, the Indian variety was a product of political agitation, transplanted from abroad and imposed from above on a society divided into numerous unatomized groups by races, creeds and castes at various levels of development from the prehistoric age to modernity. While atomization afforded opportunity for the exercise of choice, a *sine qua non* of democracy in the West, its virtual absence in India obstructed the growth of individualism and tended to keep people tied down to their tradition-bound social species. The Indian pattern of democracy did not weaken those ties.

On the contrary, it strengthened them. There were of course exceptions where individuals broke away from their caste or clan on grounds of ideology or interest or a combination of both. But these exceptions did not change the tenor of electoral behaviour in general. The exercise of franchise in blocks of caste or group was in fact convenient to political parties in terms of electoral costs and beneficial to constituents who could use collective caste pressure to promote their interest or that of any of their proteges. In short, democracy in the Indian situation conduced to social continuity by providing political sanction to the creation of vested interests in backwardness which, in turn, encouraged regimented reactions from the traditionally socially privileged. Despite modern education, individuals in both cases tended to remain bound to their respective communities in order to retain the practical advantage of communal backing to secure individual interest.

Democracy thus provided an additional, political incentive for the continuance of the traditional social order based on mutually exclusive communities, castes and tribes. It was initially encouraged by Dyarchy which provided for the downward filtration of education and extended franchise. The lower orders of society began to organize themselves into separate caste groups and wanted to have their separate entities recognized as a title to due share in politics and administration. But this tendency was especially strengthened by some eminent I.C.S. officers whose interest in social anthropology led them to study castes and tribes, not only for intellectual reasons, but also from a desire to present the variegated patterns of Indian society and politics. Their line of investigation received the support of the Government of India who drew a detailed list of what came to be broadly classified as Scheduled Castes and Scheduled Tribes. Their classification was said to be for the purposes of public employment duly recognized by statutory rules. But the fact remained that such efforts of the Government intensified caste and tribal consciousness and extended it beyond the major communities. Even the Constitution of India did not omit to recognize the claims of the Scheduled Castes and Tribes to services and posts under the Union as well as State Governments.[6] It specifically provided for the appointment by the President of a Commission to investigate all matters relating to the safeguards laid down for the Scheduled Castes and Tribes and to report to the President who was to cause such reports to be placed before each House of Parliament.[7] It is of interest to note that the Constitution did not use the terms Scheduled Castes and Scheduled Tribes in a restrictive sense. These were to be construed to include such other backward classes as were so deemed by the President in terms of social conditions and educational backwardness. The object of a constitutional provision for a separate Commission to investigate the position of backward classes was to improve their conditions through grants to be made available on the reports of the Commisssion.[8]

Indeed, the Government of India could not act otherwise. Considerations of politics and social justic both demanded it. In an unatomized and status-bound society the introduction of representative government and democracy could not but produce the effect it did: it could not but rivet the erstwhile social divisions of castes and creeds, of tribes and communities. Dyarchy actually compelled the Government of India to recognize the principle of communalism in the distribution of jobs in the public services. It began under statutory rules with the 'Muddiman Pledge[9] given in 1925. A perusal of the questions raised in the Central Assembly after its formation in 1921 reveals beyond doubt the preoccupation of legislators to secure an ever-increasing share of public employment for members of their own communities, their own caste or religion. Regional or provincial considerations were of course not absent. But the emphasis was by and large on caste and religious affiliations, two important principles of the Indian social system. The 1925 Pledge, which was heavily weighted in favour of Muslims and Anglo-Indians, was revised by a resolution of 1934 which specified additional reservations and direct recruitment in the interests of the Scheduled Castes and Tribes.

The principle of communal reservation in the public services was a political remedy to social and economic disparities. The operation of this principle was allowed to be extended by the Constitution in respect of Anglo-Indians in addition to Scheduled Castes and Scheduled Tribes. Communal representation doubtless had its value: it gave an incentive for providing more education to the lower castes, which, in turn, brought about changes in their traditional occupation patterns, their standards of living and social relationships. But it meant no structural change. The whole tendency of the political approach gave the backward classes their freedom to fight for the retention of the rights so reserved to them. It made each determined not to lose the privileges. It became politically paying on account of the ease with which votes could be mobilized by an exercise of influence with the leaders of castes, religious groups or tribes. It added to the influence and power of the bureaucracy in the distribution of patronage and certificates of backwardness as a title to privilege. But it certainly tended to weaken the territorial foundation of nationalism and democracy.

The general lack of emphasis on the reconstruction of society and the overtones of power politics under colonial rule had combined to create a situation which ran counter to the principles of an ideally rational bureaucracy in India. Other reasons too counteracted such a development. As suggested before, the presence of imperialism had engendered a trend of reactionary revivalism in politics. It led to a series of communal disturbances which assumed serious proportions by the time the British decided to quit. In the context of pre-Independence developments, revivalism in the post-Independence period expressed itself in the form of an intensified social reaction, more especially among the ranks of the petty bourgeoisie and in rural areas where the bulk of the population happened to be largely illiterate and profoundly suspicious of pro-Western liberal elites.

The leadership of the Government of India and the higher levels of its bureaucracy helped the country cope with the communal holocaust. But this could not be said of politics and administration at subordinate levels, where the principles of rationalism were neither understood nor practised in accordance with Weber's 'ideal type'. It was in these circumstances that the Indian Administrative Service was called upon to forge ahead in the task of building a new India.

This new service, as said before, was organized on the pattern of the Indian Civil Service, a career service acting on the principle of political neutrality as practised in Britain. The I.C.S. was not intended to promote the interests of one or a particular party over those of another. It was even socially uncommitted, and the various reformist social measures it took over the years to regulate social relationships were intended to maintain law and order and not interfere with the principles of the established social order. The impartiality of the British Civil Service, which shaped the character of the I.C.S., flowed from the British constitution which had no permanent social principles at its core to which that service could be committed. The socially uncommitted British Civil Service functioned as a satisfactory instrument for carrying out the policies and programmes of successive governments with divergent social philosophies. This was true not only of Britain, but also of other Western countries, more especially of the United States of America which had a written constitution, but without principles of any social policy embedded in it. That perhaps was the reason why the Government of India Act (1935), though in fact a constitution act, included no provision in the nature of directive principles of social policy as part of the Constitution Act itself. Nor did it contain any separate reference to fundamental rights which formed part of the legal system the British Government had established in India. Political neutrality thus flowed from the absence of definitive socio-economic goals.

Question of Commitment

In the post-Independence period, however, India adopted a written Constitution. It embodies certain principles of social policy which form an integral part of that Constitution. These principles were intended to determine the ends and purposes of the polity as well as of the social order the Constitution was designed to establish. It is true that the Fundamental Rights embodied in the Constitution were for the most part not dissimilar to those of other democratic constitutions. But apart from the Preamble which set the main objectives, the Constitution of India includes the Directive Principles of State Policy. Some of these Principles were reinforced by the Constitution (Twenty-fifth Amendment) Act, 1971, which inserted a new Article 31C intended to give effect to them. And since a civil servant in India is required to take an oath of loyalty to the Constitution, he commits himself through that oath to the Preamble, the Fundamental Rights and the Directive Principles which envisage the establishment of a social order based on no discrimination of caste or creed. In view of the socio-economic goals of the Constitution there naturally arose a pressing need for commitment to these on the part of the civil service.

In a paper published in *Seminar* on the question of a committed civil service, the then Home Secretary, L. P. Singh, emphasized the importance of commitment to 'professionalism', a Weberian concept, not to a party or its policy and programme. 'From whatever angle one may look at it', he said, 'there can be no doubt that India needs a civil service with professional competence and commitment. Such a service will prove a sound instrument for achieving accepted social goals that the Constitution has laid down.' He further explained his view of professional commitment as 'dedicated service to the people, the promotion of 'the welfare and happiness of the citizen and respect for his feelings and susceptibilities,' and 'principles of fairness and integrity in all his dealings.'[10] Interestingly enough, the Home Secretary quoted from his personal knowledge two examples of the practical implications of a committed civil service. The first case was that of the son of a renowned Sanskrit scholar who had been selected for appointment to a State civil service in the early 1950s. When informed that in the course of his initial training he would be required to live and dine with colleagues belonging to different castes and religious persuasions, he expressed a fear of pollution and his reluctance to dine at the same table with members of certain castes and communities. The question arose whether in view of the social content of the Constitution he should be considered qualified to carry out the policy underlying it; and if he was not, whether it would be right to appoint him to the civil service. The question specifically posed was whether a person staunchly committed to untouchability could be a fit instrument to prohibit discrimination on grounds of religion or caste under Article 15 of the Constitution, or to forbid untouchability in any form under Article 17. The final decision was not to appoint him. The second case relates to recruitment to the Delhi Police through a psychological test and the criteria to be applied at the test. The decision taken was in keeping with the principles laid down by the Constitution: that a person who had sadistic or brutal traits, or who did not unreservedly accept the basic principles of democracy, secularism, the rights to equality and freedom, and the establishment of a just social order, should not be appointed. The Home Secretary admitted that in citing these two instances his intention was not to suggest 'that it is easy to have and maintain a civil service committed to the social, among other, principles and provisions of the Costitution. The practical problems involved are indeed exceedingly difficult and complex'. Indian politics could not build the casteless society necessary to sustain a modern administration fitted to carry out the social objectives of the Constitution.

The commitment of the civil service could not be very different from the commitments of society at large. It would in fact be unrealistic to expect that the extent and depth of the commitment of the civil service in India would differ in any marked degree from that of Indian society, where social equality has through the ages remained a subject to be preached, but hardly to be practised.

However, with the growth of democracy in India, the caste-oriented features of Indian society were immediately reflected in the behaviour of ministers, not of civil servants who, under their service conditions, were to be guided in their conduct by the civil service regulations. In 1937, for instance, when popular ministries were formed in the provinces, the Viceroy was informed by a number of Governors that ministers often trusted their own caste men and not the permanent secretary to the government whom they tried to sidetrack and eliminate by bringing a parliamentary secretary to the foreground in the transaction of departmental business.[11] Since the position of the permanent secretary was recognized by statute and the functions assigned to him could not be discharged by any other agency, the Viceroy asked his Governors not to acquiesce in such a trend on any account. For under the Constitution Act (1935) it was the permanent secretary alone who could bring to the notice of the minister or Governor concerned any matter for consideration. He alone could authenticate the order of his minister and a minister, on the other hand, was not to correspond directly with subordinate officers. He could consult experts from outside, but even such consultation was to be in the presence of the permanent secretary who alone had administrative control over his department. The Viceroy in fact made it clear that there could be no question of the permanent secretary being side-tracked or short-circuited in favour of any alternative.

Even so, as the private papers of the Governors of a number of 'Congress' provinces show, several cases occurred 'where individual ministers issued orders to subordinate officers direct'[12], over the head of the secretary. Since the rule of law lacked roots in Indian soil, it was not realistic to expect the elected executive to show marked differences from the general social norms. Thus, not infrequently ministers forgot to bear in mind that, according to the principles of parliamentary democracy, they were as much servants of the state as were civil servants, and the civil servants were not their servants, but, like them, the servants of the state.

Unlike the Congress ministries of 1937–9, the 1946–56 decade witnessed a government of national talents at the Centre. It was not a party government, nor were party overtones allowed to figure to any marked degree. The magnitude of the post-Independence problems of reconstruction was national and attempts were made to meet them nationally. But the issue of drawing a distinction between party and government for the purposes of parliamentary democracy did not cease. It bedevilled the Congress ministries in 1937.[13] It appeared again when the Indian Cabinet became part of party apparatus from 1957 onwards. The experiences of 1937 were naturally re-enacted, not locally but now on an all-India scale. This not only involved controversies over the secretary-minister relationship, but also led to a search for a compliant civil service, committed not only to the ideals enshrined in the Constitution, but also to the ruling party. Writing about what a committed civil servant actually signified, Vishnu Sahay, a retired member of the I.C.S., pointed out:

In reality, the matters of high moment which interest ministers are appointments, transfers, promotions, licences and permits. These are not matters in which heart-felt comm...ment to the lofty aims of government is directly relevant. What is desired is commitment to the ministers personally. This is often effectively secured by the minister choosing his top executives from his personal followers in the civil service. Quite often, the discerning ministerial eye falls on a fellow-caste man. If this happy combination cannot be achieved on account of some old-fashioned bureaucratic regulation, there is always the private secretary or personal assistant who can be hand-picked without the strictures of seniority, service and the like. This intermediary can safely be used for telephoning to the local official how best he can prove his commitment (to the minister). The telephone has been of much use in keeping civil servants at various levels on the right path without incurring the embarrassment of written record.[14]

This view of ministerial behaviour had in fact already been foreseen by Mahatma Gandhi who, soon after Independence, was 'deeply concerned about the rot that was setting into the Congress Party'. For he had received information that Congress legislators were taking money from businessmen to get them licences, that they were indulging in black-marketing and subverting the judiciary and intimidating top officials to secure transfers and promotions for their proteges in the administration.[15]

Such ministerial behaviour could of course be attributed basically to a tradition-bound caste and status ridden society which lacks the capacity for organized and collective resistance to corruption. But even the top leadership of the ruling party was not free from the taint. While its declared political goal was parliamentary democracy, which emphasized the primacy of the party in parliament exercising power with responsibility, its radical and power-motivated wing with Nehru at its head attempted to act on the Soviet model which gives primacy to the party executive outside the legislature. In fact, his was an attempt to inject into the framework of parliamentary democracy itself a socio-economic principle on the Russian model, so that it might call for the exercise of power without responsibility by the Congress Party in which he held a commanding position. Nehru failed to foist his Soviet line as a source of personal aggrandizement, for parliamentary democracy would not fit that line. The party majority too was opposed to it. But in the name of radical socialism he did create confusion in the ranks of the party, which interfered with the proper functioning of the parliamentary system.

The relationship between government and party, which in principle involved a conflict of ends and means, came up for serious consideration in 1937 itself. Under the 1935 Act, which provided for a parliamentary form of government, the Congress formed ministries in seven of the eleven provinces. The Congress did so despite the opposition of Jawaharlal Nehru, who was not sure whether he would be able to control these ministries from outside.[16] His fears were in fact not unfounded. Soon after the formation of their ministries most of the 'Prime Ministers' of the Congress provinces developed understanding and co-operated with the Governors who were keen to observe the recognized norms of a parliamentary government. Against the advice of the Congress High Command to avoid social contact with Governors, Dr Khare, the Prime Minister of the Central Provinces, for instance, did away with such social barriers as stood in the way of understanding between himself and his Governor; Govind Ballabh Pant, the Prime Minister of U. P., was also no exception. In spite of Nehru's direct influence, Pant and his colleagues took care to attend the Governor's address to the provincial legislature and maintain the necessary social contacts. Contrary to the advice of Jawaharlal Nehru, the Prime Minister of Bombay asserted himself as the leader of his legislature party and went ahead with labour legislation intended to curb communists in the interests of law and order. He did not allow any interference by the central caucus of the party outside.

The private correspondence between the Viceroy and Governors of the Congress provinces establishes that, while the Congress ministries were keen to function within the statutory limits of parliamentary democracy, they were in practice forced ultimately to abide by the dictates of the Congress High Command because of the existing circumstances of an imperialist presence in the country. Though anxious to continue, they were even forced to resign under the mandate of the central party caucus.

In the country's colonial situation, both the British parliamentary system and the Soviet model of government were competing side by side for recognition. The former was supported by the rational and democratic majority in the Congress, and the later, backed by the radical left, sought in the party-dominated Soviet system the real source of power without official responsibility. In one case, it was the maintenance of legislative majority and the quality of performance as a title to continuance in power, while in the other it was the control of government and its patronage, without a corresponding responsibility, that gave authority and status to the party boss. The one conduced to democracy, while the other could lead to dictatorship.

On the transfer of power the country opted in favour of parliamentary democracy within the framework of a federal constitution. It was in keeping with India's historical evolution in modern times. But the trail of Sovietism did not cease. It continued even organizationally, waning or growing in strength according to the changing patterns of politics, both national and international. With the emergence of Mrs Indira Gandhi as the *de facto* boss of the Congress Party, for instance, the balance tilted noticeably in favour of Sovietism. Cases occur where the established norms of federalism and parliamentary government are superseded and governments in the states change without ascertaining the views of assemblies. Thus, for instance, a Chief Minister of Orissa, Mrs Nandini Satpathy, was forced to resign in favour of President's rule, not becuase she did not enjoy a majority in the Assembly, but because the party caucus outside, especially in New Delhi, wanted her to go. Commenting editorially on what it called 'A Disturbing Trend', the *Statesman* (Calcutta) of 19 December 1976 thus pointed out.

So the expected has happened in Orissa. To record this fact is to underline the serious political question Mrs Nandini Satpathy's resignation raises. Apart from the propriety of the ruling party seeking a Chief Minister's resignation when she enjoys the support of a majority in the Assembly, the manner of her forced departure is, to say the least, unsavoury. Whether the Congress Party chooses to replace Mrs Satpathy as Chief Minister in Orissa is its business, but the way the deed has been done is the business of the people of Orissa and the country at large. The one question being asked today is: is it right for a controlling group outside a State to create conditions of instability in a State to force the resignation of a Chief Minister?

Instead of choosing the floor of a State Assembly as the right place to test a majority, recourse was taken by rival factions to indulge in signature compaigns and a series of manoeuvres to dislodge an established ministry and effect a change of government. This development had serious repercussions on the administration. The country's civil services, however, did not come under the influence of the Soviet system which not only includes in its bureaucracy the officials of the Communist Party, but also treats it as no more than an instrument of that Party. The ministers of a government and civil servants in India remained in law separate and distinct; for both were in terms of their structure and function committed separately to the goals and purposes of the state, the common focal point of loyalty. Operationally, both were to serve as its co-ordinate agencies. The I.C.S. and its successor, the I.A.S., were organized on this principle of parliamentary government, a principle which, in terms of the mode of recruitment and conditions of service, was very much in line with that of the legal and rational bureaucracy of the Weberian model. It is true that the percentage of direct recruits in open competition was in the Indian situation limited for various reasons. The 'ideal type' of the Weberian model was necessarily modified to the extent and in a manner demanded by the compulsions of Indian politics and society. Even so, it has to be recognized that the civil service recruited on the basis of open competition by written and *viva voce* examinations established over the years a norm which was sought to be adopted as a matter of general principle by all other services.

The growing Soviet influence in the country in the post-Independence period kept voicing opinion in favour of the civil service being rendered subject to control by the ruling party. It was argued that mere attachment or professed loyalty to the principles of the Constitution was not enough. The civil service as well as the judiciary must respond to the aspirations of the 'people' and realize the way the wind of change was blowing. This was a concept of 'commitment' imbued with left overtones and advanced by Mohan Kumaramangalam, the Central Minister for Industry, who supported the Soviet line. The view was confirmed in another context by D. P. Dhar, a former Planning Minister, who held that a civil servant who was not committed to the party in power should have no place in the administration of the country. In the context of the Prime Minister's critical statement about the need for greater commitment from public servants, the subsequent controversies emerging on the subject found expression in the press as well as public platforms. The Prime Minister later clarified her earlier statement by saying that what she meant by commitment was not partisanship but professional devotion to duty, to which nobody would take any exception.

But the trouble did not end at that. The Prime Minister's earlier statement and the statements of her ministers which came in that sequence, were all traced to falterings in the implementation of development plans and their failure to achieve the results expected. While the higher echelons of the bureaucracy were for the most part honest, devoted and over-worked, the subordinate and lowere levels of government servants, besides being over-staffed in the name of 'development', had few moral examples to emulate either in society or in politics.

Administration and Plan Implementation

Nobody would dispute that plan implementation was the immediate responsibility of the administration which, of course, does not exclude the responsibility of the political leadership and its policy. The question of success or failure was a different issue. But documents[17] relating to plan implementation all unanimously indicate that, in spite of administrative changes[18] effected over the years since Independence, the development plans faltered without exception. The two co-ordinate state agencies involved in the execution of the task with the help of the existing administration were (and still are) ministers and civil servants. The manner in which they both functioned within the given framework of policy and administrative arrangements has been studied in great depth and scholarship by A.H. Hanson.[19] All that need be attempted here is briefly to provide, in terms of implementation, a coherent analysis of administration on the basis of the already known and published material.

The Planning Commission

India's Planning Commission was created on 15 March 1950 by a resolution of the Cabinet, not by an Act of Parliament. It was designed to be a separate and distinct organization from the ministries, though acting in close understanding and consultation with them at the Centre as well as in the States. Since the Prime Minister happened to be its Chairman, it could boast of a status that gave its recommendations the air of commands to central ministries and State governments. This position had the further risk of being politically reinforced when, by 1962, the Commission actually came to consist of no fewer than five minister members, all of high status in the political hierarchy of the country. They were Jawaharlal Nehru, G. L. Nanda, Morarji Desai, Krishna Menon and T. T. Krishnamachari. The original non-ministerial members, too, included politicians. But there were administrators and some business representatives also. The Commission was thus a combination of political, administrative and business experience. With the passage of time considerations of political acceptability resulted in some compromise with expertise, but the original business representation was eliminated under ideological pressures. In addition to the Minister of Finance, who sat on the Commission as its *ex officio* member, and the various central ministries working with it in collaboration, some of the important bodies that remained associated with the Commission included the

Industrial Licensing Committee, the Development Councils and the Central Statistical Organization which was governed by P. C. Mahalanobis, a theoretician in statistics and statistical adviser to the Prime Minister.

The creation of the National Development Council was suggested by the Planning Commission in the Draft Outline of the First Five-Year Plan. It was created by a resolution of the Cabinet on 6 August 1952 as an advisory body consisting of the Prime Minister, the Chief Ministers of States and Members of the Planning Commission. However, its meetings were (and still are) attended by other ministers and even by outsiders, such as eminent economists or the Governor of the Reserve Bank. Of the several associated bodies, the National Development Council was (and still is) by far the most important. It was said to rival the Planning Commission itself in importance. As defined by the Cabinet, its functions included a periodical review of the working of the National Plan, a review of social and economic policy in terms of development plans, and recommending measures not only to improve administrative efficiency, but also to ensure people's participation in the promotion of national development.

The National Development Council was meant to be an advisory body but in practice it turned out to be slightly more than that. For, though not executive in its function, its discussions have often made it clear as to how far the States are prepared to go in carrying out the Commission's centrally determined priorities. It is true that, in view of the prestige of the Commission, it was no easy task for the States to win. Moreover, the States were not only disunited but also rival clients for the Centre's favour. As the Government of India under Lord Mayo pointed out in the previous century in its Financial Resolution of 14 December 1870, there had always been a tendency on the part of 'Local Governments' to indulge in a 'scramble' for central assistance, where the most vociferous had the advantage in getting their points met.[20] Similarly, the less economy the New States practise and the more attractive their plans, the more likely are they to convince the Planning Commission of the urgency of their requirements. In spite of its limitations, the National Development Council has since its creation functioned none the less as an organized gathering 'where plans undergo adjustment in the light of the needs, pressures, prejudices and capacities of the States.'[21]

However, since 1950 the Planning Commission itself has become an *imperium in imperio*, with a tendency to reduce the ministries, States, and to an extent, even the Union Cabinet to the status of what might be called an 'agency', a trend that is prejudicial to the very principles of parliamentary democracy. In one of the Lok Sabha debates a leader of the Swatantra Party thus went to the extent of suggesting the abolition of the Planning Commission in order to 'free Cabinet Ministers' from its 'extra-constitutional intervention'.[22] There was, in addition, the political overtone in the organization of the Commission, which created bottlenecks in undertaking responsibilities of too varied a kind. These combined to strip the Commission of its basic character of a body of experts, both in the technical and administrative fields, who would make an independent survey of the problems involved and formulate plans without being influenced by extraneous considerations and day-to-day expedients. According to the Estimates Committee of the Lok Sabha, the Commission's independence and its purely advisory character could not be vouchsafed by its composition and manner of functioning, because Cabinet Ministers, including the Prime Minister, were its members. In its twenty-first report of 1957-8 the Estimates Committee thus pointed out that a 'decision, to which they are a party, taken in the Planning Commission and transmitted to the ministries to be considered by them or in the Cabinet is ... more than advice and is very nearly a final decision'. Contrary to the original object of its constitution, the Commission did not continue as an organization 'free from the burden of day-to-day administration but in constant touch with the Government at the highest policy level.'

D.R. Gadgil held a similar view on the Planning Commission. According to him, it failed because it came to mix itself with the actual formulation of public policies even in matters unconnected with development. The fault was not that of the experts who displayed competence of high order, but proceeded from the appointment of ministers and other non-experts who, in their desire to exercise power and patronage, led the Commission to extend, at the cost of its main functions, its activities over many irrelevant fields. Gadgil suggested that both the Prime Minister and Finance Minister cease to be members of the Commission and that no Cabinet Minister should be a member, except perhaps the Minister for Planning if such a Minister continued to be in the Cabinet. Indeed, his whole emphasis was on the appointment of experts, more especially in the fields of natural sciences, technology, social sciences, statistics and economics.[23]

Planning in the States

There is a basic difference between planning at the Centre and planning in the States. The Centre has to draw a viable plan for the whole of the country, while the States need not go beyond producing a number of projects to be fitted into an all-India plan. The concern of the Centre is to sort out priorities in terms of resources. But being dependent upon the Centre for finance, the States unload on it a list of what they propose to do and leave to the Planning Commission the task of relating their proposals to financial availabilities. Some States in fact regard planning as a peripheral function which is discharged by an official who combines planning with other onerous duties. The usual set-up, however, consists of a bureau of statistics or a planning department under a Secretary who also functions as a Development Commissioner exercising the status of Additional Chief Secretary.

The state administrative arrangements are not devised for the purposes of co-ordinating development programmes, the essence of planning. New responsibilities have of course been undertaken under new administrative devices. But the mode of organization and rules of procedure have changed little since British days. There has been, in addition, the old problem of built-in deparmental antagonisms, of which the most serious is that between Planning and Finance. While the first emphasizes development, the second sticks to economy. Both have merits in their respective fields, but the problem is that of striking a balance, which remains for the most part unresolved.

District Administration

The planning of a uniform system of district administration in modern India was first done by Warren Hastings (1772–85) who created on 14 May 1772 the office of Collector, with revenue and judicial functions united in the same person. Changes were from time to time effected in the constitution of that office to suit policy requirements. But imperial considerations as well as the heterogeneous character of Indian society finally combined to settle down in the post-Mutiny period to a form of district administration where the Collector united in his office on a permanent basis not only the settlement and collection of revenues, but also the administration of magisterial and criminal judicial functions. He remained the executive head of his district. In his *Minute on the Administration of Justice in British India* (1872) the Law Member of the Government of India (Sir James Fitzjames Stephen) made it clear that the social and political stability of the country would be seriously affected if the influence and authority of the District Officer were in any way diminished, more especially in the administration of law and order, the recognized mark of sovereign power in India. In spite of a division of authority under Dyarchy at the political level in the Provinces, there was little or no change in the functions of the Collector who continued, as before, to be answerable not only for general administration, but also for the administration of the 'nation building departments' placed under popular ministers.

To make the task of the Collector easier attempts were made to reconstitute the districts on a principle that provided elements of social and cultural contiguity. The introduction of even a limited measure of democracy under the 1919 Act called for such reconstitution. For, as the Government of India aptly pointed out in one of its memoranda to the Indian Statutory Commission in 1930, 'it is in the district administration that the Government establishes its most direct contact with the people. The district is a unit which has grown to be part of the people. It is not a mere administrative convenience, but may be regarded as an essential part of the organization of the community. It has established itself in this position, because it corresponds to certain fundamental characteristics of the people'.

The District Officer provided relief against petty tyrannies: it formed part of his duties to look after the promotion of agriculture, to help projects for improvement, to administer relief, to recommend suspension or remission of land revenue in the event of natural calamities, to preserve peace among agricultural classes, and, in short, to secure the welfare of the whole community living in the district. These were functions which remained traditionally attached to his office.[24] By virtue of his experience, his historical position and his status in the superior civil service, the Collector, as the head of district administration, could alone represent in their totality the policy, will and might of the Government. He continued through the ages to function in some form or other despite political instability at the centre or in the provinces. He continues so even now.

The sub-divisional system grew with the extended function of the state, especially in the post-Mutiny period, to meet the exigencies of relief operations against famines and epidemics, not only involving at places the problems of law and order on a mass scale, but also dictating the necessity of creating the self-governing institutions of local bodies as an agency to raise local resources for local needs in respect of such development activities as roads, sanitation, education, public health and the like. The sub-divisional system was aided by the erstwhile revenue agencies functioning at a still lower level of such smaller units as tehsils or talukas, whose revenue officers were also invested with the maintenance of law and order within limits. These were all governmental agencies of administration which functioned on the principle of bureaucratic despotism or, at best, on enlightened and parental principles, which in all cases remained authoritarian in the same way as Indian society itself.

Even so, there lay at the bottom of the official hierarchy the ancient institution of village council or panchayat which, though vague in terms of constitution and function, exercised traditionally a unique prestige and was a prelude to democracy, though not of course in the full modern connotation. The village community in the past consisted mainly of two elements—the proprietary class and the occupational or rural service class.[25] The proprietary element was in possession of social and economy power. Its bond of unity was kinship and jointly-held village property called coparcenary tenure comprising the bulk of joint sharers in addition to a major or chief sharer who acted as headman, influenced the village panchayat, and undertook on behalf of the government or a superimposed agency to pay for all coparceners, owning or cultivating. It was the chief sharer who served as link between the governmental or its official agency and the village community where he was primarily rooted. The occupational element, on the other hand, was bound to coparceners in an inferior relationship, cultivating their lands and rendering all kinds of rural services for them in return for the grant of what was called the *chākaran* or service lands.

The members of the village community in pre-British days were not bound by anything in the nature of a free contract. Even the owning and cultivating communities of joint sharers were kept together by the compulsions of the state of village property. What imparted corporateness to the village was the corporate character of village property which flowed from the recognition by the government or the superimposed agency of the exclusive right of the chief sharer to pay all others who possessed no separate records of right of their own. Transfer of landed property to any party outside the village became in these circumstances a rarity; for it was ultimately up to the chief proprietor or headman to allow or reject a transfer which, if at all necessary, took place within the village community itself. The general absence of legal records of rights to property not only restricted transferability but also limited the scope for social mobility. Indeed, the village community acted as a powerful instrument in the preservation of the traditional kinship-based caste order, of *status quo ante*. It was this unchanging pattern of Indian villages that led Metcalfe to de-cribe them as 'little republics', although B. R. Ambedkar, the leader of the Harijans, was perhaps unjustified in commenting that these 'village republics' have been the ruination of India.[26]

The revenue and rent laws of the British altered the old village system radically. Based on the principles of *laissez faire*, these laws defined all kinds of landed interest involved in agricultural opera-tions, and prepared through survey and settlement proceedings sepa-rate records of rights to property, which enabled individuals to transfer their interest in land freely and independently of chief proprietors. This was a result of British commercial capitalism which called for mobility in the transfer of landed property for the promotion of the colonial economy. The new economic trend was reflected in a series of administrative and judicial reforms which attempted to establish the primacy of law over custom, of legislative authority over individual discretion. Together they destroyed not only the collective responsi-bility of the village headman, but also the economy on which the corpo-rateness of the old village system was based. A Report of 1891 thus observed:

Whether ... it be *Lambardar* or landholder, the influences which have hith-erto held and controllec ·e masses are gradually being weakened under the levelling influence of British rule. Where there is a strong government giving protection equally to all, where there are impartial courts of justice and carefully prepared records of agricultural rights and holdings, the protecting arm of the more powerful individual is no longer needed by the once helpless many.[27]

Obviously, the establishment of statutory village panchayats under British rule was no act of restoration, no attempt to have the affairs of villages managed freely by villagers on their own. Their function was in fact to be restricted to the preservation of peace, and that through the agency of their traditional village watchmen, the chaukidars, who were to cease functioning as servants of village communities and become stipendiary servants of the government, under the immediate orders of local police officers. Lord Hastings, the Governor-General, resisted this move for a while. He argued that chaukidars must remain subservient to society, for he feared that if they became paid servants of the government they would behave as 'masters' of the people, and that an 'authority would be established, pregnant with the most odious tyranny'.[28] The change was for a time delayed. But by 1856 the entire chaukidari system had come to be integrated with the police force of the government. The chaukidars did become 'masters' of the people by representing the might and authority of the government in villages.

What immediately determined the creation of village panchayats under the British was the consideration of imperial security. Financial considerations soon came in, not only for the purpose of maintaining the chaukidari system, but also for what came to be known as rural development, a political dimension introduced to justify the expediency of local finance as a relief to imperial resources. Under Act VI of 1870, for instance, provisions were made to associate panchayats (town or village councils) with the management of the chaukidari system. The operation of this Act was extended in the 1890s to rural unions to seek the co-operation of villages. Schemes were proposed in 1903–4 to make village panchayats appear more attractive by giving them functions of a judicial and educational nature. But these remained inoperative for all practical purposes. The Report of the Royal Commission on Decentralization (1909) recommended a reconstitution of village panchayats with such powers as the trial of petty cases, the supervision of minor village works, the control of primary schools, and the management of fuel and fodder reserves. It also suggested certain financial allocations to enable the village panchayats to accomplish the objects of their institution. These recommendations were soon followed by those of the Bengal District Administration Committee (1915) which the Government of India had appointed to suggest measures to improve the administration of the districts, where, in view of the rising tide of revolutionary nationalism conditions had kept on steadily deteriorating. The Committee recommended that village panchayats should be reinvested with the supervision and control of the chaukidars within their local limits. Two chapters of its report were actually devoted to a discussion of local problems from the village upwards. And one of the recommendations which the Committee made was even to entrust local defence to village panchayats with powers to raise their own taxes to meet their requirements.

There was thus a growing realization that villages should be reinvested with the supervision and control of the security agencies of chaukidars as well as certain other functions of a developmental nature. But the real snag was the raising of financial resources. The villagers would not voluntarily tax themselves, nor would they collect taxes if introduced. Gokhale's Bill to establish a system of compulsory primary education had to be turned down largely on financial grounds. Moreover, villages could not function as self-government units under bureaucratic despotism. A corresponding structure of self-government was necessarily called for at higher levels. Indeed, it required a bold political decision and will to proceed on the lines suggested by the Royal Commission on Decentralization or the Bengal District Administration Committee.

History too was not of much help. Up to Lord Curzon's viceroyalty, there had been a firm determination to do what the Government thought was right for the Indian people. It did not matter whether Indians liked a measure or not. But that viceroyalty was followed by a state of indecision. The Home Government as well as the Government of India faltered. They neither ruled themselves nor let the people rule instead by concession. Dyarchy came in these circumstances. 'Nation building' departments were set up under Indian ministers. There was renewed activity in devising a legislative framework for administrative panchayats, more especially in terms of their size, which became a lively subject for debate. The constitution of local bodies was liberalized. But the Congress remained non-cooperative. Dyarchy failed to bring about any change at the grass roots level and the period that followed was one of political tension, not of rural reconstruction.

However, villages had started gaining in importance ever since the beginnings of limited democracy under Dyarchy and the resulting mass politics in the form of the non-cooperation movement under Gandhi's leadership led social workers, political scientists and administrators to try and understand the community and group behaviour of castes and tribes in multi-dimensional situations. Together they reinforced the significance of village panchayats which, in the emerging democratic context, began to be viewed in a light that had hardly any relevance to history. A perusal of the *Directions of Settlement Officers in the N. W. Provinces* (1948) and Thornton's *Notes* on them would make it abundantly clear that village communities in pre-British days were by no means a decentralized democracy or specimens of a self-govering community.[29] The person who governed was the *Lambardar* or village headman. He was a major sharer of the landed property held in common or with other sharers; and the principles on which he governed were local custom or usage, the basis of consensus, not of the rule of law or free contract, the basis of modern democracy. The old village community was of course a corporate body. But that was a result of compulsions imposed by common ancestry, common responsibility for the payment of revenue, common militia for defence and, above all, the absence of individual records of rights to property which, for fear of fraudulent, though legal, sales through manipulation of fictitious balances of revenue, obliged coparceners to remain loyal to their chief as a matter of course.[30] Another important factor which helped a headman of local influence to impose his will on the community was the weakness of the government itself, for no strong government would easily brook an arrogation of its authority by an individual, howsoever powerful.[31]

Gandhi, however, idealized the vision of rural India and attributed to it the qualities he sought to inspire in the India of his dreams. Drawn from Tolstoy and Kropotkin, his political philosophy rejected the modern state as a foreign accretion upon India, which he visualized as a federation of village republics. The nearest approach to civilization based on non-violence was, according to him, the erstwhile village republic of India.[32] The post-Independence Panchayati Raj Acts were said to have been inspired by Gandhi's own view, without the necessary material conditions ever being present or even currently available in support of that view.

Under the 1947 Act, Uttar Pradesh started with *Gaon Sabhas* or administrative panchayats, each such panchayat consisting of three to four villages with a population of about a thousand. It was later narrowed, so that each village with a minimum population of 250 had its own panchayat. This was in the 'small panchayat' group of states which also included Bombay, Madhya Pradesh and Punjab. The 'big panchayat' group of states, on the other hand, had a panchayat for every four to five villages. These included Andhra Pradesh, Bihar, Himachal Pradesh, Kerala, Madras and Rajasthan. The trend was on the whole towards a large unit. For, as the *Report of the Team for the Study of Community Projects and National Extension Service* (Balvantray G. Mehta Team) showed, 'Little panchayats constituted for small villages are generally swayed by narrower considerations and sometimes dominated by caste interests which are toned down in a bigger body, comprising a number of villages inhabited by practically all castes. Membership of such a body infuses a wider outlook and a sense of responsibility which transcends narrow and parochial considerations.[33]

A massive attempt was in the meantime made to involve the villagers and the ordinary people of India in a new movement of Community Development designed to create in the millions of rural families a strong desire to change their outlook and enthuse them for new knowledge and the will to live a better life. It was started in 1952 by the Prime Minister, Jawaharlal Nehru, who seemed to have been inspired by the Etawah Pilot Project first established in 1948 by the Government of Uttar Pradesh under the guidance of Albert Mayer, an American expert in the field. The principle on which he proceeded to work was merely to assist the village folk to acheive what they themselves desired rather than what the Government thought was good for them. It was a radical departure from the traditional line of action. Mayer's whole object was to organize a co-operative effort with villagers and government technicians pulling together as a team and removing the age-old barrier between aloof officials and docile villagers.

The Etawah Project was recognized as a model of development administration for rural reconstruction. Great emphasis was laid on the Village Level Worker (*Gram Sewak*) functioning as a social worker in the midst of a small group of villages rather than as a minor government servant. An important feature of the Project was that its organization and staff operated as an autonomous unit, not immediately subject to control by the administrators. The success of the Etawah Project was undoubted. But apart from the advantage of its support from the highest authority in the country, Mayer's single-minded leaderhip as well as the sincere services of his colleagues were in no small measure responsible for that success.

However, as the scope of the Etawah Project was enlarged, the 'felt needs' of the people became submerged in the all-India programme of Community Development and National Extension Service initiated by the government in 1952. Fifteen pilot projects were inaugurated in different states on the Etawah model of a 'block' of 60 to 100 villages under a Block Development Officer, the block being divided into circles of 5 to 6 villages under the *Gram Sewak* or the Village Level Worker. By 1958 the number of such blocks rose to 2,361, covering nearly three-fifths of rural India.[34] The Extension Service, on the other hand, covered nearly three-quarters of India's villages by 1962. The conflict between the normal system of routine administration and the exigency of developmental administration which had in practice afflicted Mayer's team at Etawah, now spread all over India. The reason was not far to seek. In the context of an authority-oriented society, the subordinate status of officers functioning on the development side could not impart speed to the implementation of development projects which the people, by nature and habit, were not inclined to treat as part of their own felt needs. They viewed the projects as the work of government, not their own. Society and politics were in fact both averse to attaching prestige to such individuals or classes as engaged in any kind of manual work, industrial or agricultural.

There was yet another difficulty. The officers on the development side were after all government servants. The rules governing their conduct and service conditions could not possibly be different from those of others functioning on the executive side. There could not be two sets of civil service regulations and secretariat rules, one for development purposes and the other for the executive. Both had to conform alike to the requirements of written orders to be recorded on files. In the absence of public spirit, a fear of punishment could alone ensure expedition in the transaction of public business. But in the framework of rules governing conditions of service punishments are not easily carried out.

In these circumstances, the Government had no alternative but to resolve the conflict by a resort to history. In 1955, all development functions were transferred to the charge of the District Officer within his district. It was hoped that by virtue of his status, influence and authority he would be able to serve as the most effective instrument of social and economic progress. This policy decision marked a shift of emphasis from his traditional revenue and magisterial functions to those of social and economic development. Free India thus carried forward the old tradition of district administration which eminent administrators like Holt Mackenzie and Sir George Campbell in the nineteenth century as well as Maxwell and Tottenham in the more recent past had built on the combined principle of function and power. The only difference was that provision was now made for a senior civil servant to function as Development Commissioner at the state headquarters and to guide Collectors in matters of development. This resolution of the top-level problem of co-ordination in the districts was an expression of a tendency to push upwards the level of effective decision-making, a tendency which had set in with a decline in standards of administration on account of a shortage of experienced administrators after Independence. The administrative machine, though sound in essentials and capable of improvement, had undoubtedly become impaired because the parts removed from it in the post-Independence period were replaced in many instances by those of inferior material, a result, as pointed out earlier, of rapid promotion and excessive expansion.

This upward push in the level of decision-making meant that a few highly-placed civil servants became loaded with unreasonably heavy work. It led to the centralization of authority and responsibilities. Simultaneously, it also highlighted the danger of relying too much upon delegation or democratic institutions, especially at the level of village panchayats. For it was realized that if peasant involvement in development work happened to grow, the role of the District Officer and his tradition of being in overall charge of district administration would not remain unchallenged. The realization was not without reason. The report of the team headed by Balvantray Mehta clearly brought out the poor performance of most village panchayats, which were torn by factional rivalries, aggravated by elections based on separatism arising out of caste distinctions. Committees were of course formed for different purposes. But the community as a whole showed no interest and panchayats were dominated by upper-caste, prosperous elements. As early as 1954 the Minister for Local Self-Government in Uttar Pradesh had made similar remarks about the panchayats. They had the power to impose taxes, but did not use it; taxes in force were not even collected; panchayat members were themselves frequent defaulters; of the funds collected at least half were absorbed by administrative costs, and there, too, a large number of panchayats rendered no accounts at all. The district boards and other local bodies were no better.[35]

It is interesting to note the similarity in the functioning of panchayats established under Regulation 13 of 1813[36] for the appointment and maintenace of chaukidars. Under this Regulation the principal residents of a 'town, village or mahalla' were to nominate up to four people to constitute a panchayat, and they were then authorized by the District Magistrate to regulate and superintend the assessment, collection and payment of chaukidars. The panchayat fixed the amount of monthly quotas in consultation with a convenient number of householders according to the known circumstances of every shopkeeper or householder. The assessment so made was modified annually and the panchayat could use its chaukidars in the collection of the rates which could be realized by means of distraint in case of neglect. However, instances soon began to occur in which members of the panchayat exempted their connexions, friends and the richer classes from payment of the usual assessment. It was naturally feared that the extension of this system to towns and villages remote from the personal control of Magistrates might lead to a further abuse of authority by the panchayats: thus, while assessment was taken over by Magistrates, chaukidars were placed immediately under the control of police *darogas*. It took time for the restoration of the self-governing institutions. But history repeated itself and experiences showed that the supersession of a large number of municipal and rural boards in the recent past should be a matter of no surprise.

Structurally, however, the importance of village panchayats and their links with the administration above could not be over-emphasized. In the zamindari and jagirdari areas it was necessary to create a new system of village administration, with village records that might facilitate the administration of revenue after the abolition of intermediaries. This immensely difficult task could not be accomplished except by a popular and/or governmental agency functioning at the level of villages. Elsewhere, too, such an agency could not be dispensed with for reasons of policy, which called for the imposition of restrictions on the rights of large landholders and the conferment of new rights on tenants and agricultural labourers. In both cases, sustained administrative action was needed at various levels reaching down to the village. Likewise, there was simultaneously the problem of guiding and co-ordinating the various technical services, each of which was trying to reach the cultivator through its own ill-trained and departmentally-minded personnel. Their goal was diffused and their attention divided. It was therefore suggested by the planners that the basic solution of these problems was to emphasize the implementation of development programmes in close co-operation and with the active support of the people. This was sought to be done by (i) establishing an appropriate agency for development at the village level which derived its authority from the village community, and (ii) linking local self-governing institutions with the agencies of the state government. The Panchayati Raj Acts, the administrative arrangements of Community Development and the National Extension Service were but expressions of opinion which believed in people's co-operation as the best means of plan implementation.

The dichotomous situation of district administration was, however, not realized; there was an obvious contradiction between the desire to promote democracy by relying on those elected by popular vote and the apparently decadent condition of most of the existing self-governing bodies. The Planning Commission none the less suggested the conferment by legislation of a large number of responsibilities on the village panchayats and a Development Commissioners' Conference held at Mysore in 1959 even went to the extent of producing a list of 41 functions which were sought to be assigned to village panchayats.[37]

Despite the condition of most self-governing institutions, the pro-panchayat trend proceeded from a decline in the administrative capacity of the bureaucracy. A 1961 O & M Division paper on 'Administrative Capacity'[38] attributed this decline to 'increasing pressures for centralization of authority and responsibilities', which limited the scope of delegation 'necessary in an administration growing rapidly in responsibilities'. Apart from the reasons already explained for centralization, the paper gave other reasons which obstructed delegation. Two were political in character: (1) the 'increase in the number of representations to the top levels of administration—particularly to the political elements in administration—one of the inevitable consequences of the democratic process', and (2) the 'liability of ministries to parliamentary accountability and public scrutiny of their policies and of the details of their activities'. While each representation meant an increase in work and called for explanations or facts, in contrast with the simplified administration of the pre-Independence period, parliamentary accountability and the fear of public criticism called for 'elaborate rules to govern decisions' at the top level and led to 'excessive reporting' and the necessity of a feed-back process in cases of doubt. These requirements could not be met except by centralization. To these were added two other factors, derived from the multiplication of the new administrative responsibilities. The first was the need for 'greater attention' from senior officials and political workers 'continuing activities'. The second, on the other hand, was the dilution of the quality of administrative personnel in the field, as able and experienced officers were 'drawn increasingly to the Secretariat to assist in the formulation of policy and its implementation'. In many cases executive activities which formed part of district administration got shifted to the Secretariat, which produced 'distortions' in the distribution of the time of senior officers and also pushed 'the decision making on comparatively minor problems to higher levels besides increasing the cost of administration'. A further reason for the concentration of authority was an obvious failure to discover, or even to seek with persistence, adequate motivation for the acceptance of responsibility by civil servants at the lower levels of the hierarchy, the levels of executive action. The O & M Paper therefore emphasized that 'while procedures and relationships are the anatomy of administration, men are its life-giving force. The development of the men and their proper motivation can make all the difference, given reasonable organization and methods of work'.[39] And it is here that, barring individual exceptions, the bureaucracy as a class was found wanting, especially at the lower executive levels.

Burdened with all his former responsibilities, the District Officer was now called upon to inspire and co-ordinate development, a function which rarely formed part of his principal concern. He was expected to share this responsibility with a committee which remained, for all practical purposes, no more than a formality. He generally transferred his burden to the District Planning Officer, but the departmental district-level officials often resented the interposition of the D.P.O., who often happened to be their junior. The role of the District Officer in fact tended to become more or less quasi-political and involved with the reception of leaders and their conferences. He hardly found the time for serious inspection which tended increasingly to become perfunctory, or for lengthy tours to rural areas where his predecessors in British days were required to spend anything up to half the year in camp. The I.C.S. tradition was of course sought to be adopted by members of the I.A.S. But this was more a gesture than reality, for the environment in which I.A.S. officers worked had changed not only in terms of society and politics but also in the nature and magnitude of the task required to be handled. In short, the union of executive and development functions in the office of Collector, though politically expedient to an extent, proved in most cases injurious to both in terms of speed and efficiency. Likewise, this situation applied in principle to the Sub-Divisional Officer within the limits of his own jurisdiction, although the establishment of the Block Development Officer reduced his importance in respect of development, which became the immediate function of the B.D.O., acting in collaboration with the concerned departmental officer in the district.

The B.D.O. became (and still is) the actual supervisor of development in the field. He was to be assisted at the block headquarters by a number of officers representing agriculture, social education, panchayats and co-operatives, usually including even an engineer, a veterinary officer and health visitor. Except in Bihar[40] and Bombay where all B.D.O.s were recruited from the revenue service, a B.D.O. belonged to no fixed service. He came either from the agriculture or veterinary departments. His was in fact an assorted group, including some university graduates and promotees from the ranks of *Gram Sevaks* or Village Level Workers.

The Village Level Worker, as said before, emerged originally from the Etawah Project and soon became an integral part of the Community Development Schemes which envisaged him as the vital link between government and people, designed to encourage popular initiative in the work of development. In practice, however, this objective remained for the most part unrealized. The duties assigned to the *Gram Sevak* formed a considerable list which included agriculture, animal husbandry and irrigation; welfare of the community; help to youth, women and those in need of special assistance. As a *Gram Sevak* he was indeed expected to serve villagers in general as a humble servant. In Bihar, where development and revenue functions were united, the *Gram Sevak* also functioned as a *Karmachari* in his revenue capacity under the immediate control of the B.D.O. In the earlier phase of their institution *Gram Sevaks* had acquired a place of pride among villagers, because when Community Development programmes were first launched, government funds were made available for distribution among village folk in the form of subventions and credits for a variety of purposes. But when this phase tapered off, their importance declined and their role became nebulous. Instead of moving through villages, some *Gram Sevaks* began to expect villagers to come to their 'offices' for their requirements. The *Gram Sevak* was in turn put in his place by the B.D.O. who summoned him to his block headquarters on the slightest grounds or displeasure. A hierarchic bureaucratic relationship came into being and a total absence of the team concept of development which the originators of Community Development had envisaged. Those who were expected to act as pioneers in a new venture of nation-building became mere cogs in the traditional bureaucratic machine, losing all sense of drive and initiative.

The Mehta Report of 1957 provided for some social checks to curb the bureaucratic and hierarchic tendencies of administration. It recommended a policy of 'democratic decentralization' on a national scale where the traditional executive agencies of the Central and State governments would divest themselves of certain responsibilities and entrust these to locally selected bodies for purposes of development planning and administration. It proposed a three-tier system of local government. The first level was to consist of the directly elected village panchayat for the development of five to six villages included in the panchayat. The *Gram Sevak* was to act as the secretary of the panchayat. The next tier was that of a *panchayat samiti*, composed of the heads of each village panchayat situated within the limits of a block and presided over by a *pradhan* or chairman elected from among the members of the *samiti*, which was invested with the control of the entire resources of the block. The Block Development Officer was to be responsible to the *samiti* as its secretary in the same way as the *Gram Sevak* was to the village panchayat. The third level was the *zila parishad* (district committee) comprising all the chairmen of the *samitis* within the district. The members of the *zila parishad* so formed were to elect their own chairman or *pramukh* and the District Officer was to function as the secretary of the *parishad*.

The Mehta Report was endorsed by a National Conference on Community Development held at Mount Abu in May 1958, and subsequently by a Conference of the local self-government ministers of all the States meeting at Hyderabad in October 1959. It was generally recognized that as Community Development expanded rapidly in the late 1950s, contact with villagers had been lost. In spite of a desire for economic improvement which the scheme stimulatd to some extent, no two-way communication had been established between the villages and the higher levels of administration.[41] The Mehta Report thus provided for links to ensure communication between the people and the government at each of the three levels of development administration in the districts. Who constituted these links? While the administrative side had its links in the *Gram Sevak*, the B.D.O. and the District Officer, their counterparts on the people's side were the *panchayat*, the *panchayat samiti* and the *zila parishad*. The links on both sides were, however, to function as a unified body, as an integral part of a common machanism of development administration. The links so provided could not achieve the object of their institution. The provision for social checks on the bureaucracy remained for the most part inoperative: the bureaucracy ruled the roost.

Indeed, there was no alternative to bureaucratic dominance. There were historical reasons for this: the original basis on which panchayats functioned was not law but custom under which they recognized hereditary privileges and punished offences according to caste considerations and the capacity of the accused to bear punishment rather than the degree of criminality. There was no rule of law, no civil or penal code based on legislative enactment, no criminal procedure, no law of evidence. All these developed in the course of about 200 years of British rule. To these were added the statutory provisions enacted since 1904 and recommended as a matter of policy by the Royal Commission of Decentralization and subsequent committees. These recommendations were later enlarged and incorporated into the Panchayat Acts of several States in the post-Independence period. The modern panchayats are thus constituted under legislative enactments and required to function within the framework of law, of which they have little appreciation. They have to act on the principle of legal and social equality which the elders of the village community often consider repugnant to caste privileges. In short, the principles of social organization in the Indian situation bore no correspondence to those which shaped the development of the political and administrative institutions of modern India. There remained over the years a huge gap between the two. How could there be proper communication between a tradition-bound panchayat and a rule-bound administration, especially in a situation where the latter at its lower levels was generally devoid of a sense of public service, while the former was found wanting in its understanding of social needs and obligations? Ill-educated and also divided on the basis of caste or group rivalries, the elected elements of popular bodies could not act as a cohesive force to keep the administrative agencies in their proper place. And in case they did succeed in forging unity, there was the provision for the use of the co-optive principle, which could enable officers at all three levels to break that unity by co-opting members and inviting them to join on the grounds of securing representation for such groups as the backward classes, women, and the like.

The task of revitalizing the institution of village panchayats as part of rural reconstruction in fact involved an educational issue of great magnitude. Without an educational programme comparable to the people's colleges in Scandinavian countries, any attempt to extend village panchayats as a step towards democratic decentralization made a mockery of democracy. In the absence of proper education and training the delegation of power to panchayats under statutory provisions intensified caste rivalries and group jealousies. It did of course tend to unsettle the traditional structure of land-based power relationships, but the effect was on the whole reactionary, reinforcing the divisive tendencies of caste instead of uniting villages as viable units of local self-government. Elections to local bodies on party lines made the situation worse by imparting political sanction to traditional social divisions.

It was precisely to obviate such tendencies that Gandhi had earlier devised his scheme of basic education, a work-based scheme for rural education which, instead of division, emphasized co-operation as an instrument of social change. It was first put to trial during 1917–18 in the organization of the peasantry in Champaran[42] and later recommended in 1938 by Zakir Husain's committee as part of a unified system of general and vocational education.[43] Unfortunately, basic education, too, was not properly implemented and its objectives remained unfulfilled.

The Higher Civil Service—Its Social Background

Despite the extraordinarily large number of responsibilities conferred by legislation on village panchayats, the hierarchy of executive administration continues to dominate the field of development. This hierarchy is vested with considerable discretionary powers which are exercised without any resistance or check from the local bodies. Other institutional sources of control no doubt exist, such as an effective legislative system, political parties, and a well-organized judiciary, all of which restrain the bureaucracy in the use of its discretionary powers. In the day-to-day functioning of administration and its decision-making, however, the effectiveness of these sources has not been as perceptible as that of the changing cultural and social background of regular recruits to the I.A.S., which constitutes the core of the higher civil service.

The increasing strength of non-elitist and lower middle-class elements in the I.A.S. started imparting to it an egalitarian character that generally distinguished it from the I.C.S. There are, no doubt, independent variables, such as caste, family upbringing and the kind of early education received, which go into the making of values reflected in bureaucratic decisions. But the socio-economic status of recruits is recognized as a major factor in effecting a change of attitude towards common people as well as towards their own environment of work, a change which recruits in recent years manifested noticeably in terms of adaptability and resilience, without making any radical departure from the basic service concept underlying the I.C.S. It is this development in the social pattern of recruitment that conduced to egalitarianism in bureaucratic thought and action, expecially at the level of the higher civil service.

A socio-economic analysis by R. K. Trivedi and D. N. Rao of 615 direct recruits to the I.A.S. from 1948 to 1960 shows that, unlike the I.C.S., the I.A.S. was not a close-knit and exclusive body.[44] The Trivedi-Rao data for 1948–60 and the figures for the very first three years of recruitment make it clear that from its very beginning the I.A.S. was a heterogeneous service. In fact, the first batch started with war-service recruits who, far from being subjected to a formal training, were sent out to the provinces without an interview before the Federal Public Service Commission. According to Srinivasavaradan, out of 1,830 officers appointed in the I.A.S. during 1948–60, 216 (11.8 per cent) belonged to the I.C.S., 91 (4.9 per cent) were war-service officers, 198 (10.8 per cent) were emergency recruits from the open market, 255 (13.8 per cent) came from the emergency recruitment of the States, 472 (25.7 per cent) were promotees from the state civil services and only 598 (32.6 per cent) were direct recruits.[45]

Educationally, too, the direct recruits of the I.A.S. cadre contained a considerable number of persons holding less than a first class degree. The corresponding position of the I.C.S. was much higher, as is shown in the following table which gives the position as on 1 January 1961:[46]

Cadre	Size	First Class		Second Class		Third Class	
		No.	%	No.	%	No.	%
I.C.S.	156	109	96.9	46	29.5	1	0.6
I.A.S. (D.R.)	615	348	56.6	245	39.9	22	3.5

Another feature that developed over the years was that the percentage of those with a first class degree in the I.A.S. did not remain steady but showed a marked decline

Up to 1960, 79 per cent of the I.A.S. direct recruits had urban backgrounds. Subsequent trends showed that, while the dominance of urban backgrounds continued, the percentage of candidates coming from rural areas showed a noticeable increase. A survey conducted by the U.P.S.C. revealed that, of the 165 candidates recommended for appointment to the I.A.S. and the Indian Foreign Service in 1975, as many as 50 came from villages, 32 from towns and 83 from cities. The survey indicated that the percentage of those from rural areas had reached 30.30 in 1975. The public school background of candidates also registered a steady rise; for the percentage of those who had studied in public schools was 29.68 in 1973 but rose to 33.94 in 1975.[47]

In terms of economic status, most direct recruits to the I.A.S. came from the middle-income group, ranging between Rs 300 to Rs 800 per month, and some from the lower group below Rs 300 per month. As the following table indicates, the position on 1 January 1961 presents a contrast with the higher economic status of the I.C.S. people:[48]

Cadre	Category A Above Rs 800	Category B Between Rs 300 and Rs 800	Category C Below Rs 300
I.C.S.	75.6%	21.2%	3.2%
I.A.S.	32.9%	58.2%	8.9%

With the downward filtration of education, we learn from the U.P.S.C. survery of 1975 that most of the direct recruits to the I.A.S. came from the lower income group.[49] This indication of a perceptible change in the social background of the Service afforded the opportunity to other sectors of the public services, as well as to the elites in the academic, technical and industrial fields, to challenge the traditional superiority of the bureaucracy.

Politically, however, this non-elitist trend in the I.A.S. and its heterogeneous composition brought it nearer the total pattern and needs of Indian democracy. The I.A.S. did retain some of the elitist attributes of the I.C.S. But its transformation from the elitist cadre of the British Raj to a mere higher civil service enabled it to fit in with the political requirements to the post-Independence period and get reconciled with the general pattern of political behaviour in government and society. As said before, clashes of course did occur between secretaries and ministers. But those who so resisted and showed independence of judgement were members of the I.C.S., the elitist cadre, who, in terms of social and economic status as well as educational and cultural attainments, had little in common with most of their political bosses.

Unlike the I.C.S., which had been a composite service, the direct recruits in the I.A.S. as on 1 January 1961 were Hindu to the extent of nearly 90 per cent; Sikh, 4.4 per cent; Christian, 2.9 per cent; and Muslim, 1.9 per cent.[50] Even though the social background of the I.A.S. was changing perceptibly in the direction of lower income groups, the pace of change was slow; for no fewer than 44.4. per cent of the I.A.S. recruits since 1948 came from families already in government service. The fathers of the remainder in 1960 and thereabout were teachers (13.4 per cent), lawyers (9.4 per cent), businessmen (9.9 per cent), agriculturists (9.0 per cent), physicians (4.2 per cent) and 'others' (9.7 per cent).[51] Subsequent development, however, showed that entrants from families with incomes of less than Rs 300 a month increased in a marked degree. The reservation of seats for members of the Scheduled Castes and Scheduled Tribes added to the number of such entrants.

It was this increasingly egalitarian leavening amongst I.A.S. officers that led them to take care of agriculturists in rural areas, and not the organizational initiative or capacity of villagers themselves. Doubtless, there were and are exceptions, where the rural folk gave evidence of a progressive outlook and the power to resist administrative bungling and arrogance on the part of petty officials. But as the evaluation reports of development administration in the districts point out, the self-governing institutions have generally been known more for their division and inaction than unity and activity. The old tradition of paternal administration has naturally to continue to ensure economic development.

Administration and Politics

It is true that the social background of the new administrative service was such that it stimulated a tendency to recognize the demands of 'mass democracy' where, as a result of education, achievement and property, new classes emerge and endeavour to supplant old values, tastes and standards of morality. But habituated as administrators are to functioning within the framework of established rules, they tend to view even new and unique situations of a sociopolitical nature as falling within the realm of administration. Commenting on the psychology of bureaucracy, Karl Mannheim pointed out: 'Every bureaucracy tends to generalize its own experience and to overlook the fact that the realm of administration and of smoothly functioning order represents only a part of the total political reality. Bureaucratic thought does not deny the possibility of a science of politics, but regards it as identical with the science of administration. Thus irrational (unpredictable) factors (characterizing politics) are overlooked, and when these nevertheless force themselves to the fore, they are treated as "routine matters of state". A classic expression of this standpoint is contained in a saying which originated in these circles: "A good administration is better than the best constitution."'[52]

This precisely was the attitude of the bureaucracy during British rule, more especially under Lord Curzon, when bureaucratic efficiency was considered a panacea for everything. Politically, the

Morely-Minto Councils marked a break from the past. But administration showed no particular appreciation of the new social forces reflected in the emergence of the nationalist movement. Commenting on the Indian situation in 1918, the Montford Report thus said: 'We must make up our minds either to rule ourselves or to let the people rule: there is no half-way house.' The bureaucracy tried to govern by concession. But when faced with the paradoxical task of having to incorporate into its system new laws to satisfy the exigencies of politics, it treated these laws as only a further elaboration of the original system. The bureaucracy thus conduced to administrative continuity, a continuity which Indian bureaucrats maintained even after the British had left.

In these circumstances, the Panchayati Raj Acts or Mehta's three-tier system of democratic decentralization which aimed to promote popular participation in development work made little dent on the administration. It viewed the change as a mere elaboration of the old system of local administration conducted within the framework of rules as routine matters, with the panchayats, samitis or parishads acting more or less as rubber stamps. This became all the more possible in a situation of mass democracy where the power of making decisions became increasingly concentrated in fewer and fewer hands, particularly those of the administrative bureaucracy. In a caste-structured society like that of India, this concentration of administrative activity in the bureaucracy became easier, for, while mass democracy helped in the emergence of an increasing number of rural elites, the elites so emerging tended to cancel each other out. This is precisely what happened under the panchayati raj scheme, which could not provide a solid base for democracy as an alternative to bureaucracy. The stratified groups or individuals functioning in panchayats tended to cancel each other out, thus ensuring the continuance of bureaucratic control and the inability of democracy in its modern connotation to stabilize at the grass roots level.

Unlike administration, which deals with the settled, recurrent and rationalized patterns of social events in a prescribed and routinized manner, politics, theoretically speaking, begins with new and unpredictable situations where rationalization has not yet penetrated and decisions are sought to be made not by reference to precedent but in a manner yet to be reduced to regulation. The sphere of politics includes, for example, the conclusion of new treaties with foreign countries, legislative enactments on new measures of taxation, electoral campaigns, steps to handle a sudden upsurge of mass revolt or strikes, the formulation of a policy to nationalize industrial or commercial undertakings, and so on. In short, administration is prescriptive and politics prospective. Both are co-ordinate instruments of the state, but while the former tends to be static and stereotyped, the latter is forward-looking. Together, they conduce to stability and progress. The arrangement, however, represents the 'ideal type' and does not wholly apply to the Indian situation. Since the grass roots democracy of the panchayati raj model acted as a mere funnel to facilitate the downward filtration of political interests, specially for electoral purposes, it is the administration that continued to dominate the rural scene and act in a routinized manner independently of what might be called the 'prospective' goal of politics, if any. In view of the poverty of politics as a higher link for society, the bureaucracy remained the virtual arbitrator.

Attempts are doubtless made in all countries to identify party interests with those of a class or society itself on ideological grounds. The peculiarity of the Indian situation, however, arose from a couple of circumstances. The first was its colonial situation which, for historical reasons, enabled the Congress to have a virtual monopoly of political power representing a variety of ideological patterns. The second, on the other hand, was the peculiar constitution of Indian society which recognized no rule of law as the guiding principle of political conduct. Politics was bound by emotion and interest, but hardly sustained by society on principles of contract-based egalitarianism. The concept of ideology, which in its totality cuts across caste barriers, was, in these circumstances, bound to be weakened because of the diffused loyalty of a party's constituent members. The individual members of the Congress Party, for instance, participated only in certain fragments of the Party's declared ideology, the totality of which was by no means a mere sum of these fragmentary individual experiences. As a totality the thought-system inherent in the Party's ideology should have been integrated systematically in order to make sure that it did not become a jumble of fragmentary views presented by individual members. But none the less the whole body of the socialistic thought-system underlying the declared ideology of the Congress Party remained more or less fragmentary, reflecting the characteristic features of its heterogeneous and mutually exclusive social elements as well as of certain individual members who functioned within its power structure. The second chapter of this work makes clear that, while criticizing the British for what they called acts of exploitation, the Indian governors and ministers made no concessions in so far as their own rates of salaries, allowances and perquisites were concerned. Such was the dilution of the Party's egalitarian ideology that not only did the President of India and his governors follow the norms established earlier for the Viceroy and British governors respectively, but cases even occurred where certain Indian governors indulged in serious irregularities and often exceeded the limits of expenditure on items of luxury.

Reservations in Government Service

In the course of our discussion of the conceptual foundations of the civil services a reference has already been made to communal representation in the all-India services recruited directly by open competition. Our main emphasis in this section will be on reservations, for Scheduled Castes and Scheduled Tribes, although the principle of reservation also applied to released Emergency Commissioned Officers, Short Service Commissioned Officers, and ex-service men.[53]

The Scheduled Castes were initially recognized as 'Depressed Classes' and categorized systematically at the time of the 1931 Census. On the basis of the list of Depressed Classes recognized in 1931 the Government of India (Scheduled Castes) Orders, 1936 was issued under the Constitution Act, 1935. The first list of Scheduled Castes after Independence was drawn in 1950; it was a revised version of that issued in 1936. Similarly, a list of backward tribes was specified under the 1935 Act for the various provinces. And, as in the case of Scheduled Castes, the first list of Scheduled Tribes was, after Independence, drawn in 1950 by making additions to the list of backward tribes prepared under the 1935 Act.

In drawing up the list of Scheduled Castes the test applied was social, economic and educational backwardness, arising from the custom of untouchability. But in the absence of a universally acceptable definition of a tribe, tribes and tribal communities could not be easily specified, for in the Indian context they had for several decades remained tribes in transition. Even so, the Constitution drew up as complete a list as could possibly be made of both Scheduled Castes and Scheduled Tribes. The two separate lists were accordingly notified by the President in terms of Articles 341 and 342 of the Constitution, and it was laid down that there would be reservations in the services and posts under the Central Government for persons belonging to the Castes and Tribes included in these lists.[54]

The reservations provided for the Scheduled Castes in 1943 amounted to 8⅓ per cent of the posts recruited directly on an all-India basis. This percentage was enhanced to 12½ in 1946. Reservations for Scheduled Tribes were, on the other hand, provided for the first time in 1950. The 1978 percentage of reservations in all-India direct recruitment was 15 for the Scheduled Castes and 7½ for the Scheduled Tribes in respect of the posts filled by open competition, either through the U.P.S.C. or by open competitive tests held by any other authority. In other cases, this percentage was $16^2{}_3$ for the Scheduled Castes and 7½ for the Scheduled Tribes. In respect of candidates for local or regional appointment, the percentage of reservation for the Scheduled Castes and the Scheduled Tribes takes into account their share in the population of the State/Union Territory concerned, subject to a minimum of 5 per cent for the Scheduled Castes. These have all been calculated on the basis of the population figures of the 1971 Census which put the percentage of the Scheduled Castes at 14.60, and that of the Scheduled Tribes at 6.94. Reservations have also been provided in respect of posts filled by promotion up to the lower rung of Class I, subject only to direct recruitment, if any, to the grade not exceeding 50 per cent. In matters of promotion the principles applied included, within the limits of reservations, departmental competitive examination, selection and seniority. The reservation orders are, however, not to apply to posts which are classified as scientific and technical as well as to posts intended for conducting research or for organizing, guiding and directing research.

The reservations so made clashed with Article 16 of the Constitution which guaranteed certain Fundamental Rights in regard to equality of opportunity in matters of public employment. The conflict was, however, sought to be met in two ways. First, a special provision was made under Article 16(4) of the Constitution. It said that nothing could prevent the state from making provision for the reservation of appointments to posts in favour of any backward class which, in the opinion of the state, was not adequately represented in the services. Reservation was thus to flow from the Constitution itself. Secondly, it was laid down by Article 335 of the Constitution that the claims of the Scheduled Castes and Scheduled Tribes were to be considered in the context of the need to maintain efficiency of administration.

However, considerations of administrative efficiency were more in the nature of a formal declaration of policy than a reality. For Scheduled Caste and Scheduled Tribe candidates were not to be judged in comparison with other candidates. The interviewing authorities and boards were in fact made aware of the need to judge them with 'relaxed standards'. Provisions of course do exist for de-reservation in case a sufficient number of candidates fit for appointment to the vacancies reserved for them are not available. But no such de-reservation is done without the prior approval of the Department of Personnel and Administrative Reforms. And even if such approval is obtained, reservations are carried forward to three subsequent recruitment years. This naturally encourages a tendency amongst interviewing boards to apply a lower standard of recruitment to avoid being dubbed inimical to the interests of Scheduled Castes and Scheduled Tribes.

As regards promotion, reservation exists also to the extent of 15 and 7½ per cent respectively for Scheduled Castes and Scheduled Tribes. It applies to promotion made on the basis of limited competitive examinations in Class II, III and IV posts in grades and services to which direct recruitment, if any, does not exceed 50 per cent.[55] Here, as in the case of recruitment, regard for efficiency had to go by default. For in such examinations for promotion Scheduled Caste and Scheduled Tribe candidates unable to acquire the general qualifying standard, have also to be considered for promotion in case they are found fit on the standard being 'relaxed' in their favour. Further, in matters of promotion by selection, until 1974 reservation was admissible in Class III and IV posts only. The principle of selection, which was more or less an exercise of executive discretion, did not apply to higher ranks. In Class II and up to the lowest rung of Class I a concession of one grading higher was admissible. With effect from 20 July 1974, however, reservation has been provided by selection in or to Class II and up to the lowest rung of Class I posts. It was also provided that in promotions by selection to posts within Class I with an ultimate monthly salary of Rs 2000 or less, Scheduled Caste and Scheduled Tribe officers who are senior enough to be considered for promotion would be included in select lists drawn up for the purpose. The only criterion for their exclusion from the select list is that they are not considered unfit for promotion.

Though recruited or promoted on the basis of a relaxed qualifying standard, members of Scheduled Castes and Scheduled Tribes can claim to rise to the highest level of the administrative hierarchy merely by virtue of an accident of birth in a particular caste or community. Though politically paying to a party or group for a time, this exclusive and communal approach to public administration has not only the risk of destroying the administrative unity of the country, which is already being impaired by its linguistic divisions, but also the danger of perpetuating the divisive character of the Indian social system, which parties and groups in politics have indiscriminately been exploiting for political gains and personal advantages. In the policy so pursued, there is of course an element of social justice in the Indian context. The British too had realized this before they introduced communal representation in the public service under the Muddiman Pledge of 1925 and its subsequent modifications. But they avoided doing anything that might compromise with ability and integrity. They did not provide for reservations in promotion, for efficiency and quality of performance were paramount.[56] Pressed by political considerations under an egalitarian cover, however, the Government has not only relaxed standards of recruitment and promotion in respect of the Scheduled Castes and Scheduled Tribes but also made certain other concessions to them. These include, for instance, relaxation in age in the matter of recruitment, which provides that the maximum age limit prescribed for direct recruitment to a service or post may be enhanced by five years. They are also allowed a 15 per cent reduction in the fees prescribed for admission to any examination or selection to a service. Provision exists for payment of railway fares to those called for departmental interviews to Class III and Class IV advertised posts, and the U.P.S.C., in any case, gives travelling allowances for interviews for all Class I and Class II posts.

The Government has, in addition, taken care to ensure that the reservations and other orders relating to concessions are followed scrupulously by the several ministries and departments. Liaison officers of the rank of Deputy Secretary have, for example, been nominated by them for work relating to special representation in various ministries and departments, including Attached and Subordinate Offices. Their business is to ensure that instructions issued from time to time in this behalf are strictly complied with. Special Cells have been set up under Liaison Officers to assist them in the discharge of their duties. Annual statements showing particulars of recruitment made have to be submitted by the appointing authorities to the administrative ministries to make sure that all possible steps are taken to comply with reservations and other orders. The Constitution also provides for the appointment of a Commissioner for Scheduled Castes and Scheduled Tribes, a Special Officer, whose duty it is to investigate matters relating to the safeguards provided under the Constitution for Scheduled Castes and Scheduled Tribes, and report to the President upon the working of those safeguards. The Commissioner, who is appointed by the President, submits his annual reports to Parliament which *inter alia* cover reservations for all Scheduled Castes and Scheduled Tribes in government services. There are, in addition, a Parliamentary Committee to ensure their welfare, and a Higher Power Committee under the chairmanship of the Prime Minister. The latter reviews from time to time the representation of Scheduled Castes and Scheduled Tribes in services and posts under the Central Government, including public sector undertakings.

The unexceptionable emphasis on special treatment for certain castes has produced distortions of two kinds. More and more people want to be listed as backward merely to become beneficiaries of special dispensations. Secondly, the benefits so provided for historical and other reasons have in practice tended to be appropriated by the more articulate in the depressed and backward communities and groups. The result is that those who are really poor and deserving are often left out. The caste-based arrangement not only hardens the age-old caste system, but creates a class within a class.

Personnel Motivation

The civil and the commercial functions of the East India Company were separated for the first time under the Regulating Act of 1773, which laid down a code of conduct for civil servants who were not to engage in the Company's commercial transactions or to accept any bribe. Warren Hastings acted on this principle and made a serious beginning to create out of the existing trading personnel a civil service better fitted to discharge civil duties.

The motivating element in the formative period of the service was, of course, not money, although the salary of a Collector, for instance, was raised to Rs 1,200 a month. It was emphasized that the power, prestige and dignity of a civil servant were not to flow from affluence, but from his integrity and uprightness of conduct. In terms of worldly gain a commercial resident maintained a standard of comfort which a Collector could never afford.[57] But an increasing emphasis on education, honesty and the conscientious discharge of public duties could enable the latter to wield an authority that might supersede the influence of wealth.

The quality of the service and its motivation, however, did not remain unrelated to emoluments. Motivation in fact soon become a function of pay structure, especially under the government of Lord Wellesley (1798-1805), who believed that the stability of British imperial interests in India lay not in 'the instruments by which kingdoms are overthrown, revolutions are accomplished, or, wars conducted', but in a civil service capable of 'an inexhaustible supply of useful knowledge, cultivated talents and disciplined morals'.[58] The emoluments of the civil service which had already registered a considerable increase under Cornwallis, thus rose further under Wellesley.[59] I.C.S. officers continued to draw a rate of pay which attracted the best talents, except when politics and inflation began to act as a deterrent, towards the close of the First World War and thereafter.[60]

However, the I.C.S. formed after all only a small proportion of the entire body of government servants. The Central Government employees, who constituted the bulk, increased enormously in numbers in the course of the Second World War and kept on increasing in the post-Independence period. It was the exigencies of social and economic development which, despite the continuous administrative expansion, caused impatience, disappointment and even a search for scapegoats. No attempt was made to screen the quality of men who held the levers of administration, or to encourage motivation in the bulk of the personnel resources available in abundance. A census conducted by the Directorate General of Employment and Training revealed that, as on 31 March 1972, there were as many as 30.56 lakh government employees as compared to 22 lakhs at the end of March 1963, most employees being non-gazetted. Of the 28.11 lakh employees in 1970, for instance, only 1.9 per cent were gazetted and the rest were non-gazetted, including for the most part clerical and inferior staff. Of the total only 3 per cent of the regular Central Government employees drew a monthly pay of Rs 500 and above, the number of persons in the different pay ranges above Rs 500 being as follows:[61]

Pay Range Rs		Number	% of total
500–749	—	49,247	1.86
750–999	—	15,463	0.58
1,000–1,499	—	10,239	0.39
1,500–1,999	—	2,241	0.08
2,000–2,499	—	603	0.02
2,500–2,999	—	332	0.01
3,000 and above	—	189	0.01

The emoluments of most Central Government employees were thus below Rs 500 a month. The salary structure and personnel administration were in fact not based on the sound principle of compensation, a principle that might improve motivation and provide an incentive for hard and sustained work. Doubtless, pay scales were duly prescribed for various posts and promotion prospects provided on some rationale. But there has been no systematic link between the quality of performance and compensation on the basis of a proper system of appraisal. The confidential character roll system, which was first introduced by Lord William Bentinck (1828–35), has, of course, existed as a mode of appraisal. But, in practice, it has often degenerated into a routine annual exercise to be completed under pressure from the administrative section of a department.

Moreover, the system of appraisal introduced under the British was punishment-oriented rather than reward-oriented: the utmost that could be done for an outstanding worker was to give him an outstanding remark about his performance, which might help in his promotion. A poor worker could no doubt be taken to task, but it was generally considered expedient to let sleeping dogs lie because of the procedural complexities necessarily involved in securing punishment. In between the outstanding and the poor worker, there were those with various shades of competence which could not adequately be handled by the system. They continued on the same incremental scale, drawing the same periodical increment with the outstanding and the poor worker. There is in fact often a progression in pay without a corresponding progression in performance—a system where performance and its appraisal remain for the most part unrelated to compensation, and does not adequately motivate personnel.

There are, of course, other reasons which tend to kill motivation. These, for example, include the want of clarity or decision at policy-making levels, a decline in the standards of honesty and administrative culture, wrong juxtaposition of power and responsibility, and the operation at times of certain inept and ill-conceived rules and regulations relating to personnel administration. But basically the pay structure and adequacy of compensation, especially at the middle and lower levels of the bureaucratic hierarchy, remains by far the most important that propel men to action.

The first Pay Commission (1946–7) threw practically no new light on the problem of pay structures and compensation. Its approach was virtually that of the Islington Commission (1912–15), which had laid down that 'Government should pay so much and so much only to their employees as is necessary to obtain recruits of the right stamp and to maintain them in such a degree of comfort and dignity as will shield them from temptation and keep them efficient for the term of their service'. Suggestions were doubtless made to meet the disparities of remuneration prejudicial to efficiency. But no consideration was given to the rise in prices except the recognition of a general principle that a man's pay should in no case be less than a living wage which, of course, had to keep in view not only the status and dignity of an officer, but also the comparable rates of pay outside, more especially in private industry. A new development which, however, engaged the attention of the first Pay Commission was a realization of the need to formulate a social policy which might lay down the ratio between the maximum and minimum salaries. On the question of fixing the intermediate salaries the Commission expressed itself in favour of maintaining or establishing satisfactory vertical relativities within a service or hierarchy of services and horizontal relativities between one set of services and another.

The second Pay Commission (1957–9), however, did not recognize that the social position a government servant was traditionally expected to maintain should itself be a factor of any importance in determining his remuneration. The second Pay Commission did consider the concept of the Government being a model employer, but this concept could lend itself to varied interpretation. One interpretation was that the state might function as a class by itself and make available to its employees a standard of comfort in terms of pay, promotion and other amenities that comparable classes outside the Government could never hope to get. However, if the state were to become a model employer in this sense, it would ordinarily expose itself to a well-founded criticism of extravagance, with the community being required to pay a price which the public service hardly merited. The Commission therefore concluded that the Government could not be a model employer in this sense. Even so, it did not mean that the Government had no special obligations as an employer, or that it should determine the remuneration and conditions of service of its employees at all levels without importing social or non-economic considerations. Once the Government accepted the social obligations of regulating wages and conditions of employment in the private sector, it became necessary that it should, as an employer, be guided by the objectives, principles and standards commended to other employers.

Naturally enough, the Government had to act as a pace-setter or model employer, a concept which envisaged a minimum wage which was to be high enough to compare favourably with the wages allowed by the best employers in the private sector. This was to apply, however, to the minimum wage levels, not the highest, which needed to be brought down so that the existing disparities might be reduced and the structure of emoluments under the Central Government made to reflect the egalitarian objectives of a socialist society. For it was argued that the Government was not only an employer but also a regulator of the employer-employee relationship. In other words, the Government did not exist to maintain its servants as a model employer at the cost of the community, but to treat them only as a means to achieve the purposes for which the Government itself was constituted.

The second Pay Commission also recognized that, since modern administration had come to assume the functions of management that required a more or less multi-disciplinary approach, all the functions of the Government, such as audit and accounts, railways and postal services, the collection of revenue or the maintenance of law and order, were to be treated as of equal importance. In the new context of socio-economic development, therefore, the old principle of a governing class of civil servants and the resultant differentials in the structure of pay were viewed as anachronistic. Attempts were naturally sought to be made to improve employer-employee relations in the Government by using industrial principles: this affected the old concept of the public service—that it had obligations to the community at large and that its ethics and traditions were opposed to officers being allowed to assert their right to strike. The 1960 strike of government servants was a logical follow-up of this new thought-pattern.

Whitley Councils to Resolve Differences

Whitleyism had first grown in Britain out of the report of a committee (under the chairmanship of J.H. Whitley) appointed to investigate employer-employee relations in industry and to suggest measures to improve those relations. In its report the committee had recommended a scheme of joint and standing industrial councils to resolve difference arising from time to time between labour and management.[62] In 1919, the principle of this recommendation was, under pressure from staff associations, adopted by the public services in England. Whitleyism in fact came to signify a scheme of joint consultation and compulsory arbitration to ensure peace and harmony between employers and employees.

In India, changes in the direction of Whitleyism began to take place after the general strike of Central Government employees in July 1960. Instructions were issued by the Government of India in September 1961 that the recognition of unions and associations, which had been withdrawn as a result of the strike, might be restored on the terms and conditions existing at the time of withdrawal.[63] Consistent with the recommendation of the second Pay Commission, a committee was appointed to organize a co-ordinated welfare programme for the entire body of Central Government employees and to advise the Government generally on welfare policies and programmes.[64] The scales of pay of the two all-India Services, the I.A.S. and I.P.S., were revised with effect from 1 April 1960 on the pattern recommended by the second Pay Commission for the Central Services, Class I.[65] Then, with the object of promoting understanding and co-operation between the Government as employer and the general body of its employees in matters of common concern, and in order further to increase the efficiency of the public service, the Government decided in 1963 to establish 'a machinery for joint consultation and arbitration of unresolved differences'.[66]

A Scheme for Joint Consultation and Compulsory Arbitration was accordingly drawn up and approved by the Government. Copies of the scheme and drafts of (i) Instructions for Recognition of Unions/Associations, (ii) a Model Constitution of the National Council, (iii) Model Instructions for the Conduct of Business of the National Council, (iv) a Model Constitution of Departmental Regional Councils, and (v) Model Instructions for the Conduct of Business of Various Councils were forwarded to ministries and departments for circulation among the Federations, Unions and Associations concerned. In order to iron out differences, meetings were then held with the representatives of major Federations, Unions and Associations on 20 January and 29 April 1964. Attempts were made to resolve differences even with individual employees' organizations, some of which declined to agree to the Scheme. The establishment of Joint Councils was thus delayed becuase of differences over the Scheme itself.[67] It took time to have differences with the individual employees' organizations duly settled. On their final settlement, the Scheme for Joint Consultation and Compulsory Arbitration for Central Government employees was inaugurated on 28 October 1966.[68]

The Scheme in its final form provided a forum for consultation and negotiation in the Joint Councils of officials and staff at the national, departmental and regional or office levels. The scope of the Councils extended to all matters relating to conditions of service and work, the welfare of employees as well as the improvement of their efficiency and standards of work. On questions of recruitment, promotion and discipline, however, the scope of joint consultation was to remain limited to matters of general principles, which did not include considerations of individual cases. The staff side or official side could of course on its own initiative seek arbitration if there was a difference of opinion between the two sides on questions related to the pay and allowances, leave and hours of work of a class or grade of employees. The Board of Arbitration was, for this purpose, to consist of three members, one drawn from a panel of five names submitted by the official side, one from a similar panel submitted by the staff side of the National Council, and a chairman who was to be an independent person.

The conditions of service relating to the conduct of government servants were laid down under the All-India Service (Conduct) Rules, 1954,[69] made in pursuance of section 3 of the All-India Services Act, 1951. The rules of conduct governing public services were examined for revision specifically by the Committee on Prevention of Corruption presided over by K. Santhanam. Its recommendations were incorporated into a new set of conduct rules issued on 30 November 1964 for the guidance of the Central Civil Service as a whole.[70] The Discipline and Appeal Rules for Central Government employees, which were first made under the 1951 Act,[71] were also revised by the Government on the recommendations of the Santhannam Committee.[72]

Broadly, the provisions of conduct rules which called for consideration by the joint consultative machinery at national or departmental levels, fell into three main categories. The first included rules restricting political and civic rights, while the second contained those bearing on service associations, trade unions and cognate matters. The third set of rules, on the other hand, laid down restrictions or prohibitions regarding public expression of opinion; criticism of the government; acquisition and disposal of property; engaging in trade and business; acceptance of gifts and free services like transport, boarding, lodging; exercise of influence to secure employment for friends and family members in firms enjoying official patronage, etc.

The representatives of staff viewed these rules as a legacy of the British Raj, as authoritarian and undemocratic. Their contention was that since these were all bureaucratic creations, they should be replaced by a new set of rules enacted by Parliament on the principles of democracy and socialism. Little did they realize that the rules so framed were in exercise of the powers conferred by the All-India Services Act, 1951, and revised in accordance with the recommendations of the Santhanam Committee which was seized with the serious problem of administrative corruption and inefficiency. A more stringent set of rules is in fact needed in the modern context, where the extended functions of the state in both administrative and economic fields have multiplied opportunities for the misuse of power and influence. As and when necessary, these may of course be modified at appropriate levels by the joint consultative machinery, so that punitive discipline may in due course be replaced by a code of conduct laid down by the service itself. But self-discipline and influence have rarely been found to be sufficient by themselves. And since the Government is answerable to the community as a whole, it becomes essential that its employees should conform to the standards of conduct which the Government lays down for them.

An Overall View

An important and noticeable development of the post-Independence period has been the increasing amenability of politics to social reactions proceeding from the introduction of adult suffrage in a status-bound society still divided into mutually exclusive groups of caste and community, professing separate religions, speaking different languages and practising diverse rites. While no political party or government could possibly afford to act independently of the manner of social organization, its thought patterns and traits of behaviour, the higher levels of the bureaucracy, who since the British days were accustomed to functioning within the framework of law and established procedure, found it difficult to bend the universality of rules to the convenience of individual ministers or governors.

As pointed out in Chapter II, cases occurred where, apart from the irregularities committed by heads of States and ministers, the Prime Minister himself was found to have made use of an authority which in law did not belong to him. While in one particular case he had expressed a desire to have a person appointed in some department or other without a reference to the Public Service Commission, in another case he acted executively in respect of the salaries, allowances and perquisites granted to ministers without the prior sanction of Parliament. But since he was endowed with a basic sense of honesty and financial integrity, he did not stand on prestige but yielded to the firmness shown by the Home Secretary in the first case and by the Comptroller and Auditor-General in the second. It was conceded that while the Public Service Commission alone was the proper agency for all government appointments, the Prime Minister or his Cabinet could not be permitted to sanction executively the disbursement of the tax-payer's money without an Act of Parliament. The Salaries of Ministers Act (1952) was the natural outcome.

Governors and ministers in general, however, stood on a different plane. They were an assortment of varying kinds and qualities, although in terms of allowances, privileges and perquisites they were all unanimous about continuing the traditions established by the Raj under the Government of India Act, 1935. Even the President, who was universally known for simplicity and abstemious habits, allowed himself the sumptuary allowance of Rs 45,000 a year that was earlier given to the British Viceroy in accordance with the rules made under the Act. All this happened during the Prime Ministership of Jawaharlal Nehru, an acclaimed radical. Though personally irreproachable, as Prime Minister he bore an immediate responsibility for a clean administration, more especially at the political level which alone could set an example for the administrative elites to emulate. It was precisely here that he failed. In view of the evidence cited in Chapter II of corruption at the political level, the comment of the Santhanam Committe about ministers, legislators and party officials could not but be treated as mild and almost sympathetic.[73]

To regulate the conduct of ministers and stop corruption at their level, the Santhanam Committee had suggested the formation of a national panel of eminent jurists, one of whom should have held a high judicial office. The idea was that, in case of a written complaint against a minister, the President should select out of this panel an *ad hoc* committee to ascertain whether or not there was a *prima facie* case for inquiry by the Central Bureau of Investigation. This suggestion had been made to justify similar inquiries into the conduct of civil servants. But the Cabinent turned down the proposal for political reasons and did not agree to go beyond ministerial conduct being recognized as a subject of inquiry by party bosses only. Ministers were permitted to associate themselves with the collection of funds for party purposes, although the Santhanam Committee had expressed itself strongly against this practice on the ground of its being destructive of public morality. The rule of law was thus to apply only to public servants, not to politicians. Politics refused to be rule-bound.

Perhaps because of the paucity of suitable models at the political level, the Committee on Prevention of Corruption pinned its faith on the higher public servants, most of whom, it said, 'maintain and function in accordance with strict standards of integrity'. But even this 'solid and hard core of public servants' had their own limitations arising from the operational control of state governments over the management of the I.A.S. which, with the gradual depletion of the I.C.S. cadre, rose steadily to higher positions in the administrative hierarchy of the country. As pointed out in the first and second chapters of this work, the States remained in most cases politically subservient to the ruling party and its influence at the Centre. But as the findings of Chapter V show, this subservience did not apply to administrative fields. Structural and functional proliferations[74] enabled State governments to manage the I.A.S. in their own way, even independently of the controlling authority of the Ministry of Home Affairs at the Centre. This was specially so in Uttar Pradesh, where cadre posts continued to be held for years by non-cadre officers without the permission of the Centre. I.A.S. officers in the State tended in fact to become increasingly subject to local influence, which, in other words, meant subservience to politics and the consequent use of political sanction for bureaucratic despotism in the administration of the States. This departure from the Weberian concept of bureaucratic neutrality portends a danger to democracy.

The position of the higher civil service at the Centre, however, continued to be better organized. Its challenges were of a superior order and so were its general abilities to handle them with ease and confidence. This became possible because of the care with which the Home Ministry selected the best talents out of the State cadres, either for its own central administrative pool or for tenure posts. Officers so selected over the years were initially members of the I.C.S. who continued to man the higher posts in the Central Secretariat as Secretaries or Heads of Departments. Their proximity to central political authority was of special advantage to them and so was their connexion with several central ministries. But what gave them an edge over their ministers and weight to their advice in policy-making was their knowledge and expertise of public business which ministers could not do without. Ministerial dependence on bureaucratic advice was an administrative necessity. Politically, too, the importance of the bureaucracy was in no way less recognized. This was particularly so after the poor performance of the Congress Party in the general elections of 1967. The C.P.I. gained politically by lending its support to the Goverment of Mrs Indira Gandhi. But the political gains of the bureaucracy were much greater. The privilege of the higher civil service and its position of prestige remained inviolate. As pointed out in Chapter IV, for instance, the Cabinet had already at the instance of the civil service reduced the powers of the Central Vigilance Comission which, in spite of the Santhanam Comittee's recommendations, was not permitted to look into bureaucratic corruption independently of the Government. The traditional supremacy of Secretaries and Heads of Departments was left unaffected. They were not to be bye-passed in any act of inquiry to be conducted by the Government against a civil servant. The position of the civil service became all the more reinforced after 1967. Despite the agitation of specialists in favour of a unified service-structure on the lines of what the Fulton Committee had recommended in Britain, the Prime Ministei continued to lend her full support to the I.A.S. and the established principles of position classification governing the existing bureaucratic organization of the country. The Government turned its face against any recommendation of the Administrative Reforms Commission which might tend to weaken the control of the civil service over the entire field of civil administration. There were of course a few exceptions, but these did not affect the structure of the bureaucratic organization as a whole.

The general trend of political development after 1967 was in fact such that the ruling party at the Centre could not but let the higher bureaucracy share power with it in its own interest and for the sake of its own security. It was possibly the state of political uncertainty that led the Congress to raise a slogan demanding what came to be known as a 'committed civil service'. The declaration of a state of emergency in June 1975 under Article 352 of the Constitution was perhaps a logical sequence of developments that had been taking place since 1967, developments which dictated the expediency of a virtual overlapping of political and administrative lines on the Soviet model. It ensured some kind of balance in the power structure of the country on the basis of an identity of interest between politics and administration, with a tilt of that balance perhaps weighted more in favour of the latter that the former.

In the context of India's authoritarian and status-bound society, both ministers and bureaucrats tried to ape the British imperial tradition by attempting to have their prestige measured in terms of their salary, the quality of their furniture and furnishings, the size of their lawns and office rooms, their allowances, privileges and perquisites. Their approach to life remained elitist and far from Gandhian. Ministers and their officers both flourished independently of the state of the national economy. Though outwardly clad in khadi, even Congress ministers, with certain exceptions, developed attitudes which differed but little from the general pattern of bureaucratic culture. In fact, politics was hardly any guide to the evolution of a new administrative culture. It is the bureaucracy and its ethos that set the norm for ministerial behaviour.

Another noticeable feature of the post-Independence period was the enormous expansion and proliferation of the administrative structure. It began during the Second World War and continued without any let or hindrance as part of the development plans after the transfer of power. However, the extent of expansion that took place in the name of development administration was more a function of patronage than administrative necessity. It symbolized the power politics which appeared in the wake of democracy, howsoever limited. Patronage as part of power politics, for instance, became noticeable initially on the introduction of Dyarchy in 1921. It led to demands for communal representation in the public services, which were sought to be met by the Muddiman Pledge and subsequent orders of the Government which flowed from the urge to use patronage as an instrument of power politics. The scope for providing employment, which had remained limited, suddenly expanded at the outbreak of the War which dictated the necessity of recruiting all kinds of human material, good, bad or indifferent. This had occurred even in the course of the First World War, but the retrenchment effect under the recommendations of the Inchcape Committee (1922) restored the balance in favour of financial stability. No such measure of retrenchment was introduced after the Second World War, although the Economy Committee appointed in 1948 did go into the whole question and suggest measures to effect economy and efficiency. In practice, the development administration absorbed most of the expanded staff. The Community Development Projects and the National Extension Service became the dumping ground for a variety of ill-equipped staff recruited through patronage and a non-competitive basis. The reorganized Central

Secretariat Service even afforded opportunities for Assistants to be not only promoted to Under Secretaryships, but also to rise to the rank of Deputy Secretary and, in some cases, of Joint Secretary also.

As already pointed out, the *Paper on Measures for the Strengthening of Administration* laid before Parliament in 1961 made several recommendations to improve the administrative machinery as a condition for the success of the Third Plan. The recommendation that a government servant retire at the age of 50 or after 25 years of service if necessary for the public interest was not implemented, even though the Committee on Prevention of Corruption made a similar recommendation. The Department of Administrative Reforms established in 1964 carried out in the meantime studies to evolve better methods and procedures of work. It focussed attention on job analysis and evaluation, identifying the kind of work performed, matching the skills of people with the skills needed in the job, and providing the basis for a rational pay policy related to the contribution made by workers. Some of the changes introduced as a result of these studies led to some reduction in unnecessary work and the consequent reduction of staff. Surplus staff was also identified by the staff Inspection Unit of the Ministry of Finance. But since the principle and mode of joint consultation were in the process of discussion between the Government and its employees' associations, no reduction of staff could be effected and the Government finally decided upon a scheme for the redeployment of surplus staff. For this purpose a Central (Surplus Staff) Cell was set up in the Ministry of Home Affairs with effect from 25 December 1966.[75]

The operation of the scheme was extended to the staff rendered surplus as a result of *suo-moto* studies of work measurement or other administrative reforms undertaken by ministries as well as due to the abolition and winding up of any organization. On transfer to the Central Cell the surplus staff continued to receive for six months the pay and allowances earned previously until they were absorbed elsewhere. To secure speedy redeployment of surplus staff a ban was therefore imposed on direct recruitment to all ministerial posts under the Central Government unless a certificate was obtained from the Central Cell to confirm that it had no suitable candidates to offer. This ban was later extended to all Class III posts (both ministerial and non-ministerial) and to certain categories of promotion posts, such as Upper Division Clerks, Head Clerks, etc. Those who joined the Central Cell were mostly Class III employees. Their number rose from 446 in 1967–8 to 1322 in 1969–70. The number of Class I employees who joined the Cell was limited to 3 throughout. The percentage of redeployment for both Class III and Class II emloyees was considerable, 2,577 out of a total of 2,872 for three years in the case of Class III, and 186 out of a total of 215 for Class II. In the case of Class I employees, however, only 3 could be redeployed out of 9 in the course of three years. There were instances of retrenchment and voluntary retirement. But these were few and far between.[76] Thus, despite the recommendations made from time to time to match staffing with work-load, no effective steps were taken to remedy the cumulative effect of surplus staffing by means of retrenchment.

But a more serious problem was that of differential growth which, as discussed before, had made the administration top-heavy by an expansion of the higher bureaucracy to a much greater extent than the lower grades. The increasing strength of the civil service from Under Secretaries upwards in the post-Independence period tended to forestall any political action that might otherwise have been taken to effect economy and prevent differential growth. This bureaucratic strength not only conduced to administrative continuity with all its privileges and perquisites, but also influenced political decisions under the cover of ministerial responsibility. It was further augmented after Nehru's death, especially as a result of the political infirmity of his party after its reverses at the 1967 elections. The political vacuum so caused meant an additional accession to bureaucratic power. It created a situation where the Government could not but adopt such advice as the bureaucracy offered in keeping with its own general interest and aversion to the retrenchment of surplus staff at any level of the administrative hierarchy.

The power of the executive has grown additionally over the years on account of yet another development—the increasing realization of the need to promote socio-economic progress as a condition for political stability. The exigencies of planned development to secure this progress necessarily called for an overlapping of political and administrative functions at different levels of decision-making. As this functional overlapping could mean a new despotism, the expediency of panchayati raj was suggested by the Mehta Committee as an instrument of decentralized democracy for the promotion of social and economic change. But the Committee's suggestion remained in practice more formal than real. Apart from the evils of caste and class domination which forestalled unity of action, most panchayat bodies came to be controlled by administrative agencies at all levels.[77]

One of the basic ills of the Indian situation has, however, flowed in modern times from social revivalism as an instrument of the struggle for political freedom. The modern political, legal and administrative institutions which the British created lacked indigenous roots. They were developed for imperial purposes and those of a limited class of educated Indian elites whom Macaulay had visualized as a potential social base for imperialism. Macaulay's hopes were not fully realized. His potential collaborators became political competitors. And since the institutions so established over the years did not have the cultural backing of society in general, political opposition to British rule became reinforced by an emotional appeal to revivalist nationalism. Even Gandhi made use of revivalism as an anti-western weapon to win freedom from that rule. It formed in fact the basis of mass politics in the course of his non-cooperation and civil disobedience movement. The current of social revivalism which mobilized the masses politically, became, on the transfer of power, a breeding ground for communal and caste politics. The cadres of political parties were no exception and in fact acted as the carriers of the germ of such politics even to non-political and voluntary organizations. The policy of the government to identify backwardness by a reference to certain castes and tribes and to distribute favours to them on that basis has further intensified the traditional social divisions and widened old gaps among communities and castes, which in the past had been sought to be reduced on the principles of religion, equity and natural justice. It is doubtful whether a caste-based democracy can ever sustain any modern administration based on the rule of law. A caste-based democracy is a kind of cancer in the Indian body politic. It is being kept in check by the higher echelons of a rule-oriented bureaucracy whose administrative culture theoretically permits little serious deviation from the universally recognized norms of public administration. The higher echelons of the bureaucracy, however, are not all-pervasive or immune from the corroding influence of political and sectarian pressures on rational administration.

Notes

I. THE GOVERNMENT

1. See B. B. Misra, *The Bureaucracy in India*, Chap. V.
2. Including any enactments, amending or supplementing that Act, such as the India (Central Government and Legislative) Act, 1946.
3. In its restricted form the amendment was moved in the Assembly by K. M. Munshi on 10 October 1949.
4. Quoted in B. Shiva Rao (ed.), *The Framing of India's Constitution: A Study*, p. 721.
5. Ibid., p. 722.
6. See Sneh Mahajan (Mrs.), 'The Working of the Indian Legislature', 1909–21 (an unpublished Ph.D. Thesis of the University of Delhi, 1974).
7. See B. B. Misra, op. cit., Chap. VI.
8. Reginald Coupland, *The Constitutional Problem in India*, p. 65.
9. See B. B. Misra, *The Bureaucracy in India*, Chap. VI and *The Indian Political Parties*, Chap. III.
10. The Report of the Joint Committee on Indian Constitutional Reforms, Vol. I, part I, Session 1933–4 (Lords), p. 76.
11. C. H. Philips (ed.), *The Partition of India: Policies and Perspectives, 1935–1947*, p. 55. See also Moore's 'British Policy and the Indian Problem', ibid., pp. 79–94. It is a clear exposition of Conservative policy towards implementing the federal provisions of the 1935 Act.
12. Article 254.
13. Article 249.
14. See Articles 200–1.
15. See Articles 352–5.
16. See Articles, 358, 359 and 19.
17. See Article 360.
18. See B. B. Misra, *The Administrative History of India, 1834–1947*.
19. See *Report of the States Reorganization Commission, 1955*, p. 5.
20. The State of Delhi, for instance, had no power to make laws with respect to public order, police, the constitution of the municipal corporation and other local authorities, improvement trusts, water supply, drainage, electricity, transport and public utility authorities, lands and buildings situated in Delhi, etc. The reason for these restrictions was that Delhi was the seat of the Central Government. See Section 21 of the Government of Part C States Act (No. XLIX) of 1951.
21. See B. B. Misra, *The Administrative History of India, 1834–1947*, Chap. IV.
22. See *Report of the Indian Statutory Commission*, ii, p.38; *Report of the Orissa Committee (O'Donnel Committee)*, i, para. 6; *Report of the States Reorganization Commission*, Chap. II.

23. In a letter to K. N. Katju, Home Minister, on 12 May 1954 Hari Bhan Upadhyaya, Chief Minister of Ajmer, enclosed a copy of a memorandum submitted to the Chairman of the States Reorganization Commission. The memorandum was a result of discussions held at a Conference of the Chief Ministers of Part C States on 10–12 May 1954. The Commission was asked to leave the existing administrative set-up of Part C States undisturbed for the present in order to ensure their economic self-sufficiency and all-round progress. See F.No. 23/9/54-Public I.

24. The tribal areas specified in Part A included the United Khasi-Jaintia Hills District, the Garo Hills District, the Lushai Hills District, the Naga Hills District, the North Cachar Hills and the Mikir Hills. Those specified in Part B included the North-East Frontier Tract and the Naga Tribal area. See Sixth Schedule to the Constitution, which provided within the State of Assam a kind of inner federation consisting of autonomous Regional and District Councils in the Tribal Areas.

25. See The Constitution (Application to Jammu and Kashmir) Order, 1954 in the *Constitution of India* amended up to 1972, Appendix, pp. 259–67. The Constitution (Seventh Amendment) Act, 1956, included Jammu and Kashmir as one of the other States. The old distinction of Part A, B or C States was abolished. The head of state of Jammu and Kashmir, however, continued to be called Sadar-i-Riyasat.

26. By the Constitution (Seventh Amendment) Act, 1956, B and C States were abolished and all States were given the same status and governed by the provisions relating to A States. C States were either amalgamated with other States or reduced to the status of Union Territories, though governed still by the Government of Part C States Act, 1951. All States thus became of one class.

27. See First Schedule to the Constitution of India as amended up to 1972 (Twenty-ninth Amendment Act), p. 156.

28. See M.H.A.F. No. 2/2/56–SR(1).

29. It provides that the President may in the public interest direct the establishment of a Council to investigate and discuss subjects in which some or all of the States may have a common interest, or make recommendation for the better coordination of policy and action.

30. Article 312.

31. Quoted in M. C. Setalvad, *Union and State Relations under the Indian Constitution*, 1974, p. 177. It was a case of the State of Madhya Pradesh for the year 1950.

32. See B. Shiva Rao, *The Making of India's Constitution: A Study*, Chap. IV.

33. Equality before law (Art. 14); prohibition of discrimination on the ground of religion, race, colour, caste, language or sex (Art. 15); equality of employment opportunity (Art. 16); abolition of untouchability (Art. 17); and abolition of titles (Art. 18).

34. Freedom of speech, etc. (Art. 19); protection in respect of conviction for offences (Art. 29); protection of life and personal liberty (Art. 21); and protection against arrest and detention (Art. 22).

35. Freedom of conscience, profession, practice and propagation of religion (Art. 25); freedom to manage religious affairs (Art. 26); freedom for payment of taxes for promotion of any religion (Art. 27); freedom as to attendance or religious instruction or religious worship in certain educational institutions (Art. 28).

36. Protection of interests of minorities (Art. 29) ; right of minorities to establish and administer educational institutions (Art. 30).

37. Right to property (Art. 31). Compulsory acquisition of property (Art. 31).

38. Remedies for enforcement of fundamental rights (Art. 32); power to Parliament to modify fundamental rights in their application to armed forces (Art. 33); restriction on fundamental rights while martial law is in force in any area (Art. 34); legislation to give effect to fundamental rights (Art. 35).

39. Prohibition of traffic in human beings and forced labour (Art. 23); and prohibition of employment of children in factories (Art. 24).

40. See B. B. Misra, *The Bureaucracy in India*, Chap. VI, on bureaucracy and democracy.

41. See B. B. Misra, *The Indian Political Parties*.

42. There was, for instance, a Communist Government in Kerala for a period of nearly two years after the General Elections of 1957. The Assembly was dissolved and President's Rule introduced in 1959, in spite of the Communist majority in the legislature.

II. THE PRESIDENT, STATE GOVERNORS AND CENTRAL MINISTERS

1. There was a controversy over re-election. Dr Radhakrishnan was an aspirant in the field. But through the intercession of Maulana Azad the controversy was set at rest. The Congress Parliamentary Board re-nominated Dr Prasad, and this was communicated to him on 1 April 1957 by Nehru himself. See *Portrait of a President: letters of Dr Rajendra Prasad written to Mrs Gyanwati Darbar*, pp. 153–5.

2. See Bimanesh Chatterjee, *The Presidential Predicament: Rajendra Prasad Remembered*, 1974, p. 36.

3. See Granville Austin, *The Indian Constitution: Cornerstone of a Nation*, 1966, p. 140.

4. See Girja Kumar and B. K. Arora (ed.), *Documents on Indian Affairs*, p. 144.

5. Quoted in K. L. Punjabi, *Rajendra Prasad: First President of India*, 1960, p. 161.

6. See pp. 40–6.

7. Bimanesh Chatterjee, op. cit., p. 37.

8. *Portrait of a President*, 1974, pp. 256, 288.

9. Article 59(3) runs as follows: 'The President shall be entitled without payment of rent to the use of his official residences and shall be also entitled to such emoluments, allowances and privileges as may be determined by Parliament by law and, until provision in that behalf is so made, such emoluments, allowances, and privileges as are specified in the Second Schedule'.

10. Under the Third Schedule to the Government of India Act, 1935 the annual salary of the Governor-General was Rs 250,800. Rajagopalachari who took over from Lord Mountbatten, raised the question of reduction in his salary, which, it was proposed, should be Rs 5,500 a month, a salary proposed for the President of the Union. The Constituent Assembly accepted the proposal and introduced a Bill on 22 February 1948 which made the reduced rate free from taxes. See *Review of the Activities of the Ministry of Home Affairs for the Year 1948*, Section XIII, F. No. 51/423/49-Public.

11. It provided that the President would be entitled to the same allowance as was being paid to the Governor-General previously.

12. See Home Ministry, F. No. 14/4/55-Public (1).

13. Secret letter No. F.R.5/56, dated 1 March 1956 from the Governor of Madras to the President of India. See Home Ministry F. No. 19/4/56-Public (1), p. 15.

14. See Bimanesh Chatterjee, op. cit., p. 105.

15. Ibid. pp. 108, 112.

16. See J. R. Siwach, *The Indian Presidency*, 1971, p. 195. The increase of 'bribery and corruption in public services' was admitted by the Home Minister as well as by the Prime Minister. See *The Statesman*, 4 Nov. 1963.

17. A sitting member of the Punjab Legislative Assembly since 1937 became Development Minister of the Congress Government in Punjab in 1952; and then Chief Minister in 1956.

18. Anees Chishti, *President Zakir Husain: A Study*, 1967, p. 6.

19. *The Statesman*, 29 April 1967, p. 7.

20. *The Times of India*, 2 Aug. 1969, p. 11.

21. *Patriot*, 2 Aug. 1969, p. 5.

22. See Sri Prakasa, *State Governors in India*, 2nd ed., 1975, pp. 108–10.

23. See Sri Prakasa, op. cit. pp. 89–112.

24. See *Report of the Committee of Governors on the Role of Governors*, 1971, p. 45.

25. Press statement dated 25 Nov. 1967, cited in Sri Prakasa, op. cit., pp. 96–7.

26. On the reports of Governors the President declared breakdowns of the constitutional machinery more than 25 times up to February 1974. See Sri Prakasa, op. cit., p. 70. See also C. P. Barthwal, 'Imposition of President's Rule: Use and Abuse of Article 356', in *Parliamentary Studies*, Vol. 15, No. 8, 1971.

27. Sir Prakasa, op. cit., pp. 73–4.

28. Sri Prakasa, op. cit., p. 71.

29. Dharma Vira, *Memoirs of a Civil Servant*, 1975, p. 136.

30. Dharma Vira, op. cit., p. 140.

31. Ibid. p. 140.

32. See Third Schedule to the Government of India Act, 1935.

33. See Second Schedule to the Constitution of India.

34. This Order came into force on 1 January 1950. See F. No. 19/5/56-Public (I) and F. No. 19/65/65-Public (I), pp. 9–10.

35. See F. No. 19/65/65–Public (I), pp. 11, 20.

36. See F. No. 19/4/60-Public (I), pp. 1–4.

37. See F. No. 19/39/60-Public (I).

38. See F. No. 19/22/59-Public (I), pp. 15–17.

39. See F. No. 19/50/60-Public (I), p. 14 (Correspondence).

40. See F. No. 19/15/60-Public (I), pp. 13–14.

41. See F. No. 60/1/49-Public (Correspondence), pp. 2–4.

42. See F. No. 60/1/49-Public (Correspondence), pp. 6–7.

43. Ibid. p. 5.

44. See F. No. 18/3/51-Public, p. 5.

45. Sri Prakasa, Minister for Commerce, to Rajagopalachari, Home Miniser, 22 Jan. 1951, F. No. 18/3/51-Public, p. 1.

46. Ibid.

47. Ibid.

48. See F. No. 22/10/48-Appt (Sp), pp. 13–15 (Notes), and pp. 13–14, 24 (Correspondence); O.M. No. 22/10/48-Appt (Sp) of 27–28 Dec. 1948 and 28 Feb. 1949, containing orders regulating the use of saloons.
49. Ibid. p. 2.
50. F. No. 15/202/51-Public, pp. 1–18; Sri Prakasa was at the time Minister for Communications. See F. No. 15/54/51-Public, p. 12/n.
51. See F. No. 15/54/51-Public (I), p. 6/n.
52. These designations were: Cabinet Minister, Minister of State and Deputy Minister.
53. See F. No. 18/25/52-Public, p. 2/n.
54. Ibid. p. 5/n.
55. F. No. 14/43/64-Public (I), p. 2.
56. This arrangement continued until Nehru's death on 27 May 1964. His successor, Lal Bahadur Shastri, was, however, allowed to draw his usual sumptuary allowance of Rs 500.
57. See F. No. 15/19/55-Public (I) (Notes and Correspondence).
58. Ibid.
59. F. No. 14/26/57-Public (I), p. 1/n.
60. Ibid. p. 2/n.
61. Narahari Rao had by now left.
62. F. No. 15/3/56-Public (I), pp. 1–4 (Correspondence), and pp. 1–2 (Notes). The same principle applied to a reference from Jammu and Kashmir.
63. See F. No. 15/223/51-Public.
64. F. No. 14/12/57-Public (I), p. 3.
65. Ibid. p. 10.
66. See F. No. 14/31/57-Public (I), pp. 2–3.
67. F. No. 12/68/63-Public (I), p. 35 (Correspondence).
68. See F. No. 12/68/63-Public (I), pp. 74–5 (Correspondence).
69. Ibid. pp. 1–3 (Corr.). See also Ibid. pp. 3–20 (Corr).
70. F. No. 14/9/57-Public (I), pp. 10–13.
71. From Govt. of Madhya Pradesh to the Sec. to Govt. of India, 15 Sept. 1961, F. No. 12/47/61-Public (I), pp. 58–9, Serial No. 41.
72. Ibid. Serial No. 34.
73. Ibid. p. 58, Serial No. 41.
74. Ibid. pp. 86–7, Serial No. 63.

III. THE ALL-INDIA SERVICES, 1946–56

1. M.H.A. File No. 20/21/49–G.S., 1949, No. I, p. 1 (Notes).
2. Ibid., pp. 13–14.
3. See B. B. Misra, *The Bureaucracy in India*, Chap. V.
4. The Constituent Assembly (Leg.) Debates, 19 November 1947, Vol. L, pp. 17–18.
4.A See M.H.A. File No. 23/3/51–AIS, p. 8/Notes.
5. In the Central Provinces and Berar, for instance, all the I.C.S. Officers (excepting the three High Court Judges) and I.P. were released on 15 August 1947. In Madras, there were 56 European Civilians and 73 Indian Civilians on 1 Jan.

1948. Of these, 41 Europeans and three Indians were released on 15 August 1947. They were granted all the leave due to them preparatory to retirement. Of the 42 European I.C.S. officers on the Bombay Establishment, 28 were on leave preparatory to retirement. Some retired prematurely on proportionate pension, while others went on leave preparatory to retirement. The bulk of the Europeans in fact left on the transfer of power. See M.H.A. File No. 31/1/48–Ests. and 51/423/49–Pub. (Review of the Activities of M.H.A. for 1948.

6. See B. B. Misra, *The Bureaucracy in India*, Chap. V. The I.A.S. and I.P.S. cadres were deemed to have come into being with effect from 21 October 1946, when agreement to constitute these new All-India Services was reached. M.H.A. File No.20/21/48–G.S. (AIS), p.12. (Note dated 7.7.48 by C.B. Gulati, Asst. Sec. to Govt).

7. See M.H.A. File No.174/47–Ests (R), Serial No. 4, App. pp.1–8.

8. See M.H.A. File No.20/69/48–G.S., pp. 6–12. The Memorandum set out the scheme for the constitution of the I.A.S. which had been agreed to by the Central Govt. and nine of the participating Prov. Govts.

9. See The All-India Services Manual (2nd ed.), corrected up to 1.8.69, pp.404–11

10. See M.H.A. File No.12/56/49–Appts. See also M.H.A. File No.37/17/47–Ests.(R), p. 3.

11. See M.H.A. File NO.37/43/47–Ests.(R), p.7.

12. This suggestion was made by Dr R.M. Ray, Secretary, F.P.S.C., in his letter to the Home Ministry dated 7 Oct. 1947. No effect, however, seems to have been given to Ray's suggestion for interview as a precondition to confirmation.

13. See M.H.A. File No.37/43/47–Ests.(R), Serial No. 24, pp.38–40/Corresp.

14. See M.H.A. File No.20/45/49–AIS, Serial Nos. 1–2.

15. See M.H.A. File No.22/2/49–C.S.

16. See M.H.A. File No.25/1/48–Pub. p.177.

17. See M.H.A. File No.20/21/48–G.S.(AIS), Serial No. 2, pp.1–3 Notes.

18. See *Review of the activities of the M.H.A. for the year 1948*, Sec. 1, para. 5, M.H.A. File No.51/423/49–Pub.

19. M.H.A. File No.21/12/48–G.S., p.1/Notes.

20. M.H.A. File No.20/62/48–G.S., p.1/Notes.

21. See M.H.A. File No.25/1/48–Pub. of 1948, pp.217–18.

22. See M.H.A. File No.21/12/48–G.S., pp. 1–3/Notes.

23. *Review of the activities of the M.H.A. for the year 1948*, Sec. 1, para. 6.

24. *Review of the activities of the M.H.A. for the year 1949*, p. 3.

25. See Ibid. p. 2.

26. See M.H.A. File No.21/24/49–AIS, Serial Nos. 1–2 (Corresp.) and pp. 1–2/Notes.

26a See M.H.A. File No.21/2/49–G.S., App. to Corresp., pp. 1–22.

27. See M.H.A. File No. 3/12/49–AIs–1949, pp. 1–6/Notes.

28. See M.H.A. File No.3/9/49-AIS (Note for Supplementaries) also M.H.A. File No.3/14/49-AIS (App., 1 p.).

29. 1,645 applicants for 1947, 1,990 for 1948 and 1,591 for 1949.

30. See Ibid, Note for Supplementaries.

31. The F.P.S.C. could not interview the war service probationers selected in March 1947. They were assigned to their respective Provinces without examination or even interview by it.

31a See M.H.A. File No.3/9/49-AIS, Notes for Supplementaries to the reply of the Home Minister, 29 Nov. 1949, to Unstarred Question No. 562 raised in the Constituent Assembly.

32. See *Review of the activities of M.H.A. for the year 1949*, p. 16; also see M.H.A File No.25/1/48-Pub. of 1948, p. 255.

33. See M.H.A. File No.21/24/49-AIS, p. 1/Notes.

34. See M.H.A. File No.20/17/49-G.S., pp. 1–29 Corresp.

35. See B. B. Misra, *The Bureaucracy in India*.

36. M.H.A. File No.16/63/49-AIS (Patel to Prithvi Singh Azad, 16 Nov. 1949).

37. See *Review of the activities of the M.H.A. for the year 1948*, Sec. VII, para. 6, in M.H.A. File No.51/423/49-Pub.

38. The maximum age prescribed for appointment to a service or post was increased by 3 years for Scheduled Caste candidates and the fee prescribed for admission to any examination or selection reduced to one-fourth in their case.

39. See *Review of the activities of the M.H.A. for the year 1948*, Sec. III, para. 2, in M.H.A. File No.51/423/49-Public. The figures of Superintendent included 8 Assistants-in-Charge for 1939 and 110 for 1948. As pointed out by the Economy Committee (1948), the Central Secretariat itself expanded tremendously during the war. During 1939–48 the number of Secretaries increased from 9 to 19; of Joint Secretaries from 8 to 35, and of Deputy Secretaries from 12 to 84. See S. R. Maheshwari, *The Evolution of Indian Administration*, p. 195.

40. *Review . . . for the year 1948*, Sec. III, para. 3.

41. Ibid. paras. 8–10.

42. In accordance with the recommendations made by the Second Pay Commission, Grade II (Superintendents) and Grade III (Assistant Superintendents) of the Central Secretariat Service carrying the scales of pay of Rs 530–30–800 and Rs 275–25–500, respectively, were merged into a single grade of Section Officers with a revised scale of Rs 350–25–500–30–590–EB–30–830–35–900 with effect from 1 July 1959. The merged grade was classified as a class II service. See *Report 1960–1*, Ministry of Home Affairs, p. 8.

43. These Committees were set up under Home Deptt. O.M. No. 33/46-Ests (R) dated 17 June 1946. The first Committee was for promotion to the post of Asst. Sec. It consisted of the Sec., Jt. Sec., Depy Sec. in charge of Secretariat Officers and a Member of the F.P.S.C. The second was for promotion of Class II posts. It consisted of the Depy. Sec. in charge of Establishment, two other Depy. Secs., and an Asst. Sec. in charge of Establishment. See M.H.A. File No. 68/16/48-Admn., pp. 1–4.

44. See *Review . . . for the year 1949*, p. 7.

45. The rules governing the quasi-permanent service were first issued on 17 March 1949. See M.H.A. File No. 135/56-Pub. I, p. 8, para. 53.

46. Ibid. pp. 12–13; also *Review . . . for the year 1948*, Sec. V, paras. 1–6.

47. The Committee consisted of Seth Kasturbhai Lalbhai (Chairman), B. Das, S. K. Patil, Jaipal Singh and Ishwar Dayal. It submitted its report on 30 April 1949. See M.H.A. File No. 2/8/49-RE, pp. 53–6. See also ibid. pp. 46–7 (*The Hindustan Times*), 17 Dec. 1949 re. the proposals of the Economy Committee.

48. See *The Illustrated Weekly of India*, Vol. LXX, No. 18, dated 1 May 1949 in M.H.A. File No. 2/8/49-RE. The figure of purely civil expenditure given by *The Hindustan Times* of 18 June 1949 stood as follows: 1938–9, Rs 24.5 crores; 1945–6,

Rs 90.8 crores; and 1948–9, Rs 144.5 crores. See Ibid.

49. Ibid. pp. 46–8, 53–6, containing the proposals of the Committee, including retrenchment.

50. *Mail* (Madras), 20 May 1949, in M.H.A. File No. 2/8/49-RE.

51. Ibid.

52. See *The Hindustan Times*, 18 June 1949, M.H.A. File No. 2/8/49-RE, p. 6. The Prime Minister 'felt that there was too large an army of clerks and chaprassis in the Secretariat and that we should do something to curtail their numbers.' For, they were 'a swarm of low paid men—most of them idle and doing no particular work'. See Ministry of Transport File No. RE31–14/49–RE, Report (N. Gopala-swamy Ayyangar) on the Reorganization of the Machinery of Government.

53. See M.H.A. File No. 1/27/50-AIS, 1950, App. B (R. C. Dutt, to Chief Secs, 7 Feb. 1950). The Indian Police Cadre similarly comprised the Indian Police and the Indian Police Service.

54. See M.H.A. File No. 20/62/48-G.S.

55. See Govt. of India to Chief Secs. of all Part A State Govts, 7 Feb. 1950, M.H.A. File No. 1/27/50-AIS, App. B.

56. The I.A.S. was deemed to have been constituted with effect from 21 Oct. 1946, the date of the Agreement in question.

57. Persons recruited to the I.A.S. from open competition, war service, the open market or from the Provincial Services were all entitled to its membership after confir-mation. See M.H.A. File No. 20/69/48.-G.S., Serial No. 1, pp. 1–2/Notes. The I.C.A. Rules were designed to cover three categories of officers: the I.C.S., the listed post-holders (pre-15 August 1947) and members of the I.A.S, direct recruits and promotees, after 15 Aug. 1947.

58. See M.H.A. File No. 40/49-AIS and No. 1/27/50-AIS, 1950. Annexure to these Rules contains the Memorandum regarding the constitution of the I.P.S. as agreed on 21 Oct. 1946.

59. M.H.A. File No. 1/27/50-AIS, 1950, App. A.

60. See M.H.A. File No. 1/27/50-AIS, 1950 (Notes).

61. Enacted on 29 Oct. 1951.

62. Sec 3. Provision for consultation with Jammu and Kashmir was first intro-duced by the All-India Services (Amendment) Act, 1958 (No. 25 of 1958) enacted on 3 Sept. 1958.

63. Sec. 4.

64. The Act was passed on 6 Sept. 1963. The Indian Forest Service was constituted with effect from 1 July 1966, the Indian Medical and Health Service from 1 Feb. 1969, and the Indian Service of Engineers was in the process of being constituted in 1969. See *All-India Services Manual*, 2nd ed., p. 3.

65. See M.H.A. File Nos. 3/1/52-AIS(II) and 4/3/53-AIS(II).

66. See M.H.A. File No. 135/56-Public I, p. 29. These rules are mostly printed and may be seen in the *All-India Services Manual*, 2nd ed., corrected up to 1 Aug. 1969. The orders passed from time to time by the Home Ministry are specially noteworthy.

67. See *All-India Services Manual*, 2nd ed., 1969, pp. 412, 555.

68. Members of the I.C.S, however, retained their separate and special right to their Family Pension Fund and Provident Fund.

69. This was in addition to a joint cadre for the Union Territories.

70. *All-India Services Manual*, 1969, pp. 377-98, 404–11. The total authorized strength of 9 of the provincial cadres was stated to be only 834 in 1949. See M.T. File No. 1(2)/49-R.E., App. to Notes, pp. 1–2. The figure 834 was, however, not inclusive of I.C.S. officers in the judiciary.

71. See R. A. Gopalaswami to P. K. Sundaram, Min. of Transport (Depy. Sec.), 13 Oct. 1948 in M.H.A. File No. 1(1)/49-RE, pp. 1–4/Corresp.

72. Ibid. p. 5.

73. See Min. of Transport (Reorganization Wing) File No. 1(2)/49-RE, App. to Notes.

74. The Financial Services were recruited, in addition to the I.C.S., from the Indian Audit and Accounts Service, Military Accounts Dept, Imperial Customs Service, and the Income-Tax Dept.

75. See Min. of Transport (Reorganization Wing) File No. 1(2)/49-RE, pp. 8–14.

76. The two pools together comprised (1) the available I.C.S. officers, (2) I.A.S. officers, (3) members of the Central Services, Class I, serving as feeder services for the Finance-Commerce Pool, and (4) of the Central Secretariat Service in its reorganized form.

77. See M.H.A. File No. 1(1)/49-R.E., pp. 19–20/Corresp.

78. See M.H.A. File No. 1(1)/49-R.E., p. 21/Corresp.

79. It might be raised to Rs 3,750 after five years if the officer was retained in the post in the interest of the public service.

80. When the post was held by an I.C.S. officer, pay on the above scale was to be fixed at a stage corresponding to his length of service.

81. See *Report of the Ministry of Home Affairs*, 1950–1, p. 4.

82. Ibid. 1953–4, p. 1.

83. Ibid. 1954–5, p. 1.

84. Ibid. 1954–5, p. 1.

85. See *Reprint of Study Team on the Machinery of the Goverment of India*, Feb. 1968, Part II, Vol. II, p. 29.

86. See M.H.A. File No. 1(1)/49-RE, pp. 15–16/Corresp.

87. Ibid. p. 16/Corresp. See also Finance Dept. Notification No. F.23(6)-Ex.II/42, 30 April 1942, defining the constitution and functions of an Establishment Committee for the Finance-Commerce Pool.

88. See M.H.A. File No. 1(1)/49-RE, p. 22, 18 July 1939.

89. Ibid. pp. 23–4, Finance Dept. O.M. No. F.25(9)-Ex. II/39, 8 Sept. 1939.

90. Ibid. pp. 25–6/Corresp.

91. Ibid. pp. 2–3/Notes. Instead of being required to complete a minimum period of 18 years before appointment to the post of Jt. Sec. according to earlier practice cases occurred where persons holding the post had less than 13 years' service; nor were approved lists of officers prepared and maintained to ensure appointment on grounds of merit alone.

92. An Appointment Committee was set up in 1950. This Committee consisted of the Prime Minister, the Home Minister and the Minister administratively concerned with the case. It dealt with all appointments in the Secretariat at the level of Depy. Sec. and above. This Committee also considered cases where a Ministry happened to depart from the advice of the Public Service Commission.

93. In 1951 the Board came to be headed by the Cabinet Secretary. Appointments to the post of Secretary were excluded from its purview in 1951 and of Additional

Secretary in 1954. See *Report by Study Team on Machinery of the Government*, 1968, ii.
p. 27. The *Descriptive Memoirs* of the Ministry of Home Affairs for December 1955
thus wrote about the Central Establishment Board: 'It consists of five members
of whom two are chosen from the Secretariat of the Ministries primarily concerned with economic administration (i.e. Ministries of Finance, Commerce and
Industry and Production) and the remaining three from the Secretaries of other
Ministries. The Cabinet Secretary is the ex-officio Chairman of the Board. The
Establishment Officer to the Government of India acts as Secretary. The Board
makes recommendations to Government for selection of officers to Secretariat
posts of and above the rank of Under Secretary (except posts of Secretary) and to
certain other non-Secretariat posts . . . . The Board is, however, not concerned
with statutory appointments made by the President . . . or appointments of
ambassadors, Heads of Indian Missions abroad and other high dignitaries
under the aegis of the Min. of Ext. Affairs'. M.H.A. File No. 135/56-Public I.

94.   M.H.A. File No. 1(2)/49-RE, p. 15 (Appendix to Notes).
95.   See M.H.A. File No. 20/21/49-GS, pp. 6–7/Corresp.
96.   See *Report of the Ministry of Home Affairs*, 1950–1, pp. 3–4.
97.   See M.H.A. File No. 113/56-Public I, pp. 67–8. About 400 persons were sought
      to be recruited from both the sources. The *Report* of the Min. of Home Affairs for
      1958–9 shows that 182 persons were recruited from the State Services and 86
      from the open market. See p. 2 of the *Report*.
98.   Ibid. Since the gap in the I.P.S. was not considerable, it was filled by increased
      intake from the annual competitive examination and by promotion from the
      State Police Services.
99.   Ibid. p. 73.
100. See M.H.A. File No. 113/56-Public I, p. 11/Notes. Financial assistance from
      public funds in the form of regular pensions, however, became later available not
      only to all kinds and conditions of 'Freedom Fighters', but also to legislators.
101. Ibid. p. 16/Notes.
102. Ibid. p. 12/Notes.
103. Ibid. p. 15/Notes.
104. Under Art. 320(5) of the Constitution this power to make regulations came to be
      vested in the President and the Governor of the State.
105. The term 'His Majesty' was substituted by 'under the Government of India or
      the Government of a State' under Article 320(3) of the Constitution.
106. The term 'His Majesty' in (d) and in (e) was substituted by 'under the Govern-
      ment of India or the Government of a State or under the Crown in India or under
      the Government of an Indian State'. The rest of the provisions were bodily lifted
      and made part of Art. 320(3) of the Constitution.
107. The use of the term 'in his discretion' in respect of the President or the Governor
      was omitted under Art. 320(3) of the Constitution.
108. It provided for continuance of the existing laws and their adaptation until these
      were altered, repealed or amended by a competent legislature.
109. *First Report of the Union Public Service Commission*, 1951, p. 3.
110. M.H.A. File No. 20/220/49-Ests., Serial No. 1, p. 2/Corresp.
111. Ibid. p. 1/Notes.
112. Ibid. p. 2/Notes.
113. Ibid. p.5/Corresp.

114. This committee was to consist of a member of the F.P.S.C., a representative of the Ministry concerned and two experts.
115. Ibid. p. 136/Corresp.
116. Ibid. p. 140/Corresp.
117. Ibid. p. 141/Corresp.
118. See M.H.A. File No. 79/56-Public I, pp. 1, 17.

IV. ADMINISTRATIVE CHANGES 1957–72

1. See Address to Services by the Prime Minister at Kurnool, 9 December 1955, M.H.A. File No. 79/56-Public I.
2. Memorandum prepared for the Cabinet by N. Gopalaswami Ayyangar, 20 May 1948, Min. of Transport File No. RE-31(14)/49-RE.
3. See *Report of the Ministry of Home Affairs*, 1950–1, App. I, p. 45.
4. See *Report of the Study Team: Machinery of the Government of India*, Part I, p. 67.
5. Ibid. p. 67.
6. Ibid. p. 68.
7. Memorandum, para. 6.
8. Min. of Transport File No. 31(14)/49-RE. See Notes by R. A. Rangaswami, 12 Nov. 1949.
9. Ibid. V. Shanker's general note of discussion between Patel and Ayyangar, 13 Nov. 1949.
10. The Defence Committee was started in 1947. It formed part of the Cabinet Sect.
11. The Economic Committee also formed part of the Cabinet Sect. Its functions were to coordinate all governmental activities in the economic field and generally regulate the working of the national economy; to determine priorities in regard to Central and State development schemes, and to deal with resource mobilization for developmental purposes.
12. Its function was to secure the efficient and smooth conduct of parliamentary business; to consider official attitudes towards non-official bills and resolutions, and to maintain a review of state legislation.
13. It formed part of the Home Ministry. Its functions were to consider all recommendations for Secretariat appointments of the rank of Deputy Secretary and above: other appointments carrying a salary of Rs 2,000 p.m. and above; and to decide all cases of disagreement relating to appointments between the Ministry concerned and the U.P.S.C. Home Ministry.
14. The Administrative Organization Committee was under the Home Ministry. Its functions included approval of detailed schemes of reorganization; supervision of implementation of the schemes; resolution of differences between ministries, and all other measures designed to secure economy and efficiency. See App. I and Annexure to *Report of the Ministry of Home Affairs*, 1950–1.
15. The function of this Committee was to advise the Economic Committee in the fulfilment of its objectives.
16. See *Report of the M.H.A.*, 1950–1 (App. I)
17. The Central Secretariat Service (Reorganization and Reinforcement) Scheme which the Cabinet approved in 1948, provided for two grades of officers called Superintendent and Assistant Superintendent. These were to be designated as

Section Officers and placed in grades I and II respectively.

18. The Ayyangar Committee's *Report on the Reorganization of the Machinery of Government*, para. 15, p. 17.

19. M.H.A. File No. 21/4/50-RE, p. 16 (from *The Hindustan Times*, New Delhi 25 March 1950).

20. Ibid. p. 25 (from *Free Press Journal*, Bombay, 3 June 1950).

21. See *Report of the Economy Committee of the Ministry of Home Affairs*, Annexure III, para. 15 and *Descriptive Memoir of the Ministry of Home Affairs*, M.H.A. File No. 135/56-Public I, pp. 19–21, 26 (Abstract of Establishment).

22. Min. of Transport File No. RE.31–14/49 (Memorandum for the Cabinet, 20 May 1948, para. 13).

23. *Report on the Machinery of the Government of India and its Procedure of Work*, New Delhi, A.R.C., 1968, para. 56.

24. Gorwala, *The Role of the Administrator: Past, Present and Future*, Poona, 1952, p. 12.

25. *Mundhra Inquiry: the Full Story*, a report of the inquiry held by the Chagla Commission, p. 69

26. Ibid. p. 66.

27. Ibid. p. 66.

28. Ibid. p. 80.

29. See *The Vivian Bose Board of Inquiry Report*, p. 36.

30. Writing about the resignation of T. T. Krishnamachari, M. C. Chagle observes: 'When it came to the question of T. T. K.'s resignation, I know that he (Jawaharlal Nehru) had set his face firmly against T. T. K.'s quitting and I also know first hand that it was entirely due to Maulana Azad's intervention that the Prime Minister was compelled to call for the resignation of his Finance Minister. Azad is reported to have told Nehru that it would cause a national scandal if after the disclosures in my report he continued to retain T.T.K. in the Cabinet. I know Nehru was very angry with me, and did not hesitate to show his displeasure. When T.T.K. ultimately resigned, the Prime Minister went to the airport in person to bid him farewell, a gesture that was unique in the annals of our parliamentary history.' *Roses in December: An Autobiography*, Bombay, 1973.

31. *Patriot* (New Delhi), 10 Nov. 1966.

32. See Lok Sabha Debates, 28 April 1969, c. 267 and Rajya Sabha Debates, 1 May 1969.

33. See B. B. Misra, *The Bureaucracy in India*, Chap. VI.

34. *Administrative Reforms Commission: Report of the Study Team on Personnel Administration*, p. 178.

35. *Personnel Administration—The Need for Change* (Report of the Conference held during 5–9 March, 1968), Delhi, Aug. 1968. It is a publication of the Institute itself.

36. *Third Report*, p. 7.

37. See Appendix 2 to *Seventh Report of the Union Public Service Commission*, pp. 16–17.

38. *Third Report of the U.P.S.C.*, p. 7.

39. See *Report of the Study Team on Personnel Administration*, Aug. 1967, Delhi, 1969, p. 1.

40. Ibid. p. 1.

41. *Report*, p. 18.

42. See *Census of Central Government Employees* for relevant years, The first such census was conducted by the Min. of Finance in 1948 at the instance of the first Pay

Commission. From then onwards and up to 1959 the censuses were conducted by the Central Secretariat Organization (except for 1952 when no census was undertaken). Since 1960, it began to be done by the Directorate General of Employment and Training, Min. of Labour and Rehabilitation. The number of regular employees in 1972 was 27, 51, 313.

43. *Report*, p. 19.
44. Ibid. p. 21.
45. Ibid. p. 19.
46. See Annexure 2(4), Table I, in *Report of the Study Team on Personnel Administration*, 1967.
47. See *Census of Central Government Employees* for relevant years.
48. Table II of Annexure 2(4) of the *Report*, p. 266.
49. See Ibid. Table III, p. 267.
50. p. 21.
51. See also A. D. Gorwala, *Report on Public Administration*, New Delhi, 1951, pp. 60–1.
52. *Seventh Report of Organization and Methods Division, 1961–4*, p. 2.
53. Ibid. p. 2 and *The First Five Year Plan*, Planning Commission, 1952, pp. 122–3.
54. Ibid. p. 3, and Paul H. Appleby, *Public Administration in India: Report of a Survey*, New Delhi, 1953, p. 63.
55. See *Seventh Report of Organization and Methods Division, 1961–4*, pp. 4–5.
56. See *Third Annual Report of O and M Division, 1956–7*, pp. 5–22.
57. Ibid. pp. 21–2. See also *Sixth Report of Organization and Methods Division, 1959–61*.
58. *Sixth Report of O and M Division, 1959–61*, p. 58. The studies completed are given on pp. 61–3.
59. Ibid. pp. 58–9.
60. Ibid. p. 2.
61. See *Papers on Measures for Strengthening of Administration*, O and M Division, 21 Sep. 1961.
62. Ibid. p. 58.
63. Ibid. p. 58–9.
64. *The Statesman*, 4 Nov. 1963.
65. Ibid. 4 Nov. 1963.
66. *The Times of India*, 17 Nov. 1963. As many as 39 Commissions and Committees had been appointed at the Centre in the course of sixty years, including 17 since independence. See *The Hindustan Times*, 17 Nov. 1963. The Administrative Reforms Division was expected to make use of the material available in these reports.
67. The group comprised S. S. Khera, Cabinet Secretary; V.T. Dehaja, Secretary in the Finance Ministry and V. T. Pimpudkar, Joint Secretary, Home Ministry.
68. *Report*, Department of Administrative Reforms, Ministry of Home Affairs, 1964–5, p. 1.
69. See *Seventh Report of O and M Division, 1961–64*, p. 1.
70. *Report*, Dept. of Administrative Reforms, 1964–5.
71. *Report*, Dept. of Administrative Reforms, 1965–5, p. 5.
72. Ibid. p. 9 and Annexure II, p. 24.
73. *Annual Report*, 1965–6, p. 12.
74. G. S. Pathak, a member of the Commission, accepted a governorship, while H. C. Mathur, another member died in the third year of the Commission's work. In

1970, the last year of the Commission's work, these five members included K. Hanumanthaiya, H. V. Kamath, D. Mookerjee, a retired judge, V. Shankar and T. N. Singh.

75. The names of the central committees on administrative reforms appointed since 1947 are given in S. R. Masheshwari, *Indian Administration*, 2nd ed., 1973, pp. 304–5.

76. See *Report*, Dept. of Adm. Reforms, 1966–7, p. 3.

77. Ibid. p. 4.

78. *Report*, Dept. of Adm. Reforms, 1967–8, pp. 3–4.

79. See *Seventh Report of O and M Division, 1961–4*, p. 15.

80. These are compiled in *The Administrative Reforms Commission* by S. R. Maheshwari, Agra, 1972.

81. The maximum suggested for the Cabinet was 16, and for the Council of Minister 45.

82. *Ninety-third Report of the Estimates Committee*, New Delhi, 1966, pp. 18–19.

83. See *Personnel Administration—The Need for Change*, Indian Institute of Public Administration, August 1968 (Inaugural Address of K. Hanumanthaiya), pp. 60–5.

84. See *Report on the Management of the Indian Administrative Service*, Dept. of Adm. Reforms, 1968 (cyclostyled copy), pp. 18–19.

85. *Report on Personnel Administration* (Chairman, R. K. Patil), Aug, 1967, p. 1.

86. Ibid. pp. 29–31.

87. See *Personnel Administration—The Need for Change*, I.I.P.A., p. 81.

88. Ibid. p. 81.

89. Inclusive of the I.A.S., the Central Services, Class I; the Central Secretariat Service, Class I; and persons promoted from the State Civil Services.

90. See *Report* (R. K. Patil), pp. 80–1.

91. See *Personnel Administration—The Need for Change*, I.I.P.A., p. 96.

92. *Report* (R. K. Patil), p. 89.

93. See *Annual Report*, 1961–2, p. 3.

94. See *Annual Report*, 1963–4, M.H.A., p. 1.

95. See *All-India Services Manual*, 2nd ed., corrected up to 1.8.69, pp. 647—9.

96. See *Annual Report*, 1969–70, M.H.A., p. 3.

97. See *Report of the Ministry of Home Affairs*, 1964–5 to 1969–70.

98. See Annexure III of the *Report of the Study Team on Promotion Policies, Conduct Rules, Discipline and Morale* (Chairman, K. N. Nagarkatti), pp. 351–7. The Report was published in 1968 but submitted in December 1967.

99. Ibid. p. 31.

100. See B. Sivaraman, *The Role of Civil Services in the Administration of India*, Training Division, Dept. of Personnel, Cabinet Secretariat, New Delhi, Sept. 1970 (cyclostyled copy), pp. 27–8. These figures represent perhaps the result of reduction effected in consequence of the ARC's recommendations.

101. Source: Department of Personnel and Administrative Reforms, Government of India. These findings were made available to me by the courtesy of the Director, India Institute of Public Administration, New Delhi. They were collected from the Central Secretariat for the purpose of the long term/IAS training course, 1975–6.

102. The Indian Economic Service and the Indian Statistical Service were two of the

new Central Services constituted in February 1964 after a screening of the existing holders of posts in the two Services conducted by a Selection Committee of the U.P.S.C. See *Report* M.H.A., 1964–5, p. 3. A decision to constitute these two new Central Services was first notified in the Gazette of India Extraordinary, dated 1 November 1961. As advised by the Indian Economic Service Board and the Indian Statistical Service Board, the Ministry of Home Affairs was to be the controlling authority of these two Services, each consisting of four grades, all being Class I posts, ranging from Rs 1,300–1,800 (Director) to Rs 400–950 (Assistant Director). Recruitment to Grade IV of these services was to be made by the U.P.S.C. by open competition and other grades by a Sel. Com. of the U.P.S.C., which was to screen departmental candidates for promotion to higher grades. See *Report*, M.H.A., 1961–2, p. 1.

103. See B. B. Misra, *The Bureaucracy in India*, Chapter IV.
104. *Report*, 1960–1, M.H.A., p. 3.
105. See *Report*, 1963–4, M.H.A., pp. 10–11, 1964–5, p. 5.
106. See *Report*, M.H.A., 1969–70, p. 14.
107. See *Report*, 1969–70, M.H.A., pp. 15–16.

V. THE MANAGEMENT OF THE ADMINISTRATIVE SERVICE

1. The proceedings of the conference of provincial Premiers and their reaction to Sardar Patel's plea for a 'Central Administrative Service' have been analysed in B. B. Misra, *The Bureaucracy in India: An Historical Analysis of Development up to 1947*, Chapter V.
2. *Report on the Management of the Indian Administrative Service*, Dept. of Adm. Reforms, Govt. of India (1968). Vol. I, App. I, p. 175 (cyclostyled copy).
3. See Home Dept. File No. 32/46-Ests (R), para. 2 of the Minutes of the Premiers' Conference.
4. *Report on the Management of the Indian Administrative Service*, May 1968, Vol. I, p. 2.
5. The Commission's Study Team on the 'Centre-State Relationship' took pains to point out that quality was the *raison d'etre* for the existence of an elite service and that the task of the Government was such that it could not be performed except by men of the highest ability and character.
6. See *Report on the Management of the Indian Administrative Service*, 1968, Vol. I, pp. 4–5.
7. See *Report on the Management of the Indian Administrative Service*, 1968, Vol. I, pp. 4–5.
8. Ibid. pp. 6–8.
9. Ibid. p. 196.
10. Ibid. p. 7.
11. Ibid. Vol. II, pp. 209–43.
12. Ibid. Vol. II, p. 214.
13. Ibid. Vol. II, p. 234.

14. The size of the select list during 1960–4 was as follows:

Year	No. of officers in the select list	Promotion quota
1960	31	19
1961	35	24
1962	36	28
1963	62	28
1964	75	28

Large select lists went hand in hand with large-scale creation of ex-cadre posts with a view to giving benefit in the matter of pay and seniority to a select list of officers on their subsequent absorption into the IAS. Ibid., Vol. II, pp. 239–40.

15. Ibid. Vol. II, p. 214–15. The all-India average growth, excluding Punjab, was 32 per cent.
16. Ibid. Vol. II, p. 215.
17. Ibid. Vol. I, p. 28.
18. Ibid. Vol. I, p. 29.
19. See B. B. Misra, *The Bureaucracy in India*, Chapter V.
20. See *All-India Services Manual*, 2nd ed., p. 425.
21. Ibid. p. 427.
22. Ibid. p. 375.
23. See *Report on the Management of the Indian Administrative Service*, 1968, Vol. I, p. 155.
24. See M.H.A., File No. 21/22/49-G.S., App. to Corresp. p. 1–22.
25. *All-India Service Manual*, 2nd ed., p. 463.
26. Ibid. p. 463 f.n.
27. Under M.H.A. Notification No. 1/46/67-AIS(II)-A dated 21 Nov. 1968 appointment to the Selection Grade and posts carrying pay above the time-scale of pay in the IAS was required to be made by selection on merit, with due regard to seniority. Ibid. p. 463.
28. Ibid. p. 374.
29. *Report on the Management of the Indian Administrative Service*, 1968, Vol. I, p. 90.
30. Ibid. pp. 92–3.
31. Ibid. pp. 102–3.
32. As pointed out earlier, these objectives were to provide a body of competent personnel that was common to the Union and the States and had an all-India outlook.
33. See *Report on the Management of the Indian Administrative Service*, 1968, Vol. I, p. 119.
34. Ibid. Vol. II, p. 79.
35. Ibid. Vol. II, p. 276–7.
36. Ibid. Vol. I, p. 122.
37. Ibid. Vol. II, p. 82.
38. Ibid. Vol. II, pp. 278–9.
39. Cited in B. B. Misra, *The Administrative History of India, 1834–1947*, p. 496.
40. B. Sivaraman, *The Role of the Civil Services in the Administration of India*, Training Division, Dept. of Personnel, Sept. 1970, p. 3 (cyclostyled copy).

41. Para. 324.
42. See A. H. Hanson. *The Process of Planning, A Study of India's Five-Year Plans*, 1966, p. 39.
43. See B. B. Misra, *The Administrative History of India 1934–1947*, pp. 197, 494 and 549.
44. See *Report on the Management of the Indian Administrative Service*, 1968, Vol. I, p. 133.
45. Ibid. Vol. I, p. 135.
46. The education and training of the ICS has been discussed by the author in Chapter IV of the *Bureaucracy in India*.
47. See M.H.A., File No. 12/56/49-Apptts-1949, p. 1.
48. Ibid. p. 4.
49. See M.H.A., File No. 37/43/47-Ests(R), pp. 1–6. Desai wanted personal assessment by tutors on the basis of what the Training Division of the British Treasury and the Imperial Staff College did in England.
50. See Dr. R. M. Ray, Sec. F.P.S.C., to Sec., Govt of India, 7 Oct. 1947, M.H.A. File No. 37/43/47-Ests(R), Corresp., pp. 4–9.
51. See M.H.A. File No. 27/2/48-G.S., Corresp., pp. 1–25 (training of IAS probationers in the provinces).
52. See M.H.A. File No. 27/17/48-G.S. (Report on the working of the IAS Training School), pp. 3–9.
53. The person who made the complaint in a letter of 13 August 1948, was Lakshminarayan Sahu, Member of the Central Assembly, who had received complaints from other persons. See M.H.A. File no. 27/2/49-G.S., 1949, p. 1.
54. M.H.A. File No. 27/2/49-G.S.-1949, p. 2 (Corresp.)
55. See M.H.A. File No. 27/17/48-G.S., p. 17.
56. Ibid. p. 5. Out of 145 working days in a term, for instance, 132 were spent at the School and 13 on visits. Ibid. p. 17.
57. See *The First Five-Year Plan*, pp. 121–2.
58. See *Journal of the National Academy of Administration*, V (1960), pp. 2–3.
59. Ibid. p. 5.
60. A list of such institutions is given in S. R. Maheshwari, *Indian Administration*, pp. 239–40.
61. See Bishwanath Prasad, *The Indian Administrative Service*, Delhi, 1968, f.n., pp. 229–30.
62. See V. T. Krishnamachari, *Report on Indian and State Administrative Services and Problems of District Administration*, Delhi, 19–63.
63. See B. Sivaraman, op. cit. (cyclostyled copy), pp. 23–4.
64. Ibid. p. 49.
65. *Twenty-third Report of the Union Service Commission*, 1 April 1972 to 31 March 1973, p. 27.
66. Ibid. pp. 47–9.
67. Ibid. pp. 68–9.
68. See App. to this Chap. for the Regulations and Schedule taken from the *Ninth Report of the U.P.S.C.*, 1 April 1958 to 31 March 1959, pp. 65–7.
69. See App. IV to *Thirteenth Report of the U.P.S.C.*, p. 28, and App. IV to *Twenty-first Report*, pp. 70–71.
70. It was reconstituted in 1968 in the light of recommendations of the Scientific

Advisory Committee to the Cabinet set up in 1956. See *Twenty-first Report of the U.P.S.C.*, pp. 5⌐-8.

71. Ibid. p. 58.
72. Ibid. p. 68–9.
73. *Twenty-third Report of the U.P.S.C.*, p. 8.
74. Ibid. p. 8.
75. Article 124(4) of the Constitution.
76. See Article 148(1).
77. Provisio (b) to clause (1) of Article 217.
78. Article 317(1).
79. See *Twentieth Report of the U.P.S.C.*, p. 2; also *Nineteenth Report of the U.P.S.C.*, para 5.
80. A Member of the Union Public Service Commission was to hold office under Article 316(2) of the Constitution for a period of six years, or until he attained the age of sixty-five, whichever was earlier.
81. Recommendation No. 14(1)
82. Cited in the *Twenty-third Report of the U.P.S.C.*, p. 20.
83. Ibid. p. 21.
84. Ibid. p. 70.
85. Ibid. p. 70.
86. *Twenty-second Report of the U.P.S.C.*, p. 3.

VI. STANDARDS OF ADMINISTRATIVE MORALITY

1. See B.B. Misra, *The Judicial Administration of East India Company in Bengal 1765–82.*
2. Cited in B.B. Misra, *The Central Administration of the East India Company, 1773–1834*, p. 386.
3. See B.B. Misra, *The Indian Middle Classes*, pp. 162–8.
4. Ibid. p. 145.
5. Home (Judl.) A Progs., March 1874, No. 280, para. 6.
6. See B. B. Misra, *The Bureaucracy in India: An Historical Analysis of Development to 1947*, Chap. IV.
7. See B.B. Misra, *The Indian Middle Classes*, pp. 81–2.
8. See B.B. Misra, *The Bureaucracy in India*, Chap. V.
9. *Report of the (Santhanam) Committee on the Prevention of Corruption*, Govt, of India, March 1964, p. 10. The Committee was appointed following a debate in Parliament on 6 June 1962 when Lal Bahadur Shastri, Home Minister, suggested that a formal committee should look into the whole question of corruption and recommended measures.
10. Ibid. pp. 10–11.
11. Ibid. p. 12.
12. See *Report of the Study Team on Economic Administration*, April 1967, Annexure 1, pp. 289–97.
13. *The Santhanam Committee Report*, p.12.
14. Ibid. p. 7.

15. Ibid. p. 14. In its issue of 22 June 1967 *Patriot* (New Delhi) pointed out that the C.B.I. annual report showed a steady rise in new graft cases which alone had increased from 551 in 1956 to 2208 in 1966. See also *Annual Reports of the Central Vigilance Commission* from 1964 to 1973, containing department-wise statistics of complaints and action taken by ministries and departments.
16. *The Santhanam Committee Report*, pp. 12–13.
17. See 240 (2).
18. See 240 (3).
19. Art. 311 (1).
20. Art. 311 (2).
21. Proviso to clause (2) to Art. 311.
22. See M.H.A. File No 24/6/49–AIS, 1949.
23. Ibid. Sardar Patel's Note dated 23 June 1949.
24. *Santhanam Committee Report*, 1964, p. 12.
25. Appendix II to the *Santhanam Committee Report*, p. 294.
26. Ibid. p. 294.
27. See App. III to the *Santhanam Committee Report*, p. 296.
28. M.H.A. File No. 24/124/64—AVD., App. to Corresp., pp. 3–4.
29. Ibid. p. 5. After the resignation of C.D. Deshmukh in 1956 the Govt. of India became a purely party concern of the Congress.
30. Ibid. p. 204.
31. The task of working out the details of such a machinery was later assigned to the Department of Administrative Reforms, which was then under contemplation.
32. See M.H.A. File No. 24/88/64—AVD, pp. 81–5.
33. See M.H.A. File No. 24/124/64—AVD, App. to Corresp., p. 11.
34. Ibid. p. 13.
35. *The Statesman*, 29 Aug. 1964.
36. Ibid. 29 August 1964.
37. *Indian Express*, New Delhi, 4 April 1964.
38. *Santhanam Committee Report*, p. 180.
39. See *Report of the (Das) Commission of Inquiry*, 11 June 1964, p. 1.
40. *Indian Express*, 4 April 1964.
41. *Patriot*, 1 Nov. 1964.
42. Ibid. para 12.
43. M.H.A. File No. 24/88/64–AVD, p. 36.
44. Ibid.
45. See *The Statesman*, 30 May 1976.
46. Ibid. 30 May 1976.
47. See *Annual Report*, Department of Administrative Reforms, 1965–6, p. 21.
48. See *The Hindustan Times*, 25 June 1976, p. 8.
49. Interim Report of the Administrative Reforms Commission, Oct. 1966, pp. 12–13.
50. See G.S. Bhargava, *A Study of Political Corruption in India*, Delhi, 1974.
51. M.H.A. File No. 29/27/64 AVD, p. 5.
52. Ibid. p. 9.
53. Ibid. p. 13.
54. Ibid. pp. 21–2.
55. See *Observer*, 28 June 1964.

56. See *The Statesman*, 23 June 1964.
57. See *Monopolies and Public Policy—A Round Table Discussion*, People's Publishing House, Aug. 1972, p. 19 (paper by V.C. Shukla).
58. Ibid. p. 19.
59. B.B. Misra , *The Indian Middle Classes*, pp. 248–50.
60. See *Lok Udyog*, Vol. VII, No. 10, Jan. 1974, pp. 13–14.
61. Railways and Canal Irrigation are two important examples of departmental management of the public sector which date back to the middle of the nineteenth century.
62. See *Seventy-eighth Report of Estimates Committee* (1968–9), Fourth Lok Sabha, Ministry of Home Affairs, Central Bureau of Investigation, New Delhi, Lok Sabha Secretariat, 1969. For the staffing pattern of the CVC see its *Annual Report*. Its strength varied between 135 to 159 during 1964–73.
63. See Kailash Prakash, 'The Vigilance set-up of the Government of India', in the *Indian Journal of Public Administration*, Vol. XVIII, Oct-Dec., 1972, p. 539 and p. 558.
64. See App. II to the *First Annual Report of the Central Vigilance Commission*, pp. 26–31.
65. See *First Annual Report of the Central Vigilance Commission* (1 April 1964 to 31 March 1965), p. 3.
66. Ibid. p. 59.
67. See *Ninth Annual Report of the Central Vigilance Commission* (April 1972 to March 1973), p. 50.
68. Ibid. p. 59.
69. Ibid. p. 59.
70. See *Second Annual Report of the Central Vigilance Commission* (April 1965 to March 1966), pp. 67.
71. The *Ninth Annual Report of the Central Vigilance Commission* quotes instances where the Council of Scientific and Industrial Research (CSIR) violated its own rules and byelaws in making oppointments 'to favour unduly a particular candidate or candidates' (see p. 51). The UPSC, which earlier did the recruitment, could not now intervence.
72. See *Third Annual Report of the Central Vigilance Commission* (April 1966 to March 1967), p. 4.
73. Ibid. pp. 4–5.
74. See *Ninth Annual Report of the Central Vigilance Commission* (April 1972 to March 1973), pp. 51–2.
75. Ibid. p. 52.

VII. SOME GENERAL REFLECTIONS

1. See Donald J. Kingsley, *Representative Bureaucracy*.
2. *Report on Indian Constitutional Reforms (1918)*, Reprint, 1928, para 141.
3. Ibid. para 141.
4. MSS. Eur. C. 144, no. 17, f. 2.
5. See B.B. Misra, *The Bureaucracy in India*, Chap. VI.
6. See Article 335.

7. Article 338.
8. Article 240.
9. See B.B. Misra, *The Bureaucracy in India*, Chap. VI.
10. *Seminar*, January–December 1973, No. 168.
11. The post of Parliamentary Secretary was created by Congress ministries on taking office 1937.
12. Zetland Papers, I.O. MSS. Ext.D.609/4, p. 313 (Sept. 1937).
13. See B.B. Misra, *The Bureaucracy in India*, Chap. VI.
14. *Seminar*, January–December 1973, No. 168.
15. Durga Das, *India from Curzon to Nehru and After*, p. 276. Gandhi expressed this concern in an interview with Durga Das.
16. See B.B. Misra, *The Bureaucracy in India*, Chap. VI.
17. These include the Estimate Committee's *Report on Administrative, Financial and other Reforms* (1953–4); the first Appleby *Report on Public Administration in India* (1953); *Review of the First Five-Year Plan*; the *Report of the Team for the Study of Community Projects and National Extension Service* (Balvantray G. Mehta, Leader, 1957); the *Fifth Evaluation Report* of the Planning Commission's Programme Evaluation Organization (1958); and the Planning Commission's *Report on Indian and State Administrative Services and Problems of District Administration* by V.T. Krishnamachari.
18. See Chapter IV of this study.
19. See A. H. Hanson, *The Process of Planning: A Study of India's Five Year Plans, 1950–64*, London, 1966.
20. See B.B. Misra, *The Administrative History of India, 1834–1947*, pp. 376–7.
21. A. H. Hanson, op. cit., p. 62.
22. Lok Sabha Debates, 14th sess., 2nd ser., viii, 4651–52. Also see S.P. Jagota, 'Some Constitutional Aspects of Planning' in Ralph Braibanti and Joseph J. Spengler, eds., *Administration and Economic Development in India*, 1963.
23. Gadgil, *Planning*, p. 110.
24. See B.B. Misra, 'Evolution of the Office of Collector', in *Indian Journal of Public Administration*, July–September, 1965.
25. See B.B. Misra, *The Indian Middle Classes*, pp. 309–12; and *The Administrative History of India*, pp. 414–20.
26. *Indian Legislative Assembly Debates*, VII, 39.
27. N. W. P. *Admn. Rep.*, 1890–1, quoted in Miller, *Condition of Agricultural and Labouring Classes* (Parl. Branch Collection 220), para 92.
28. Minutes of the G.G. (Lord Moira) and Members of Council on the political state of India. I.O. (now C.R.O.), Home Misc., 603–4, 1815–17. This was the period when the government of the East India Company was involved in a series of wars with the country powers.
29. See Parl. Papers 999 of 1853, Revenue (India) LVII B. 61, Section V (Record of Rights, paras. 76–183) and App. No. 4, pp. 457–65, containing Thornton's *Notes*.
30. See B.B. Misra, *The Central Administration of the E.I. Company 1773–1834*, pp. 145–7.
31. See Maine, *Village Communities in the East and West*, London, 1876; and *Early History of Institutions*, London, 1880.
32. See S. N. Agarwal, *Gandhian Constitution for Free India*, Allahabad, 1946, p. 58.

33. Vol. III (Parts I and II, Dec. 1957), Part II, p. 3.

34. See Hugh Tinker, 'The Village in the Framework of Development' in Ralph Braibanti and Joseph J. Spengler (eds.), *Administration and Economic Development in India*, London, 1963.

35. See *Report of the Congress Village Panchayat Committee; Fifth Evaluation Report; Mehta Report; Report of the U.P. Panchayat Raj Amendment Act Committee.*

36. See B.B. Misra, *The Central Administration of the E.I. Co.*, pp. 362–6.

37. See National Conference on Community Development at Mysore City, *Main Recommendations and Conclusions*, pp. 1–29.

38. See *Papers on Measures for Strengthening of Administration*, O & M Division, Cabinet Secretariat, 1961, pp. 25, 30–3.

39. Ibid. p. 33.

40. In Bihar the BDOs hold charge of both revenue and development functions.

41. See *Seventh Evaluation Report on Community Development and Some Allied Fields* (New Delhi; Programme Evaluation Organization, Planning Commission, Govt. of India, 1960), pp. 121–35.

42. The papers connected with Gandhi's view on basic education were handed over to the authorities of Gandhi Nidhi (New Delhi) by this author who had collected them while editing the *Select Documents on Mahatma Gandhi's Movement in Champaran* 1917–18. For Gandhi's ideas about education for villagers see also *Selected Documents*, 414–16, 430–3 and 457–8.

43. See B.B. Misra, *The Indian Middle Classes*, pp. 296–9.

44. See 'Regular Recruits to the IAS—A Study', in the *Journal of the National Academy of Administration*, V. 3 (1960).

45. See T. C. A. Srinivasavaradan, 'Some Aspects of the Indian Administrative Service', *Indian Journal of Public Administration*, VII (1961), pp. 26–31. According to Trivedi-Rao, only 31.2 per cent entered the IAS by direct recruitment during 1948–60. The total number of direct recruits who so entered was 615, which included casualties also.

46. See R. K. Trivedi and D. N. Rao, 'Higher Civil Service in India—A Sample Survey', *Journal of the National Academy of Administration*, VI. 3 (1961), p. 48.

47. See *The Statesman*, Calcutta, 19 Aug. 1976. p. 5.

48. See Trivedi and Rao, 'Higher Civil Service in India', op. cit., p. 45.

49. See *The Statesman*, Calcutta, 19 Aug. 1976, p. 5.

50. See Trivedi and Rao, 'Higher Civil Service in India', op. cit., p. 43.

51. See Trivedi and Rao, 'Regular Recruits to the IAS—A Study', op. cit., p. 58, and 'Descriptive Rolls' of the IAS probationers maintained by the National Academy of Administration, Mussoorie, for 1961–2.

52. Karl Mannheim, *Ideology and Utopia*, translated by Louis Wirth and Edward A. Shils, London, 1936, p. 106.

53. S. Krishnan, *Reservation in Services*, a manuscript paper read at the Institute of Secretariat Training and Management, 22 Aug. 1974. It was kindly lent to me by the author for such use as I deemed fit to make for research purposes.

54. These lists were subject to being revised by the President or by an Act of Parliament.

55. According to a Supreme Court judgement, reservations in excess of 50 per cent of vacancies arising in a year would be denying equality of opportunity.

56. Reservation in posts filled by promotion was introduced in 1963–4 in the case of

Class III and Class IV appointments to start with. See *Ministry of Home Affairs Report*, 1963–4, p. 7.

57. See W. W. Hunter, *The Annals of Rural Bengal*, pp. 353 ff.

58. Cited in B. B. Misra, *The Bureaucracy in India*, p. 66.

59. See B.B. Misra, *The Central Administration of the East India Company, 1773–1834*, pp. 80–1.

60. See B.B. Misra, *The Bureaucracy in India: An Historical Analysis of Development up to 1947*.

61. I am indebted to Mr. S. Krishnan (Personnel Dept. of the Govt. of India) who allowed me to use his manuscript paper on 'Compensation and Benefits in Public Service' prepared for a lecture on 28 April 1972.

62. See *Great Britain, Accounts and Papers*, 1917–18, Vol. XVIII, End. 8606, 'Interim Report on Joint Standing Industrial Councils'.

63. See *Ministry of Home Affairs Report*, 1961–2, p. 10.

64. See *Ministry of Home Affairs Report*, 1960–1, pp. 12–13.

65. See *Ministry of Home Affairs Report*, 1962–3, p. 2.

66. See *Ministry of Home Affairs Report*, 1963–4, p. 6.

67. See *Ministry of Home Affairs Report*, 1964–5, pp. 8–9.

68. See *Ministry of Home Affairs Report*, 1966–7, pp. 22–4.

69. It was revised under the All-India Services (Conduct) Rules, 1968. See *The All-India Services Manual*, 2nd ed., pp. 194.

70. See *Ministry of Home Affairs Report*, 1964–5, p. 6.

71. See *The All-India Services Manual*, 2nd ed., p. 241.

72. See *Ministry of Home Affairs Report*, 1965–6, p. 6. These rules were revised again in 1969. See p. 222.

73. The comment of the Committee has been quoted in Chapter VI.

74. The extent and manner of proliferation have been discussed by B. S. Khanna in 'Aspects of the Evolution of Public Administration in India: Experiences and Lessions' in *Research Bulletin (Arts)*, Punjab University, Vol. V, No. 1, April 1974.

75. *Ministry of Home Affairs Report*, 1969–70, p. 14. The 1967–8 *Report* of the Ministry mentions 25 Feb. 1966 as the date for the establishment of the Cell. See p. 23 of the *Report*.

76. See *Ministry of Home Affairs Report*, for relevant years.

77. See *The Times of India*, 15 Sept. 1976, p. 6, containing an article by H. Kusum Kakar, which examined the ills of panchayati raj in some depth.

Select Bibliography

Original Files of the Ministry of HomeAffairs,
Government of India

F. No. 174/47-Ests (R).	Indian Administrative Service.
F. No. 20/21/48-G.G. (A15).	I.A.S. deemed to have been started with effect from 21.10.1946.
F. No. 45/34/47-Ests(R).	Combined Competitive Examination, July 1947.
F. No. 30/47–43-G.G.(A).	Disciplinary Rules governing Secretary of State's Services.
F. No. 37/44/47-Ests(R).	Indian Administrative Service—need for military training.
F. No. 4/1/48-R	Reorganization of the machinery of Government.
F. No. 27/16/48-G.S.	I. A. S. Training School.
F. No. 27/2/48-G.S.(AIS)	Training of I. A. S. probationers in the Provinces.
F. No. 1/48-R.E.	Economy Committee's Report on Min. of Ext. Affairs.
F. No. 68/16/48-Admn.	Promotion Committee in the Home Department.
F. No. 31/1/48-Ests.	Indianization in the I.C.S. and I.P.
F. No. 20/69/48-G.S.	Promotees to I.A.S. permitted to suffix I.A.S. against names.
F. No. 21/12/48-G.S.	Emergency Recruitment Scheme.
F. No. 25/1/48-Public.	Emergency Recruitment—fall in standards.
F. No. 20/62/48-G.S.	Emergency Recruits—a threat to I.C.S. seniority.
F. No. 27/17/48-G.S.	Report on the Functioning of the Training School.
F. No. 13/51/48-G.S.	Irregular confirmation of stenographers after 16 April 1947.

F. No. 102/48-R.	Reorganization—Sardar Patel to N. Gopalaswami Ayyanagar.
F. No. 12/18/48-Apptts.	Competitive examination—question of Scheduled Castes.
F. No. 20/48-G.S.	I.A.S.—communal representation—Statement.
F. No. 60/225-Ests.	Limitations of Govt. to alter the service conditions of the I.C.S.
F. No. 4/2/48-R.	Question re. Special Recruitment Board.
F. No. 68/49/48-Admn.	Chief Secretaries Conference (31.3.48).
F. No. 20/52/48-G.S.	I. P. officers and I.A.S. examination.
F. No. 20/47/48-G.S.	Question whether promotees to A.I.S. were to be regular members.
F. No. 20/21/48-G.S.(A.I.S.).	Ad Hoc Committee to select P.C.S. men for I.A.S. posts—Central and Provincial. Centre's concern for common standard—provinces interested in patronage.
F. No. 12/12/48-Apptts.	I.A.S. and I.P.S.—general conditions of service.
F. No. 76/3/48-Admn.	R. A. Gopalaswamy, I.C.S., appointed OSD in Home to assist reorganization of Government.
F. No. 20/34/48-G.S.-Ests.	Women in government services.
F. No. 20/67/48-G.S.	Eligibility of women for public services.
F. No. 20/22/48-G.S.	I.A.S. recruitment—provincial bias in Members of interview boards.
F. No. 51/423/49-Public	Review of the activities of the Ministry of Home Affairs for the year 1948.
F. No. 27/2/49-G.S.	I.A.S. Training School Courses—correspondence.
F. No. 21/2/49-G.S.	Combined competitive examinations, Dec. 1949.
F. No. 21/24/49-AIS.	I.A.S. recruitment and training.
F. No. 22/2/49-G.S.	Concessions to war services reviewed since 1945.
F. No. 3/12/49-AIS.	No. of officers recruited to the I.A.S. since 15 Aug. 1947—P.C.S. men more than 50%, and only 39 out of 342 recruited by competition.
F. No. 20/45/49-AIS.	Recruitment to I.A.S. from war service closed.
F. No. 20/17/49-G.S.	Training of emergency recruits—courses.
F. No. 60/1/49-Public.	Salaries and allowances and other

	perquisites and advantages of Ministers at the Centre and in the Provinces.
F. No. 59/2/49-Public.	Assurances and promises of Home Minister.
F. No. 2/8/49-R.E.	Report of the Economy Committee—authorized strength of the superior services—press reports.
F. No. 16/53/49-AIS.	Scheduled Castes appointments—Patel's comment.
F. No. 1(2)/49/-R.E.	Central Cadre of the A.I.S.—draft scheme.
F. No. 1(1)/49/-R.E.	Procedure relating to selection of officers to superior administrative posts under the central government organization of general administrative post.
F. No. 3/14/49-AIS.	Review of I.A.S. examination held in Dec. 1949.
F. No. 3/9/49-AIS.	Appointment to I.A.S. made during 1947–49 from various categories.
F. No. 60/220/49-Ests.	Persons with technical and specialist qualifications—special procedure of recruitment.
F. No. 20/21/49-G.S.	Prime Minister's suggestion to expedite recruitment and training—history of efforts to meet man-power gap.
F. No. 12/56/49-Apptts.	I.A.S. (Probationary Service and Seniority of Recruits) Rules, 1947.
F. No. 25/46/49-AIS.	Government Servants Conduct Rules.
F. No. 23/2/49-AIS.	Fixation of pay of P.C.S. men in I.C.S. and I.A.S..
F. No. 23/13/49-AIS.	Conditions of service.
F. No. 20/13/49-G.S.	Relative seniority of the I.A.S. and the I.C.S.
F. No. 23/4/49-G.S.	Pay fixation of P.C.S. men promoted to the I.A.S.
F. No. 23/11/49-AIS.	Pay of P.C.S. men promoted to the I.A.S. Conditions of service re. pay fixation.
F. No. 40/246/49-P. II.	I.A.S. (Probationary Service) Rules, 1947.
F. No. 20/39/49-AIS, S.No.I	
F. No. 9/7/49-Ests.	Case of I.M. Lall, I.C.S.; disciplinary action.
F. No. 24/6/49-AIS.	I.M. Lall restored to the Indian Civil Service; settlement of his claims.

F. No. 17/2/49-G.S.   Secretariat of the Economic Committee of the Cabinet.

F. No. 1/9/49-R.E.   Central Statistical Organization.

F. No. 26/10/49-Ests.   Conduct Rules governing Secretary of State's Services.

F. No. 31(14)/49-R.E.   Report (of N. Gopalswami Ayyangar) on the reorganization of the machinery of Government; discussion with Prime Minister Nehru and Deputy Prime Minister Patel (major file), containing memorandum for the Cabinet dated 20 May 1948.

F. No. 15/18/49-AIS.   Selection Board for recruitment of officers under the Central Government.

F. No. 12/58/49-Apptts.   Appointment of women—question of physical fitness.

F. No. 20/17/49-G.S.   Training courses for emergency recruits to the I.A.S.

F. No. 15/4/49-G.S.   Selection Board under the Central Government.

F. No. 20/26/49-G.S.   I.A.S. and I.P.S.—communal composition returns.

F. No. 43/49/49-Apptts.   Recruitment to Central Services—communal reservations and domicile qualifications.

F. No. 12/39/49-Apptts.   Special Recruitment Board—charge of bribery.

F. No. 12/21/49-Apptts.   I.A.S. allotment, subject to State Govt.'s approval.

F. No. 61/2/49-Ests.   Provincial Public Service Commission—reconstitution.

F. No. 21/21/49-AIS(1).   Question of agriculture as an optional subject of combined competitive examination for the I.A.S.

F. No. 3/5/49-G.S.   Qualification for the I.A.S. examination—university degree.

F. No. 20/16/49-G.S.   I.A.S.—question of seniority.

F. No. 20/50/48-G.S.   Appointment of non-I.A.S. to I.A.S. cadre post on a permanent basis not permitted.

F. No. 60/110/50-Ests.   Procedure of selection of officers to superior administrative posts under the Central Govt.

F. No. 1/27/50-AIS.   Notes on the statutory validity of the 'Agreement' of 21 October 1946 consti-

	tuting the I.A.S./I.P.S.—question raised by the West Bengal Govt.—I.A.S.——Indian Civil Administrative Cadre Rules 1950 instead of joint I.A.S. and I.C.S. cadre.
F. No. 60/117/50-Ests.	Reorganization of the machinery of Govt.
F. No. 1/4/50-R.E.	Cabinet decision on reorganization.
F. No. 60/119/50-Ests.	Reorganization—'Minorities' and 'Departments'.
F. No. 21/4/50-R.E.	Reorganization—Transport Minister N. Gopalaswami Ayyangar's Report submitted to Govt. in November 1949 and placed before Parliament in August 1950 with Cabinet decision on implementation.
F. No. 4/3/53-AIS(II).	All-India Services Act, 1951—finalization of the draft I.A.S. (Probation) Rules framed under it.
F. No. 15/223/51-Pub.	Ministers and Governors—whether they are entitled to take staff when not travelling on official duty.
F. No. 10/61/51-AIS(I).	Use of the suffix 'I.A.S.' by substantive holders of listed posts in the I.C.S.
F. No. 21/12/51-AIS.	Combined competitive examination of 1950—strict adherence to age limit emphasized.
F. No. 3/1/52-AIS(II).	I.A.S.—framing of regulations governing appointment by competition.
F. No. 20/19/53-R.E.	Proposal to set up O & M Division.
F. No. 2/38/54-AIS.	I.A.S.—question of minimum height of women candidates.
F. No. 23/9/54-Pub.	Part C States—Memorandum to States Reorganization Commission regarding their future.
F. No. 27/20/54-Pub.I.	Amendment of GAP (Governor's Allowances and Privileges) Order, 1950.
F. No. 27/11/54-Pub.I.	Purchase or import of articles by Governors duty free.
F. No. 14/4/55-Pub.I	Sumptuary allowances of the President of India.
F. No. 19/11/56-Pub.I.	Imposition of Income Tax on certain allowances of Governors.

F. No. 19/21/56-Pub.I.   Governor of Bombay, Maharaj Singh, taking advantage of customs free import of articles imported two landrovers for his use.

F. No. 19/7/56-Pub.I.   GAP Order 1950—purchase of motor car for the use of the Governor of Bihar.

F. No. 19/10/56-Pub.I.   Replacement of motor cars for the use of the Andhra Pradesh Governor.

F. No. 113/56-Pub. I.   Informal Consultative Committee of MPs, and Scheme for Special Recruitment to the Indian Administrative Service.

F. No. 135/56-Pub. I.   Descriptive Memoir of the Ministry of Home Affairs.

F. No. 19/31/57-Pub. I.   State Reorganization (Governor's Allowance and Privilege) Order, 1957—Purchase of Cars.

F. No. 19/50/57-Pub.I.   Whether the wife of a Governor is entitled to tour outside the State at State cost, and whether the ADC to the Governor can accompany her at State cost in such circumstances.

F. No. 19/29/57-Pub.I.   State Reorganization (Governor's Allowance and Privilege) Order 1957—purchase refrigerators.

R. No. 19/32/57-Pub.I.   Appointment of Governors by President Rajendra Prasad.

F. No. 14/15/59-RPS.   Recruitment policy compulsory notification of vacancies to the Employment Exchange.

F. No. 19/22/59-Pub.I.   Governor of Madras—purchase of a car.

F. No. 19/4/60-Pub. I.   Governor of Uttar Pradesh—maintenance of railway saloon.

F. No. 19/50/60-Pub. I.   Rajasthan Governor—demand for new carpets and chandeliers and furnishing for banquet hall, guest house, suites, etc.

F. No. 19/15/60-Pub. I.   Punjab Governor—excess expenditure on maintenance, etc.—special order of the President requested.

F. No. 19/39/60-Pub. I.   An additional fourth car for the Governor of Uttar Pradesh.

F. No. 12/47/61/-Pub. I.   Ministers—corrupt practice—case of A.I.C.C. meeting at Raipur in Madhya Pradesh at Government cost.

F. No. 19/83/61-Pub. I.   Huge expenditure incurred on the furnishing of the Raj Bhavan of Gujarat without proper permission.

F. No. 19/53/61-Pub. I.   Punjab Governor's case—excess expenditure on furnishing, etc. regularized *ex post facto* in spite of AG's objections.

F. No. 24/124/64-AVD.   Measures for the prevention of corruption—Constitution of Special Consultative Group on Anti-corruption and Administrative Vigilance.

F. No. 19/85/65-Pub.I.   Earlier Orders of 1936, 1950, 1957 and 1960 on the subject of Governors' allowances and privileges revised to meet the excessive and increasing demands of Governors, especially of the Governor of Punjab (important file showing not only the continuance of the British imperial tradition but a scale of expenditure far in excess of that).

Printed Documents and Reports

Acts

The All-India Services Act, 1951 (No. LXI of 1951).

The Government of Part C States Act, 1951 (No. XLIX of 1951).

The States Reorganization Act, 1956 (No. 37 of 1956).

The Andhra Pradesh and Madras (Alternation of Boundaries) Act, 1959 (No. 56 of 1959).

The Rajasthan and Madhya Pradesh (Transfer of Territories) Act, 1959 (No. 47 of 1959).

The Bombay Reorganization Act, 1960 (No. 11 of 1960).

The Acquired Territories (Merger) Act, 1960 (No. 64 of 1960).

The State of Nagaland Act, 1962 (No. 27 of 1962).

The Punjab Reorganization Act, 1966 (No. 31 of 1966).

The Andhra Pradesh and Mysore (Transfer of Territories) Act, 1968 (No. 36 of 1968).

The Bihar and Uttar Pradesh (Alternation of Boundaries) Act, 1968 (No. 24 of 1968).

The Madras State (Alternation of Name) Act, 1968 (No. 55 of 1968).

The North-Eastern Areas (Reorganization) Act, 1971 (No. 81 of 1971).

Constitution

The Government of India Act, 1935.

The Constitution of India, 1949.

The Constitution of India (As modified up to 1st January, 1973). Commemorative Edition, Government of India, Ministry of Law and Justice, New Delhi, 1973.

Basu, D. D. (ed.), *Constitutional Documents*, Calcutta, 1969.

Shiva Rao, B. (ed.), *The Framing of India's Constitution*, Vols. I to IV, Indian Institute of Public Administration, New Delhi, 1968.

Reforms Office: Provisional Constitutional Orders, 1946–47.

Administrative Reforms Commission

Report of the Study Team on Personnel Administration (Chairman: R. K. Patil), August 1967, Delhi. 1969.

Report of the Study Team (Machinery of the Government of India and its Procedures of Work), Part I, March 1967.

Report of the Study Team (Machinery of the Government of India and its Procedures of Work), Part II, Vol. II (Annextures), February 1968.

Study Team on Promotion, Policies, Conduct Rules, Discipline & Morale (Report), Chairman: K. N. Nagarkatti, New Dellhi, 1967.

Reports on Public Sector Undertakings, October, 1967; Economic Administration, July 1968; Machinery for Planning, March 1968.

All India Services Manual, second edition (corrected up to 1–8–1969), issued by the Government of India, Ministry of Home Affairs, New Delhi, 1969.

Census of Central Government Employees, 1963, 1965, 1966–69, 1971–72.

Papers on Measures for Strengthening Administration, O & M Division, Cabinet Secretariat, New Delhi, 1961.

Report on Indian Constitutional Reforms (reprint), Calcutta, 1928.

Report on the Management of the Indian Administrative Service, Department of Administrative Reforms, Ministry of Home Affairs, Government of India, Vol. I (Report) and Vol. II (Special Appendix), May 1968 (cyclostyle copy).

Report of the Royal Commission on Decentralization in India, Vol. I, 1909.

Review of the Activities of the Ministry of Home Affairs for the year 1949, New Delhi, 1950.

Report, Ministry of Home Affairs, Government of India (Annual) from 1950–1 to 1972–3.

Reports of the Central Vigilance Commission (Annual), first to ninth reports, 1964–5 to 1972–3.

Reports of Organization and Methods Division (Annual), Cabinet Secretariat, Government of India, 1956–64.

Report of the Committee on Prevention of Corruption, Government of India, Ministry of Home Affairs (Chairman: K. Santhanam), New Delhi, 1964.

Report of the Commission of Inquiry (S. R. Das Commission), 1963, appointed by the Government of India to report on allegations made against Sardar Partap Singh Kairon, Chief Minister of Punjab.

Reports of the Union Public Service Commission (Annual) for the period from 1950 to 1973.

Report of the Bengal Administration Enquiry Committee, 1944–5, Calcutta, 1945.

The Civil Service, Vol. I, Report of the Committee, 1966–8 (Chairman: Lord Fulton), HMSO, London, 1968 (Comnd. 3638).

Estimate Committee's Report on Administrative, Financial and other Reforms, 1953–4.

First Appleby Report on Public Administration in India, 1953.

Review of the First Five Year Plan.

Report of the Team for the Study of Community Projects and National Extension Service (Balvantray G. Mehta, leader, 1957).

Fifth Evaluation Report of the Planning Commission's, Programme Evaluation Organization, 1958.

Planning Commission's Report on Indian and State Administrative Services and Problems of District Administration by V. T. Krishnamachari.

Seventh Evaluation Report on Community Development and Some Allied Fields, New Delhi, 1960.

SOME SECONDARY WORKS

Agarwal, S. N., *Gandhian Constitution for Free India*, Allahabad, 1946.

Austin, G., *The Indian Constitution; Cornerstone of a Nation*, Delhi, 1972.

Basu, Durga Das, *Constitutional Documents*, Vol. I, Calcutta, 1969.

Bhargava, G. S., *A Study of Political Corruption in India*, Delhi, 1971.

Blunt, Sir Edward, *Social Service in India*, London, 1939.

Braibanti, Ralph (ed.), *Administration and Economic Development*, London, 1963.

——, *Asian Bureaucratic Systems Emergent From the British Imperial Traditions*, Durham, 1966.

Chagla, M. C., *Roses in December*, Bombay, 1973.

Chanda, A., *Federalism in India*, London, 1965.

Colaro, F. T. R. and Shukla, K. S., *Reluctance of the Public to Aid the Police in the Detection of Crime and Crime Reporting at Police Stations*, New Delhi, 1973 (cyclostyled copy).

Coupland, R., *The Indian Problem, 1833–1935* (Report on the Constitutional Problem in India), Part I, London, 1943.

Darbar, Gyanwati, *Portrait of a President*: Letters of Dr Rajendra Prasad written to Mrs Gyanwati Darbar, Delhi, 1974.

Dharma Vira, *Memoirs of a Civil Servant*, Delhi, 1975.

Gorwala, A. D., *Report on Public Administration*, New Delhi, 1951.

—— , *The Role of the Administrator, Past, Present and Future*, Poona, 1952.

Hanson, A. H., *The Process of Planning*, London, 1966.

Kingsley, Donald G., *Representative Bureaucracy*, London.

Maine, H. S., *Village Communities in the East and West*, London, 1876.

—— , *Early History of Institutions*, London, 1880.

Mannheim, Karl, *Ideology and Utopia*, tr. by Louis Wirth and Edward A. Shils, London (reprint), 1968.

Menon, V. P., *The Transfer of Power*, Madras, 1968.

Misra, B. B., *The Bureaucracy in India, An Historical Analysis of Development up to 1947*, Delhi, 1977.

—— , *The Indian Political Parties, An Historical Analysis of Political Behaviour up to 1947*, Delhi, 1976.

—— , *The Administrative History of India, 1834–1947*, Bombay, 1970.

—— , *The Central Administration of the East India Company, 1773–1834*, Manchester, 1958.

—— , (ed.), *The Select Documents on Mahatma Gandhi's Movement in Champaran, 1917–18*, Patna, 1961.

—— , *The Judicial Administration of the East India Company in Bengal*, Delhi, 1961.

—— , *The Indian Middle Classes*, London, 1961.

Mundhra Inquiry: The Full Story, A report of the Inquiry held by the Chagla Commission.

Muttalib, M. A., *The Union Public Service Commission*, Delhi, 1967.

Philips, C. H. (ed.), *The Partition of India: Policies and Perspectives*, London, 1970.

Punjabi, K. L., *Rajendra Prasad: First President of India*, London, 1960.

Prasad, B., *The Indian Administrative Service*, Delhi, 1968.

Setalvad, M. C., *Union and State Relations under the Indian Constitution*, 1974.

Singh, Nagendra, *President Speaks* (A compilation of speeches made by President V. V. Giri), Delhi, 1970.

Sivaraman, B., *The Role of Civil Services in Administration in India*, Dept. of Personnel, Cabinet Secretariat (cyclostyled copy).

Sri Prakash, *State Governors in India*, Delhi 1975.

Sydenham & Combe, Lord, *The Federation of India: A Dangerous Illusion* (pamphlet issued by the Indian Empire Society, No. 11), London, 1931.

White, Leonard D., *Introduction to the Study of Public Administration*, 4th ed., Delhi, 1958.

Index